Switching *to the* Mac

THE MISSING MANUAL

*The book that
should have been
in the box*

Switching *to the* Mac
THE MISSING MANUAL

David Pogue

POGUE PRESS™
O'REILLY®

Beijing • Cambridge • Farnham • Köln • Paris • Sebastopol • Taipei • Tokyo

Switching to the Mac: The Missing Manual
by David Pogue

Published by Pogue Press/O'Reilly & Associates, Inc.,
1005 Gravenstein Highway North, Sebastopol, CA 95472.

March 2003:	First Edition.
May 2003:	Second Printing.
July 2003:	Third Printing.

ISBN: 0-596-00452-4

[5/03] M

Table of Contents

Part Two: Moving In

Part Five: Appendixes

The Missing Credits

About the Author

 David Pogue is the weekly computer columnist for the *New York Times*, a technology correspondent for CBS News, and the creator of the Missing Manual series. He's the author or co-author of 25 books, including eight in this series and six in the "For Dummies" line (including *Magic, Opera, Classical Music,* and *The Flat-Screen iMac*). In his other life, David is a former Broadway show conductor, a magician, and a pianist (*www.davidpogue.com*).

He welcomes feedback about Missing Manual titles by email: *david@pogueman.com.* (If you need technical help, however, please refer to the sources in Appendix A.)

About the Creative Team

Nan Barber (copy editor) co-authored *Office X for the Macintosh: The Missing Manual* and *Office 2001 for Macintosh: The Missing Manual.* As the principal copy editor for this series, she has edited the titles on iPhoto, Mac OS 9, AppleWorks 6, iMovie, Dreamweaver 4, and Windows XP. Email: *nanbarber@mac.com.*

John Rizzo (technical editor) runs the MacWindows Web site the Internet's largest resource for making Macs and Windows work together (*www.macwindows.com*). He also writes about Macintosh hardware and software at CNET.com, MacHome, and Macworld. John is the author of several books, including the upcoming *Thinking Mac OS X.* In the pre-Web era, he was a columnist for such now-defunct magazines as *MacWeek* and *MacUser.*

Joseph Schorr (Chapter 6) is a frequent contributor to *Macworld,* co-author of *iPhoto: The Missing Manual* and *iPhoto 2: The Missing Manual,* and a senior product manager at Extensis, Inc. He wrote *Macworld*'s "Secrets" column for several years and co-authored six editions of *Macworld Mac Secrets.* He began collaborating with David Pogue in 1982—on musical comedies at Yale.

Phil Simpson (design and layout) works out of his office in Stamford, Connecticut, where he has had his graphic design business since 1982. He is experienced in many facets of graphic design, including corporate identity, publication design, and corporate and medical communications. Email: *pmsimpson@earthlink.net.*

Acknowledgments

The Missing Manual series is a joint venture between the dream team introduced on these pages and O'Reilly & Associates: Tim O'Reilly, Mark Brokering, and company.

I'm grateful to all of them, and also to a few people who did massive favors for this book. They include Brook Stein, Apple's "Switch" guru who cheerfully reviewed the chapters to offer suggestions and corrections; Ken Bereskin, Apple's director of world-wide marketing for Mac OS X; AOL's Nicholas Graham and Jane Lennon for their helpful migration tips; David Karp, who provided many great suggestions; Tuncer Deniz, editor-in-chief of *Inside Mac Games,* who helped with a list of key games; and to John Cacciatore for his proofreading smarts. Thanks to David Rogelberg for believing in the idea, and above all, to Jennifer, Kelly, and Tia, who make these books—and everything else—possible.

The Missing Manual Series

Missing Manual books are designed to be superbly written guides to computer products that don't come with printed manuals (which is just about all of them). Each book features a handcrafted index; cross-references to specific page numbers (not just "See Chapter 14"); and a promise never to use an apostrophe in the possessive word *its.* Current and upcoming titles include:

- *Mac OS X: The Missing Manual, Second Edition* by David Pogue

- *Mac OS X: The Missing Manual, Panther 10.3 Edition* by David Pogue

- *iPhoto 2: The Missing Manual* by David Pogue, Joseph Schorr, & Derrick Story

- *iMovie 3 & iDVD: The Missing Manual* by David Pogue

- *Dreamweaver MX: The Missing Manual* by David Sawyer McFarland

- *Filemaker Pro: The Missing Manual* by Geoff Coffey

- *Mac OS X Hints: Jaguar Edition* by Rob Griffiths

- *Office X for Macintosh: The Missing Manual* by Nan Barber, Tonya Engst, & David Reynolds

- *AppleWorks 6: The Missing Manual* by Jim Elferdink & David Reynolds

- *Mac OS 9: The Missing Manual* by David Pogue

- *Windows XP Home Edition: The Missing Manual* by David Pogue

- *Windows XP Pro: The Missing Manual* by David Pogue, Craig Zacker, & L.J. Zacker

Introduction

W hy are people replacing or supplementing their Windows PCs with Macs all of a sudden? Maybe Apple's "Switch" ad campaign is working. Maybe people are noticing how cool Macs look nowadays. Or maybe they've just spent too many hours trying to troubleshoot Windows, or even understand it.

In any case, there's never been a better time to make the switch. Mac OS X version 10.2 has been hailed as the best operating system on earth—it's gorgeous, easy to understand, and virtually crash-proof. Apple's computers are in top form, too, complete with features like built-in Ethernet, DVD burners, and FireWire (IEEE 1394) ports. Among laptops, the story is even better: Apple's PowerBooks and iBooks cost less than similarly outfitted Windows laptops, yet weigh less and last twice as long on a battery charge.

That's not to say, however, that switching to the Mac is all sunshine and bunnies. The Macintosh is a different machine, running a different operating system—and built by a company with a different philosophy, a fanatical perfectionist/artistic zeal. When it comes to their missions and ideals, Apple and Microsoft have about as much in common as a melon and a shoehorn.

In any case, you have three challenges before you. First, you'll probably want to copy your Windows stuff over to the new Mac. You'll need to move both your files (photos, MP3s, Microsoft Office documents) and some data that's trickier to extract (email messages, address books, buddy lists, and so on).

Second, you have to assemble a suite of Macintosh programs that do what you're used to doing in Windows. Sometimes that's easy: most programs from Microsoft,

Adobe, Macromedia, and other major players are available in nearly identical Mac and Windows formats. Occasionally, it's more difficult: many second-tier programs are available only for Windows, and it takes some research (or Chapter 7 of this book) to help you find Macintosh replacements.

Finally, you have to learn Mac OS X itself. In some respects, it resembles the latest versions of Windows: there's a taskbar-like thing, a Control Panel–like thing, and, of course, a Trash can. At the same time, hundreds of features you thought you knew have been removed, replaced, or relocated. (If you ever find yourself groping for an old favorite feature, see Appendix B, the "Where'd It Go?" dictionary.)

Note: In Mac OS X, the X is meant to be a Roman numeral, pronounced "ten." Unfortunately, many people see "Mac OS X" and say "Mac O.S. ex." That's a sure way to get funny looks in public.

What the Mac Gives You

This isn't a Mac-vs.-Windows book. Windows certainly has its virtues—a larger software library and much greater acceptance in the corporate world, for example. But since you've already made the decision to investigate the Mac, you might enjoy looking over a list of *its* perks.

The main thing you gain by moving to Mac OS X is stability. You and your Mac may go for years without ever witnessing a system crash. Oh, it's technically possible for Mac OS X to crash—but few have actually witnessed such an event. Rumors of such crashes circulate on the Internet like Bigfoot sightings. (If it ever happens to you, turn promptly to Appendix A.)

Underneath the shimmering, translucent desktop of Mac OS X is Unix, the industrial strength, rock-solid OS that drives many a Web site and university. It's not new

---

FREQUENTLY ASKED QUESTION

All About "Jaguar"

What's this business about Jaguar?

Like Microsoft, Apple develops its wares in secret, giving new products code names to throw outsiders off the scent. Apple's code names for Mac OS X and its descendants all refer to big cats: Mac OS X was Cheetah, 10.1 was Puma, and 10.2 was Jaguar.

Usually, the code name is dropped as soon as the product is complete, at which time the marketing department gives it a new name. In Mac OS X 10.2's case, though, Apple thought that the Jaguar name was cool enough that it stuck

with it for the finished product. The name even seems to suggest the new system's speed and power. That's why the CD and the box feature jaguar fur as a design element.

In most countries, the word "Jaguar" even appears on the box—but not everywhere. In the United Kingdom, for example, jaguar fur appears on the box and the CD, but Apple carefully refrains from using the term "Jaguar." That's a result of threatening memos from the automaker. Evidently, Jaguar Cars, Ltd. worries that consumers might be confused and—when shopping for a $75,000 sports car—might walk out with a $130 software kit by mistake.

---

by any means; in fact, it's decades old, and has been polished by generations of pro-grammers. That's precisely why Apple CEO Steve Jobs and his team chose it as the basis for the NeXT operating system, which Jobs worked on during his twelve years away from Apple and which Apple bought in 1997 to turn into Mac OS X.

But crash resistance is only the big-ticket item. Here are a few other joys of becoming a Mac fan:

- **No viruses.** There isn't yet a single virus that runs in Mac OS X. (Even Microsoft Word macro viruses don't run "correctly" in Mac OS X.) For some people, this is a good reason to move to Mac OS X right there.

- **No nagging.** Unlike Windows XP, Mac OS X isn't copy-protected. You can install the same copy on your desktop and laptop Macs, if you're so inclined. When you buy a new Mac, you're never, ever asked to type in a code off a sticker. Nor must you "register," "activate," sign up for ".NET Passport," or endure any other friendly suggestions unrelated to your work. In short, Mac OS X leaves you alone.

- **Sensational software.** Mac OS X comes with several dozen useful programs, from Mail (for email) to a 3-D, voice-activated Chess program. The most famous pro-grams, though, are the famous Apple "i-Apps": iTunes for working with MP3 files, iMovie for editing video, iPhoto for managing your digital photos, and so on. You also get iChat, an AOL-compatible instant messaging program, and iCal, a calendar program that syncs with Palm organizers. (This book covers the basics of all of them.)

- **Simpler everything.** Most applications in Mac OS X show up as a single icon. Behind the scenes, they may have dozens of individual software crumbs, just like programs do in Windows—but Mac OS X treats that single icon as though it's a folder. All of the support files are hidden away inside, where you don't have to look at them. As a result, all you have to do to remove a program from your Mac is drag the one application icon to the Trash, without having to worry that you're leaving scraps behind.

- **Desktop features.** Microsoft is a neat freak. Windows XP, for example, is so op-posed to your using the desktop as a parking lot for icons, it actually interrupts you every 60 days to sweep all your infrequently used icons into an "Unused" folder.

The Mac approach is different. Mac people often leave their desktops absolutely littered with icons. As a result, Mac OS X offers a long list of useful desktop fea-tures that will be new to you, the Windows refugee.

For example, *spring-loaded* folders let you drag an icon into a folder within a folder within a folder with a single drag, without leaving a wake of open win-dows. An optional second line under an icon's name tells you how many items are in a folder, what the dimensions are of a graphic, and so on. And there's a useful column view, which lets you view the contents of many nested folders at a glance. (You can think of it as a horizontal version of Windows Explorer.)

There's also a handy Search bar for searching the window you're in, plus a speedy system-wide Find command. No longer are Web searching and disk searching functions combined in a single, sluggish Search program.

- **Advanced graphics.** What the programmers get excited about is the set of advanced graphics technologies called *Quartz* (for two-dimensional graphics) and *OpenGL* (for three-dimensional graphics). For the rest of us, these technologies translate into a beautiful, translucent look for the desktop (a design scheme Apple calls Aqua); smooth-looking (*antialiased*) onscreen lettering; and the ability to turn any document on the screen into an Adobe Acrobat (PDF) file (page 186).

- **Advanced networking.** When it comes to hooking up your Mac to other computers, including those on the Internet, few operating systems can touch Mac OS X. It offers advanced features like *multihoming*, which, for example, lets your laptop switch automatically and invisibly from its cable modem settings to its dial-up modem settings when you take it on the road.

  Macs and Windows PCs can "see" each other on a network automatically, so that you can open, copy, and work on files on each other's machines as though the age-old religious war between Macs and PCs had never even existed.

- **Voice control, keyboard control.** You can operate every menu in every program entirely from the keyboard or—new in 10.2—even by voice. These are terrific timesavers for efficiency freaks. In fact, the Mac can also read aloud *any text in any program,* including Web pages, email, your novel, you name it. In fact, you can even turn the Mac's spoken performance into an MP3 file, ready to transfer to a CD or a portable music player to enjoy on the road.

- **Full buzzword compliance.** You can't read an article about Mac OS X without hearing certain technical buzzwords that were once exclusively the domain of computer engineers: *preemptive multitasking, multithreading, symmetrical multiprocessing, dynamic memory allocation,* and *memory protection,* for example.

  Apple is understandably proud that Mac OS X offers all of these sophisticated, state-of-the-art operating system features. Unfortunately, publicizing them means exposing the rest of us to a lot of fairly unnecessary geek terms. What it all adds up to, though, is that Mac OS X is very stable, that a crashy program can't crash the whole machine, that the Macintosh can exploit multiple processors, and that the Mac can easily do more than one thing at once—downloading, playing music, and opening a program, for example—all simultaneously.

- **A command-line interface.** In general, Apple has completely hidden from you every trace of the Unix operating system that lurks beneath Mac OS X's beautiful skin. For the benefit of programmers and other technically oriented fans, however, Apple left uncovered a tiny passageway into that far more complex realm—Terminal, a program in your Applications→Utilities folder.

  This isn't a Unix book, so you won't find much instruction in using Terminal here. If you like, though, you can capitalize on the *command-line interface* of Mac

OS X. In other words, you can type out cryptic commands, which the Mac executes instantly and efficiently, in an all-text window.

About This Book

Switching to the Mac: The Missing Manual is divided into five parts, each containing several chapters:

- Part 1, **Welcome to Macintosh,** covers the essentials of the Macintosh. It's a crash course in everything you see on the screen when you turn on the machine: the Dock, icons, windows, menus, scroll bars, the Trash, aliases, the menu, and so on.

- Part 2, **Moving In,** is dedicated to the actual process of hauling your software, settings, and even peripherals (like printers and monitors) across the chasm from the PC to the Mac. It covers both the easy parts (copying over your documents, pictures, and music files) and the harder ones (transferring your email, address books, buddy lists, and so on).

- Part 3, **Making Connections,** lets you know where to find your Internet settings on the old Windows machine—and where to plug them in on the Macintosh. It also covers Apple's Internet software suite: Mail, Address Book, Web browsers like Safari and Internet Explorer, and chat programs like iChat.

- Part 4, **Putting Down Roots,** treads in more advanced topics—and aims to turn you into a Macintosh power user. It teaches you how to set up private accounts for people who share a single Mac, navigate the System Preferences program (the Mac equivalent of the Windows Control Panel), and operate the 35 freebie bonus programs that come with Mac OS X.

Note: Some of the material in this book is adapted from the bestselling *Mac OS X: The Missing Manual,* Second Edition. That book is a much fatter, more in-depth guide to Mac OS X (and a worthy investment if you, like thousands before you, grow into a true Macoholic).

At the end of the book, you'll find three appendixes. The first covers Mac OS X troubleshooting and installation. The second is the "Where'd it go?" Dictionary—an essential reference for anyone who occasionally (or frequently) flounders to find some familiar control in the new, alien Macintosh environment. Finally, Appendix C is a master list of all the secret keystrokes that do useful things in Mac OS X.

About→These→Arrows

Throughout this book, and throughout the Missing Manual series, you'll find sentences like this: "Open the System folder→Libraries→Fonts folder." That's shorthand for a much longer instruction that directs you to open three nested folders in sequence, like this: "On your hard drive, there's a folder called System. Open that.

Inside the System folder window is a folder called Libraries; double-click it to open it. Inside *that* folder is yet another one called Fonts. Double-click to open it, too."

Similarly, this kind of arrow shorthand helps to simplify the business of choosing commands in menus, such as →Dock→Position on Left, as shown in Figure I-1.

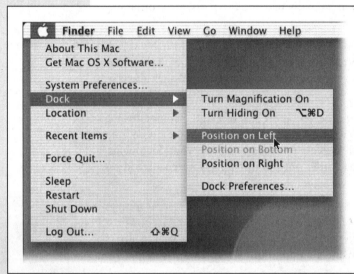

Figure I-1:
In this book, arrow notations help to simplify folder and menu instructions. For example, "Choose →Dock→ Position on Left" is a more compact way of saying, "From the menu, choose Dock; from the submenu that then appears, choose Position on Left," as shown here.

About MissingManuals.com

If you visit *www.missingmanuals.com* and click the "Missing CD-ROM" link, you'll find a neat, organized, chapter-by-chapter list of the shareware and freeware mentioned in this book. (As noted on the inside back cover, having the software online instead of on a CD-ROM saved you $5 on the cost of the book.)

The Web site also offers corrections and updates to the book (to see them, click the book's title, then click Errata). In fact, you're invited and encouraged to submit such corrections and updates yourself. In an effort to keep the book as up-to-date and accurate as possible, each time we print more copies of this book, we'll make any confirmed corrections you've suggested. We'll also note such changes on the Web site, so that you can mark important corrections into your own copy of the book, if you like.

In the meantime, we'd love to hear your own suggestions for new books in the Missing Manual line. There's a place for that on the Web site, too, as well as a place to sign up for free email notification of new titles in the series.

The Very Basics

To use this book, and indeed to use any kind of computer, you need to know a few basics. This book assumes that, as somebody who's used Windows, you're already familiar with a few terms and concepts:

- **Clicking.** To *click* means to point the arrow cursor at something on the screen and then—without moving the cursor at all—to press and release the button on the mouse (or your laptop trackpad). To *double-click,* of course, means to click twice in rapid succession, again without moving the cursor at all. And to *drag* means to move the cursor while pressing the button.

  When you're told to ⌘-*click* something, you click while pressing the ⌘ key (which is next to the Space bar). Such related procedures as *Shift-clicking, Option-clicking,* and *Control-clicking* work the same way—just click while pressing the corresponding key at the bottom of your keyboard.

- **Menus.** The *menus* are the words at the top of your screen: File, Edit, and so on. (The at the top left corner of your screen is a menu, too.) Click any of these to make a list of commands appear, as though they're written on a window shade you've just pulled down.

  Some people click to open a menu and then release the mouse button; after reading the menu command choices, they click again on the one they want. Other people like to press the mouse button continuously after the initial click on the menu title, drag down the list to the desired command, and only then release the mouse button. Either method works fine.

- **Keyboard shortcuts.** If you're typing along in a burst of creative energy, it's sometimes disruptive to have to take your hand off the keyboard, grab the mouse, and then use a menu (for example, to use the Bold command). That's why many experienced Mac fans prefer to trigger menu commands by pressing certain combinations on the keyboard. For example, in most word processors, you can press ⌘-B to produce a **boldface** word. When you read an instruction like "press ⌘-B," start by pressing the ⌘ key; while it's down, type the letter B, and then release both keys.

- **Icons.** The colorful inch-tall pictures that appear in your various desktop folders are the *icons*—graphic symbols that represent each program, disk, and document on your computer. If you click an icon one time, it darkens; you've just *highlighted* or *selected* it, in readiness to manipulate it by using, for example, a menu command.

If you've mastered this much information, you have all the technical background you need to enjoy *Switching to the Mac: The Missing Manual.*

Part One:
Welcome to Macintosh

1

How the Mac Is Different

W hen you get right down to it, the job description of every operating system is pretty much the same. Whether it's Mac OS X, Windows XP, or Billy Bob's System-Software Special, any OS must serve as the ambassador between the computer and you, its human operator. It must somehow represent your files and programs on the screen so that you can open them; offer some method of organizing your files; present onscreen controls that affect your speaker volume, mouse speed, and so on; and communicate with your external gadgets, like disks, printers, and digital cameras.

In other words, Mac OS X offers roughly the same features as recent versions of Windows. That's the good news.

The bad news is that they're called different things and parked in different spots. As you could have predicted, this rearrangement of features can mean a good deal of confusion for you, the Macintosh foreigner. For the first few days or weeks, you may keep instinctively reaching for certain familiar features that simply aren't where you expect to find them, the way your tongue keeps sticking itself into the socket of the newly extracted tooth.

To minimize the frustration, read this chapter first. It makes plain the most important and dramatic differences between the Windows method and the Macintosh way.

The One-Button Mouse

Every Windows mouse ever made has two buttons. You use the left one for selecting things, and the right one for making shortcut menus appear (Figure 1-1).

Apple, on the other hand, thinks that two mouse buttons is one too many. An Apple mouse has only one mouse button—the equivalent of the Windows left mouse button. You use it exclusively for selecting and clicking things.

That's not to say that you can't "right-click" things on the Mac—you can, as shown in Figure 1-1. On the Mac, though, you're supposed to produce shortcut menus by holding down the Control key as you click things on the screen. (Furthermore, they're not called *shortcut menus* on the Mac; they're called *contextual menus,* because the list of commands that appears depends on what you're clicking and when.)

Tip: If this Control-clicking business bothers you, as it does certain hard-core Windows veterans, you're welcome to provide your own two-button USB mouse. Most are very inexpensive. The instant you plug a two-button mouse into your USB port, you'll be able to right-click on the Mac just as you do in Windows.

Although you generally don't need to install driver software for USB mice, it's worth checking the manufacturer's Web site for Mac OS X drivers. They may give your two-button mouse even more features.

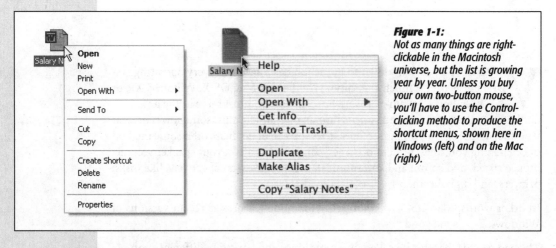

Figure 1-1:
Not as many things are right-clickable in the Macintosh universe, but the list is growing year by year. Unless you buy your own two-button mouse, you'll have to use the Control-clicking method to produce the shortcut menus, shown here in Windows (left) and on the Mac (right).

On, Off, and Sleep

If you're the only person who uses your Mac, finishing up a work session is simple. You can either turn off the machine or simply let it go to sleep, in any of several ways.

Sleep Mode

It's clear that Apple expects its customers *not* to shut down their machines between sessions, because the company has gone to great lengths to make doing so inconvenient. (For example, pressing the Power button on most Mac models no longer offers you the option to shut down.)

That's OK. *Sleep mode* (called Standby on the PC) consumes very little power, keeps everything you were doing open and in memory, and wakes the Mac up almost immediately when you press a key or click the mouse. To make your machine sleep, use any of these techniques:

- Choose →Sleep. (The menu, available no matter what program you're using, is at the upper-left corner of your screen.)

- Press Control-Eject. In the dialog box shown in Figure 1-2, click Sleep (or just press S).

- Press the Power button on your machine. On most current models, doing so makes it sleep immediately.

- Just walk away, confident that the Energy Saver control panel described on page 293 will automatically send the machine off to dreamland at the specified time.

Figure 1-2:
Once the Shut Down dialog box appears, you can press the S key instead of clicking Sleep, R for Restart, Esc for Cancel, or Enter for Shut Down.

Restart

You shouldn't have to restart the Mac very often. But on those rare occasions, including severe troubleshooting mystification, here are a few ways to do it:

- Choose →Restart.Click Restart (or press Enter) in the confirmation dialog box.

- Press Control-⌘-Eject. (On older laptops that lack a separate Eject key, substitute F12.)

- Press Control-Eject to summon the dialog box shown in Figure 1-2. Click Restart (or type R).

Shut Down

To shut down your machine completely (when you don't plan to use it for more than a couple of days or when you plan to transport it, for example), do one of the following:

- Choose →Shut Down. A simple confirmation dialog box appears; click Shut Down (or press Enter).

- Press Control-Option-⌘-Eject. (It's not as complex as it looks—the first three keys are all in a tidy row to the left of the Space bar.)

- Press Control-Eject to summon the dialog box shown in Figure 1-2; click Shut Down (or press Enter).

Note: The Macintosh has no equivalent of the modern PC's Hibernate mode.

Log Out

If you share your Mac with other people, you should *log out* when you're done. Doing so ensures that your stuff is safe from the evil and the clueless when you're out of the room. To do it, choose →Log Out (or press Shift-⌘-Q). When the confirmation dialog box appears, click Log Out (or press Enter), or just wait for two minutes. The Mac hides your world from view and displays the Login dialog box, ready for the next victim. Logging out is described in greater detail in Chapter 12.

Tip: If you press Option as you release the mouse when choosing the Restart, Shut Down, or Log Out commands, you eliminate the "Are you sure?" confirmation dialog box. The mouse click you save each time can really add up.

The Menu Bar

It won't take you long to discover that on the Macintosh, there's only one menu bar. It's always at the top of the screen. The names of these menus, and the commands inside them, change to suit the window you're currently using. That's a bit different from Windows, where a separate menu bar appears at the top of every window.

Mac and Windows devotees can argue the relative merits of these two approaches until they're blue in the face. All that matters is that you know where to look when you want to reach for a menu command. On the Mac, you always look upward.

Finder = Windows Explorer

In Mac OS X, the "home base" program—the one that appears when you first turn on the machine, showing you the icons of all your folders and files—is called the Finder. This is where you manage your folders and files, throw things away, manipulate disks, and so on. (You may also hear it called the *desktop*.)

Getting used to the term Finder is worthwhile right up front, because it comes up so often. For example, the first icon on your Dock (page 65) is labeled Finder, and clicking it always takes you back to your desktop.

Dock = Taskbar

At the bottom of almost every Mac OS X screen sits a tiny row of photorealistic icons. This is the Dock, a close parallel to the Windows taskbar. (As in Windows, it may be hidden or placed on the left or right edge of the screen instead—but those are primarily options preferred by power users and eccentrics.)

On the Dock, all your *open* programs and windows are denoted by small black triangles beneath their icons. Clicking these icons takes you to the corresponding files, folders, disks, documents, and programs; and if you click and hold (or Control-click) an open program's icon, you'll see a pop-up list of the open windows in that program, along with Quit and a few other commands.

When you close a program, its icon disappears from the Dock (unless you've secured it there for easy access, as described on page 70).

Tip: Just as in Windows, you can cycle through the various open programs on your Dock by holding down the ⌘ key and pressing Tab repeatedly. In Mac OS X 10.2 and later, in fact, you can just *tap* ⌘-Tab to switch back from the program you're using into the one you used most recently.

What you may find confusing at first, though, is that the Dock also performs one function of the Windows Start menu: It provides a "short list" of programs and files that you use often, for easy access. To add a new icon to the Dock, just drag it there (put programs to the left of the divider line; everything else goes on the right). To remove an icon from the Dock, just drag the icon away from the Dock. As long as that item isn't actually open at the moment, it disappears from the Dock with a little animated puff of smoke when you release the mouse button.

The bottom line: On the Mac, a single interface element, the Dock, exhibits characteristics of *both* the Start menu (it lists frequently used programs) and the taskbar (it lists currently open programs and files).

Chapter 3 describes the dock in more detail.

Menulets = Tray

Most Windows fans refer to the row of tiny status icons at the lower-right corner of the screen as the *tray,* even though Microsoft's official term is the notification area. (Why use one syllable when eight will do?)

Macintosh fans wage a similar battle of terminology when it comes to the little menu-bar icons shown in Figure 1-3. Apple calls them Menu Extras, but Mac fans prefer to call them *menulets.*

In any case, these menu-bar icons are the direct cousins of the Windows tray—that is, each is both an indicator and a menu that provides direct access to certain set-

Figure 1-3:
The little icons at the upper-right corner of the Mac OS X screen are called Menu Extras or menulets. Each is generally both a status indicator and a pop-up menu.

tings in System Preferences. One lets you adjust your Mac's speaker volume, another lets you change the screen resolution, another shows you the remaining power in your laptop battery, and so on.

To summon the various menulets, you usually must turn on a certain checkbox. These "Show" checkboxes lurk on the various panes of *System Preferences* (Chapter 13), which is the Mac equivalent of the Control Panel. (To open System Preferences, click the light-switch icon on the Dock, or choose its name from the menu.)

Here's where to find this magic on/off checkbox for each of the menulets (in the order shown in Figure 1-3):

- **Bluetooth status** is for connecting to Bluetooth devices, "pairing" your Mac with a cell phone, and so on. *To find the "Show" checkbox:* Open System Preferences→Network. From the Show pop-up menu, choose Bluetooth. (It's available only if you've installed Apple's Bluetooth software.)

- **Eject disc.** This one's the oddball: There's no checkbox in System Preferences to make it appear. In fact, the fact that it even exists is something of a secret.

  To make it appear, open the System→Library→CoreServices→Menu Extras folder, and double-click the Eject.menu folder. That's it! The Eject menulet appears.

  You'll discover that its wording changes: "Open Combo Drive," "Close DVD-RAM Drive," "Eject [Name of Disk]," or whatever, to reflect your particular drive type and what's in it at the moment.

- **PPPoE status** (PPP over Ethernet) lets you control certain kinds of DSL connections. *To find the "Show" checkbox:* Open System Preferences→Network→PPPoE.

- **Dial-up modem status** lets you connect or disconnect from the Internet. *To find the "Show" checkbox:* Open System Preferences→Network. From the Show pop-up menu, choose Internal Modem. Click the Modem tab.

- **Displays** adjusts screen resolution. *To find the "Show" checkbox:* Open System Preferences→Displays.

- **AirPort status** lets you turn your AirPort card on or off, and join existing AirPort wireless networks. (AirPort is Apple's name for the popular 802.11 wireless networking standard.) *To find the "Show" checkbox:* Open System Preferences→Network. From the Show pop-up menu, choose AirPort. (It's available only if you've installed Apple's AirPort software.)

- **Speaker volume,** of course, adjusts your Mac's speaker volume. *To find the "Show" checkbox:* Open System Preferences→Sound.

- **Battery status** shows how much power remains in your laptop's battery (laptops only). *To find the "Show" checkbox:* Open System Preferences→Energy Saver→Options. (Two battery icons appear in Figure 1-3, because it's a PowerBook G3 with, of course, two batteries.)

- **Menu-bar clock** tells the time, in analog or digital form (choose your preference from the menulet itself). *To find the "Show" checkbox:* Open System Preferences→ Date & Time→Menu Bar Clock tab.

To remove a menulet, just drag it off of your menu bar while pressing the ⌘ key (or turn off the corresponding checkbox in System Preferences). You can also rearrange them by ⌘-dragging them horizontally.

Keyboard Differences

The Mac and PC keyboards are different, too. Making the switch involves two big adjustments: Figuring out where the special Windows keys went (like Alt and Ctrl)— and figuring out what to do with the special Macintosh keys (like ⌘ and Option).

Where the Windows Keys Went

Here's how to find the Macintosh equivalents of familiar PC keyboard keys:

- **Ctrl key.** The Macintosh offers a key labeled Control, but it isn't the equivalent of the PC's Ctrl key. (It's primarily for helping you "right-click" things, as described above.)

  Instead, the Macintosh equivalent of the Ctrl key is the ⌘ key. It's right next to the Space bar, bearing both the cloverleaf symbol and the Apple logo. It's pronounced "command," although novices can often be heard calling it the "pretzel key," "Apple key," or "clover key."

  Most Windows Ctrl-key combos correspond perfectly to ⌘ key sequences on the Mac. The Save command is now ⌘-S instead of Ctrl-S, Open is ⌘-O instead of Ctrl-O, and so on. (Mac keyboard shortcuts are listed at the right side of each open menu, just as in Windows.)

- **Alt key.** On most Mac keyboards, a key on the bottom row of the Macintosh keyboard, between the Space bar and the ⌘ key, is labeled *both* Alt and Option (at least on Macs sold in the U.S.). This is the closest thing the Mac offers to the old Alt key, and it's generally called the Option key.

  In many situations, keyboard shortcuts that involve the Alt key in Windows use the Option key on the Mac. For example, in Microsoft Word, the keyboard shortcut for the Split Document Window command is *Alt*-Ctrl-S in Windows, but *Option*-⌘-T on the Macintosh.

  Still, these two keys aren't exactly the same. Whereas the Alt key's most popular function is to control the menus in Windows programs, the Option key on the Mac is a "miscellaneous" key that triggers secret functions and secret characters.

  For example, when you hold down the Option key as you click the close or minimize button on a Macintosh window, you close or minimize *all* open desktop windows. (See page 22 for more on window controls.) And if you press the Option key while you type R, G, or 2, you get the ®, ©, and ™ symbols in your document. (See page 369 to find out how you can see which alphabet letters turn into which symbols when you press Option.)

- **Windows logo key.** As you probably could have guessed, there is no Windows key on the Macintosh. Then again, there's no Start menu to open by pressing it, either.

Tip: If you connect a USB Windows keyboard to the Mac, it works fine—and the Windows-logo key works like the Mac's ⌘ key.

- **Backspace and Delete.** On the Mac, the backspace key is labeled Delete, although it's in exactly the same place as the Windows Backspace key.

  The Delete key (technically, the *forward delete* key, because it deletes the character to the right of the insertion point) is a different story. On a desktop Macintosh, it's labeled with the word *Del* and a little forward-delete X symbol.

  On laptop Macs, this key is missing. You can still perform a forward delete, though, by pressing the regular delete key while pressing the Fn key in the lower-left corner of the laptop keyboard.

- **Enter.** Most full-size Windows keyboards have *two* Enter keys: one at the right side of the alphabet keyboard, and one at the lower-right corner of the number pad. They're identical in function; pressing either one serves to "click" the OK button in a dialog box, for example.

  On the Mac, the big key on the number pad still says Enter, but the key on the alphabet keyboard is usually labeled Return. Most of the time, their function is identical—once again, either can "click" the OK button of a dialog box. Every now and then, though, you'll run across a Mac program where Return and Enter do different things. In Microsoft Word for Mac OS X, for example, Shift-*Return* inserts a line break, but Shift-*Enter* creates a page break.

Note: See page 202 for a summary of the Mac's text-navigation keystrokes.

What the Special Mac Keys Do

So much for finding Windows keys you're used to. There's another category of keys worth discussing, however: keys on the modern Macintosh keyboard that you've never seen before. (If you're using a very old Macintosh, you may not have these special keys.) For example:

- ◀̶, ◀)), ◀. These keys give you one-touch control of your Mac's built-in speaker—a great feature when, for example, you intend to use your laptop in a library or in church. (Yes, every Macintosh has built-in speakers. You're welcome to attach external stereo ones, but you don't have to.) The three symbols here mean Quieter, Louder, and Mute. (Press Mute a second time to turn speakers back on.)

• ⏏. This key, in the upper-right corner of the keyboard, means Eject. When you press it, your Mac's CD or DVD drawer opens so that you can insert or remove a disc. Or, if your Mac has a *slot-loading* CD or DVD drive (one that slurps in the disc rather than providing a tray for it), pressing the Eject key spits out whatever disc is in the machine.

If you have an older Mac whose keyboard doesn't have this key, the F12 key serves the same purpose.

Tip: You have to hold this key down for a moment; just tapping it generally doesn't do anything. That's to prevent you from ejecting a disc by accident and knocking over your coffee.

Disk Differences

Working with disks is very different on the Mac. Whereas Windows is designed to show the names (letters) and icons for your disk *drives,* the Mac shows you the names and icons of your *disks.* You'll never see an icon for an empty drive, as you do in Windows.

As soon as you insert, say, a CD, you see its name and icon appear on the screen. In fact, *every* disk inside, or attached to, a Macintosh is represented on the desktop by an icon (see Figure 1-4). That's why the icon for your primary hard drive (usually named Macintosh HD) has probably been sitting in the upper-right corner of your screen since the first time you turned on the Mac.

If you prefer the Windows look, in which no disk icons appear on the desktop, it's easy enough to re-create it on the Mac, as shown in Figure 1-4.

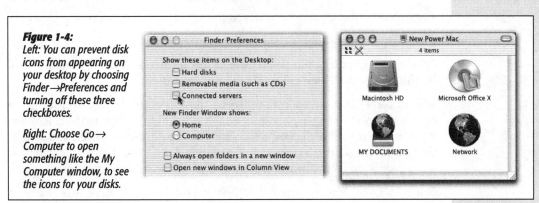

Figure 1-4:
Left: You can prevent disk icons from appearing on your desktop by choosing Finder→Preferences and turning off these three checkboxes.

Right: Choose Go→ Computer to open something like the My Computer window, to see the icons for your disks.

Ejecting a disc from the Mac is a little bit different, too, whether it's a CD, DVD, Zip disk, floppy, shared network disk, iDisk (page 125), iPod, or non-startup hard drive. You can go about it in any of these ways:

- Click the disk icon on the screen, and then press the Eject key as described above.

- Control-click (or right-click) the disk's desktop icon. From the contextual menu that appears, choose Eject (Figure 1-5).

- Click the disk's icon and then choose File→Eject (or press ⌘-E).

- Drag the icon of the disk onto the Trash icon at the end of the Dock. (You'll see its icon turn into a giant Eject symbol, the Mac's little acknowledgment that it knows what you're trying to do.)

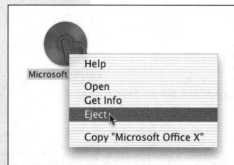

Microsoft

| Help |
| Open |
| Get Info |
| Eject |
| Copy "Microsoft Office X" |

Figure 1-5:
The Macintosh provides at least four different ways to make a physical disk pop out of its drive (floppy, Zip, CD, DVD). The same methods unmount *(remove from your screen) any other kind of disk (network disk, iDisk, hard drive, or whatever).*

For you, the Windows veteran, the main thing to remember here is that you *never eject a Macintosh disk by pushing the Eject button* (if there even is one) on the disk drive itself.

Where Your Stuff Is

The folders of Mac OS X bear some resemblance to those in Windows. For example:

Applications Folder

Applications is Apple's word for *programs,* although among ordinary humans, you'll hear the terms used interchangeably.

When it comes to managing your programs, the Applications folder (which you can open by choosing Go→Applications) is something like the Program Files folder in Windows—but without the worry. You should feel free to open this folder and double-click things. In fact, that's exactly what you're supposed to do. This is your complete list of programs. (What's on your Dock is more like a Greatest Hits subset.)

Better yet, on the Mac, programs bear their real, plain-English names, like Microsoft Word, rather than "eight-dot-three"-letter abbreviations, like WINWORD.EXE. Most are self-contained in a single icon, too (rather than being composed of hundreds of little support files), which makes copying or deleting a program extremely easy.

Home Folder

Your documents, files, and preferences, meanwhile, sit in an important folder called your *Home folder*. Inside are folders that closely resemble the My Documents, My Pictures, and My Music folders in Windows—except that on the Mac, they don't say "My."

The long way to find it is to open the Macintosh HD (hard drive) window, double-click the Users folder inside it, and then double-click the folder inside *it* that bears your name and looks like a house (see Figure 1-6). Here, at last, is the window that you'll eventually fill with new folders to organize, back up, and so on.

Figure 1-6:
For the most part, the folders you care about on the Mac are the Applications folder in the main hard drive window (top) and your own Home folder (middle and bottom). You're welcome to save your documents and park your icons almost anywhere on your Mac (except inside the System folder or other people's Home folders). But keeping your work in your Home folder makes backing up and file sharing easier.

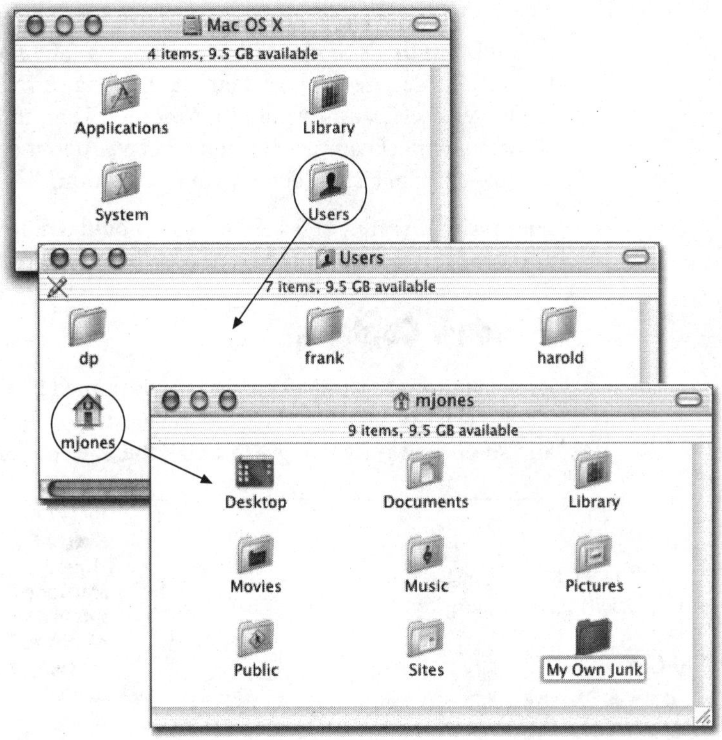

Fortunately, Mac OS X is rife with shortcuts for opening this all-important folder.

- Choose Go→Home.

- Press Shift-⌘-H.

- Click the Home icon on the toolbar (page 72).

- Click the Home icon on the Dock. (If you don't see one, consult page 74 for instructions on how to put one there.)

The rationale for forcing you to keep all of your stuff in a single folder is described in Chapter 12. (Windows 2000 and Windows XP work very similarly.) For now, it's enough to note that the approach has some advantages. For example, by keeping such tight control over which files go where, Mac OS X keeps itself pure—and very, very stable.

Furthermore, keeping all of your stuff in a single folder makes it very easy for you to back up your work. It also makes life easier when you try to connect to your machine from elsewhere in the office (over the network) or elsewhere in the world (over the Internet).

System Folder

This folder is the same idea as the WINDOWS or WINNT folder on a PC, in that it contains hundreds of files that are critical to the functioning of the operating system. These files are so important that moving or renaming them could render the computer useless, as it would in Windows. That, in fact, is why the System folder shows up almost completely empty when you first open it. Thousands of files lurk within—they're just hidden for your protection.

For maximum safety and stability, you should ignore Mac OS X's System folder just as thoroughly as you ignored the old Windows folder.

Window Controls

As in Windows, a window on the Mac is framed by an assortment of doodads and gizmos (Figure 1-7). You'll need these to move a window, close it, resize it, scroll it, and so on. But once you get to know the ones on a Macintosh, you're likely to be

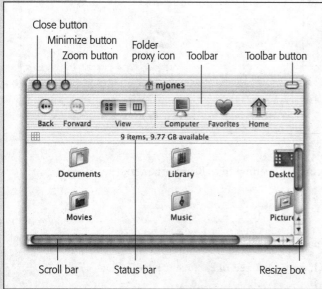

Figure 1-7:
When Steve Jobs unveiled Mac OS X at a Macworld Expo in 1999, he said that his goal was to oversee the creation of an interface so attractive, "you just want to lick it." Desktop windows, with their juicy, fruit-flavored controls, are a good starting point.

pleased by the amount of thought those fussy perfectionists at Apple have put into their design.

Here's an overview of the various Mac OS X window-edge gizmos and what they do.

Title Bar

When several windows are open, the darkened window name and colorful upper-left controls tell you which window is *active* (in front). Any windows in the background have gray, dimmed lettering and gray upper-left control buttons. As in Windows, the title bar also acts as a *handle* that lets you move the entire window around on the screen.

Tip: Here's a nifty keyboard shortcut: You can cycle through the different open windows in one program without using the mouse. Just press ⌘-' (that's the tilde key, to the left of the number 1 key). With each press, you bring a different window forward within the current program. It works both in the Finder and in your programs.

After you've opened one folder that's inside another, the title bar's secret *folder hierarchy menu* is an efficient way to backtrack—to return to the enclosing window. Figure 1-8 reveals everything about the process after this key move: press the ⌘ key as you click the name of the window. (You can release the ⌘ key immediately after clicking.)

Tip: Instead of using this title bar menu, you can also jump to the enclosing window by pressing ⌘-up arrow. Pressing ⌘-down arrow takes you back into the folder you started in. (This makes more sense when you try it than when you read it.)

Figure 1-8:
Press ⌘ and click a window's title bar (top) to summon the hidden folder hierarchy menu (bottom). By choosing the name of a folder from this menu, you open the corresponding window. The Finder isn't the only program that offers this trick, by the way. It also works in most other Mac OS X–compatible programs.

One more title bar trick: By double-clicking the title bar, you *minimize* the window (as described on the next page).

Tip: The Option key means "apply this action to all windows." For example, Option-double-clicking any title bar minimizes *all* desktop windows, sending them flying to the Dock. Option-clicking the close button closes all open desktop windows, and so on. (The Option-key trick doesn't close all windows in every program, however—only those in the current program. Option-closing an Internet Explorer window closes *Internet Explorer* windows, but your desktop windows remain open. Moreover, Option-closing doesn't work in Microsoft Office programs.)

Close Button

As the tip of your cursor crosses the three buttons at the upper-left corner of a window, tiny symbols appear inside them: x, –, and +. The most important window gadget is the close button—the red, droplet-like button in the upper-left corner (see Figure 1-4). It closes the window, exactly like the X button at the upper-*right* corner in Windows. Learning to reach for the upper-left corner instead of the upper-right will probably confound your muscle memory for the first week of using the Macintosh.

Tip: If, while working on a document, you see a tiny dot in the center of the close button, Mac OS X is trying to tell you that you haven't yet saved your work. The dot goes away when you save the document.

Figure 1-9:
Clicking the minimize button sends a window scurrying down to the Dock, collapsing in on itself as though being forced through a tiny, invisible funnel. If you collapse a document window in this way (as opposed to a desktop window), a tiny icon appears on the corner of its minimized image to identify the program it's running in.

Or you can avoid that frustration by learning to use the keyboard shortcut: ⌘-W (for *Window*)—a keystroke that's somewhat easier than the Windows version (Alt-F4), which for most people is a two-handed operation. If you get into the habit of dismissing windows with that deft flex of your left hand, you'll find it far easier to close several windows in a row, because you don't have to aim for successive close buttons.

Minimize Button

Click this yellow drop of gel to minimize any Mac window, sending it shrinking, with a genie-like animated effect, into the right end of the Dock, where it now appears as an icon. It's exactly like minimizing a window in Windows, except that it's now represented by a Dock icon rather than a taskbar button (see Figure 1-9). To bring it back, click the newly created Dock icon (see Chapter 3 for more on the Dock).

Tip: If you enjoy the ability to roll up your windows in this way, remember that you actually have a bigger target than the tiny minimize button. The entire striped title bar becomes a giant minimize button when you double-click anywhere on it.

Better yet, you can also minimize a window from the keyboard by pressing ⌘-M. That's a keystroke worth memorizing on Day One.

Zoom Button

A click on this green geltab (see Figure 1-7) makes a desktop window just large enough to show you all of the icons inside it. If your monitor isn't big enough to show all the icons in a window, the zoom box resizes the window to show as many as possible. In either case, a second click on the zoom button restores the window to its original size. (The Window→Zoom Window command does the same thing.)

This should sound familiar: It's a lot like the maximize button at the top right of a Windows window. On the Macintosh, however, the window never springs so big that it fills the entire screen, leaving a lot of empty space around the window contents; it only grows enough to show you as much of the contents as possible.

The Folder Proxy Icon

Each Macintosh title bar features a small icon next to the window's name (Figure 1-10), representing the open window's actual folder or disk icon. In the Finder, dragging this tiny icon (technically called the *folder proxy icon*) lets you move or copy the folder to a different folder or disk, to the Trash, or into the Dock, without having to close the window first. (When clicking this proxy icon, hold down the mouse button for a half second, or until the icon darkens. Only then are you allowed to drag it.) It's a handy little function with no Windows equivalent.

Tip: In a program like Microsoft Word, dragging this proxy icon lets you move the actual file to a different disk or folder—without even leaving the program. It's a great way to make a backup of the document that you're working on without interrupting your work.

Figure 1-10:
When you find yourself confronting a Finder window that contains useful stuff, consider dragging its proxy icon to the Dock. You wind up installing its folder or disk icon there for future use. That's not the same thing as minimizing the window, which only puts an icon for the window into the Dock, and only temporarily at that.

The Finder Toolbar

Chapter 3 describes this fascinating desktop-window element in great detail.

Toolbar Button

Mac OS X prefers to keep only one Finder window open at a time. That is, if a window called United States is filled with folders for the individual states, double-clicking the New York folder doesn't open a second window. Instead, the New York window replaces the United States window (Figure 1-11). Modern versions of Windows work exactly the same way.

So what if you've now opened inner folder B, and you want to backtrack to outer folder A? In that case, just click the tiny left-arrow button labeled Back, shown in Figure 1-11, or use one of these alternatives:

• Choose Go→Back

• Press ⌘-[(left bracket)

• Press ⌘-up arrow

None of that will help you, however, if you want to copy a file from one folder into another, or compare the contents of two windows. In such cases, you'll probably want to see both windows open at the same time.

You can open a second window using any of these techniques:

• Choose File→New Finder Window (⌘-N).

Tip: The window that appears when you do this is the Computer window, which usually isn't where you find the folders you want to work with. Changing this setting should be one of your first bits of business in Mac OS X.

To do so, choose Finder→Preferences and click the Home button (near the center of the dialog box that appears). Now every new Finder window shows you your Home folder (page 20), which contains all your files—a much more useful arrangement.

• ⌘-double-click a disk or folder icon.

• Double-click a folder or disk icon on your desktop.

Figure 1-11:
In an effort to help you avoid window clutter, Apple has designed Mac OS X windows so that double-clicking a folder in a window (top) doesn't actually open another window (bottom). Every time you double-click a folder in an open window, its contents replace whatever was previously in the window. If you double-click three folders in succession, you still wind up with just one open window.

- Choose File→Preferences, and turn on "Always open folders in a new window." Now when you double-click a folder, it always opens into a new window of its own.

Another alternative is to switch to "hidden-toolbar mode" (not the official Apple terminology). The upper-right corner of every Finder window contains a little button that looks like a half-inch squirt of Crest toothpaste. When you click it, you enter hidden-toolbar mode. (You can also enter hidden-toolbar mode by pressing ⌘-B, the equivalent for the View→Hide Toolbar command.)

In this mode, two things happen. First, the Finder window toolbar, identified in Figure 1-7, slides out of sight. Second, double-clicking a folder now opens a new corresponding window.

You can return to regular Mac OS X mode by clicking the toolbar button again, by pressing ⌘-B again, or by choosing View→Show Toolbar.

Note: You'll find this little white toolbar-control nubbin in a number of toolbar-endowed programs, including Mail, Internet Explorer, System Preferences, and others. Clicking it makes the toolbar go away.

Scroll Bars

In general, scroll bars work on the Mac just as they do in Windows.

Tip: One key difference: Out of the box, the Mac scroll bar's scroll-up arrow and scroll-down arrow are nestled together, at the same end of the scroll bar (the bottom, for example). To "fix" them so that they sit at opposite ends as in Windows, choose ⌘→System Preferences. Click General. Where it says "Place scroll arrows," click "At top and bottom."

Mac OS X, however, introduces a new scroll bar option called "Scroll to here." Ordinarily, when you click in the scroll bar track above or below the gelatinous handle, the window scrolls by one screenful. But your other option is to turn on "Scroll to here" mode in the General panel of your System Preferences (see page 295). Now when you click in the scroll bar track, the Mac considers the entire scroll bar a proportional map of the document and scrolls directly to the spot you clicked. That is, if you click at the very bottom of the scroll bar track, you see the very last page.

It's worth noting, however, that the true speed expert eschews scroll bars altogether. The Mac has the usual complement of navigation keys: Page Up, Page Down, Home, and End (although these don't always work the way you're used to; see page 203). And if you bought a non-Apple mouse that has a scroll wheel on the top, you can use it to scroll windows, too, without pressing any keys at all.

Tip: Avoiding the scroll bars also gives you the option to scroll a Finder window diagonally. Position your mouse inside a Finder window (list views not included) or even an Internet Explorer window. While pressing ⌘ and Option, you can drag—and scroll—in any direction. As you drag, the cursor changes shape, becoming a white-gloved butler's hand. Where can you get that kind of service these days?

Resize Box

The lower-right corner of every standard Mac OS X window is ribbed, a design that's meant to imply that you can grip it by dragging. Doing so lets you resize and reshape the window, just as on the PC.

Unfortunately, you can't also change the shape of a Macintosh window by dragging its *edges,* as you can in Windows.

Status Bar

If you choose View→Show Status Bar, you get a handy information strip just beneath the title bar in every Finder window. It tells you how many icons are in the window ("14 items," for example) and the amount of free space remaining on the disk.

Tip: If the window is very narrow, the status bar shows only the number of icons in the window (such as "1 item"). To see how much free space is on the disk, *click* the "1 item" text. Mac OS X changes it to show you the remaining free-space statistic. Click again to return to the item count.

Terminology Differences

There are enough other differences between Mac and windows to fill 17 pages. Indeed, that's what you'll find at the end of this book: an alphabetical listing of every familiar Windows feature and where to find its equivalent on the Mac.

As you read both that section of the book and the chapters that precede it, however, you'll discover that some functions are almost identical in Mac OS X and Windows, but have different names. Here's a quick-reference summary.

Windows term	**Macintosh term**
Control Panel	System Preferences
Drop-down menu	Pop-up menu
Program	Application
Properties	Get Info
Recycle Bin	Trash
Search command	Find command
Shortcut menus	Contextual menus
Shortcuts	Aliases
Taskbar	Dock
Tray (notification area)	Menulets
Windows Explorer	Finder
WINDOWS folder	System folder

Windows and Icons

When you turn on a Mac with the latest version of Mac OS X, you hear a startup chime from the Mac's built-in speakers. You see the Apple logo as the machine warms up, followed by an animated, liquidy blue progress bar. (Don't tell anyone, but behind this shimmering façade, what's actually loading is *Unix,* the operating system preferred by geeks the world over.)

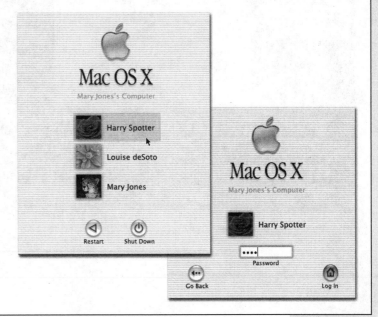

Figure 2-1:
Left: On Macs configured to accommodate different people at different times, one of the first things you see upon turning on the computer is this dialog box. Click your name. (If the list is long, you may have to scroll to find your name—or just type the first couple of letters of it.)

Right: At this point, you're asked to type in your password. Type it and then click Log In (or press Return or Enter; on the Mac, pressing these keys always "clicks" the blue, pulsing button in a dialog box). If you've typed the wrong password, the dialog box vibrates, in effect shaking its little dialog-box head, suggesting that you guess again.

Logging In

What happens next depends on whether you are the Mac's sole proprietor or share it with other people in an office, school, or household.

- **If it's your own Mac,** and you've already been through the Mac OS X setup wizard described in Appendix A (including the "What's your time zone?" and "What's your name?" screens that appear the first time you turn on a new Mac), no big deal. You arrive at the Mac OS X desktop.

- **If it's a shared Mac,** you may encounter the Login dialog box, shown in Figure 2-1. Click your name in the list. Type your password if you're asked for it, and click Log In (or press Return). You arrive at the desktop. Chapter 12 offers much more on this business of user accounts and logging in.

The Elements of the Mac OS X Desktop

Most of the objects on your screen should seem familiar. They are, in fact, cousins of elements you already know from Windows. Here's a quick tour (see Figure 2-2).

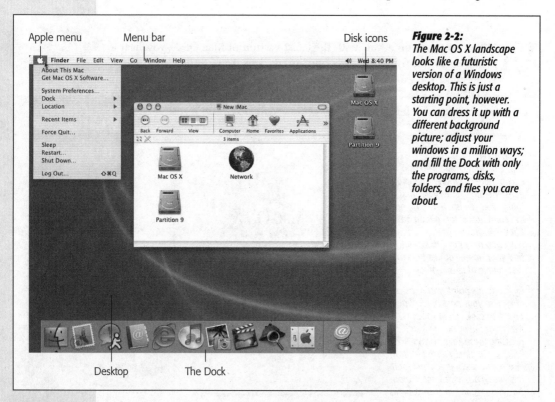

Apple menu   Menu bar   Disk icons

Figure 2-2:
The Mac OS X landscape looks like a futuristic version of a Windows desktop. This is just a starting point, however. You can dress it up with a different background picture; adjust your windows in a million ways; and fill the Dock with only the programs, disks, folders, and files you care about.

Desktop   The Dock

Note: If your desktop looks absolutely nothing like this—no menus, no icons, almost nothing on the Dock—then somebody in charge of your Mac has turned on *Simple Finder mode* for you. Details on page 271.

Disk icons

As noted in Chapter 1, the icons of your hard drive and any other disks attached to your Mac generally appear on your desktop for quick access.

The Dock

This ribbon of translucent, almost photographic icons is a launcher for programs, files, folders, and disks you use often.

In principle, the Dock is very simple:

• Programs go on the left side. Everything else goes on the right, including documents, folders, and disks. (Figure 2-2 shows the dividing line.)

• You can add a new icon to the Dock by dragging it there. Rearrange Dock icons by dragging them like tiles on a puzzle. Remove a Dock icon by dragging it away from the Dock, and enjoy the animated puff of smoke that appears when you release the mouse button. (You can't remove the icon of a program that's currently open, however.)

• Click something *once* to open it. A tiny triangle underneath a program's icon lets you know that it's open.

• Each Dock icon sprouts a pop-up menu, similar to a shortcut menu. A folder can show you a list of what's inside, for example. To see the menu, hold the mouse button down on a Dock icon, or Control-click it, or (if you have a two-button mouse) right-click it.

You can change the Dock's size, move it to the sides of your screen, or hide it entirely. Chapter 3 contains complete instructions for using and understanding the Dock.

The menu

The menu at the top left of the screen houses important Mac-wide commands that used to be scattered—sometimes illogically—in other menus. For example, the Sleep, Restart, and Shut Down commands now appear here, where they're always available.

The menu bar

The first menu in every program, in boldface, tells you at a glance what program you're in. The commands in this Application menu include About (which tells you what version of the program you're using), Preferences, Quit, and commands like Hide Others and Show All (which help you control window clutter, as described on page 81).

The File and Edit menus come next, exactly as in Windows. The last menu is almost always Help. It opens a miniature Web browser that lets you search the online Mac Help files for explanatory text.

Icon View

Chapter 1 provides a tour of the various gizmos around the *edges* of a window (the close button, Resize box, and so on)—but what about what's *inside* a window?

As it turns out, you can view the files and folders in a desktop window in any of three ways: as icons, as a single list, or in a series of neat columns. To switch from one view to another, click one of the corresponding icons in the toolbar (see Figure 2-3), or choose View→as Icons (or View→as Columns, or View→as List).

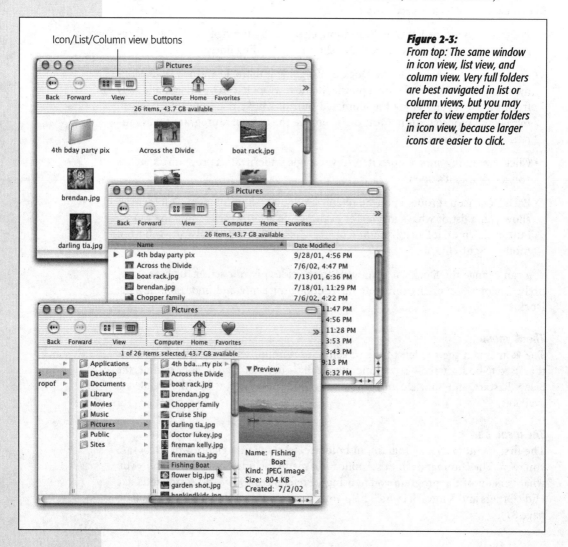

Figure 2-3:
From top: The same window in icon view, list view, and column view. Very full folders are best navigated in list or column views, but you may prefer to view emptier folders in icon view, because larger icons are easier to click.

In icon view, each file, folder, and disk is represented by a small picture—an *icon*. This humble image, a visual representation of electronic bits and bytes, is the cornerstone of the entire Macintosh religion. (Maybe that's why it's called an icon.)

If you then choose View→Show View Options (or press ⌘-J), you'll discover a wealth of interesting display options for this view.

Icon Sizes

Mac OS X can scale your icons to almost any size without losing any quality or smoothness (Figure 2-4). At the top of the View→Show View Options window (Figure 2-5), click either "This window only" or "All windows," to indicate whether you want to change the icon sizes in just the frontmost window or everywhere on the Mac. Then drag the "Icon size" slider back and forth until you find a size you like. (For added fun, make little cartoon sounds with your mouth.)

Text Size

You can also control the type size of icon names. In fact, if you choose "This window only" at the top of the dialog box, you can actually specify a different type size for *each window* on your machine. You might want smaller type to fit more into a crammed-full list view without scrolling, and larger type in less densely populated windows. (Your choices range from 10 to 16 points, and you can't choose a different font.)

Figure 2-4:
Mac OS X lets you choose an icon size to suit your personality. For picture folders, it can often be very handy to pick a jumbo size, in effect creating a slide-sorter "light table" effect. Just use the slider in the View Options dialog box, shown in Figure 2-5.

Windows XP–style Labeling

This 10.2 feature lets you create, in effect, a *multiple-column* list view in a single window (see Figure 2-5).

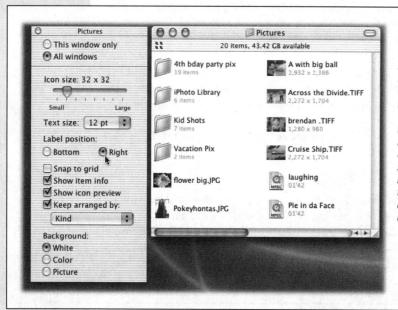

Figure 2-5:
Thanks to the beefed-up View Options palette (left), Mac OS X can now display icon names on the right, and even show a second line of file info, in any icon view. You now have all the handy, freely draggable convenience of an icon view, along with the compact spacing of a list view. This is nothing new if you're used to Windows XP, where this attractive arrangement debuted.

"Show Item Info"

While you've got the View Options dialog box open, try turning on "Show item info." Suddenly you get a new line of information about any disk or folder icon in the window, in tiny blue type. For example:

- **Folders.** The info line lets you know how many icons are inside each one without having to open it up.

- **TIFF, GIF, PDF files.** Certain other kinds of files may show a helpful info line, too—for example, TIFF-format graphics files display their dimensions, in pixels. (For some reason, JPEG files don't reveal their dimensions.)

- **Sounds and QuickTime movies.** The light-blue bonus line tells you how long the sound or movie takes to play. For example, "02' 49" means two minutes, 49 seconds.

You can see these effects illustrated in Figure 2-5.

Show Icon Preview

This option pertains primarily to graphics, which Mac OS X often displays only with a generic icon (stamped JPEG or TIFF or PDF). But if you turn on "Show icon preview," Mac OS X turns each icon into a miniature display of the image itself, as shown in Figure 2-5.

Window Backgrounds

Here's another Mac OS X luxury: You can fill the background of any icon-view window on your Mac with a certain color—or even a photo.

Color-coordinating or "wallpapering" certain windows is more than just a gimmick; it can serve as a timesaving psychological cue. Once you've gotten used to the fact that your main Documents folder has a sky-blue background, you can pick it out like a sharpshooter from a screen filled with open windows. Color-coded Finder windows are also especially easy to distinguish at a glance when you've minimized them to the Dock.

Note: Background colors and pictures disappear in list or column view, and in windows that "belong" to Mac OS X itself, such as the hard drive window and the Users folder.

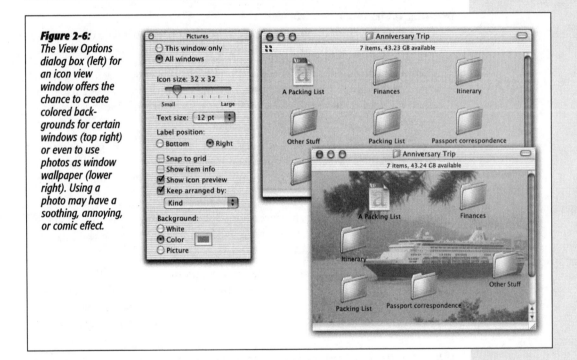

Figure 2-6:
The View Options dialog box (left) for an icon view window offers the chance to create colored backgrounds for certain windows (top right) or even to use photos as window wallpaper (lower right). Using a photo may have a soothing, annoying, or comic effect.

The bottom of the View Options dialog box (Figure 2-6) offers three choices:

- **White.** This is the standard option.

- **Color.** When you click this button, you see a small rectangular button beside the word Color. Click it to open the Color Picker, the Mac's standard color-wheel dialog box that, in this case, you can use to choose a new background color for the window. (Unless it's April Fool's day, pick a light color. If you choose a dark one—like black—you won't be able to make out the lettering of the icons' names.)

• **Picture.** If you choose this option, a Select button appears. Click it to open the Select a Picture dialog box, already open to your Library→Desktop Pictures folder. Choose a graphics file (one of Apple's—in the Desktop Pictures folder—or one of your own). When you click Select, you'll see that Mac OS X has superimposed the window's icons on the photo. As you can see in Figure 2-6, low-contrast or light-background photos work best for legibility.

Tip: The Mac has no idea what sizes and shapes your window may assume in its lifetime. Therefore, Mac OS X makes no attempt to scale down a selected photo to fit neatly into the window. If you have a high-res digital camera (a three- or four-megapixel model), you may see only the upper-left corner of a photo as the window background. Use a graphics program to scale the picture down to something smaller than your screen resolution for better results.

Keeping Icons Neat and Sorted

It's easy enough to request a visit from an electronic housekeeper who tidies up your icons, aligning them neatly to an invisible grid. For example:

• **Aligning individual icons to the grid.** Press the ⌘ key while dragging an icon or several highlighted icons. (Don't push down the key until after you begin to drag.) When you release the mouse, the icons you've moved all jump into neatly aligned positions.

• **Aligning all icons to the grid.** Choose View→Clean Up (if nothing is selected) or View→Clean Up Selection (if some icons are highlighted). Now *all* icons in the window (or those you've selected) jump to the closest positions on the invisible underlying grid.

This is a temporary status, however—as soon as you drag icons around, or add more icons to the window, the newly moved icons wind up just as sloppily positioned as before you used the command.

If you'd rather have icons snap to the nearest underlying grid positions *whenever* you move them, choose View→Show View Options. In the resulting dialog box, turn on "Snap to grid." Make sure the proper button is selected at the top of the window ("This window only" or "All windows"), and then close the window.

Note: You can override the grid setting by pressing the ⌘ key when you drag. In other words, when grid-snapping is turned *off*, ⌘ makes your icons snap into position; when grid-snapping is turned *on*, ⌘ lets you drag an icon freely.

Note, by the way, that neither of these grid-snapping commands—View→Clean Up and the "Snap to grid" option—moves icons into the most compact possible arrangement. If one or two icons have wandered off from the herd to a far corner of the window, they're merely nudged to the closest grid points to their present locations. They aren't moved all the way back to the group of icons elsewhere in the window.

To make them jump back to the primary cluster, read on.

- **Sorting all icons for the moment.** If you choose View→Arrange→by Name, all icons in the window snap to the invisible grid *and* sort themselves alphabetically. Use this method to place the icons as close as possible to each other within the window, rounding up any strays. The other subcommands in the View→Arrange menu, such as →by Size, →by Date Modified, and so on, work similarly, but sort the icons according to different criteria.

As with the Clean Up command, View→Arrange serves only to reorganize the icons in the window at this moment. Moving or adding icons in the window means you'll wind up with icons out of order. If you'd rather have all icons remain sorted *and* clustered, try this:

- **Sorting all icons permanently.** This arrangement is the ideal solution for neat freaks who can't stand seeing icons out of place. It maintains sorting and alignment of all icons in the window, present and future. Now if you add more icons to the window, they jump into correct alphabetical position; if you remove icons, the remaining ones slide over to fill in the resulting gap.

To make it happen, choose View→Show View Options. In the resulting dialog box, turn on the "Keep arranged by" checkbox. From the pop-up menu, specify what order you want your icons to snap into. Close the window. As shown at right in Figure 2-7, your icons are now locked into sorted position, as compactly as possible.

Figure 2-7:
Use the View Options dialog box (left) to turn on permanent-cleanliness mode (right). A tiny four-square icon (circled) appears just below the window's close button. That symbol is supposed to remind you that you've turned on the Mac's spatial lockjaw feature, so that you don't get frustrated when you try to drag an icon into a new position and discover that it won't budge.

You can also apply any of the commands described in this section—Clean Up, Arrange, Keep Arranged, and so on—to icons lying loose on your *desktop*. Even though they're not technically in any window at all, you can specify small or large icons, automatic alphabetical arrangement, and so on. Just click the desktop before using the commands in the View menu.

List View

In windows that contain a lot of icons, the list view is a powerful weapon in the battle against chaos. It shows you a tidy table of your files' names, dates, sizes, and so on. Here's how to master these columns:

Sorting the List

As in Windows, the column headings in a list view aren't just signposts—they're buttons, too. Click Name for alphabetical order, Date Modified to view newest first, Size to put the largest files at the top, and so on.

It's especially important to note the tiny, dark gray triangle that appears in the column you've most recently clicked. It shows you which way the list is being sorted.

Tip: You can also change the sorting order from the keyboard. Just press Control-Tab to highlight each successive column heading, sorting the list by that criterion in the process. Add the Shift key to move *leftward* through the column headings.

Flippy Triangle Keystrokes

The keystrokes for opening and closing flippy triangles in a list view are worth committing to memory.

Pressing the Option key when you click a flippy triangle lets you view a folder's contents *and* the contents of any folders inside it. The result, in other words, is a longer list that may involve several levels of indentation.

If you prefer to use the keyboard, substitute the right-arrow key (to expand a selected folder's flippy triangle) or left-arrow key (to collapse the folder listing again). Here again, adding the Option key expands all levels of folders within the selected one.

Suppose, for example, that you want to find out how many files are in your Pictures folder. The trouble is, you have organized the graphics files within that folder in several category folders. And you realize that the "how many items" statistic in the status bar shows you how many icons are

visible in the window. In other words, you won't know your total photo count until you've *expanded* all the folders within the Pictures folder.

You could perform the entire routine from the keyboard like this: Get to your own Home folder (see page 20) by pressing Option-⌘-H. Select the Pictures folder by typing the letter P. Open it by pressing ⌘-O (the shortcut for File→Open) or ⌘-down arrow. Highlight the entire contents by pressing ⌘-A (the shortcut for Edit→Select All).

Now that all folders are highlighted, press Option-right arrow. You may have to wait a moment for the Mac to open every subfolder of every subfolder. But eventually, the massive list appears, complete with many levels of indentation. At last, the "items" statistic in the status bar (see page 29) gives you a complete, updated tally of how many files are in all of those folders combined.

Flippy Triangles

One of the Mac's most distinctive features is the tiny triangle that appears to the left of a folder's name in a list view. In its official documents, Apple calls these buttons *disclosure triangles;* internally, the programmers call them *flippy triangles.*

When you click one, you turn the list view into an outline, in which the contents of the folder are displayed in an indented list, as shown in Figure 2-8. Click the triangle again to collapse the folder listing. You're saved the trouble and clutter of having to open a new window just to view the folder's contents.

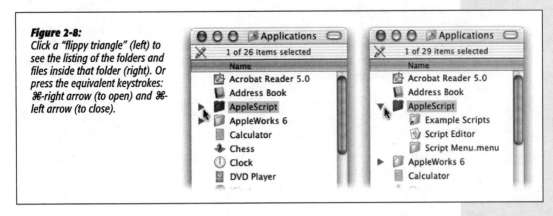

Figure 2-8:
Click a "flippy triangle" (left) to see the listing of the folders and files inside that folder (right). Or press the equivalent keystrokes: ⌘-right arrow (to open) and ⌘-left arrow (to close).

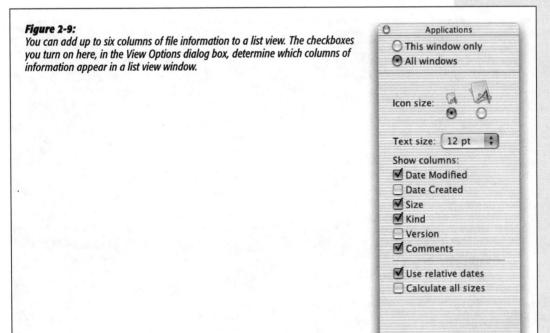

Figure 2-9:
You can add up to six columns of file information to a list view. The checkboxes you turn on here, in the View Options dialog box, determine which columns of information appear in a list view window.

By selectively clicking flippy triangles, you can, in effect, peer inside of two or more folders simultaneously, all within a single list view window. You can move files around by dragging them onto the tiny folder icons.

Which Columns Appear

Choose View→Show View Options. In the palette that appears, you're offered on/off checkboxes for the different columns of information that Mac OS X can display, as shown in Figure 2-9.

Other View Options

The View Options for a list view include several other useful settings (choose View→Show View Options, or press ⌘-J). As always, be sure to click either "All windows" or "This window only" before closing the window, so that your changes will have the scope of effect that you intended.

- **Icon size.** These two buttons let you choose a standard icon size for the current window. You can choose regular size or tiny size; unlike icon view, list view doesn't give you a size slider.

- **Text size.** As described on page 35, you can change the type size for your icon labels, either globally or one window at a time.

- **Show columns.** Turn on the columns you'd like to appear in the current window's list view, as described in the previous section.

FREQUENTLY ASKED QUESTION

Calculate All Sizes

When I sort my list view by size, I see only dashes for folder sizes. What am I doing wrong?

Nothing at all. When viewing a Finder window, you see a Size statistic for each *document*. For *folders and disks*, however, the Mac normally gives you only an uninformative dash.

As a Windows refugee, of course, that's old news. Windows PCs *never* show folder-size or disk-size information in a list view.

Here's what's going on: It can take a computer a long time to add up the sizes of all files inside a folder. Your System→Library folder alone, for example, contains over 1,500 files. Instead of making you wait while the Mac does all of this addition, Mac OS X simply shows you a dash in the Size column for a folder.

On occasion, however, you really *do* want to see how big your folders are. In such cases, choose View→Show View Options, turn on "Calculate all sizes," and close the palette. You'll see the folder sizes slowly begin to pop onto the screen, from the top of the window downward, as the Mac crunches the numbers for the files within.

But now consider this anomaly: Suppose you've opted to sort a particular window by folder size—in other words, you've clicked the word Size at the top of the column. Turning on "Calculate all sizes" bewilders the unprepared, as folders arbitrarily begin leaping out of order, forcing the list to rearrange itself a couple of times per second.

What's happening, of course, is that all folders *begin* at the bottom of the list, showing only dashes in the Size column. Then, as the Mac computes the size of your folders' contents, they jump into their correct sorted order at what may seem to be random intervals.

- **Use relative dates.** In a list view, the Date Modified and Date Created columns generally display information in a format like this: "Saturday, February 2, 2003." (It may not be written out as fully; the Mac uses shorter date formats as the column gets narrower.) But when the "Use relative dates" option is turned on, the Mac substitutes the word "Yesterday" or "Today" where appropriate, making recent files much easier to spot.

- **Calculate all sizes.** The box on the facing page describes this option for showing the disk-space totals for folders.

Rearranging Columns

You're stuck with the Name column at the far left of a window. But you can rearrange the other columns just by dragging their gray column headers horizontally, just as in Windows.

Adjusting Column Widths

Adjusting their widths works the same as in Windows, too. Place your cursor carefully on the dividing line between two column headings. When the cursor sprouts horizontal arrows from each side, you can drag horizontally. Doing so makes the column to the *left* of your cursor wider or narrower.

If you make a column too narrow, Mac OS X shortens the file names, dates, or whatever by removing text from the *middle*. An ellipsis (...) appears to show you where the missing text would have appeared. For example, suppose you've named a Word document called "Madonna—A Major Force for Humanization and Cure for Depression, Acne, and Migraine Headache." If the Name column is too narrow, you might see only "Madonna—A Major...Migraine Headache."

Tip: You don't have to make the column mega-wide just to read the full text of a file whose name has been shortened. Just point to the icon's name without clicking. After a moment, a yellow, floating label appears—something like a tooltip in Microsoft programs—to identify the full name.

And if you don't feel like waiting, hold down the Option key. As you whip your mouse over truncated file names, their tooltips appear instantaneously. (Both of these tricks work in any view—icon, list, or column.)

Column View

Icon view and list view should certainly be familiar from your old PC. But *column* view is probably something new—and welcome.

The goal is simple: To create a means of burrowing down through nested folders without leaving a trail of messy, overlapping windows in your wake.

The solution, a distant relative of the tree view known as Windows Explorer, is shown in Figure 2-10. It's a list view that's divided into several vertical panes. The first pane shows the icons of all your disks, including your main hard drive. (The Network icon gives you access to other computers on your office network, if you have one.)

When you click a disk (once), the second pane shows a list of all the folders on it. Each time you click a folder in one pane, the pane to its right shows what's inside. The other panes slide to the left, sometimes out of view. (Use the horizontal scroll bar or the Shift-Tab keystroke to bring them back.) You can keep clicking until you're looking at the file icons inside the most deeply nested folder.

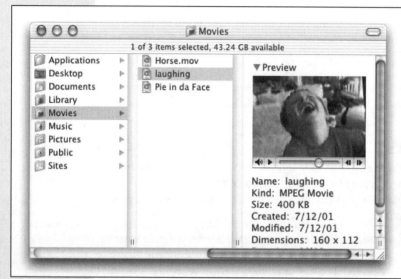

Figure 2-10:
If the rightmost folder contains pictures, sounds, or movies, Mac OS X even lets you look at them or play them, right there in the Finder. If it's a certain kind of text document (Apple- Works or PDF, for example), you actually see a tiny image of the first page. If it's any other kind of document, you see a blowup of its icon and a few file statistics. You can drag this jumbo icon anywhere—into another folder, for example.

If you discover that your hunt for a particular file has taken you down a blind alley, it's not a big deal to backtrack, since the trail of folders you've followed to get here is still sitting there before you on the screen. As soon as you click a different folder in one of the earlier panes, the panes to its right suddenly change, so that you can now burrow down a different rabbit hole.

The beauty of column view is, first of all, that it keeps your screen tidy. It effectively shows you several simultaneous folder levels, but contains them within a single window. With a quick ⌘-W, you can close the entire window, panes and all. Second, column view provides an excellent sense of where you are. Because your trail is visible at all times, it's much harder to get lost, wondering what folder you're in and how you got there, than in any other window view.

Note: Column view is always alphabetical. There's no way to sort the lists by date, for example, as you can in list view.

Column View by Keyboard

You can operate this entire process by keyboard alone, a great timesaver for keyboard fans. For example:

- You can jump from one pane to the next by pressing the right or left arrow keys. Each press highlights the closest *icon* in the next or previous pane.

- You can use any of the commands in the Go menu, or their keyboard equivalents, to fill your columns with the contents of the corresponding folder—Home, Favorites, Applications, and so on.

- The Back command—clicking the Back button on the toolbar, pressing ⌘-[(left bracket) or choosing Go→Back—works just as it would in a Web browser, by letting you retrace your steps backward. You can use this command over and over again until you return to the column setup that appeared when you first switched to column view.

- Within a pane, press the up or down arrow keys to highlight successive icons in the list. Or type the first couple of letters of an icon's name to jump directly to it.

- When you finally highlight the icon you've been looking for, press ⌘-O or ⌘-down arrow to open it (or double-click it, of course). You can open any icon in any column, not just the one you've pinpointed in the rightmost column.

Manipulating the Columns

The number of columns you can see without scrolling depends on the width of the window. In no other view are the zoom button (page 25) and resize box (page 29) so important.

That's not to say, however, that you're limited to four columns (or whatever fits on your monitor). You can make the columns wider or narrower—either individually or all at once—to suit the situation. Figure 2-11 shows the details.

Figure 2-11:
You can make all the columns wider or narrower simultaneously by dragging any of the small handles (circled) at the bottom of the columns. To make a single column wider or narrower, Option-drag the column handle at its lower-right.

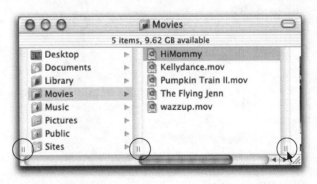

View Options

Just as in icon and list view, you can choose View→Show View Options to open a dialog box—a Spartan one, in this case—offering a bit more control over your column views.

Note: Any changes you make here affect *all* column views.

- **Text size.** Choose your preferred size for icon labels in column views.

- **Show icon.** For maximum speed, turn off this option. Now you'll see only file names, not the tiny icons next to them.

The Go to Folder Command

Sometimes a Unix tentacle pokes through the user-friendly Aqua interface. Mac OS X has places where you can use Unix shortcuts instead of the mouse.

One classic example is the Go→Go to Folder command (Shift-⌘-G). It brings up a box like the one shown here.

The purpose of this box is to let you jump to a certain folder on your Mac directly by typing its Unix *folder path.* Depending on your point of view, this special box is either a shortcut or a detour.

Go to the folder:

/Users/mjones/Movies/

Cancel   Go

For example, if you want to see what's in the Documents folder of your Home folder, you could choose Go→Go to Folder, then type this:

/Users/mjones/Documents

Then click Go or press Return. (In this example, of course, *mjones* is your short account name.)

In other words, you're telling the Mac to open the Users folder in your main hard drive window, then your Home folder inside that, and then the Documents folder inside *that.* Each slash means, "and then open." (As in this example, you can leave off the name of your hard drive.) When you press Enter, the folder you specified pops open immediately.

Of course, if you really wanted to jump to your Documents folder, you'd be wasting your time by typing all that. Unix (and therefore Mac OS X) offers a handy shortcut that means, "home folder." It's the tilde character (~) at the upper-left corner of your keyboard.

To see what's in your Home folder, then, you could type just that ~ symbol into the "Go to" box and then press Return. Or you could add some slashes to it to specify a folder inside your Home folder, like this:

~/Documents

You can even jump to someone *else's* Home folder by typing a name after the symbol, like this:

~chris

If you get into this sort of thing, here's another shortcut worth noting: If you type nothing but a slash (/) and then press Return, you jump immediately to the Computer window, which provides an overview of all your disks, plus a Network icon.

Note, too, that you don't have to type out the full path—only the part that drills down from the *window you're in.* If your Home folder window is already open, for example, you can open the Pictures folder just by typing *Pictures.*

But the Go to Folder trick *really* turns into a high-octane timesaver if you use *tab completion.* After each slash, you can type only enough letters of a folder's name to give Mac OS X the idea—*de* instead of *desktop,* for example—and then press the Tab key. Mac OS X instantly and automatically fills in the rest of the folder's name.

For example, instead of typing */applications/Microsoft Office X/clipart/standard,* you could type nothing more than */ap/mi/cl/st,* remembering to press Tab after each pair of letters. Now *that's* how to feel like a Unix programmer.

- **Show preview column.** The far-right Preview column (see Figure 2-10) can be handy when you're browsing graphics, sounds, or movie files. The rest of the time, it can get in the way, slightly slowing down the works and pushing other, more useful columns off to the left side of the window. If you turn off this checkbox, the Preview column doesn't appear.

Tip: No matter what view you're in, remember this if you ever start dragging an icon and then change your mind: press the Esc key while the mouse button is still down. The icon flies back to its precise starting place. (Too bad real life doesn't have a similar feature for returning a spilled glass of grape juice back to the tabletop.)

What's in Your Home Folder

As noted in Chapter 1, your Home folder (choose Go→Home) will be your primary activity center on the Mac. It stores not only your documents, music files, photos, and so on, but also all of your preference settings for the programs you use. Because you'll be spending so much time here, it's worth learning about the folders that Apple puts inside here. You're free to rename or delete them, except as noted. Solely as a convenience, Mac OS X creates the following folders:

- **Desktop folder.** When you drag an icon out of a window and onto your Mac OS X desktop, it may *appear* to show up on the desktop, but that's just an optical illusion. In truth, nothing in Mac OS X is ever *really* on the desktop. It's actually in this Desktop *folder*, and mirrored on the desktop area.

  You can entertain yourself for hours by proving this to yourself. If you drag something out of your Desktop folder, it also disappears from the actual desktop. And vice versa. (You're not allowed to delete or rename this folder.)

- **Documents.** Apple suggests that you keep your actual work files in this folder. Sure enough, whenever you save a new document (when you're working in AppleWorks or Word, for example), the Save As box proposes storing the new file in this folder, as described in Chapter 4.

  Your programs may also create folders of their own here. For example, if Microsoft Entourage is your email program, you'll find a Microsoft User Data folder here (which contains your actual mail files). If you use a Palm organizer, you'll find a Palm folder here for your palmtop's calendar and phone book data. And so on.

- **Library.** The *main* Library folder (the one in your main hard drive window) contains folders for fonts, preferences, help files, and other files essential to the operation of Mac OS X.

  But you have your *own* Library folder, too, right there in your Home folder. It stores exactly the same kinds of things, but they're *your* fonts, *your* preferences, and so on.

This setup may seem redundant if you're the only person who uses your Mac. But it makes perfect sense in the context of families, schools, or offices where numerous people share a single machine. Because you have your own Library folder, you can have a font collection, sounds, and other preference settings that are in effect only when *you're* using the mac. (It's best not to move or rename this folder.)

- **Movies, Music, Pictures.** These folders, of course, are designed to store multimedia files. They're the precise equivalents of such Windows folders as My Music, My Pictures, and so on. The Mac OS X programs that deal with movies, music, and pictures will propose these specialized folders as storage locations. For example, when you plug a digital camera into a Mac OS X computer, the iPhoto program automatically begins to download the photos on it—and stores them in the Pictures folder. Similarly, iMovie is programmed to look for the Movies folder when saving its files, and iTunes stores its MP3 files in the Music folder. (More on these programs in Chapter 14.)

- **Public.** If you're on a network, or if others use the same Mac when you're not around, this folder can be handy. It's the "Any of you guys can look at these files" folder. Other people on your network, as well as other people who sit down at this machine, are allowed to see whatever you've put in here, even if they don't have your password. (If your Mac isn't on an office network and isn't shared, you can throw away this folder.) Details on sharing the Mac are in Chapter 13; networking info is in Chapter 5.

- **Sites.** Mac OS X has a built-in *Web server*—software that turns your Mac into an Internet Web site that people all over the world can connect to. (This feature is practical only if your Mac has a full-time Internet connection.) This Mac OS X feature relies on a program called the Apache Web server, which is so highly regarded in the Unix community that programmers lower their voices when they mention it.

For now, it's enough to note that this is the folder where you will put the actual Web pages you want available to the Internet at large.

File Icons

Just as in Windows, every document, program, folder, and disk on your Mac is represented by an icon. In Mac OS X, icons look more like photos than cartoons, and you can scale them to any size—but otherwise, icons work just as they do in Windows. They're your ticket to moving, copying, and deleting your files and folders.

File Names

A Mac OS X icon's name can have up to 255 letters and spaces. Better yet, you're about to discover the first of many degrees of freedom that come with a move to the Mac: Punctuation is permitted. For the first time in your life, you can name a file, say, "Update 11/15/03," without getting yelled at by your operating system. In fact, you can use any symbol you want except for the colon (:), which the Mac uses behind the scenes for its own folder-hierarchy designation purposes.

To rename an icon, begin with one of these two methods:

• Click once squarely on the icon's name.

• Click once on the icon, and then press Return or Enter.

Either way, a rectangle now appears around the name (see Figure 2-12). At this point, the existing name is highlighted; just begin typing to replace it, just as in Windows.

Tip: If you simply want to add letters to the beginning or end of the file's existing name, press the left or right arrow key immediately after pressing Return or Enter. The insertion point jumps to the corresponding end of the file name.

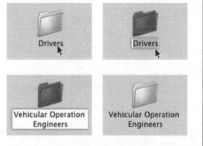

Figure 2-12:
Click an icon's name (top left) to produce the renaming rectangle (top right), in which you can edit the file's name. Once the existing name is highlighted, begin typing to replace it (bottom left). When you're finished, press Return, Enter, or Tab to seal the deal, or just click somewhere else.

DON'T PANIC

Long and Short File Names

Hey, what's the deal with long file names? I tried saving an AppleWorks document, and it didn't let me use more than 31 letters!

As you can read in Chapter 4, not all Mac programs have been written expressly for Mac OS X. Some predate Mac OS X, and others have merely been adapted to run in Mac OS X (*Carbonized,* as the geeks say). Many pre–Mac OS X programs still limit you to 31 letters when naming a new document in the Save As dialog box.

Over time, software companies may get with the program and rejigger their software to overcome this anachronistic glitch. For now, though, all is not lost.

Even though you can use only 31 letters when saving a new document from, say, AppleWorks or Internet Explorer, you're welcome to *rename* the file in the Finder, using all 255 characters Mac OS X permits. When you reopen the document in the original program, you'll see an abbreviated name in the title bar (a file that, at the desktop, is called *My Visit to Bill Gates's House, and Why I'll Take the Apple Bumper Sticker off My Car Next Time* opens into AppleWorks as something like *My Visit to Bill Gates's H#B6C5).*

The good news is that behind the scenes, Mac OS X still remembers its long name. Even if you edit and re-save the document, you'll still find its long file name intact when you view its icon at the desktop.

A space is considered alphabetically *before* the letter A. To force a particular folder to appear at the top of a list view window, type a space before its name.

Selecting Icons

To highlight a single icon in preparation for printing, opening, duplicating, or deleting, click the icon once with the mouse. (In a list or column view, you can also click any visible piece of information about that file—its name, size, kind, date modified, and so on.) The icon darkens, and its name changes color.

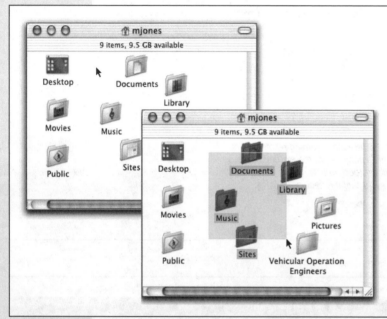

Figure 2-13:
You can highlight several icons simultaneously by dragging a box around them. To do so, drag from outside of the target icons (left) diagonally across them (right), creating a transparent gray rectangle as you go. Any icons touched by this rectangle are selected when you release the mouse. If you press the Shift or ⌘ key as you do this, any previously highlighted icons remain selected.

Selecting Icons from the Keyboard

For the speed fanatic, using the mouse to click an icon is a hopeless waste of time. Fortunately, you can also select an icon by typing the first couple letters of its name.

When looking at your home window, for example, you can type *M* to highlight the Movies folder. If you actually intended to highlight the *Music* folder instead, press the Tab key to highlight the next icon in the window alphabetically. You can use the arrow keys, too, to highlight a neighbor-ing icon. (Pressing Tab has no effect in column view, however.)

After highlighting an icon in this way, you can manipulate it using the commands in the File menu or their keyboard equivalents: open (⌘-O), put in the Trash (⌘-Delete), Get Info (⌘-I), duplicate (⌘-D), or make an alias (⌘-L), as described later in this chapter. By turning on the special disability features described on page 324, you can even *move* the highlighted icon using only the keyboard.

You can highlight *multiple* files in preparation for moving or copying them en masse, using the same techniques you're used to in Windows. You can select all of them in a window (press ⌘-A or choose Edit→Select All), drag diagonally (see Figure 2-13), or select individual icons by ⌘-clicking them one at a time. (If you include a particular icon by mistake, ⌘-click it to remove it from the selected cluster.)

The ⌘ key trick is especially handy if you want to select *almost* all the icons in a window. Press ⌘-A to select everything in the folder, then ⌘-click any unwanted icons to deselect them.

Tip: In a list view, you can also select a group of consecutive files by clicking the first one you want, and then Shift-clicking the last file. All the files in between are automatically selected, along with the two icons you clicked.

Moving and Copying Icons

In Mac OS X, there are two ways to move or copy icons from one place to another: by dragging them, or by using the Copy and Paste commands.

Copying by Dragging

You can drag icons from one folder to another, from one drive to another, from a drive to a folder on another drive, and so on. You can cancel the copying process by pressing either ⌘-period or the Esc key.

Understanding when the Mac copies a dragged icon and when it just *moves* the icon bewilders many a beginner. However, the scheme is fairly simple:

• Dragging from one folder to another (on the same disk) *moves* the icon; dragging from one disk to another *copies* the folder or file. So far, this is the same as Windows.

• Option-dragging it (that is, pressing the Option key while dragging) *copies* the icon instead of moving it. Doing so within a single folder produces a duplicate of the file called "[Whatever its name was] copy."

• Dragging an icon from one disk to another while pressing ⌘ *moves* the file or folder, in the process deleting it from the original disk. (Press ⌘ just *after* you start to drag.)

Copying by Using Copy and Paste

You can also use the Copy and Paste commands to get files from one window to another, too. Highlight the icon or icons you want to move, choose Edit→Copy, open the window where you want to put the icons, and then choose Edit→Paste. You get a second set of the copied icons, exactly as in Windows.

Well, *almost* exactly like Windows. On the Mac, you can't *cut* and copy icons to move them. You can only *copy* icons to make a copy of them.

Spring-Loaded Folders

Here's a common dilemma: You want to drag an icon not just into a folder, but into a folder nested *inside* that folder.

Instead of fiddling around, opening and closing one window after another, you can instead use the spring-loaded folders feature (see Figure 2-14), a Mac OS X 10.2 delicacy with no equivalent in Windows. It works like this: Drag the icon onto the first folder—but keep your mouse button pressed. After a few seconds, the folder window opens automatically, centered on your cursor. Still keeping the button down, drag onto the inner folder so that its window opens, too. Now drag onto the *inner* inner folder—and so on. (If the inner folder you intend to open isn't visible in the window, you can scroll by dragging your cursor close to any edge of the window.)

When you finally release the mouse, all the windows except the last one close automatically. You've neatly placed the icon into the core of the nested folders.

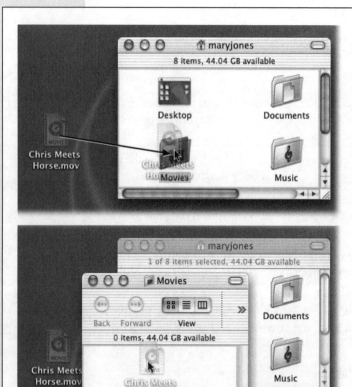

Figure 2-14:
Top: To make spring-loaded folders work, start by dragging an icon onto a folder or disk icon. Don't release the mouse button. Wait for the window to open automatically around your cursor (or tap the Space bar if you don't feel like waiting).

Bottom: Now you can either let go of the mouse button to release the file in its new window, or drag onto yet another, inner folder. It, too, will open. As long as you don't release the mouse button, you can continue until you've reached your folder-within-a-folder destination.

Aliases (Shortcuts)

Highlighting an icon and then choosing File→Make Alias (or pressing ⌘-L) generates an *alias,* a specially branded duplicate of the original icon (see Figure 2-15). It's precisely the same idea as a file *shortcut* in Windows: When you double-click the alias, the original file opens. Because you can create as many aliases as you want of a single file, aliases let you, in effect, stash that file in many different folder locations simultaneously.

Tip: Another way to create an alias is by Control-clicking a normal icon and choosing Make Alias from the contextual menu that appears. You can also create an alias by Option-⌘-dragging the icon out of its window.

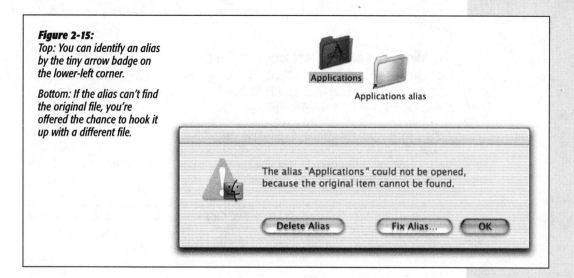

Figure 2-15:
Top: You can identify an alias by the tiny arrow badge on the lower-left corner.

Bottom: If the alias can't find the original file, you're offered the chance to hook it up with a different file.

Applications

Applications alias

The alias "Applications" could not be opened, because the original item cannot be found.

Delete Alias   Fix Alias...   OK

An alias takes up almost no disk space, even if the original file is enormous. Aliases are smarter than Windows shortcuts, too: Even if you rename the alias, rename the original file, move the alias, and move the original, double-clicking the alias still opens the original icon.

And that's just the beginning of alias intelligence. Suppose you make an alias of a file that's on a removable disk, such as a Zip disk. When you double-click the alias on your hard drive, the Mac requests that particular disk by name. And if you double-click the alias of a file on a different machine on the network, your Mac attempts to connect to the appropriate machine, prompting you for a password (see Chapter 5)—even if the other machine is thousands of miles away and your Mac must dial the modem to connect.

Tip: Mac OS X makes it easy to find the file an alias "points" to without actually having to open it. Just highlight the alias and then choose File→Show Original (⌘-R). Mac OS X immediately displays the actual, original file, sitting patiently in its folder, wherever that may be.

The Trash

No single element of the Macintosh interface is as famous as the Trash, which now appears as a wire wastebasket at the end of the Dock. It is, of course, the same thing that Microsoft calls the Recycle Bin: a waiting room that holds files and folders you intend to delete.

You can either drag files or folders onto the Trash icon, or you can save a little effort by using the keyboard alternative: highlighting the icon and then pressing ⌘-Delete.

Rescuing Files and Folders from the Trash

File and folder icons sit in the Trash forever—or until you choose Finder→Empty Trash, whichever comes first. The Trash never reaches a fullness level where it empties automatically, as it does in Windows.

If you haven't yet emptied the Trash, you can open its window by clicking the wastebasket icon once. Now you can review its contents: icons that you've placed on the waiting list for extinction. If you change your mind, you can rescue any of these items by dragging them out of the Trash window.

Tip: If dragging something to the Trash was the last thing you did, you can press ⌘-Z—the keyboard shortcut for the Edit→Undo command. This not only removes it from the Trash, but also returns it to the folder from whence it came. This trick works even if the Trash window isn't open.

Emptying the Trash

If you're confident that the items in the Trash window are worth deleting, use any of these three options:

- Choose Finder→Empty Trash.

- Press Shift-⌘-Delete.

- Control-click the wastebasket icon, then choose Empty Trash from the contextual menu. This method has two advantages. First, it doesn't bother asking "Are you sure?" (If you're clicking right on the Trash and choosing Empty Trash from the pop-up menu, it's pretty darned obvious you *are* sure.) Second, this method nukes any locked files (see the following Tip) without making you unlock them first.

If the Macintosh asks you to confirm your decision (see Figure 2-16), click OK.

Tip: By highlighting a file or folder, choosing File→Get Info, and turning on the Locked checkbox, you protect that file or folder from accidental deletion (see Figure 2-16).

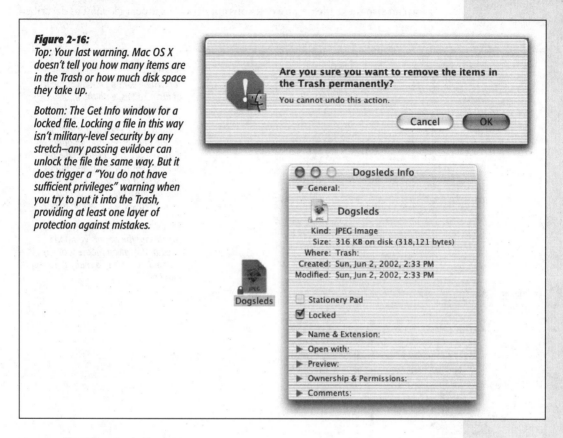

Figure 2-16:
Top: Your last warning. Mac OS X doesn't tell you how many items are in the Trash or how much disk space they take up.

Bottom: The Get Info window for a locked file. Locking a file in this way isn't military-level security by any stretch—any passing evildoer can unlock the file the same way. But it does trigger a "You do not have sufficient privileges" warning when you try to put it into the Trash, providing at least one layer of protection against mistakes.

Get Info (Properties)

By clicking an icon and then choosing File→Get Info, you open an important window like the one shown in Figure 2-17. It's a collapsible, multipanel screen that provides a wealth of information about a highlighted icon—the Mac version of icon properties. Click a triangle to expand a corresponding information panel. For example:

- **General.** Here's where you can view (and edit) the name of the icon, as well as see its size, creation date, most recent change date, Locked status, and so on. If you click a disk, this info window shows you its capacity and how full it is. If you click the Trash, you see how much stuff is in it. This is the panel that always opens the first time you summon the Get Info window.

- **Name & Extension.** On this screen, you can read and edit the name of the icon in question. The "Hide extension" checkbox refers to the file name extension (*.doc* or *.txt*, for example).

As in Windows, many Mac OS X documents, behind the scenes, have file name extensions—but Mac OS X, like Windows XP, comes factory set to hide them. By turning off this checkbox, you can make the suffix reappear for an individual file. (You can also make file name extensions appear or disappear *globally*, as described on page 85.)

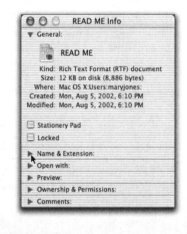

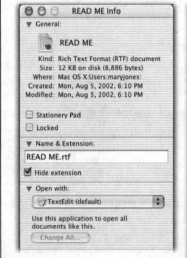

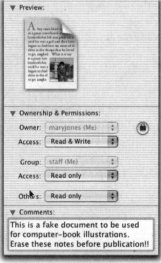

Figure 2-17:
Top: The Get Info window appears at first like this, with the information panels "collapsed."

Bottom: Click each flippy triangle to open its corresponding panel of information. The resulting dialog box can easily grow taller than your screen (it's shown here split in half because the book isn't tall enough to show the whole thing).

That's a good argument for either (a) closing the panels you don't need at any given moment or (b) running out to buy a really gigantic monitor.

• **Content index.** As noted on page 63, Mac OS X's Find program can locate files based on the *words inside them*, regardless of the actual names of the files. It can perform this magic only in folders that have been *indexed* (analyzed by the operating system), however. This panel lets you know when a folder was last indexed, and allows you to index the folder manually or to delete the existing index file to save disk space.

- **Memory.** You'll see this option only when showing info for Classic programs (page 95). There are three different memory statistics: Suggested Size (the software company's official recommendation), Minimum Size (below which the program won't even run—a number you shouldn't change), and Preferred Size. This final number is the one you should feel free to adjust, arming the program with more memory if it seems unstable in your Classic world (Chapter 4).

- **Open with.** Use the controls on this screen to specify which program will open when you double-click this document or all documents of this type. (Details on page 86.)

- **Preview.** On this panel, you see a large, handsome thumbnail image. In the case of spreadsheets, word processing documents, HTML documents, and so on, this is nothing to write home about—just a magnified version of the generic document icon.

  But when you're examining pictures, text files, PDF files, sounds, clippings, and movies, this feature can be extremely useful. As you click each icon, you see a magnified thumbnail version of what's actually *in* that document. A controller lets you play sounds and movies, where appropriate, for example.

- **Ownership & Permissions.** This is available for all kinds of icons. If other people have access to your Mac (either from across the network or when logging in in person), this panel lets you specify who is allowed to open or change this particular icon. See Chapter 12 for a complete discussion of this hairy topic.

- **Comments.** Here, you can type in random comments for your own reference. Later, you can view these remarks in any list view (if you've made the Comments column visible).

Here and there, you may even see other panels in the Get Info window, especially when you get info on application icons. For example, iPhoto offers a Plug-ins panel that lets you manage add-on software modules, some programs offer a Languages panel, and so on.

Finding Files 1: The Search Bar

To find a certain file in a folder (or a folder *in* that folder), Mac OS X offers a tool that's far simpler and more convenient than the lumbering Search program of Windows. It's called the Search bar (Figure 2-18).

If you don't see this little round-ended box at the top of every Finder window, then check these conditions:

- Your Finder toolbar must, in fact, be visible (see page 73).

- The window must be wide enough to reveal the Search bar.

- The Search bar must be on the toolbar to begin with (page 74).

If all is well, and the Search bar is staring you in the face, here's how to use it:

1. **Open the window you want to search. Click inside the Search bar.**

   You're about to search in this window *and all folders inside it.*

2. **Type a few letters of the file or folder name you're seeking.**

   If you're trying to find a file called *Pokémon Fantasy League.doc,* just *pok* or *leag* would probably suffice.

Figure 2-18:
The Search bar is a kind of software sieve that lets you screen out the rabble in a window filled with files.

3. **Press Return or Enter.**

   A Search Results window opens, revealing, item by item, a list of the files and folders whose names contain what you typed in step 2 (see Figure 2-19).

   While the searching is going on, the "sprocket" icon whirls away in the upper-left corner. To pause or cancel the search in progress, click the ⊠ button. Once you've halted the search in this way, you can click the ⟨⟩ icon above the scroll bar to resume the original search.

What to Do with Search Results

You can manipulate the list of search results much the way you'd approach a list of files in a standard Finder list view window. You can move up or down the list by pressing the arrow keys, scroll a "page" at a time with the Page Up and Page Down keys, and so on. Or you can proceed in any of these ways:

Find out where something is

If you click *once* on any item in the results list, the bottom half of the window becomes a folder map that shows you where that item is (see Figure 2-19).

To get your hands on the actual icon, choose File→Open Enclosing Folder (⌘-R). The Search Results window retreats to the background, as Mac OS X highlights the actual icon in question, sitting there in its window wherever it happens to be on your hard drive.

Open the file (or open one of the folders it's in)

If one of the found files is the one you were looking for, double-click it to open it (or highlight it and press ⌘-O). In many cases, you'll never even know or care *where* the file was—you just want to get into it.

You can also double-click to open any of the *folders* that appear in the map in the bottom half of the window. For example, in Figure 2-19, you could double-click the AppleWorks 6 icon to open it, or the Applications folder to open *it,* and so on.

Manipulate the file

You can move, delete, rename, or (by Option-⌘-dragging out of the window) make an alias of an item in the found-files list, exactly as you would any file.

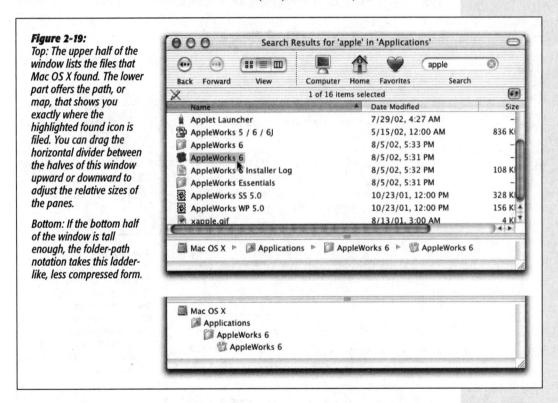

Figure 2-19:
Top: The upper half of the window lists the files that Mac OS X found. The lower part offers the path, or map, that shows you exactly where the highlighted found icon is filed. You can drag the horizontal divider between the halves of this window upward or downward to adjust the relative sizes of the panes.

Bottom: If the bottom half of the window is tall enough, the folder-path notation takes this ladder-like, less compressed form.

Adjust the list

By clicking the column headings, you can sort the list of found files in various ways: by name, size, date, and so on. (You can reverse the order by clicking the same heading a second time.) You can also make the window bigger by dragging the lower-right corner handle, adjusting the relative widths of the columns by dragging the column-name dividers, or rearranging the columns horizontally by dragging their names. All of this works exactly as it does in a Finder list view window.

Copy a file

To copy a file, Option-drag it out of the Search Results window and onto the desktop, into a different window, or onto a disk or folder icon.

Start over

If you'd like to repeat the search using a different search phrase, back out of the Search Results window and return to the window where you began the search. Just click the Back button in the toolbar, or press ⌘-[.

Give up

If none of these avenues suits your fancy, you can simply close the Search Results window as you would any other window (⌘-W).

Finding Files 2: The Find Program

The Search bar is simple, fast, and above all, convenient. It's always there, happy to serve you, no matter what window you're in.

It's not, however, the most powerful search program on earth. It searches only for icon's names, not their sizes, dates, and so on. And it can't look for words *inside* your files.

There is a program that can perform these more complex searches, though. In fact, no modern self-respecting operating system would be without it. To meet this file-finding tool, choose File→Find (or press ⌘-F). The shockingly simple dialog box shown in Figure 2-20 appears next.

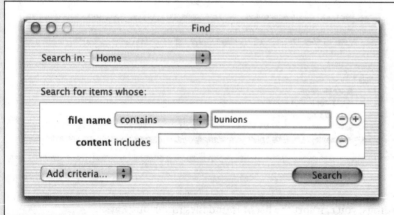

Figure 2-20:
The first time you use it, the new Find program opens up ready to search by file name and file content, as shown here, because those are the most common kinds of search. But don't settle—Find has many more tricks up its software sleeve.

As you'll soon discover, the Find program can hunt down icons using extremely specific criteria. If you spent enough time setting up the search, you could actually use this program to find a document whose name begins with the letters *Cro*, is between 34 and 95 K in size, was created after 5/1/03 but before the end of the year, was changed within the last week, has the file name suffix *.doc,* and contains the phrase "attitude adjustment." (Of course, if you knew *that* much about a file, you'd probably know exactly where it is, too, without having to use the Find program. But you get the picture.)

To use the Find program, you need to feed it two pieces of information: *where* you want it to search, and *what* to look for. You can make both of these criteria as simple or complex as you like.

Where to Look

The pop-up menu at the top of the window lets you specify *where* you want Find to do its searching. Your choices are:

- **Everywhere.** You want to round up *every* file with a certain name (or containing certain text), wherever it may be on your Mac, your iDisk (*page 123*), or even on your network.

- **Local disks.** You're saying, "I just want to search my own machine. I don't care about the network, Internet-based disks, or whatever."

- **Home.** Home refers to your own Home folder (*page 20*).

- **Specific places.** If you know that the file you're trying to find is in a certain folder, or on a certain disk, drag the folder or disk's icon directly into the "Specific places" list. Mac OS X will confine its search to these items, as shown in Figure 2-21.

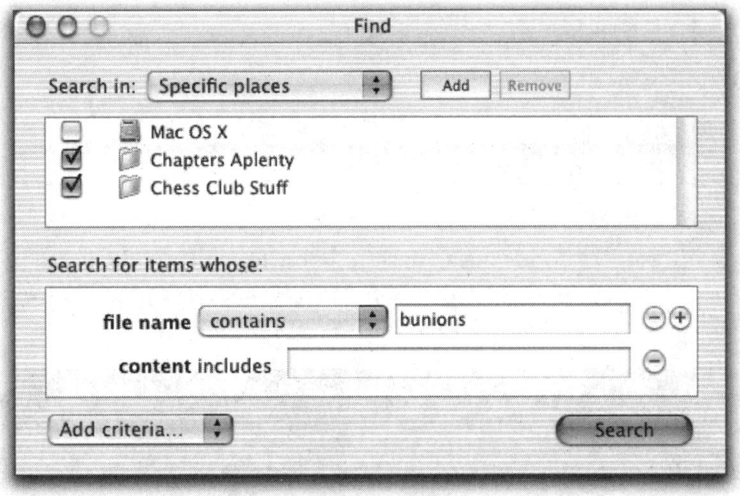

Figure 2-21:
To limit (and thereby speed up) a search, you can drag a folder, or set of folders, off the desktop and into this list. (Alternatively, click the Add button above the list.) The folder names appear there, marked with checkboxes. In fact, they'll still be listed here every time you open the Find program—until you drag them out of the window to the Trash can, or highlight them and then click the Remove button above the list.

What to Look For

The first time you open the Find program after turning on your Mac OS X 10.2 machine, two boxes appear that need filling in: "File name" and "content" (that is, words inside the files).

But those are only starting points. In all, Find lets you define a search using up to eight different criteria (date modified, file size, and so on). Figure 2-22 illustrates how detailed this kind of search can be.

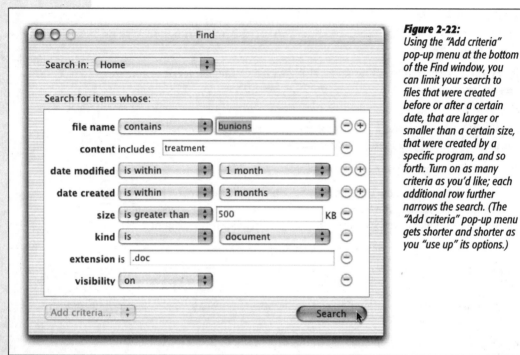

Figure 2-22:
Using the "Add criteria" pop-up menu at the bottom of the Find window, you can limit your search to files that were created before or after a certain date, that are larger or smaller than a certain size, that were created by a specific program, and so forth. Turn on as many criteria as you'd like; each additional row further narrows the search. (The "Add criteria" pop-up menu gets shorter and shorter as you "use up" its options.)

To add one to the list, choose from the "Add criteria" pop-up menu at the bottom of the Find window. A new row appears in the Find window, where you can specify *what* date, *what* file size, and so on.

To delete a row from the Find window, click the – button at the right side of the window.

Most of the information types are self-explanatory (file name, date created, and so on). But a few are worth noting:

- **Content.** Sooner or later, it happens to everyone: a file's name doesn't match what's inside it. Maybe a marauding toddler pressed the keys while playing KidPix, inadvertently renaming your doctoral thesis "xggrjpO#$5%////." Or maybe you just can't remember what you called something.

  For this purpose, Find can search for words *inside* your files, regardless of their names. Just type the word or phrase you seek into the "content includes" box (see Figure 2-23).

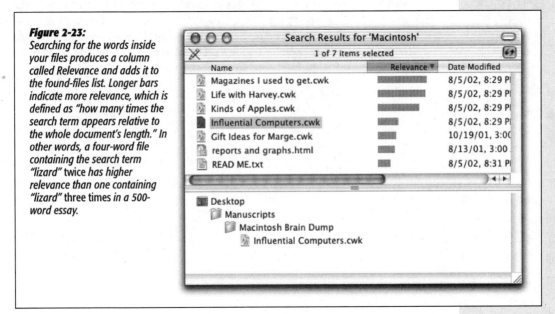

Figure 2-23:
Searching for the words inside your files produces a column called Relevance and adds it to the found-files list. Longer bars indicate more relevance, which is defined as "how many times the search term appears relative to the whole document's length." In other words, a four-word file containing the search term "lizard" twice has higher relevance than one containing "lizard" three times in a 500-word essay.

- **Comments.** This box lets you find files whose Get Info boxes' *Comments* field (page 57) includes certain text. If you religiously fill in these Comments boxes, you've got yourself one heck of a powerful file-labeling (and file-finding) tool. You could type your client's name (Jenkins, for example) into the comment boxes of relevant files, and then, at any time, round up all Jenkins documents at once.

- **Extension.** Here's the option you need when rounding up all files of a certain type, using their file name extensions as a "handle." You'd type *.doc* here to find all Word files, *.jpg* to find all JPEG graphics, and so on.

- **Visibility.** Your hard drive is absolutely *teeming* with invisible files, including the thousands of Unix files that make up Mac OS X. Using this command, you can take a look at them. (It's not wise to move or throw away invisible files, however. In fact, Apple made them invisible expressly so you wouldn't tamper with them.)

Tip: You can add a certain criterion row to your Find setup *more than once,* for even more specific searches. To find files you created between two specific dates, for example, you could set up two "date created" rows, one that specifies the starting date and one for the ending date. Just click the + button at the right end of a row to add a second, duplicate row (this trick works only for file name and date searches).

Find the Files and Use Them

Once you've set up your search—a process that, in extreme cases, can take all afternoon—click the Search button or press Return to set the search in motion.

A new window, called Search Results, opens up immediately, although it may take some time for any files to appear in the list. At this point, you should proceed as described on page 58 (as it turns out, the Search bar and the Find program produce precisely the same Search Results window). Double-click a found file to open it, drag it to the desktop to move it, and so on.

Dock, Desktop, and Toolbar

W hen you stop to think about it, the Mac OS X environment owes most of its different, photo-realistic looks to three key elements: the Dock at the bottom edge of the screen, the toolbar at the top of every Finder window, and the shimmering, sometimes animated backdrop of the desktop itself. This chapter shows you how to use and control these most dramatic elements of Mac OS X.

The Dock

As noted briefly in Chapter 1, the Dock is a launcher (like the Windows Start menu) and "what's open" listing (like the Windows taskbar) rolled into one. Only a tiny triangle beneath a program's icon tells you that it's open.

Apple starts the Dock off with a few icons it thinks you'll enjoy: QuickTime Player, iTunes, iChat, and so on. But using your Mac without putting your *own* favorite

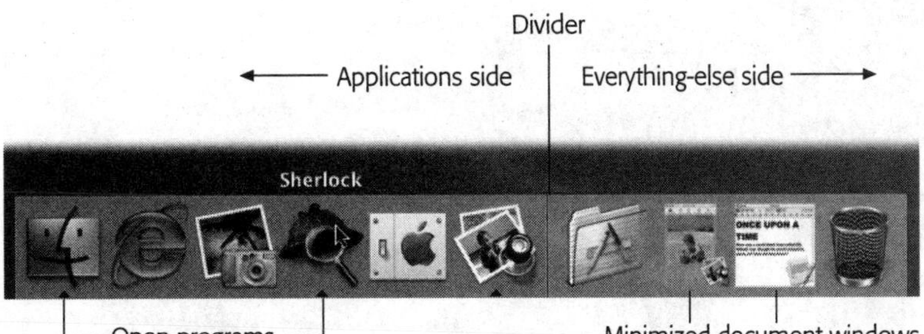

Figure 3-1:
To add an icon to the Dock, just drag it there. Note that you haven't moved the original file. What you've actually done is install a copy of its icon onto your Dock–like a Macintosh alias or Windows shortcut, you might say.

Divider
◄———— Applications side   Everything-else side ————►
Sherlock
└— Open programs —┘   Minimized document windows

icons on the Dock is like buying an expensive suit and turning down the free alteration service. At the first opportunity, you should make the Dock your own.

The concept of the Dock is simple: Any icon you drag onto it (Figure 3-1) is installed there as a large, square button. A single click, not a double-click, opens the corresponding icon. In other words, the Dock is an ideal parking lot for the icons of disks, folders, documents, and programs you frequently use.

Tip: You can install batches of icons onto the Dock all at once—just drag them as a group.

Here are a few aspects of the Dock that may throw you at first:

- **It has two sides.** The fine dark line running down the middle of the Dock in Figure 3-1 is a divider line. Everything on the left side is a program. Everything else goes on the right side: files, documents, folders, and disks.

- **Its icon names are hidden.** To see the name of a Dock icon, point to it without clicking. You'll see the name appear just above the icon.

- **Folders and disks are hierarchical.** If you retain nothing else in this chapter, remember this: If you *hold down* the mouse button on a folder or disk icon on the right side of the Dock, a list of its contents sprouts from the icon. It's a hierarchical list, meaning that you can burrow into folders within folders this way. See Figure 3-2 for an illustration.

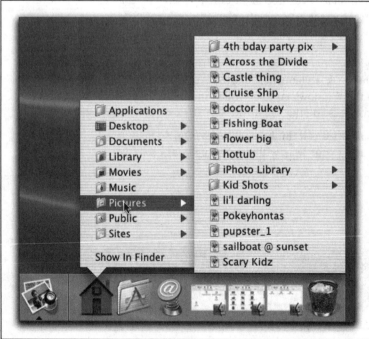

Figure 3-2:
As long as you keep the mouse button pressed, you can burrow into folders within folders—either with the intention of opening a file or folder (by releasing the mouse button as you point), or just to see what's inside.

Tip: To make the pop-up menu appear instantly, just Control-click the Dock icon, or (if you have a two-button mouse) right-click it.

- **Programs appear there unsolicited.** Nobody but you can put icons on the *right* side of the Dock. But program icons appear on the left side of the Dock automatically whenever you open a program (even one that's not listed in the Dock). Its icon remains there for as long as it's running.

Organizing and Removing Dock Icons

You can move the tiles of the Dock around just by dragging them horizontally. As you drag, the other icons scoot aside to make room. When you're satisfied with its new position, drop the icon you've just dragged.

To remove a Dock icon, drag it away. Once your cursor has cleared the Dock, release the mouse button. The icon disappears, its passing marked by a charming little puff of animated cartoon smoke. (Mac OS X won't let you remove the Finder, the Trash, or the Dock icon of a program or document that's currently open.)

Three Ways to Get the Dock out of Your Hair

The bottom of the screen isn't necessarily the ideal location for the Dock. Because most screens are wider than they are tall, the Dock eats into your limited vertical screen space. Worse, a bottom-feeding Dock can actually overlap your document windows, interfering with your work.

In these situations, you have three ways out: Hide the Dock, shrink it, or rotate it 90 degrees.

GEM IN THE ROUGH

Living Icons

Mac OS X brings to life a terrific idea, a new concept in mainstream operating systems: icons that *tell* you something. As shown here, for example, you can often tell documents apart just by looking at their icons.

Furthermore, some program icons actually change over time. The Clock program (in your Applications folder), for example, is a living icon that actually ticks away the time, right there in the Dock. The Mail icon (see Chapter 10) displays a live counter that indicates how many new email messages are waiting for you. (After all, why should you switch into the Mail program if you'll only be disappointed?) The America Online icon sprouts a flag to let you know if an instant message is waiting. And if you minimize a QuickTime movie while it's playing, it shrinks down and continues playing right there in the Dock.

Think of the possibilities. At this rate, one day the Internet Explorer icon could change to let us know when interesting new Web pages have appeared, the Quicken icon could display your current bank balance, and the Microsoft Word icon could change every time Microsoft posts a bug fix.

Auto-hiding the Dock

To turn on the Dock's auto-hiding feature, choose →Dock→Turn Hiding On (or press Option-⌘-D).

In other words, a hidden Dock works just like a hidden taskbar in Windows. When it's hidden, you can make it slide into view by moving the cursor to the Dock's edge of the screen. When you move the cursor back to the middle of the screen, the Dock slithers out of view once again. (Individual Dock icons may occasionally shoot upward into desktop territory when a program needs your attention—cute, very cute—but otherwise, the Dock lies low until you call for it.)

Tip: You may prefer to hide and show the Dock by pressing the hide/show keystroke, Option-⌘-D. The Dock pops on and off the screen without requiring you to move the cursor.

Shrinking and enlarging the Dock

The official way to resize Dock icons goes like this: Choose →Dock→Dock Preferences. In the resulting dialog box, drag the Dock Size slider, as shown in Figure 3-3.

There's a much faster way to resize the Dock, however: Just position your cursor directly on the Dock's divider line, so that it turns into a double-headed arrow (shown in Figure 3-4). Now drag up or down to shrink or enlarge the Dock.

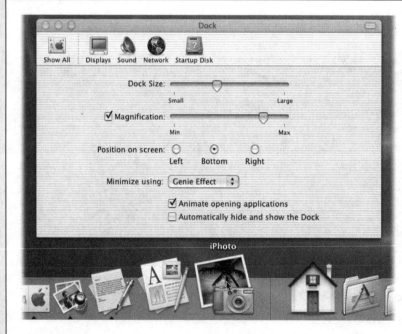

Figure 3-3:
To find a comfortable setting for the Magnification slider, choose →Dock→Dock Preferences. Leave the Dock Preferences window open on the screen, as shown here. After each adjustment of the Dock Size slider, try out the Dock (which still works while the Dock Preferences window is open) to test your new settings.

Tip: If you press Option as you drag, the Dock snaps to certain canned icon sizes—those that the programmer actually drew. (You won't see the in-between sizes that Mac OS X calculates on the fly.)

As noted in Figure 3-4, you may not be able to *enlarge* the Dock, especially if it contains a lot of icons. But you can make it almost infinitely *smaller*. Which makes you wonder: How can you distinguish between icons if they're the size of molecules?

The answer lies in the →Dock→Turn Magnification On command. What you've just done is trigger the swelling effect shown in Figure 3-3. Now your Dock icons balloon to a much larger size as your cursor passes over them. It's a weird, rippling, magnetic sort of animated effect that takes some getting used to.

Figure 3-4:
See the secret cursor that resizes the Dock? If you don't see any change in the Dock size as you drag upward, you've reached the size limit. Never fear: Mac OS X won't make your Dock icons so big that they burst the sides of your screen.

Moving the Dock to the sides of the screen

Yet another approach to getting the Dock out of your way is to rotate it, so that it sits vertically against a side of your screen. You can rotate it in either of two ways:

- **The menu way.** From the →Dock submenu, choose "Position on Left," "Position on Right," or "Position on Bottom," as you see fit.

- **The mouse way.** While pressing Shift, drag the Dock's divider line, as though it's a handle, directly to either side of the screen.

You'll probably find that the right side of your screen works better than the left. Most Mac OS X programs put their document windows against the left edge of the screen, where the Dock and its labels might get in the way.

Note: When you position your Dock vertically, the "right" side of the Dock becomes the bottom. In other words, the Trash now appears at the bottom of the vertical Dock. So as you read references to the Dock in this book, mentally substitute the phrase "bottom part of the Dock" when you read references to the "right side of the Dock."

Using the Dock

Most of the time, you'll use the Dock as either a launcher (click an icon once to open the corresponding program, file, folder, or disk) or as a status indicator (the tiny black triangles, identified in Figure 3-1, indicate which programs are running).

But the Dock has more tricks than that up its sleeve. You can use it, for example, to pull off any of the following stunts.

Switch Applications

The Dock does much of what the Windows taskbar does—and more. For example, it lets you:

- Jump among your open programs by clicking their icons.

- Jump among your open programs by pressing ⌘-Tab. (That keystroke highlights successive icons on the Dock from left to right. Add the Shift key to move backwards—right to left—across the Dock.)

- ⌘-drag a document (such as a text file) onto a Dock application button (such as the Microsoft Word icon) to open the former with the latter.

- Hide all windows of the program you're in by Option-clicking another Dock icon.

This is just a quick summary of the Dock's application-management functions. You'll find the full details in Chapter 4.

Use Secret Menus

It turns out that if you Control-click a Dock icon—or, if you're in no hurry, hold down the mouse button on it—a hidden menu sprouts out (Figure 3-5).

If you've clicked the icon of an open application, you get some incredibly useful commands. For example:

- **[Window names].** At the top of the shortcut menus of most running-application Dock icons, you'll find at least one tiny, neatly labeled window icon, like those shown in Figure 3-5. This useful feature means that you can jump directly not just to a certain program, but to a certain *open window* in that program.

  For example, suppose you've been using Word to edit three different chapters. You can use its Dock icon as a Window menu to pull forward one particular chapter—even from within a different program.

- **Keep In Dock.** Whenever you launch a program, Mac OS X puts its icon in the Dock—marked with a little black triangle—even if you don't normally keep its icon there. As soon as you quit the program, its icon disappears again from the Dock.

  If you understand that much, then the Keep In Dock command makes a lot of sense. It means, "Hello, I'm this program's icon. I know you don't normally keep me on your Dock, but I'd be happy to stay here even after you quit my program. Just say the word."

- **Show In Finder.** Choose this command to highlight the actual icon (in whatever folder window it happens to sit) of the application, alias, folder, or document you've clicked. You might want to do this when, for example, you're using a program that you can't quite figure out, and you want to jump to its desktop folder in hopes of finding a Read Me file there.

Tip: If you really want to reveal an icon in the Finder, there's a much faster way: ⌘-click its Dock icon. This takes you there instantly. (You can even ⌘-click an item that's listed in one of the Dock's pop-up menus, illustrated in Figure 3-5, to highlight *its* icon.)

- **Quit.** You can quit any program directly from its Dock shortcut menu.

Tip: If you hold down Option—even after you've opened the pop-up menu—the Quit command changes to say Force Quit. That's your emergency hatch for jettisoning a locked-up program.

Figure 3-5:
Control-click a Dock icon, or click and hold on it, to open the secret menu. The names at the top of this shortcut menu are the names of the windows currently open in that program. The checkmark next to a window's name indicates that it's the frontmost window of that program (even if the program is in the background).

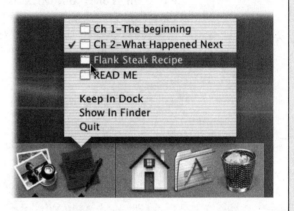

- **Do your filing.** Once you've tried stashing a few important folders on the right side of your Dock, there's no going back. You can pretty much forget all the other navigation tricks you've learned in Mac OS X. After all, the folders you care about are always there, ready for opening with a single click.

Better yet, they're easily accessible for *putting away* files. You can drag files directly into the Dock's folder icons as though they're regular folders. In fact, if you press ⌘ just before releasing the mouse, docked folder icons don't even scoot out of the way, as they usually do to accommodate something you're adding to the Dock. The folder icon you want just sits there—a sitting duck for whatever you're filing.

Great Things to Put on Your Dock

Now that you know what the Dock's about, it's time to set up shop. Install the programs, folders, and disks you'll be using most often.

They can be whatever you want, of course, but don't miss these opportunities:

- **Your Home folder.** Many Mac fans immediately drag their hard drive icons onto the right side of the Dock—or, perhaps more practically, their Home folders (see page 20). Now they have quick access to every file in every folder they'll ever use.

- **The Applications folder.** Here's a no-brainer: Stash the Applications folder here, so you'll have quick pop-up menu access to any program on your machine.

- **The Documents folder.** The Documents folder in your Home folder is another primary center for your Mac activity. Stash it here for quick access.

- **The Shared folder.** If you're using the Mac's *accounts* feature (Chapter 12), this is your wormhole between all accounts—the one place you can put files where everybody can access them (page 277).

- **The System Preferences folder.** Once you stash a folder full of the System Preferences panels onto your Dock (not just the System Preferences icon itself), you'll never again waste time opening System Preferences, clicking the Show All button, and clicking the panel you want. Want to adjust one of your Mac's settings? Leap directly to it from your Dock. (Instructions on page 324; see Chapter 13 for more on System Preferences.)

The Finder Toolbar

At the top of every Finder window is a row of navigation and function icons. One click on any of these icons takes you directly to the corresponding disk or folder, or triggers the corresponding command.

The first time you run Mac OS X, for example, you'll find these icons on the toolbar:

- **Back, Forward.** As in Windows, the Mac OS X Finder works something like a Web browser. Only a single window remains open as you navigate the various folders on your hard drive.

  The Back button returns you to whichever folder you were just looking at. (Instead of clicking Back, you can also press ⌘-[, or choose Go→Back—particularly handy if the toolbar is *hidden*, as described on page 73.)

  The Forward button springs to life only *after* you've used the Back button. Clicking it (or pressing ⌘-]) returns you to the window you just backed out of.

- **View controls.** The three tiny buttons next to the Forward button switch the current window into icon, list, or column view, respectively (page 34).

- **Computer, Home, Favorites, Applications.** Click these buttons to open the corresponding folders, no matter where you are at the moment.

Tip: The Go menu lists the same folders itemized above (among others), for use when you've hidden the toolbar. The menu also displays the keyboard equivalents for summoning these folders.

- **Search.** This is your Find command, as described on page 60.

Removing or Shrinking the Toolbar

The only problem with the Finder toolbar is that it takes up a good chunk of screen space. Between the toolbar, the Dock, and the unusually large icons of Mac OS X, it almost seems like an Apple conspiracy to sell big screens.

Fortunately, you can eliminate the toolbar with one click on the white, oval toolbar button in its upper-right corner. You can also hide the toolbar by choosing View→Hide Toolbar or pressing ⌘-B. (The same keystroke, or choosing View→Show Toolbar, brings it back.)

But you don't have to do without the toolbar altogether. If its consumption of screen space is your main concern, you may prefer to simply collapse it—to delete the pictures but preserve the text buttons.

To make it so, choose View→Customize Toolbar. As shown in Figure 3-6, the dialog box that appears offers a Show pop-up menu at the bottom. It lets you choose picture buttons with Icon Only, or, for the greatest space conservation, Text Only. You can see the results without even closing the dialog box. (Figure 3-7 illustrates the three possible arrangements.)

Click Done or press Enter to make your changes stick.

Note: In Text Only mode, the three View buttons become a little pop-up menu. Furthermore, the Search bar turns into a one-word button called Search. Clicking it brings up the Find dialog box (page 60), which is actually much more powerful than the Search bar.

Figure 3-6:
While this window is open, you can add additional icons to the toolbar by dragging them into place from the gallery before you. You can also remove icons from the toolbar by dragging them up or down off the toolbar, or rearrange them by dragging them horizontally.

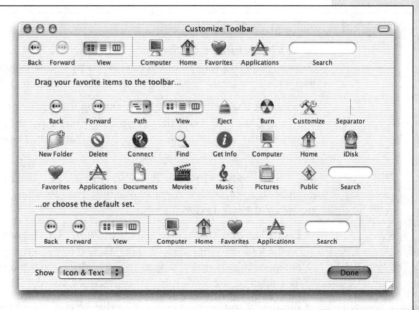

Adding Your Own Icons to the Toolbar

As it turns out, Apple *doesn't* presume to know which icons you want on your Finder toolbar. Mac OS X not only offers a collection of beautifully designed icons for alternate (or additional) toolbar buttons, but makes it easy for you to add *anything* to the toolbar, turning it into a supplementary Dock.

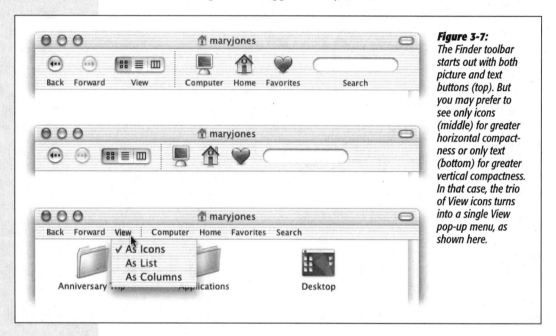

Figure 3-7:
The Finder toolbar starts out with both picture and text buttons (top). But you may prefer to see only icons (middle) for greater horizontal compactness or only text (bottom) for greater vertical compactness. In that case, the trio of View icons turns into a single View pop-up menu, as shown here.

Apple's toolbar icon collection

To see the optional toolbar icons that Apple has prepared for you, choose View→Customize Toolbar. The window shown in Figure 3-6 appears.

This is your chance to rearrange the existing toolbar icons or delete the ones you don't use. You can also add any of Apple's buttons to the toolbar simply by dragging them from the "gallery" upward onto the toolbar itself. The existing icons scoot out of your cursor's way, if necessary.

Most of the options listed in the gallery represent shortcuts to certain folders, or duplicate the functions of menu commands. Here are a few of the options that don't appear on the standard toolbar:

- **Path.** Most of the gallery elements are buttons, but this one creates a *pop-up menu* on the toolbar. When clicked, it reveals and lets you navigate the hierarchy—the *path*—of folders that you open to reach whichever window is open. (*Equivalent:* ⌘-clicking a window's title bar, as described on page 23.)

- **Eject.** This button ejects whichever disk or disk image is currently highlighted. (*Equivalent:* The File→Eject command, or the Eject key on your keyboard.)

- **Burn.** If your Mac has a compatible CD burner (see Chapter 8), this button "burns" a blank CD with the folders and files you've dragged onto it. (*Equivalent:* The File→Burn CD command.)

- **Separator.** This is the only gallery icon that doesn't actually do anything when clicked. It's designed to set apart *groups* of toolbar icons.

- **Delete.** This option puts the highlighted file or folder icons into the Trash. (*Equivalent:* the File→Move to Trash command, or the ⌘-Delete keystroke.)

Tip: The New Folder and Delete icons are among the most valuable ones to put on your toolbar. They represent functions you'll probably use often.

- **Connect.** If you're on an office network, opens the Connect to Server dialog box so that you can tap into another computer. (*Equivalent:* The Go→Connect to Server command, or the ⌘-K keystroke.)

- **Get Info.** This button opens the Get Info window (page 55) for the icon you've highlighted.

- **Default set.** If you've made a mess of your toolbar, you can always reinstate its original, factory-installed arrangement just by dragging this rectangular strip directly upward onto your toolbar.

Note: If a window is too narrow to show all the icons on the toolbar, you will see, at the right end of the toolbar, a >> symbol. Click it for a pop-up menu that names whichever icons don't fit at the moment. (You'll find this toolbar behavior in many Mac OS X programs—System Preferences, Mail, Address Book, and so on—not just the Finder.)

Adding your own stuff

As useful as some of Apple's toolbar-gallery icons may be, the toolbar really takes off only when you add your own icons. You can drag *any icons at all* onto the toolbar—files, folders, disks, programs, or whatever—to turn them into one-click buttons. Together, the Dock and the toolbar offer so many parking places for icons, you may never pine for the Start menu again.

Note: You don't need to choose View→Customize Toolbar to add your own icons to the toolbar. Just drag them from the desktop or any folder window directly onto the toolbar, at any time.

Rearranging Toolbar Icons

You can drag toolbar icons around, rearranging them horizontally, by pressing ⌘ as you drag.

Removing Toolbar Icons

Taking an icon off the toolbar is almost as easy as putting it on. While the Customize window is open, just drag them clear away from the toolbar—or when the Customize window *isn't* open, just ⌘-drag icons clear away from the toolbar at any time. (Watch your Trash on the Dock turn into a pair of snipping scissors as you do it. Cute!)

Designing Your Desktop

In some ways, just buying a Macintosh was a renegade act of self-expression. But that's only the beginning. Now it's time to fashion the computer screen itself according to your personal sense of design and fashion.

System Preferences

Cosmetically speaking, Mac OS X offers two dramatic full-screen features: desktop backgrounds and screen savers. (That's not counting the pictures and colors you can apply to individual folder windows, as described on page 37.)

The command center for both of these functions is the System Preferences program (the equivalent of the Windows Control Panel). Open it by clicking the System Preferences icon on the Dock, or by choosing its name from the menu.

When the System Preferences program opens, you can choose a desktop picture by clicking the Desktop button, or a screen saver by clicking the Screen Saver button. For further details on these System Preferences modules, see Chapter 13.

Desktop Sounds

Desktop *sounds* are tiny sound effects that accompany certain mouse drags in Mac OS X 10.2, which you can turn on to keep yourself awake.

To turn them on, open System Preferences, click the Sound icon, and turn on "Play user interface sound effects."

The result is so subdued and sparse, you might not even notice anything is different. But you'll hear a little *plink/crunch* when you drop an icon onto the Trash, and a little *whoof!* when you drag something off the Dock and into oblivion. Use this feature with discretion when working in a library, neurosurgical operating room, or church.

Programs and Documents

The beauty of life in the Era of Switchers is that most of the big-boy programs are available in nearly identical versions for both the Mac and Windows. Microsoft Word, Excel, PowerPoint, Outlook Express, and Internet Explorer; Adobe Photoshop, Photoshop Elements, Illustrator, InDesign, and GoLive; FileMaker Pro; Macromedia FreeHand and Dreamweaver; and many other programs are available for both Mac and Windows. Sometimes you have to buy the Mac version separately; sometimes they're all on the same CD.

Note: Even if you have one of these combo Mac-Windows software discs, you may want to avoid it if it doesn't contain a *Mac OS X* version of the software. A pre-2000 version of, say, Photoshop, designed for Mac OS 9 or earlier might be more of a hassle than it's worth.

The beauty of programs like these is that the documents you create with the Mac versions are generally *identical in format* to the ones created in Windows. A Microsoft Word document, for example, requires no conversion when transferred from a Mac to a PC or vice-versa. It is what it is: a .doc file.

Same thing with Excel spreadsheets (.xls), PowerPoint slide shows (.ppt), Photoshop documents (.psd), and on and on. You may occasionally encounter a tiny formatting difference—a line thickness change, a movie file that requires a plug-in—but most documents open flawlessly when moved between Macs and PCs. Chapter 7 offers more detail on finding Mac versions of your favorite PC programs.

But even if switching to the Mac OS X versions of your programs is relatively easy, learning how Mac OS X programs *in general* operate may require some study. As this chapter makes clear, the relationship between programs and their documents differs in several substantial ways from the way things work in Windows.

Launching Mac OS X Programs

Most of the techniques for launching (opening) a program work just as they do in Windows. For example:

- Double-click an application's icon (in the Applications folder, for example).

- Click a program's icon on the Dock or the Finder toolbar (Chapter 3).

- If a program's icon is already highlighted, press ⌘-O (short for File→Open) or ⌘-down arrow.

- Use the submenus of the menu's Recent→Applications command.

- Use the Go→Favorites command.

- Open a *document* icon in any of these ways, or drag a document onto the icon of a program that can open it (whether in the Dock, the Finder toolbar, or in a folder window).

As the program opens, its icon jumps up and down eagerly in your Dock (unless you've turned off this feature using the Finder→Preferences command).

The Application Menu

Once a program is open, you'll notice a few changes to the menu bar at the top of the screen. The first menu appears with bold lettering and identifies the program you're using. It might say Internet Explorer, Microsoft Word, or Stickies, for example.

This Application menu (Figure 4-1) offers a number of commands pertaining to the program as a whole and its windows, including About, Quit, and Hide.

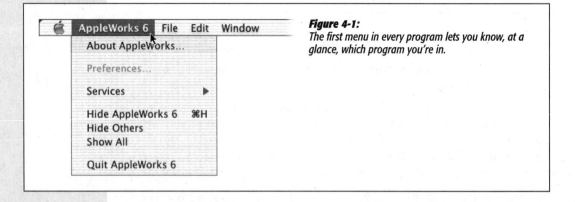

Figure 4-1:
The first menu in every program lets you know, at a glance, which program you're in.

Quitting Programs

In Macintosh lingo, you don't *exit* a program when you're finished with it, you *quit* it. And the command to do so isn't in the File menu—it's at the bottom of the Application menu.

But Mac OS X offers three much more fun ways to quit a program.

- Press ⌘-Q, which is the keyboard equivalent for the Quit command.

- Control-click a program's Dock icon and choose Quit from the pop-up menu.

- When you've highlighted a Dock icon by pressing ⌘-Tab to rotate through the running programs, type the letter Q without releasing the ⌘ key. The program quits instantly.

Force Quitting Programs

Mac OS X is a rock-solid operating system, but that doesn't mean that *programs* never screw up. Individual programs are just as likely to freeze or lock up as they are in, say, Windows.

In such cases, you have no choice but to *force quit* the program—or, in Windows lingo, to terminate it or "end its task." Fortunately, doing so doesn't destabilize your Mac, meaning you don't have to restart it. In fact, you can usually reopen the very same program and get on with your life.

Figure 4-2:
Top: You can force quit a program from the Dock thanks to the Option key.

Bottom: When you press Option-⌘-Esc or choose Force Quit from the menu, a tidy box listing all open programs appears. (This is the equivalent of the Windows Task Manager.) Just click the one you want to abort, click Force Quit, and click Force Quit again in the confirmation box.

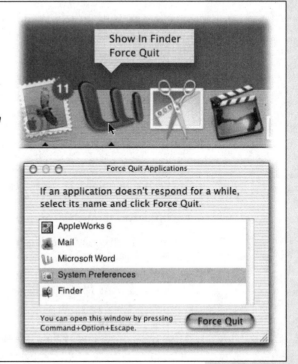

You can force quit a stuck program in any of several ways. First, you can Control-click its Dock icon (or just hold your mouse down on it). Once the pop-up menu appears, press Option so that the Quit command now says Force Quit (see Figure 4-2). Bingo: That program is outta here.

Second, you can press Option-⌘-Esc, the Mac's version of the Windows "three-fingered salute." Third, you can choose →Force Quit. Either way, proceed as shown in Figure 4-2.

Again, force quitting isn't bad for your Mac. The only downside to force quitting a program is that you lose any unsaved changes to your open documents.

Juggling Programs with the Dock

Mac OS X includes an elegant solution to tracking the programs you've opened: the Dock.

Chapter 3 describes the navigational features of this multipurpose icon row—but once you've actually opened a program or two, it takes on a whole new purpose in life.

Switching Programs

The primary purpose of the Dock is simple: to let you know which programs are running. Only one can be in front, or *active*, at a time.

One way to switch to a different program is to click its icon on the Dock. Doing so makes the program, along with any of its open windows and toolbars, pop to the front.

The New, Improved "Alt-Tab"

Exactly in Windows, you can also switch between programs with a keystroke—in Mac OS X, it's ⌘-Tab. (To move *backward* through the open programs, press *Shift-⌘-Tab*.)

Better yet, a single press of ⌘-Tab takes you to the program you used *most recently*, and another press returns you to the program you started in. Imagine that, for example, you're doing a lot of switching between your Web browser and your email program. If you have five other programs open, you don't waste your time ⌘-Tab-bing your way through *all* open programs just to "get back" to your Web browser.

Yet you can still cycle through *all* open programs if you want to—the trick is to keep the ⌘ key pressed. Now, with each press of the Tab key, you highlight the Dock icon of another program, in left-to-right Dock order. Release both keys when you reach the one you want. Mac OS X brings the corresponding program to the front.

Hiding Programs

If the open programs on your Mac are like overlapping sheets of paper on a messy desk, then *hiding* a program makes that individual sheet transparent. When a program is hidden, all of its windows, tool palettes, and button bars disappear. You can bring them back only by bringing the program to the front again (by clicking its Dock icon again, for example).

If your aim is to hide only the program you're currently using, Mac OS X offers a whole raft of approaches to the same problem. Many of them involve the Option key, as listed here:

- Option-click any visible portion of the desktop. The program you were in vanishes.

- Option-click any other program's icon on the Dock. You open that program or (if it's already open) bring all of its windows to the front *and* hide all the windows of the one you were using.

- Option-click any visible portion of another program's windows. Once again, you switch programs, hiding the one you were using at the time.

- From the Application menu—the boldfaced menu that bears the program's name—choose Hide [Program Name].

- Press ⌘-H. This may be the easiest and most useful trick of all (although it doesn't work in every program). Doing so hides the program you're in; you then "fall down" into the next running program.

Tip: Consider this radical, timesaving proposal: *Never quit* the programs you use frequently. Instead, simply hit ⌘-H whenever you're finished working in a program. That way, the next time you need it, the program launches with zero wait time. Because Mac OS X's virtual-memory scheme is so good, there's almost no downside to leaving your programs open *all the time*.

To un-hide a program and its windows, click its Dock icon again, or choose the Show All command in the Application menu.

Hiding All Other Programs

Choosing Hide Others from your program's Application menu means, "hide the windows of every program but this one." It even hides your Finder (desktop) windows, although desktop icons remain visible. (In most programs, you're offered a keyboard shortcut for this command: Option-⌘-H. That's one small step for keystrokes, one giant leap for productivity geeks.)

If this trick interests you, you might also enjoy its Mac OS X–only corollary, described next.

The Bring-Forward, Hide-All-Others Trick

Here's a fantastic Mac OS X secret with no counterpart in Windows. It's a terrific technique that lets you bring one program to the front (along with all of its open windows), and hide all other windows of all *other* open programs—all with one click. You might think of it as Hero mode, or Front-and-Center mode, or Clear My Calendar mode.

In any case, the trick is to Option-⌘-click the lucky program's icon on the Dock. As it jumps to the fore, all other windows on your Mac are instantly hidden. (You can bring them back, of course, by clicking the appropriate Dock icons.)

Minimizing Individual Windows

In Mac OS X, you can hide or show individual windows, just as in Windows. In fact, Apple offers at least four ways to do so:

- Click the minimize button on its title bar, as shown in Figure 4-3.

- Double-click the window's title bar.

- Choose Window→Minimize Window, if your program offers such a command.

- Press ⌘-M.

In any case, the affected window shrinks down until it becomes a new icon on the right side of the Dock. Click that icon to bring the window back.

Tip: If you press the Option key as you perform any of these techniques, you minimize *all* of the program's open windows to the Dock. (If you had several document windows open, they turn into side-by-side document icons on the Dock.) This isn't the same thing as hiding the entire program, as described above—you remain in the same program, but now all of its windows are hidden.

Unfortunately, there's no way to bring them all back at once. You have to click their Dock icons one by one.

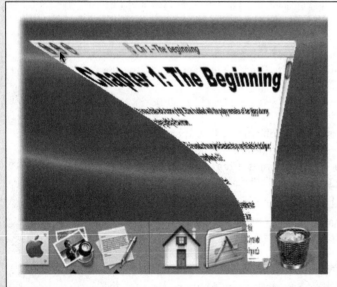

Figure 4-3:
When you click the center button on a window's title bar, you minimize that window, getting it out of your way and off your screen. It's now represented by a window icon on your Dock, which you can click to reopen the window.

Using the Dock for Drag-and-Drop

As described on the next page, the Mac is smart about the relationship between documents and applications. If you double-click a Word document icon, for example, the Word program opens automatically and shows you the document.

But these days, it's occasionally useful to open a document using a program *other* than the one that created it. Perhaps, as is often the case with downloaded Internet graphics, you don't *have* the program that created it, or you don't know which one was used.

In such cases, the Dock is handy: Just drag the mystery document onto one of the Dock's tiles, as shown in Figure 4-4. Doing so forces the program to open the document—if it can.

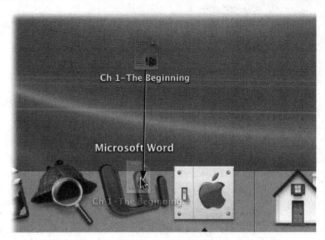

Figure 4-4:
To open a document using a program that didn't create it, drag the document icon onto the corresponding Dock tile. This technique is ideal for opening a downloaded graphics file into your favorite graphics program (such as AppleWorks or GraphicConverter). It's also useful for opening a Read Me file into your word processor, such as Word, instead of the usual TextEdit program.

How Documents Know Their Parents

Every operating system needs a mechanism to associate documents with the applications that created them. When you double-click a Microsoft Word document icon, for example, it's clear that you want Microsoft Word to launch and open the document.

In Windows, almost every document bears a three-letter file name suffix. If you double-click something called *memo.doc,* it opens in Microsoft Word. If you double-click *memo.wri,* it opens in Microsoft Write, and so on.

Mac OS 9 uses a similar system, except that you never saw the identifying codes. Instead, it relies on invisible, four-letter *creator codes* and *type codes.* So why would you, a state-of-the-art Mac OS X maven, care what Mac OS 9 does? Because it's a Macintosh–Unix hybrid, Mac OS X uses *both* creator codes (like Mac OS 9) *and* file name suffixes (like Windows).

It's possible to live a long and happy life without knowing anything about these codes and suffixes. But if you're prepared for a little bit of technical bushwhacking, you may discover that understanding creator/type codes and file name suffixes can be useful in troubleshooting, keeping your files private, and appreciating how Mac OS X works.

Type and Creator Codes

Many Macintosh documents come complete with invisible, behind-the-scenes, four-letter *type* and *creator* codes (see Figure 4-5).

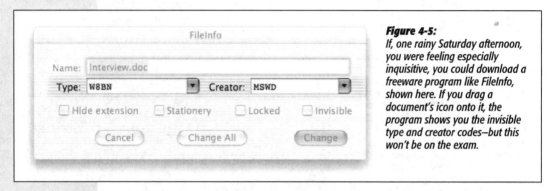

Figure 4-5:
If, one rainy Saturday afternoon, you were feeling especially inquisitive, you could download a freeware program like FileInfo, shown here. If you drag a document's icon onto it, the program shows you the invisible type and creator codes—but this won't be on the exam.

The *creator* code for a program and the documents it creates are identical—MSWD for Microsoft Word, 8BIM for Photoshop, and so on. That's the entire point: The creator code tells the Mac which program to open when you double-click a particular document.

The *type* code, on the other hand, specifies the document's file format. Photoshop, for example, can create graphics in a multitude of different formats: GIF, JPEG, TIFF, and so on. If you inspect your Photoshop documents, you'll discover that they all share the same creator code, but have a wide variety of type codes.

When you double-click a document, Mac OS X checks to see if it has a creator code. If so, it then consults an invisible database of icons and codes. This database is the master index that lists the correspondence between creator codes and the applications that generate them. Together, the type and creator codes also specify which *picture* appears on a particular icon.

If the desktop file discovers a match—if, say, you double-clicked a document with creator code BOBO, which corresponds to the AppleWorks entry in your desktop database—then the corresponding program opens the document, which now appears on your screen.

File Name Extensions

In Mac OS X, plenty of documents don't have type and creator codes. Documents created by *Cocoa* applications (page 96), for example, generally don't.

That's because Mac OS X is a Unix operating system. In Unix, type and creator codes are unheard of. Instead, what determines which program opens when you double-click a document is its *file name extension,* just as in Windows. A file name extension is identifiable by a suffix following a period in the file's name, as in *Letter to Mom.doc.*

The bottom line is that Mac OS X offers *two different* mechanisms that associate documents with the programs that created them. Mac OS X looks for type/creator codes first. Where they're absent, the file name suffixes kick in.

Hiding and Showing File Name Extensions

Exactly as in recent versions of Windows, Mac OS X comes set to *hide* most file name extensions, on the premise that they make the operating system look more technical and threatening. If you'd like to see them, however, choose Finder→Preferences and turn on "Always show file name extensions." Now examine a few of your documents; you'll see that their names now display the previously hidden suffixes.

You can hide or show these suffixes on an icon-at-a-time basis, too (or a clump-at-a-time basis). Just highlight the icon or icons you want to affect and then choose File→Get Info. In the resulting Info window, proceed as shown in Figure 4-6.

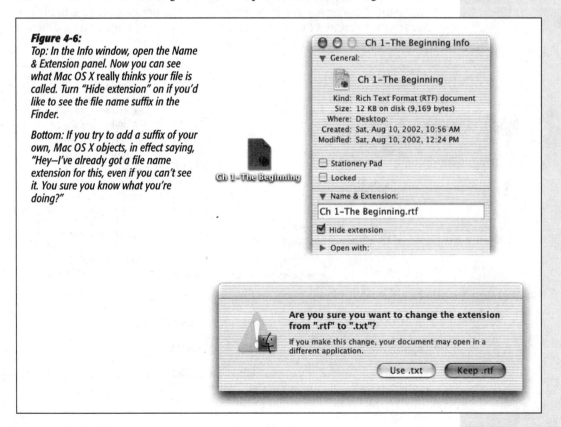

Figure 4-6:
Top: In the Info window, open the Name & Extension panel. Now you can see what Mac OS X really thinks your file is called. Turn "Hide extension" on if you'd like to see the file name suffix in the Finder.

Bottom: If you try to add a suffix of your own, Mac OS X objects, in effect saying, "Hey—I've already got a file name extension for this, even if you can't see it. You sure you know what you're doing?"

Reassigning Documents to Programs

Unfortunately, type and creator codes aren't of much use when you encounter a document created by a program you don't have. If I email you a MIDI file (a file-exchange format for music) that I exported from my Finale sheet music program, you won't be able to open it simply by double-clicking, unless you, too, have Finale installed. Even if you have a different sheet music program on your hard drive, just double-clicking the MIDI file won't, by itself, open it.

The file name extension system, meanwhile, has problems of its own. File name extensions are even less likely to pinpoint which parent program should open a particular document. Suppose you've downloaded a graphic called Sunset.jpg. Well, almost any program these days can open a JPEG graphic—AppleWorks, Word, Preview, Internet Explorer, and so on. How does Mac OS X know which of these programs to open when you double-click the file?

The solution is simple. You can *reassign* a document to a specific program (or all documents of its kind). Here's the rundown:

Reassigning a certain document—just once

Double-clicking a graphics file generally opens it in Preview, the graphics viewer included with Mac OS X (see page 350). Most of the time, that's a perfectly good arrangement. But Preview can only *display* graphics, not edit them. What if you decide to edit a graphics file? You'd want it to open, just this once, into a different program—GraphicConverter, for example.

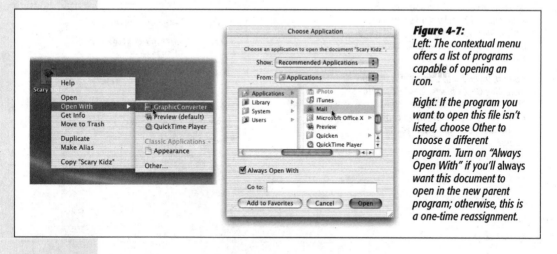

Figure 4-7:
Left: The contextual menu offers a list of programs capable of opening an icon.

Right: If the program you want to open this file isn't listed, choose Other to choose a different program. Turn on "Always Open With" if you'll always want this document to open in the new parent program; otherwise, this is a one-time reassignment.

To do so, you must access the Open With command. You can find it in two places:

- Highlight the icon, and then choose File→Open With.

- Control-click the file's icon (or right-click it, if your mouse has two buttons). From the contextual menu, choose Open With.

In any case, study the submenu for a moment (Figure 4-7, left). The program whose name says "(default)" indicates which program *usually* opens this kind of document. From this pop-up menu, choose the name of the program you'd *rather* open this particular file, right now, just this once.

Reassigning a certain document—permanently

After opening a TIFF file in, say, Photoshop for editing, you haven't really made any changes in the fabric of your Mac universe. The next time you double-click that file, it will open once again in Preview.

If you wish this particular file would *always* open in Photoshop, the steps are slightly different. Highlight the icon, and then choose File→Get Info. Open the "Open with" panel. Choose a new "parent" program's name from the pop-up menu. You'll see that the word "(default)" changes position, now tacking itself onto the name of the new program you've chosen.

Tip: You can use this method to reassign the parenthood of a whole *flock* of selected icons at once. Once you've selected them, just choose File→Get Info, open the "Open with" panel, and choose a new program from the pop-up menu. The message at the top of the window—"22 items," for example—reminds you that you're changing the whole batch at once.

In fact, if you follow up by clicking Change All beneath the pop-up menu, you can reassign *all* TIFF files to open in Photoshop, not just the specific one or batch that you highlighted. Mac OS X asks you to confirm by clicking Continue or pressing Enter. From now on, double-clicking any similar kind of document (one that has the same file name extension) opens it in the newly selected program.

Controlling Menus from the Keyboard

In Windows, of course, you can operate every menu in every program from the keyboard—and every control in every dialog box—thanks to the power of the Alt key.

Mac OS X offers full keyboard control, too, although it's not quite as convenient as in Windows. Once you've turned on this feature (see below for instructions), the possibilities include:

- **Menu bar.** The first menu on your screen drops down when you press a Control-key combination of your choice (such as Control-M). At this point, you can highlight individual commands on that menu by pressing the up or down arrow keys, open a different menu by pressing the right and left arrow keys (or Tab and Shift-Tab), and "click" a menu command by pressing Enter. You can also close the menu without making a selection by pressing Esc, ⌘-period, or the Space bar.

- **Dock.** Operate the Dock by keyboard alone? Sure, that's easy enough: Just press ⌘-Tab to cycle through the open programs.

But ⌘-Tab just highlights successive icons of *open programs* on the Dock. It skips over the icons of folders, disks, documents, and programs that aren't yet open.

If you turn on Full Keyboard Access, you get much more flexibility. For instance, once you've pressed the "highlight the Dock" Control-key stroke of your choice, you can highlight *any* icon on the Dock by pressing the right or left arrow keys (or, once again, Tab and Shift-Tab).

Then, once you've highlighted a Dock icon, you click it by pressing Enter. If you change your mind, once again, press Esc, ⌘-period, or the Space bar.

Tip: Once you've highlighted a disk or folder icon on the Dock, you can press the up arrow to make the list of its contents appear. Using the arrow keys, you can now highlight and open virtually anything in any disk or folder on the Dock. Similarly, once you've highlighted the icon of an application that has several windows open, you can press the up and down arrows to highlight the name of an individual window. When you press Enter, that window pops to the front.

- **Window (active) or next window behind it.** This command lets you switch windows using keyboard control. Each time you press Control-F4, you bring the next window forward, eventually cycling through *every window in every open program*. Add the Shift key to cycle through them in the opposite order.

- **Toolbar.** This one works in most programs that display a Mac OS X–style toolbar: System Preferences, Sherlock, the iPhoto editing window, and so on. (Ironically, this one does *not* work in the Finder.) It also works *only* if you've turned on the "Any control" button at the bottom of the dialog box shown in Figure 4-8.

  When you press Control-F5, you highlight the first button on that toolbar. Move the "focus" by pressing the arrow keys or Tab and Shift-Tab. Then tap the Space bar to click the highlighted button.

- **Utility window (palette).** In a few programs that feature floating tool palettes, Control-F6 highlights the frontmost palette. At this point, use the arrow keys to highlight the various buttons on the palette. You can see the effect when, for example, you're editing text in TextEdit and you've also opened the Font palette. Pressing Control-F6 highlights the Font palette, taking the focus off your document.

Turning on Full Keyboard Access

Apple made sure that this feature was turned *off* by default, to avoid freaking out people who sometimes set their sandwiches down on the keyboard between bites. But it's easy enough to turn on.

Start by opening System Preferences, as described on page 281. Click Keyboard, and then click the Full Keyboard Access tab (Figure 4-8). Turn on "Turn on full keyboard access." You've just powered up one of Mac OS X's most useful timesavers.

Tip: In the future, you can skip all of these steps. Just turn keyboard control on or off by pressing Control-F1 (that is, the F1 key at the top of your keyboard).

Figure 4-8:
The Full Keyboard Access panel of the Keyboard control panel lets you specify how you'd like to control your menus and other Mac OS X interface elements without using the mouse.

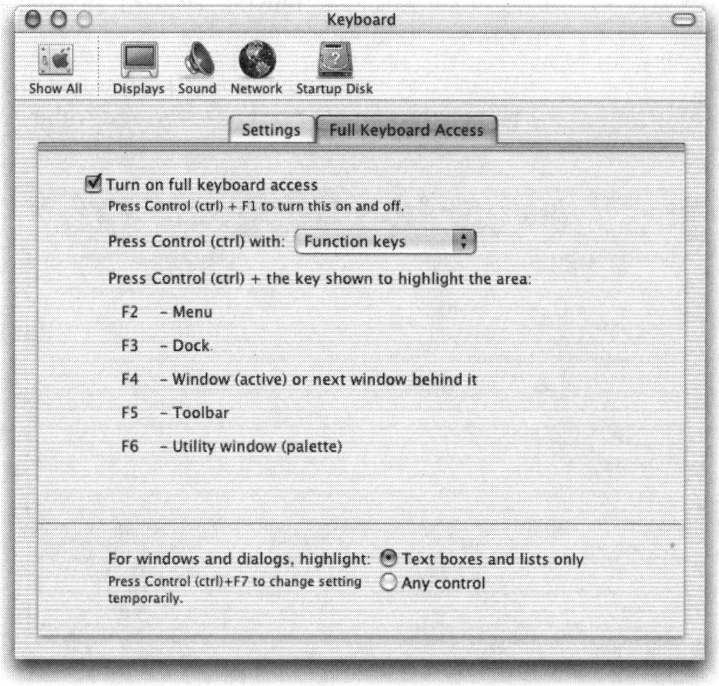

Using the "Press Control (Ctrl) with" pop-up menu, instruct the Mac how you'll be triggering commands. You have the following three choices:

- **Function keys.** In any program, no matter what you're doing, you'll be able to seize control of the menus by pressing Control-F2. Similarly, you'll activate the Dock, toolbars, palettes, and other elements by pressing Control-Fkey combinations, as illustrated in Figure 4-8.

- **Letter keys.** This option will probably give you a lot less trouble remembering how to operate the various keyboard-controllable elements of your Mac. Just press Control-M to highlight the menu bar, Control-D to highlight the Dock, and so on.

- **Custom keys.** This option lets you define your *own* keystrokes for operating the various keyboard-controllable elements. Just remember that the Control key is always required, along with any letter, number, or function key you want to trigger the five options listed in the dialog box.

Note: In Microsoft Office programs and several others, these key combinations may already be assigned to certain functions. Mac OS X will "intercept" these keystrokes.

Although you might not know it by studying the dialog box, Mac OS X also lets you navigate *any dialog box* from the keyboard. The choices at the bottom of the window specify how it works:

- When "Text boxes and lists only" is turned on, the Tab key moves your insertion point only from one text box to the next within a dialog box.

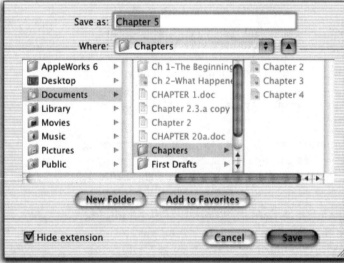

Figure 4-9:
Top: The Windows Save dialog box, an inevitable part of computing, displays a list of the folders on your hard drive. But how do you know where you are? What folder is this one inside of?

Bottom: In Mac OS X, you can see a familiar column display that matches the Finder, making it much easier to figure out what you're doing and how you got here.

- When you turn on "Any control," pressing Tab highlights the next control of *any* type, whatever it may be—radio button, pop-up menu, and so on. Press the Space bar to click a button or open a pop-up menu. (Once a menu is open, use the arrow keys to highlight commands on it, and the Space bar to click your choice.)

Tab-key navigation doesn't work in every dialog box in every program. When it does work, though, it's extremely useful.

The Save and Open Dialog Boxes

When you create a new document and then choose File→Save, you get Apple's version of the Save dialog box: the Save *sheet* (Figure 4-9).

Tip: In Mac OS X, a quick glance at the close button in the upper-left corner of a document window tells you whether or not it's been saved (see Figure 4-10). When a small dot appears in the red button, it means you've made changes to the document that you haven't yet saved. Time to press ⌘-S! The dot disappears as soon as you save your work.

In Windows (and, by the way, earlier versions of the Mac OS), the Save dialog box appears dead center on the screen, where it commandeers your entire operation. You aren't allowed to do anything more in the current program until you click Save or Cancel to close the dialog box. Moreover, because it seems stuck to your *screen* rather than to a particular *document,* you can't clearly see which document you're saving—a real problem when you quit out of a program that has three unsaved documents open.

In most Mac OS X programs, a little Save dialog box called a *sheet* slides directly out of the document's title bar (see Figure 4-10). Now there's no mistaking which document you're saving.

Better still, you can think of this little Save box as a sticky note attached to the document. It will stay there, neatly attached and waiting, even if you switch to another program, another document within the same program, the desktop, or wherever. When you finally return to the document, the Save sheet will still be there, waiting for you to type a file name and save the document.

Simplified Navigation

Of course, *you,* savvy reader, have never saved a document into some deeply nested folder by accident, never to see it again. But millions of novices (and even a few experts) have fallen into this trap.

When the Save sheet appears, however, a pop-up menu shows you precisely where Mac OS X proposes putting your newly created document: in the Documents folder of your own Home folder—the Mac's version of the My Documents folder. For many people, this is an excellent suggestion. If you keep everything in your Documents folder, it will be easy to find, and you'll be able to back up your work just by dragging a single folder (the Documents folder) to a backup disk.

But the Where pop-up menu gives you direct access to some other places you might want to save a newly created file. They include:

- **Desktop.** Just type a name for the file, choose Desktop from this pop-up menu, and then click Save. (You can also simply press ⌘-D.)

  You've just ensured that your file won't fall accidentally into some random folder. Instead, the newly minted document will be waiting for you on the desktop when you quit your program or close its window. From there, you can drag it into any folder you like.

Tip: To open the Where pop-up menu—or any pop-up menu, for that matter—you don't have to click the tiny, blue, double-headed triangle button at the right end. You can click anywhere on the pop-up menu, such as where it says Documents.

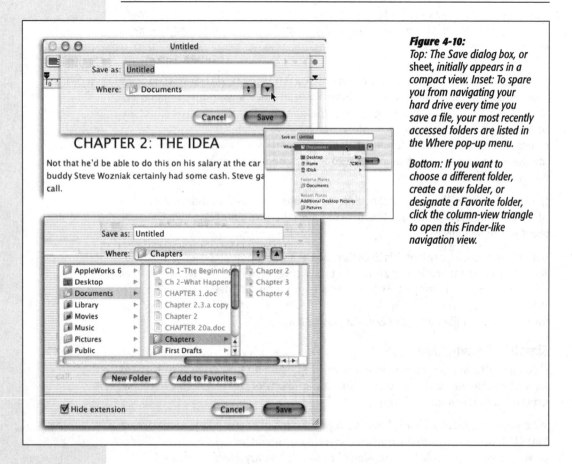

Figure 4-10:
Top: The Save dialog box, or sheet, initially appears in a compact view. Inset: To spare you from navigating your hard drive every time you save a file, your most recently accessed folders are listed in the Where pop-up menu.

Bottom: If you want to choose a different folder, create a new folder, or designate a Favorite folder, click the column-view triangle to open this Finder-like navigation view.

- **Home.** Choosing this item from the pop-up menu (or pressing Shift-⌘-H) takes you directly to your Home folder, which is described on page 20.

- **iDisk.** If you've signed up for Apple's .Mac service (page 123), you can save documents directly onto your Internet-based iDisk hard drive just by choosing this command. (Actually, you can't save icons into your iDisk window—you must save them into a folder *within* your iDisk. That's why the submenu of this iDisk command lists the various folders on your iDisk, as described in Chapter 5.)

  When you do so, your Mac will connect to the Internet and pull your iDisk onto the screen so that you can save your new document there. All of this can take some time, even if you have a high-speed connection.

- **Favorite Places.** This part of the pop-up list is a duplicate of the Favorites menu in the Finder. Its purpose is to list the disks, servers, folders, and other items you use frequently, so that you don't need to burrow through your folders every time you want access.

- **Recent Places.** This part of the menu lists folders and disks you've accessed recently. Once again, the idea is to provide quick access to the folder locations on your hard drive that matter to you—without excessive navigation.

Column View Navigation

When you save a file, the options in the Where pop-up menu have you covered 90 percent of the time. Most people work with a limited set of folders for active documents.

But when you want to save a new document into a new folder, or a folder that isn't listed in the Where pop-up menu, all is not lost. Click the large black triangle shown in Figure 4-9. A familiar scene appears: a compact version of a Finder-window column view, as described on page 43.

Tip: Your first instinct should be to widen this window, making more columns available. Do so by carefully dragging the lower-right corner of the dialog box. Mac OS X will remember the size you like for this Save sheet independently in each program.

Click a column, or press Tab, to highlight the column view itself. Now, using the same techniques described on page 43, you can navigate your entire Mac system. Most of the usual keystrokes and mouse clicks work here. For example, press the arrow keys to navigate the columns, or type the first letters of disk or folder names to highlight them.

Highlight the name of the folder in which you want to save your newly created document, or use these options:

- **New Folder.** Click this button to create a new folder *inside* whatever folder is highlighted in the column view.

- **Add to Favorites.** The Save sheet provides a quick way to add a particular folder to your list of Favorites. Just highlight the folder in the column view and then click Add to Favorites. The favorite folder appears instantly in the Where pop-up menu—in the Favorites section, of course.

The point is that the *next* time you save a new document, you won't even have to bother with the column view. You'll be able to jump quickly to the favorite folder you've just specified.

Tip: You can drag the icon of any folder or disk *from your desktop* directly into the Save or Open sheet. Mac OS X instantly displays the contents of that folder or disk. This shortcut can save you time when you want to save a file into, or open a file from, a deeply nested folder that's already visible in the Finder.

The Open File Dialog Box

The dialog box that appears when you choose File→Open is almost identical to the Save File sheet, except that it offers *both* the Where list of frequently used folders *and* the column view (see Figure 4-11). Because you encounter it only when you're opening an existing file, this dialog box lacks the New Folder button, Save button, file name field, and so on.

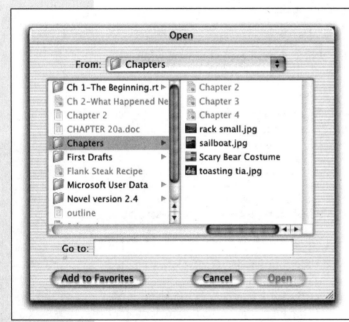

Figure 4-11:
Mac OS X's Open dialog box shows you only icons for disks, folders, and documents that you can actually open at this moment. For example, when working in Preview as shown here, Word and TextEdit documents appear dimmed and unavailable, while picture files show up fine.

Once again, you can begin your navigation by seeing what's on the desktop (⌘-D) or in your Home folder (Shift-⌘-H). Once again, you can open a folder or disk by double-clicking its name in the column-view list, or navigate the list by pressing the arrow keys. And once again, you can drag a folder or disk off of your desktop directly into the dialog box to specify a certain location.

When you've finally located the file you want to open, do so by double-clicking it or highlighting it (which you can do from the keyboard), and then pressing Return, Enter, or ⌘-O.

Most people don't encounter the Open File dialog box nearly as often as the Save File dialog box. That's because the Mac offers many more convenient ways to *open* a file—double-clicking its icon in the Finder, choosing its name from the →Recent Items command, and so on—but only a single way to *save* a new file.

Tip: Instead of using the column view to specify a folder, you can also use the Go To box at the bottom of the Open sheet. That is, you can type a folder path (such as *~/pictures* or *~/pi* and a Tab) into the blank. And if you have no idea what these codes refer to, see the box on page 46.

Three Kinds of Programs: Cocoa, Carbon, Classic

Mac OS X was supposed to make life simpler. It was supposed to eliminate the confusion and complexity that the old Mac OS had accumulated over the years—and replace it with a smooth, simple, solid system.

Five years from now, that's exactly what Mac OS X will be. For the moment, however, you're stuck with running three different kinds of programs, each with different characteristics: *Cocoa, Carbon,* and *Classic*.

The explanation involves a little bit of history and a little bit of logic. To take full advantage of Mac OS X's considerable technical benefits, software companies must write new programs for it from scratch. So what should Apple do—send out an email to the authors of the 18,000 existing Mac programs, suggesting that they throw out their programs and rewrite them from the bottom up?

At big companies like Microsoft and Adobe, such a suggestion would wind up on the Joke of the Week bulletin board.

Instead, Apple gave software companies a break. It wrote Mac OS X to let programmers and software companies choose precisely how much work they wanted to put into compatibility with the new system. The various levels include:

- **Do nothing at all (Classic).** Let's face it: Software companies go out of business, unprofitable product lines are dropped, and shareware authors go off to law school. All of them leave behind orphaned programs that run only in the old Mac OS.

  Your Mac OS X machine can still run this entire library of older software. When you try to open one of these older programs, Mac OS X launches a Mac OS 9 *simulator* called the Classic environment (page 95). Suddenly your screen is taken over by the ghost of Mac OS 9. Sure, you leave behind all the trappings (and benefits) of Mac OS X—its new look, the Dock, crash protection, and so on—but at least you're still running your favorite programs.

- **Update the existing programs (Carbon).** If software companies are willing to put *some* effort into getting with the Mac OS X program, they can simply adapt, or update, their existing software so that it works with Mac OS X. The resulting software looks and feels almost every bit like a true Mac OS X program—you get the crash protection, the good looks, the cool-looking graphics, the Save sheets, and so on—but behind the scenes, the bulk of the computer programming is the same as it was in Mac OS 9. These are what Apple calls *Carbonized* programs, named for the technology (Carbon) that permits them to run in Mac OS X.

Carbonized programs include Microsoft Office, AppleWorks, iTunes, Photoshop, FileMaker, Internet Explorer, and, believe it or not, the Finder itself.

- **Write new programs from scratch (Cocoa).** As Mac OS X becomes a bigger and bigger hit, more and more programmers and software companies create new programs exclusively for it. The geeks call such programs *Cocoa* applications—and they're the best of all. Although they may look exactly like Carbonized programs, they feel a little bit more smooth and solid. More important, they offer a number of special features not offered by Carbonized programs.

Many of the programs that come with Mac OS X are true Cocoa applications, including iChat, iCal, Safari, iPhoto, TextEdit, Stickies, Mail, Address Book, and so on.

Tip: Having trouble keeping the definitions of Carbon and Cocoa straight? You wouldn't be alone; it's like reading a novel where two characters' names start with the same letter. Here's one way to remember: *Carbon* programs are generally the *older* ones, those that might require Carbon-dating techniques to calculate their ages.

The Cocoa Difference

Here are some of the advantages offered by Cocoa programs. It's worth reading—not to make you drool about a future when *all* Mac programs will fall into this category, but to help clear up any confusion you may have about why certain features seem to be only occasionally present.

Note: The following features appear in almost all Cocoa programs. That's not to say that you'll *never* see these features in Carbonized programs; the occasional Carbon program may offer one of these features or another, too. That's because programmers have to do quite a bit of work to bring them into Carbon applications—and almost none to include them in Cocoa.

The Fonts Panel

Mac OS X comes with about 100 beautiful fonts that Apple licensed from commercial type companies—about $1,000 worth, according to Apple.

When you use a Carbon program, you usually access these fonts the same way as you do in Windows: using a Font menu. But when you use a Cocoa program, you get the Fonts panel, which makes it far easier to organize, search, and use your font collection (see Figure 4-12).

See how the Font panel is divided into columns (if the window is wide enough)? The first column, Collections, contains the names of font-list subsets, such as Fun or Modern. This arrangement makes it easier to locate the kind of font you're look-ing for. You can make your own collections, too, by choosing Edit Collections from the Extras pop-up menu at the bottom of the panel.

The second column, Family, shows the names of the actual fonts in your system. The third, Typeface, shows the various style variations—Bold, Italic, Condensed, and so on—available in that type family. (Oblique and Italic are roughly the same thing; so are Bold and Black.)

The last column lists a sampling of point sizes. Of course, you can actually use any point size you want by typing any number into the box at the top of the Sizes list; these common sizes are just listed to save you a little typing.

Tip: The Font panel is great and all that, but you may have noticed that it doesn't actually *show* you the fonts you're working with—something of an oversight in a window designed to help you find your fonts. The Show Preview command in the Extras pop-up menu adds a display section to the top of the Font panel, where you can see the font's name displayed *in* its own font.

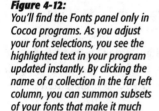

Figure 4-12:
You'll find the Fonts panel only in Cocoa programs. As you adjust your font selections, you see the highlighted text in your program updated instantly. By clicking the name of a collection in the far left column, you can summon subsets of your fonts that make it much easier to home in on what you're looking for.

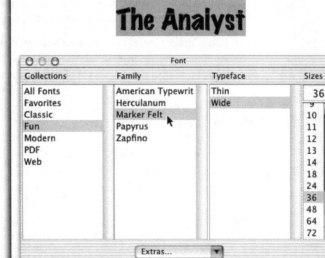

Services

Nestled in the Application menu of every Mac OS X program is a command called Services. Unfortunately, these commands are dimmed when you use most *Carbon-ized* programs; they become available only when you use *Cocoa* programs.

Here's a sampling of the most useful commands in the Services menu.

Note: Not all of these Services work in all programs—even Cocoa programs. Implementing them is left to the discretion of the programmers. In these early days of Mac OS X, a little unpredictability along these lines is par for the course.

Grab

Grab is a screen-capture program in your Applications→Utilities folder. You use it to turn what you see onscreen into graphics files. This is especially handy when writing computer books or training manuals.

Mail

This handy command springs to life only after you've highlighted some text in a Cocoa program—or a file in the Finder.

- **Send File.** This convenient option appears only if you've highlighted an icon in the Finder. In one swift step, this command opens the Mac OS X Mail program (Chapter 10), creates a new outgoing message, and attaches your highlighted file. All you have to do is address the message, click send, and exult in the tedium you've been spared.

- **Send Selection.** In one step, the Mail Text command launches Mail and pastes the highlighted text into the body of a new email message.

- **Send To.** This command is useful only if you've highlighted an email *address* in a text document. This command, too, switches to Mail and creates an outgoing message—but this time, Mac OS X pastes the text you've highlighted into the "To:" field.

Make New Sticky Note

This command copies whatever text you've highlighted, switches to your Stickies program (page 354), creates a new sticky note, and pastes your selected material in it. If you're the kind of person who keeps your life—passwords, favorite URLs, to-do list, notes, and so on—in Stickies, this one can save you considerable hassle.

Speech

Mac OS X doesn't just display text onscreen—it can actually *read it* out loud.

- **Start Speaking Text.** Start by highlighting some text in a Cocoa program. Then choose this command, and presto: The Mac actually reads the text out loud, using the character voice you've chosen in System Preferences (page 321).

- **Stop Speaking.** This command makes the Mac shut up.

Summarize

When you choose this command after highlighting some text, the Mac analyzes the sentences you've highlighted and, after a moment, launches Summary Service. This little program, which you probably never even knew you had, displays a greatly shortened version of the original text. Bear in mind that Summary Service doesn't actually do any creative rewriting. Instead, it chooses the most statistically significant sentences to include in the summary. Figure 4-13 offers details.

Tip: To save the summarized document as a TextEdit document, choose File→Save As.

Figure 4-13:
Use the Summarize command to create a one-paragraph summary (front right) of a longer passage (back left). Once the summary appears in the Summary Service program, you can make the summary more or less concise by dragging the Summary Size slider. You can also ask it to display the most statistically relevant paragraphs instead of sentences, just by clicking the appropriate radio button at the lower left. (Note: Even Summary Services can't come up with something coherent if the original wasn't.)

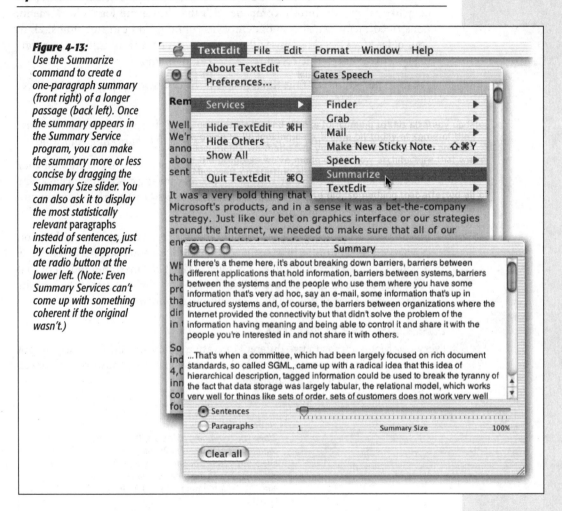

Back to Mac OS 9

If only we could move into Mac OS X and live there! Unfortunately, *software* makes the world go 'round, and it'll be a long time before every program you'd ever want to use has been written or rewritten for Mac OS X.

That doesn't mean you can't use them at all, though. You can certainly run your old favorites within Mac OS X—by flipping back into Mac OS 9. There are two ways to do that:

• **Run Classic.** You can think of the Classic program as a Mac OS 9 simulator or emulator. It runs automatically whenever you double-click the icon of a pre–Mac OS X program.

At that point, the Classic (Mac OS 9) world takes over your screen, looking exactly like a 1999 Macintosh, complete with the old startup logo, old menu, nonstriped menu bar, and so on. Once it's running, you can run almost all of your older Mac OS 9 programs without a hitch. Your Mac is running two operating systems at once, which requires quite a bit of memory.

For most people, most of the time, Classic is the easiest, quickest, and most effective way to run older Mac programs.

• **Restart the Mac in Mac OS 9.** Unfortunately, Classic is only a simulator. Because Mac OS X continues to run beneath it, it isn't actually controlling your Mac.

Whenever a certain program "reaches for" a particular piece of circuitry on your Mac, such as the FireWire or USB jack, it comes up empty-handed. That's why many scanners, digitizing tablets, and even printers don't work when you run programs in the Classic mode.

Fortunately, if you bought a Mac model that was introduced before 2003, you can also restart your Mac in Mac OS 9, just as though you don't have Mac OS X installed at all. At this point, you've got just a Mac OS 9 machine, and all of that older gear works just as it always did. Of course, you don't get any of the benefits of Mac OS X, such as its stability and multitasking prowess.

Classic: Mac OS 9 in Mac OS X

Every new Mac comes with two different operating systems: 9 and X. It's easy to spot them, as shown in Figure 4-14. The icon called System Folder (whose icon is marked by a 9) is the Mac OS 9 system software.

Figure 4-14:
When you're running Mac OS X, the System Folder that contains Mac OS 9 is clearly marked by the golden 9. Only one System Folder per disk may bear this logo, which indicates that it's the only one officially recognized by the Mac. (As the programmers say, it's the "blessed" System Folder.)

When you double-click the icon of a pre–Mac OS X program, your Mac instantly concludes: "Well, this program won't run in Mac OS X, so I'll just go ahead and launch your Mac OS 9 simulator."

At this point, a progress bar appears in a floating window, as shown in Figure 4-15. During the startup process, you'll see a little Classic (numeral 9) icon in your Dock, just to help you understand what's going on.

When all the bouncing stops, you'll see a number of changes onscreen. Your Apple menu is now rainbow-striped, as it was in the days before Mac OS X. The menu bar is light gray, its fonts are smaller, and its menus and commands are different. In short, you've now gone back in time to Mac OS 9.

Note: As an entire operating system, Mac OS 9 could well be the subject of an entire book unto itself—like *Mac OS 9: The Missing Manual.*

Figure 4-15:
Top: Starting up Classic involves waiting for the progress bar to fill up.

Bottom: If you click the flippy triangle below the progress bar, you summon what looks like the full screen of a Macintosh floating within your own Mac's monitor, displaying the standard extensions and control panel icons, the Mac OS 9 logo, and other landmarks of the traditional Mac OS 9 startup process. (Note that the title bar identifies which Mac OS 9 System Folder you're starting up from.)

Once Classic is running, you're free to use the Mac OS 9 program you originally double-clicked—or any other Mac OS 9 programs, for that matter.

Remember, you're running two operating systems simultaneously. When you click a Mac OS X program's icon on the Dock, you bring forward *both* that program and Mac OS X itself. When you double-click a Mac OS 9's Dock icon (or click inside a Mac OS 9 program's window), you bring forward both that program *and* Mac OS 9. You can copy and paste information between the programs running in these two worlds—or even drag-and-drop highlighted material.

It's important to note, however, that Mac OS 9 is no more stable now than it ever was. One buggy program can still freeze or crash the entire Classic bubble. At that point, you may have to exit the Mac OS 9 portion of your machine, losing unsaved changes in any of your Mac OS 9 programs, just as though it were a Mac OS 9 machine that had locked up.

On the other hand, even when your Classic world goes down, you won't have to restart the whole computer. Mac OS X soldiers on, unaffected, and all your Mac OS X programs remain safe, open, and running.

There's really no good reason to quit the Classic simulator, ever. Because Classic is a genuine Mac OS X program, it doesn't consume any memory or horsepower to speak of when it's in the background. You may as well leave it open so that you won't have to wait for the startup process the next time you use a Mac OS 9 program.

Restarting in Mac OS 9

Classic fakes out your older software fairly well—but your Mac is not *actually* running Mac OS 9. Anytime a piece of software tries to communicate with some physical component of your Mac, such as the SCSI, USB, FireWire, or serial ports, it will bruise its knuckles on the stainless steel dome of Mac OS X, which is *really* in charge of your ports. That's why add-on equipment from the pre–Mac OS X era, including USB-to-serial adapters, printers, SCSI cards, and scanners, may not run properly in Classic-environment programs.

What this kind of equipment really needs, of course, is Mac OS X–specific driver software. If drivers exist (check the manufacturer's Web site), you can once again use your gear.

Otherwise, you have only one alternative when you want your external gadgets to work properly with your Mac: Restart the Mac *in* Mac OS 9. (As noted earlier, this is an option only on models introduced before 2003.) When you're finished with your printing or scanning, you can restart the Mac again, this time with Mac OS X "in charge." This ability to switch back and forth between two radically different operating systems on the same computer is called *dual booting*.

The key to switching back and forth between Mac OS 9 and Mac OS X is the Startup Disk control panel (or System Preferences panel).

Switching from X to 9

Suppose you're running Mac OS X, and you need to duck back into Mac OS 9 to use your scanner. The routine goes like this:

1. **Open System Preferences.**

   Click the System Preferences icon on the Dock, or choose menu→System Preferences. The System Preferences screen appears.

2. **Click Startup Disk.**

   You now see the panel shown at top in Figure 4-16. The icons here represent the various System folders, both Mac OS 9 and Mac OS X flavors, that your Mac has found on all disks currently attached to your Mac.

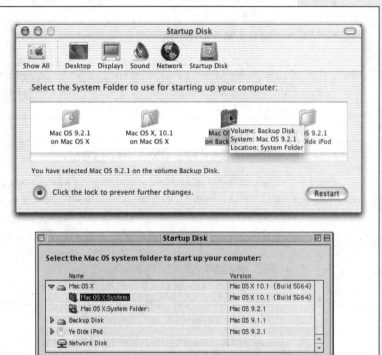

Figure 4-16:
Top: If you're running Mac OS X, you can indicate that you'd like Mac OS 9 to seize control at the next startup by using the Startup Disk system preference panel. If you're having trouble telling the System Folders apart (because, after all, System Preferences reveals only their System versions and disk names, not their folder names), point to the folder icon until the identifying yellow balloon appears.

Bottom: If you're running Mac OS 9, use the Startup Disk control panel to specify that you want Mac OS X to be in charge at the next startup.

3. **Click the Mac OS 9 System Folder you want to be in charge, and then click Restart.**

   The Mac asks, "Are you sure you want to set the Startup disk and restart the computer?"

4. Click "Save and Restart" (or press Enter).

Your Mac restarts in Mac OS 9, ready to use all your old add-on equipment and software (but without the benefit of Mac OS X's stability, good looks, and other features).

Switching from 9 to X

The officially prescribed method of returning to Mac OS X is very similar.

5. Choose →Control Panels→Startup Disk.

The Startup Disk control panel appears, as shown in Figure 4-16. Click the flippy triangle next to a disk's name, if necessary, to see the list of System folders on it.

6. Click the specific Mac OS X System folder you want to be in charge, and then click Restart.

Mac OS X starts up.

Tip: If you have both Mac OS 9 and Mac OS X installed on the same hard drive or disk partition, use this shortcut instead: Just hold down the letter X key while the Mac is starting up. (Hold it down until the Mac stops chiming.) You'll go straight to Mac OS X.

Installing Mac OS X Programs

In general, new programs arrive on your Mac via one of two avenues: on a CD or via an Internet download. The CD method is slightly simpler; see "Performing the Installation" later in this section.

For help installing downloaded programs, on the other hand, read on.

.sit, .tar, and .gz

Programs you download from the Internet generally arrive in a specially encoded, compressed form, as shown in Figure 14-17. The downloaded file's name usually ends with one of these file name extensions:

- **.sit** indicates a *StuffIt* file, the Macintosh file-compression standard—the equivalent of .zip files in Windows.

- **.tar** is short for *tape archive*, an ancient Unix utility that combines (but doesn't compress) several files into a single icon, for simplicity in sending.

- **.gz** is short for *gzip*, a standard Unix compression format.

- **.tar.gz** or **.tgz** represents one *compressed* archive containing *several* files.

Some Web browsers, such as Internet Explorer for the Mac, automatically convert these compression and archiving formats into usable form. Once you return to your desktop, you may well see *several* of these files, representing various stages of decompression and decoding (see Figure 4-17).

If not, just remember that *StuffIt Expander*, which is in your Applications→Utilities folder, can turn all of them back into usable form. If your browser didn't spur it into action automatically, as described above, double-click your downloaded compressed file to spur Expander into action.

Disk Images (.dmg files)

Once you've unstuffed (or untarred) a downloaded program, it often takes the form of a disk-image file, whose name ends with the letters *.dmg*. Disk images are extremely common in Mac OS X.

All you have to do is double-click the .dmg icon. After a moment, it magically turns into a disk icon on your desktop, which you can work with just as though it's a real disk (Figure 4-17). For example:

- Double-click it to open it. The software you downloaded is right inside.

- Remove it from your desktop by dragging it to the Trash (whose icon turns into a big silver Eject key as you drag), highlighting it and pressing ⌘-E (the shortcut for File→Eject), or Control-clicking it and choosing Eject from the contextual menu. (You've still got the original .dmg file you downloaded, so you're not really saying goodbye to the disk image forever.)

Figure 4-17:
Downloading a new program from the Internet may strew your desktop with icons. After the installation is complete, you can delete all of them. (But keep the .dmg file if you think you might want to install the software again later.)

Cleaning Up after Decompression

When the StuffIt Expander progress-bar dialog box disappears, you may have several icons on your desktop. Some are useful, some you're free to trash.

- **The original compressed file.** As illustrated in Figure 4-17, it's safe to throw away the .sit, .tar, .gz, or .tgz file you originally downloaded (after it's decompressed, of course).

Tip: If you get tired of cleaning up after your downloads in this way, you can tell StuffIt Expander to delete the pieces *automatically.* To do so, double-click the StuffIt Expander icon (in Applications→Utilities). From the StuffIt Expander menu, choose Preferences. Turn on both "Delete after expanding" checkboxes, and then click OK.

- **The .dmg file.** Once you've turned it into an actual disk-drive icon (Figure 4-17, bottom), installed the software from it, and ejected the disk-drive icon, you can delete the .dmg file. Keep it only if you think you might need to reinstall the software someday.

- **The disk image itself.** This final icon, the one that contains the actual software or its installer, doesn't exist as a file on your hard drive. It's a phantom drive, held in memory, that will go away by itself when you log out. So after installing its software, feel free to drag it to the Trash (or highlight it and press ⌘-E to eject it)— or just let it sit there until it goes away the next time you restart the Mac.

Performing the Installation

Working with .tar, .gz, and .dmg files are all skills unique to downloading Mac OS X programs from the Internet. Installing software from a CD is much more straightforward.

In either case, once you've got a disk icon on your desktop (either a pseudo-disk from a disk image or a CD you've inserted), you're ready to install the software. You can install many Mac OS X programs just by dragging their icons or folders to your hard drive. Others offer a traditional installer program that requires you to double-click, read and accept a license agreement, and so on.

In both cases, *where* you decide to install the new program is suddenly a big issue. You have the following alternatives:

- **In the Applications folder.** Most programs sit in your Applications folder. Most of the time, this is where you'll want to install new programs. Putting them in the Applications folder makes it available to anyone who uses the Mac.

Note: You can't put anything in your Applications folder unless you have an *administrator account,* as described on page 267.

- **In your Home folder.** This option is valuable only if you share your Mac with other people, as described in Chapter 12. If that's your situation, you may occasionally want to install a program privately, reserving it for your own use only. In that case, just install or drag it into your Home folder (see page 20). When other people log onto the machine, they won't even know that you've installed that new program.

If you don't have an administrator account, this is your only option.

Uninstalling Software

There's no Add/Remove Programs program on the Macintosh, and there never was one. To uninstall a program, you just drag it (or its folder) to the Trash.

In general, this simple act removes all traces of a program (except perhaps its preference file, which may remain in your Home→Preferences folder). The Macintosh doesn't have a Registry, and most pieces of an application are actually hidden inside its icon (see the box below).

POWER USERS' CLINIC

When Programs Are Actually Folders

You may have noticed that OS X programs don't seem to have 50,000 support files strewn across your hard drive.

To open Internet Explorer, you don't first open an Internet Explorer *folder;* you can just double-click the Internet Explorer icon itself. That's a much better arrangement than in Mac OS 9 or Windows, where many programs must remain in special folders, surrounded by libraries, dictionaries, foreign language components, and other support files and folders.

The question is: Where did all those support files go?

Mac OS X features something called *packages* or *bundles,* which are *folders that behave like single files.* Every properly written Mac OS X program looks like a single, double-clickable application icon. Yet to the Mac, it's actually a folder that contains both the actual application icon *and*

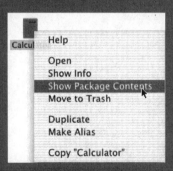

all of its support files, which are hidden for your convenience.

If you'd like to prove this to yourself, try this: Choose Go→Applications. See the Calculator program in the list? Control-click it. From the contextual menu, choose Show Package Contents. You're asking Mac OS X to show you what's inside the Calculator "application icon" folder.

The Calculator package window opens, revealing a Contents folder full of strange-looking, Unix-named folders and files that, behind the scenes, are pieces of the Calculator program itself.

The application-as-folder trick is convenient, because it means that you can uninstall the program by dragging this single icon to the Trash without worrying that you're leaving behind its entourage of support files.

Part Two:
Moving In

2

Five Ways to
Transfer Your Files

A huge percentage of "switchers" do not, technically speaking, *switch*. More often, they *add*. They may get a Macintosh (and get *into* the Macintosh), but they keep the old Windows PC around, at least for a while. If you're in that category, get psyched. It turns out that communicating with a Windows PC is one of the Mac's most polished talents.

That's especially good news in the early days of your Mac experience. You probably have a good deal of stuff on the old Windows machine that you'd like to bring over to the Mac. Somewhere along the line, somebody probably told you how easy this is to do. In fact, the Mac's reputation for simplicity may even have played a part in your decision to switch.

In any case, this chapter describes the process of building a bridge from the PC to the Mac, so that you can bring all your files and settings into their new home. It also tells you where to *put* all of them. (The following chapter is dedicated to the slightly hairier process of getting your email and addresses copied over.)

As it turns out, files can take one of several roads from your old PC to your new Mac. For example, you can transfer them on a disk (such as a CD or Zip disk), by a network, or as an attachment to an email message.

Transfers by Disk

One way to transfer Windows files to the Mac is to put them onto a disk that you then pop into the Mac. (Although Windows can't read Mac disks without help from special software, the Mac can read Windows disks.)

This disk can take any of these forms:

- **A floppy disk.** Apple eliminated built-in floppy drives from its computers in 1997, but any Mac can be equipped with an external, add-on floppy drive for about $60. Of course, if all of your old Windows files fit on a floppy disk, you must be a casual PC user indeed!

- **An external hard drive.** If you have an external USB or IEEE 1394 (what Apple calls *FireWire*) hard drive, you're in great shape. While it's connected to the PC, drag files and folders onto it. Then unhook the drive from the PC, attach it to the Mac, and marvel as its icon pops up on your desktop, its contents ready for dragging to your Mac's built-in hard drive. (An iPod music player works great for this process, too, because it *is* a FireWire hard drive.)

The only downside here is that USB hard drives are pretty slow, and not very many PCs have FireWire connectors.

WORKAROUND WORKSHOP

How to Save Some Effort—and 17 Percent

This chapter is all about (a) hooking up your PC to your Mac so that you can transport your files across the great divide, and (b) figuring out where to *put* the files that you bring over.

If you're willing to spend a little money, however, it's possible to automate some of this process. The ticket is a software-and-cable kit called Move2Mac (from Detto, *www.detto.com*).

You install the software on both your PC and your Mac, and then you connect the two with the included, specialized, one-way USB cable (or parallel-to-USB cable, if your PC is that old). A wizard guides you through the process of choosing which PC files you want brought over to the Mac—and the list of options is enormous. You can tell the program to bring over your documents, pictures, music, video files, desktop wallpaper, sounds, Internet Explorer favorites, Internet connection settings, Outlook Express address book, AIM screen names, and many other kinds of files. (Notably

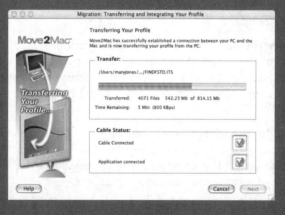

absent from the list: email. Move2Mac can't bring over the messages from any Windows email program, and it can't bring over the address book from any program except Outlook Express. For these transfers, see Chapter 6.)

As part of the process, Move2Mac does everything it can to put the moved files and folders into the right places on the Mac. For example, the PC's My Documents folder arrives in your Home→Documents folder, with most of its folders-within-folders structure intact.

Move2Mac requires Windows 98 or later on the PC (a Windows 95 version is available separately with a parallel-to-USB cable) and costs the average person about $60.

But because you had the good taste to buy this book, you can buy the kit for $10 off. Buy it wherever you like, make your best deal, and then use the rebate coupon page at the back of this book for details.

• **A Zip, Jaz, or Peerless drive.** One great thing about these various backup drives from Iomega is that they're cross-platform. Copy stuff onto a disk while the drive is connected to the PC. Then, if the drive has a USB or FireWire connector, simply move the whole drive over to the Mac. (For best results, install Iomega's Macintosh driver software beforehand.)

Unfortunately, if your drive connects to the PC using a *parallel* connector, scratch this idea off the list; the Mac has no parallel port. (Note: You can't use *USB 2.0* disk drives with the Mac, either.)

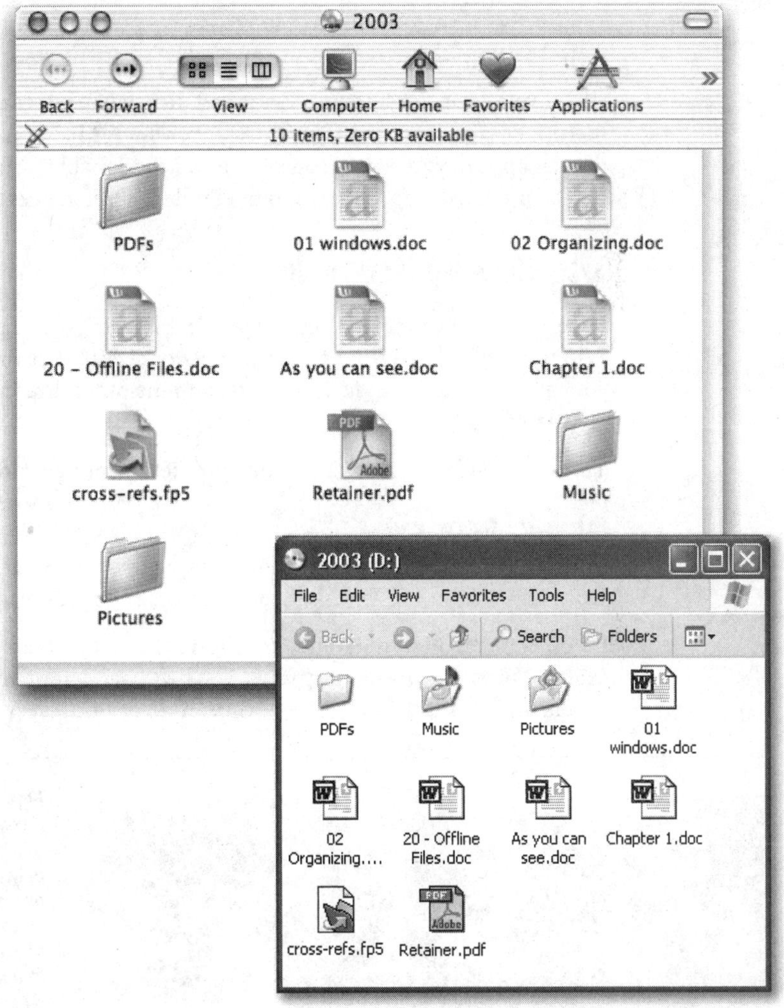

Figure 5-1:
Burned CDs generally show up with equal aplomb on both Mac and Windows, regardless of which machine you used to burn it. Here's a CD burned on a Windows XP Pro machine (bottom), and what it looks like on the Mac (top)—same stuff, just a different look and different sorting order. Double-click this disk icon to open its window and then drag files to and from it (or its window), rename files, delete files, and so on.

- **A CD or DVD.** If your Windows PC has a CD or DVD burner, here's another convenient method. Burn a disc in Windows, eject it, and then pop it into the Mac (see Figure 5-1). As a bonus, you wind up with a backup of your data (the disc itself).

Note: If you're given a choice of file format when you burn the disc in Windows, choose ISO 9660. That's the standard format that the Macintosh can read.

- **Move the hard drive itself.** This is a grisly, very technical maneuver best undertaken by serious wireheads—but it can work. You can install your PC's hard drive directly into a Power Mac, as long as it was prepared using the older FAT or FAT32 formatting scheme. (The Mac can read FAT hard drives, but *not* NTFS hard drives.)

When you insert a Windows-formatted disk, whatever the type, its icon appears at the upper-right corner of your desktop, where Mac disks like to hang out. (If it doesn't appear, you or someone you love has probably fiddled with the "Show these items on the desktop" settings in the Finder→Preferences dialog box.)

Transfers by Network

Here's one of the best features of Mac OS X: It can "see" shared disks and folders on Windows PCs that are on the same network. Seated at the Mac, you can open or copy files from a PC. In fact, you can go in the other direction, too: Your old PC can see shared folders on your Mac.

This really isn't a networking book, but there's enough room for a crash course.

Ethernet Networks

Most people connect their personal computers using either of two connection systems: Ethernet or Wi-Fi (that is, 802.11b or, in Apple's terminology, AirPort).

If you connect all of the Macs, PCs, and Ethernet printers in your small office to a central *Ethernet hub*—a compact $25 box with jacks for five, ten, or even more computers and printers—you've got yourself a very fast, very reliable network. (Most

Ethernet jack   Ethernet hub

Figure 5-2:
If your PC has an Ethernet jack (left), you're in for some easy networking. It looks like an overweight telephone jack, and every Mac OS X–compatible Macintosh has one. It connects to an Ethernet hub (right) via Ethernet cable (also known as RJ-45), which looks like an overweight telephone wire.

people wind up trying to hide the Ethernet hub in the closet, and then running the wiring either along the edges of the room or inside the walls.)

You can buy Ethernet cables, plus the Ethernet hub, in any computer store or (less expensively) from an Internet-based mail-order house. Hubs aren't platform-specific. (And a word of advice: All recent Macs offer built-in *100BaseT* or even *Gigabit Ethernet* cards, so don't hobble your network speed by buying a slower, *10baseT* hub.)

Tip: If you want to connect only two machines—your PC and your Mac, for example—you don't need an Ethernet hub at all. Instead, you can connect a standard Ethernet cable directly from your Mac to your PC's Ethernet adapter. This is a sensational system that places no limits on the amount of data that you can transfer—and it's *fast.*

That's if your Mac was made in 2002 or later. If you have an older model (Power Mac or PowerBook G3, colored iMac or iBook, 15-inch flat-panel iMac, and so on), you have to use an Ethernet *crossover cable* rather than a regular Ethernet cable—about $8 from a computer store or online mail-order supplier. Run it directly between the Ethernet jacks of the two computers.

Ethernet is the best networking system for many offices. It's fast, easy, and cheap.

Wireless Networks

By buying a $150 Wi-Fi (802.11b) base station for your office, you catapult yourself into the second most popular home-networking world: *wireless* networking. Once you've installed a corresponding wireless card into both the Mac and the PC, they can then communicate without a cable in sight, as long as the machines are within 150 feet (as the termite burrows) from the base station. If you think about it, the AirPort system is a lot like a cordless phone, with the computers as the handsets.

Apple, having recognized that both "Wi-Fi" and "802.11b" are extremely geeky names, made up its own term for this kind of networking: AirPort. For example, the card that you buy for your Mac is called an AirPort card, and Apple's version of the base station is called an AirPort base station. (Macs must use Apple's cards, but they can connect to any brand of base station.)

Note: The very latest Macs, furthermore, can accommodate AirPort *Extreme* cards, which communicate with AirPort Extreme base stations. That's Apple's name for 802.11*g* networking, which is compatible with the far more common 802.11b equipment—but in the presence of other 802.11g gear, transfers data five times as fast.

After having wired your network (or unwired it, as the case may be), your network is ready. Your Mac should "see" any Ethernet or shared USB printers, in readiness to print. You can now play network games or use a network calendar. And you can now turn on *file sharing,* one of the most useful and sophisticated features of the Mac OS.

Seated at the Mac: Seeing the PC

Suppose you have a Windows machine on the network. Thanks to Mac OS X's Windows-friendly networking smarts, you can bring selected folder icons to your Mac's screen, and manipulate their contents just as though they were sitting on your Mac's own hard drive.

Before the Mac and PC can begin chatting, though, Windows must be made ready to share its folders—and that entails installing a special software blob called File and Printer Sharing for Microsoft Networks. Do you have it? Here's how to tell:

Figure 5-3:
Top: To share a folder in Windows, right-click it, choose Properties, and turn on "Share this folder on the network."

Bottom: Back in the safety of Mac OS X, open the Connect to Server dialog box. What you see here depends on the complexity and structure of your network. You may see individual computers listed, network "clusters" as shown here, or a mix of the two.

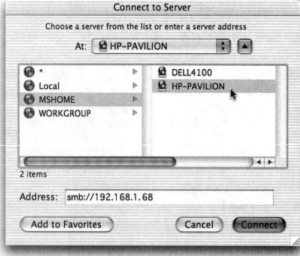

- **Windows XP, Windows Me, Windows 2000.** You have this software already. Skip ahead to step 1.

- **Windows 95, 98, or NT.** If your PC has never been part of an office network, then it probably *doesn't* have the necessary software installed.

   To install it, choose Start→Control Panel; in the Control Panel window, open Network. If you don't see "File and printer sharing for Microsoft Networks," click the Add button, double-click Service, select "File and printer sharing for Microsoft Networks," click OK, and insert the Windows installation CD when you're asked for it. See Windows Help for details.

In any case, you should now be ready to commence the cross-platform network hookup, like this:

1. **On your Windows PC, share a folder.**

   You have to specify which folders you want to make available on the network. In Windows XP, for example, you right-click a folder, choose Properties from the shortcut menu, click the Sharing tab, and turn on "Share this folder on the network" (Figure 5-3, top left). In the "Share name" box, type a name for the folder as it will appear on the network (no spaces are allowed).

Note: If you've never shared a folder on this PC before, you may not see the "Share this folder" option. In its place, you'll see a link that runs the Network Setup Wizard. Go ahead and run that, supplying a computer and workgroup name when prompted, and then restart the PC to turn on sharing. Then start over with step 1.

   Repeat for any other folders you want to make available to your Mac.

2. **On the Mac, choose Go→Connect to Server (⌘-K).**

   The Connect to Server dialog box appears, as shown at bottom in Figure 5-3. Any PCs on your network should show up automatically in the list.

   They may appear as individual computer names, or—if you've used Microsoft's Network Setup Assistant—you may see only the icon of their *workgroup* (network cluster). Unless you (or a network administrator) changed it, the workgroup name is probably MSHOME or WORKGROUP.

Tip: If you don't see any sign of your PCs, read the troubleshooting box on page 119.

---

3. **Click the Windows workgroup name, if necessary.**

   Now the names of the individual PCs on the network appear on the right side of the dialog box (Figure 5-3, bottom).

4. **Double-click the name of the computer you want.**

   The Authentication dialog box appears, as shown at top in Figure 5-4.

5. **Type your name and password, if necessary, and then click OK.**

If you have an account on the Windows PC, great—use that name and password. If the PC isn't in a corporation where somebody administers access to each machine, you may be able to leave the password blank.

Tip: If you do have to enter a password, consider turning on "Add to keychain." You won't need to type the password again the next time.

The SMB Mount dialog box now appears (Figure 5-4, lower left). Its pop-up menu lists the *shares* (that is, shared folders and disks) on the selected PC.

6. **From the pop-up menu, choose the name of the shared folder that you want to bring to your Mac desktop (Figure 5-4, bottom left). Click OK.**

At long last, the shared folder on the Windows machine appears on your desktop with a network-drive icon (Figure 5-4, lower right). From here, it's a simple matter to drag files from one machine's icon to another, open Word documents that live on the PC using Word for the Mac, and so on.

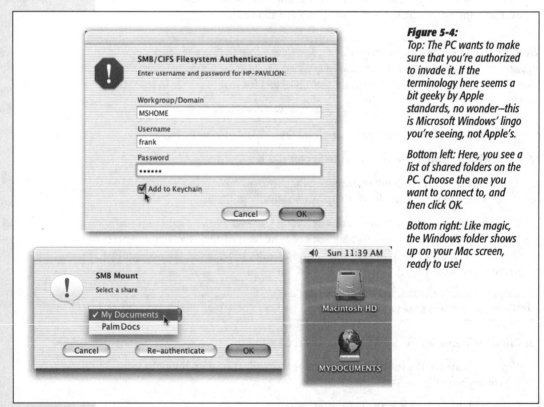

Figure 5-4:
Top: The PC wants to make sure that you're authorized to invade it. If the terminology here seems a bit geeky by Apple standards, no wonder—this is Microsoft Windows' lingo you're seeing, not Apple's.

Bottom left: Here, you see a list of shared folders on the PC. Choose the one you want to connect to, and then click OK.

Bottom right: Like magic, the Windows folder shows up on your Mac screen, ready to use!

Seated at the PC: Seeing the Mac

Not only can your Mac see other PCs on the network, but they can see the Mac, too. Here's how you prepare the Mac for visitation from a PC.

1. **On the Mac, open System Preferences. Click the Sharing icon.**

   Now you see a list of the different ways your Mac can share its goodies with the outside world via network.

2. **Turn on Windows File Sharing (Figure 5-5, top).**

   If there are other *Macs* on the network, you may also want to turn on Personal File Sharing, too. Now your Mac will be available for visitation by other Macs on the same network.

3. **Click Show All, and then click Accounts. Create an account, if necessary.**

   As a security precaution, nobody can tap into your machine unless you've first given them a name and password—that is, an *account*. Chapter 12 describes this process in detail.

   Of course, if you already *have* an account on the Mac, no problem—your existing account will work just fine. You just have to tell the Mac that you're allowed to visit, like this:

TROUBLESHOOTING MOMENT

When Your Mac Can't See the PC

For most people, the magic of Mac OS X 10.2's "Macs and PCs can see each other on the network" feature is that it works automatically, the first time, every time.

But if the Connect to Server box doesn't show the PCs on the network, it may be that you need to introduce your Mac to the Windows workgroup.

Open the Directory Access program in your Applications→Utilities folder. Click the padlock, sign in as an administrator, and then double-click the SMB item in the list.

When you get the dialog box shown here, type (or choose) the precise name of the Windows workgroup you'd like

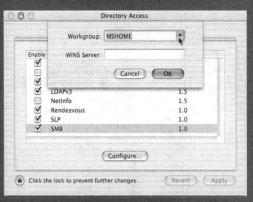

your Mac to "belong" to, and then click OK. Quit Directory Access and choose Go→Connect to Server once again. This time, your Mac should see the PCs.

Finally, note that the PC won't show up in the Connect to Server window if it's not on the same network segment as your Mac—a possibility if you work in a big corporation. In that case, ask your network administrator what the PC's *IP address* is (its numerical network address).

Once you know that key piece of information, you can bring that PC to your Mac desktop by typing *smb:// 111.222.33.444* into the text box at the bottom of the dialog box (substitute the real IP address, of course).

---

4. **Click the account name, and then click Edit User. In the resulting dialog box, turn on "Allow user to log in from Windows" (Figure 5-5, second from top).**

A "Password reset required" message appears. As it points out, you have to change this person's password (although there's nothing to stop you from putting in precisely the same password as before).

5. **Enter the new password (twice), and then click OK. Click OK to get past the Keychain notice, and then click Save.**

That's it: Your Mac is ready for invasion. Quit System Preferences, if you like.

6. **On the Windows machine, open the My Network Places or Network Neighborhood icon.**

Your Mac's icon should appear here, bearing a name like "Samba 2.2.3a (Robinscomputer)." (No, Microsoft isn't trying to give you dance lessons. Samba is the Mac's version of the SMB file sharing protocol that Windows uses.)

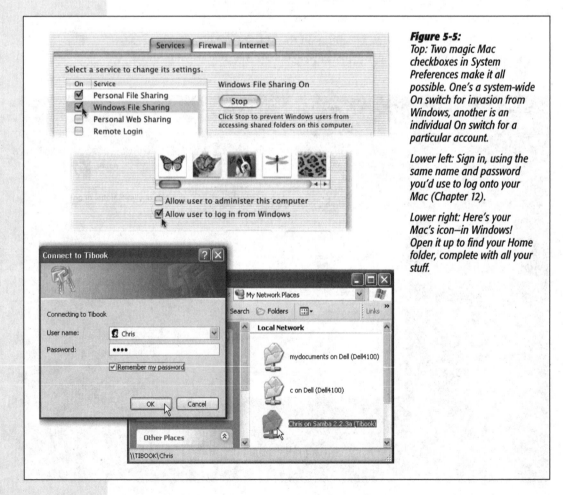

Figure 5-5:
Top: Two magic Mac checkboxes in System Preferences make it all possible. One's a system-wide On switch for invasion from Windows, another is an individual On switch for a particular account.

Lower left: Sign in, using the same name and password you'd use to log onto your Mac (Chapter 12).

Lower right: Here's your Mac's icon—in Windows! Open it up to find your Home folder, complete with all your stuff.

7. **Double-click the icon's name, sign in (Figure 5-5, bottom), and then go to town.**

In the final window, you see your actual Home folder—on a Windows PC. You're ready to open its files, copy them back and forth, or whatever.

Tip: Want more flexibility than this one-folder-at-a-time sharing system? Dave *(www.thursby.com)* is a $150 Mac–Windows file and printer sharing program that's more powerful, more flexible, and more complex than the procedure described in these pages.

Transfers by Email

If you've got a lot of stuff to bring over from your PC, you'll probably want to use one of the disk- or network-based transfer systems described earlier in this chapter. Although sending files as email attachments might seem to be a logical plan, it's very slow. Furthermore, remember that most Internet service providers limit your email box to 5 or 10 megabytes. Trying to send more than that at once will clog your system.

But for smaller transfer jobs or individual files, sending files as plain old email attachments works just fine.

If you have trouble, or if you can't open the attachments at the other end, consider the following potential snags.

TROUBLESHOOTING MOMENT

When Your PC Can't See the Mac

If your Mac doesn't show up in the My Network Places (or Network Neighborhood) window of the PC, you may have to knock it into submission.

If this is your first attempt at Mac–PC communication, try restarting the PC. The My Network Places window updates itself only once per session.

If that doesn't work, on the PC, click the "View workgroup computers" link in the left-side task pane. In the next window, click the "Microsoft Windows Network" link.

Finally, you arrive at the Microsoft Windows Network window, which contains icons for the various workgroups on the network. Double-click the icons until you find your Mac. Log in as described in Figure 12-1. Thereafter, your Home

folder will show up like any other folder in the My Network Places window, saving you the trouble of going through all this again.

If your PC sees the Mac but doesn't let you sign in, on the other hand, the troubleshooting tactic is slightly different. Go to the Mac and open System Preferences. Open the My Account panel and change your password to something else. Click OK—and then change the password *back again*, if you like. The point is that changing your password (even if you change it right back) shocks both the Mac and PC into re-memorizing it.

Now when you sign in from the PC, the Mac should recognize you—and let you in.

File Compression and Encoding

The technology behind email attachments is somewhat technical, but it's extremely useful in understanding why some attachments don't make it through the Internet alive.

When you send an email attachment, your email program does two things. First, surprising as it may seem, the Internet cannot, in fact, transmit *files*—only pure text. Your email program, therefore, takes a moment to *encode* your file attachment, converting it into a stream of text code to be reconstructed by your recipient's email program.

This encoding business is a problem chiefly when sending files *from* a Mac *to* a Windows machine—and only rarely a problem, at that. The Mac can understand almost any encoding format—MIME, Base64, AppleDouble, whatever—but Windows machines don't understand something called BinHex. If your Mac-to-Windows attachments aren't coming through alive, make sure your Mac email program isn't using the BinHex scheme for attachments. (Fortunately, none of the popular Mac email programs uses BinHex unless you explicitly tell it to.)

But there's a second, more common problem: Your email program may also *compress* the attached file so that it takes less time to send and receive. Most Mac email programs compress outgoing files using the StuffIt method—but Windows recipients can't open StuffIt files.

When sending files from the Mac to Windows, therefore, you should turn off the StuffIt compression option in your email program. (Alternatively, you can download StuffIt Expander for Windows, available at no charge from *www.aladdinsys.com,* which can open StuffIt attachments.)

Note: America Online is a particular problem. When you attach multiple files to a single email message, AOL uses StuffIt compression automatically—and you can't override this behavior. When sending files to Windows from AOL, therefore, attach only a single file per email message.

Problems Receiving Windows Files

When your Mac receives Windows files by email, the problems aren't so severe. Most email programs, including Mail and Entourage, decompress and decode file attachments automatically. When they don't, you can drag the downloaded file onto the icon of the free utility program, StuffIt Expander (which is in your Applications→ Utilities folder). StuffIt Expander can convert most Internet files back into human form.

It's worth noting again, however, that not every Windows file *can* be opened on a Macintosh, and vice versa. A file whose name ends in *.exe,* for example, may be a double-clickable Windows application that doesn't run on the Mac (at least, not unless you've gone to the expense and trouble of installing a Windows emulator program like Virtual PC). See the table on page 131 for some examples of files that transfer well from Windows to Mac and don't need conversion or adapters of any kind.

Transfer by iDisk

If your Windows PC is not, in fact, in the same home or office as the Mac, connecting the two using Ethernet or a wireless network may not be a practical proposition. But even if you can't connect them into *a* network, you can still connect them via *the* network: the Internet.

It turns out that, for $100 per year, Apple will be only too happy to admit you to a club it calls *.Mac* ("dot-mac"). It offers a number of handy Internet features that tie in nicely to Mac OS X. For example, you can turn a group of your digital pictures in Apple's free iPhoto program into a full-blown Web page, posted online for all the world to see, with only two mouse clicks. You also get an email account *(yourname@mac.com)* that you can access either from the .Mac Web site no matter where you are in the world, or using a standard email program. And you get a backup program that automatically backs up designated files and folders onto a safe, Internet-based hard drive that will still be there even if your office goes up in flames.

For most people, though, the crown jewel of the .Mac services is the iDisk, which appears on your desktop as though it's a 100 MB hard drive. Anything you drag into the folders inside this icon gets copied to Apple's secure servers on the Internet. (If

Figure 5-6:
The .Mac Web site features special tabs across the top. For example, the iCards feature lets you send attractively designed electronic greeting cards by email to anyone on the Internet. The Backup feature works in conjunction with a basic backup program that you can download from this site. Webmail and HomePage are the other second-tier features. The best feature, however, is iDisk.

that's not enough space for you, Apple is happy to rent you a larger allotment in exchange for more money.)

Because you can pull the iDisk onto *any* computer's screen—Mac or Windows—anywhere in the world, it makes a handy universal transfer disk.

The iDisk from Windows

You can bring your iDisk onto the screen of any computer, even a Windows PC. That's what makes it handy as a file-transfer vehicle when you're making the big move to Mac. You can bring the iDisk icon to your PC's screen, fill it up with files, and then retrieve those files on the Mac when you return home.

The procedure varies by Windows version, but the general idea is the same: You're going to create a new "network place" that uses the address *http://idisk.mac.com/yourname,* where *yourname* is your .Mac account name.

The first step goes like this:

- **Windows XP:** In any folder window, choose Tools→Map Network Drive.

- **Windows 2000:** In any folder window, choose Tools→Map Network Drive. Click "Web folder or FTP site."

- **Windows 98:** Open My Computer. Double-click the Web Folders icon; double-click Add Web Folder.

In each case, you should now type in this address as the location to add: *http://idisk.mac.com/yourname,* as shown in Figure 5-7. Click Browse, OK, or whatever button looks promising.

When you're asked for a name and password, type in your usual .Mac name and password.

After a minute or two, you'll find the icon for your iDisk in the My Computer window, sitting there as though it's a very slow hard drive attached to the PC. (In Windows XP, for example, it's in the Network Drives category, called something like "Frank23 on 'idisk.mac.com.'")

Tip: From now on, you'll be able to summon your iDisk by double-clicking its icon in the Network Places folder.

When you're ready to copy your PC's files onto the iDisk, there's only one rule: You can't create your own folders on the iDisk. You must put your files and folders into one of the folders *already on the iDisk,* such as Documents or Pictures. If you try to drag an icon directly into the iDisk window, or onto the iDisk icon, for example, you'll get an error message.

Otherwise, only the iDisk's 100 MB ceiling can stand in your way. (And even then, Apple is happy to expand your storage space—for a fee.)

Figure 5-7:
You can think of the iDisk as an Internet-based data bucket that lets you slosh files back and forth between distant computers, such as a Mac and a PC.

The iDisk on the Mac

Apple must really love the iDisk concept, because it has devised about 300 different ways to pull the iDisk icon onto your Mac's screen:

- Choose Go→iDisk (or press Shift-⌘-I), as shown in Figure 5-8.

- Click the iDisk icon on the toolbar of any Finder window, if you've put it there (page 74).

- From within any program, choose File→Save As or File→Open. In the Save or Open dialog box, choose iDisk from the Where pop-up menu (see Figure 5-8).

- Choose Go→Connect to Server. At the bottom of the resulting dialog box, type *http://idisk.mac.com/yourname* (substitute your actual account name for *yourname*). Press Enter. In the next dialog box, type your .Mac name and password, and then click Connect. (This is the quickest approach if you're using somebody else's Mac OS X machine.)

• Visit *www.mac.com* and click the iDisk icon. Type in your name and password, and then click Enter. Finally, click Open Your iDisk. (Clearly, this is a lot more work than the one-click methods described above. Use this technique when you're using a Mac OS 9 machine away from home, for example.)

At this point, using iDisk is exactly like using a very slow—but very safe—hard drive. You can drag files or folders from your hard drive into one of the folders that appear on the iDisk, or, more to the point, copy your old Windows files *from* the iDisk to your *Mac's* hard drive (into your Home folder, for example).

Tip: Inside the Software folder on your iDisk is an entire software collection you didn't even know you had. Inside are various folders containing both Apple software updates and the most popular Mac OS X shareware and freeware programs. After reviewing these programs, drag the software you want to your hard drive or your desktop. You can open or install it from there. (Fortunately, none of this eats into your 100 MB limit.)

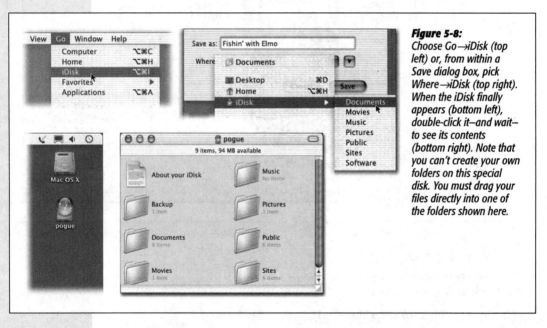

Figure 5-8:
Choose Go→iDisk (top left) or, from within a Save dialog box, pick Where→iDisk (top right). When the iDisk finally appears (bottom left), double-click it—and wait— to see its contents (bottom right). Note that you can't create your own folders on this special disk. You must drag your files directly into one of the folders shown here.

You can leave the iDisk's icon onscreen for as long as you like. If you have a full-time Internet connection, great: you can consider the iDisk a permanent fixture of your Macintosh. But even if you have a dial-up Internet account, you can leave the iDisk on your screen. Whenever you double-click it or save something onto it, your modem automatically dials the Internet and opens the pipes you need to feed your iDisk.

Transfer by Bluetooth

Bluetooth isn't really designed to be a networking technology; it's designed to elimi-nate cables between various gadgets. But if your Mac and a PC each have Bluetooth adapters, you can share files between them as though there's no language barrier at all. (Apple sells a Bluetooth adapter for any USB Mac for $50, and builds it directly into certain models, like the 2003 PowerBook and Power Mac models.)

The Mac's Bluetooth adapter comes with a nondenominational file-exchange pro-gram called Bluetooth File Exchange; not all Windows Bluetooth adapters come with such a program. But if yours does (3Com's adapters do, for example), you should be able to shoot files between the machines with the greatest of ease—and no setup whatsoever.

Where to Put Your Copied Files

Where to put your copied files? Easy one: in your Home folder.

In fact, it's a good idea to keep just about *everything* in your Mac's Home folder. That way, it's protected from inspection by other people who use the computer, it's easy to find, and it's easy to back up.

Some of the "where to put it" answers are pretty obvious:

- **My Documents.** Put the files and folders in the PC's My Documents folder into your Home→Documents folder. Here's where you should keep all your Microsoft Office files, PDF files, and other day-to-day masterpieces.

- **My Music.** In recent versions of Windows, a My Music folder is designed to hold all of your MP3 files, AIFF files, WAV files, and other music. As you could prob-ably guess, these files belong in your Home→Music folder.

  At least for starters. After that, you'll probably want to open Apple's music player—called iTunes—and choose File→Add to Library. Navigate to, and select, your Home→Music folder so that iTunes imports all your files. Now you'll be able to sort, play, and organize them.

- **My Pictures.** The latest Windows versions also offer a My Pictures folder, which is where your digital camera photos probably wind up. Mac OS X has a similar folder: the Home→Pictures folder.

  Here again, after copying your photos and other graphics faves over to the Mac, you're only halfway home. If you fire up iPhoto (in your Applications folder), choose File→Import, and choose the Pictures folder, you'll be able to find, orga-nize, display, and use your photos in spectacular ways.

- **My Videos.** As you can probably guess, the My Videos folder of Windows XP contains the video clips you've downloaded from your camcorder (presumably so that you can edit them with Microsoft's Movie Maker software). Once you've moved them to your Home→Movies folder, though, you're in for a real treat: You can now edit your footage (if it's *digital* footage) with iMovie 3, which, to put it kindly, runs rings around Movie Maker.

Other elements of your Windows world, though, are trickier to bring over. For example:

Desktop Pictures (Wallpaper)

You can say whatever you like about Microsoft's sense of design (and plenty of devoted Macintosh fans have plenty to say on this topic). But especially in recent versions of Windows, the desktop pictures, better known in the Windows world as wallpaper, are pretty cool. Fortunately, you're welcome to bring them over to your Mac and use them on your own desktop.

To find the graphics files that make up the wallpaper choices in Windows XP and Windows Me, for example, proceed like this:

1. **Open My Computer, double-click your hard drive's icon, and open the WINDOWS or WINNT folder.**

   If you see a huge "These files are hidden" message at this point, or if the window appears empty, click "Show the contents of this folder" or "View the entire contents of this folder" at the left side of the window.

2. **In the WINDOWS or WINNT window, open the Web folder.**

   You're looking for a folder inside it called Wallpaper.

3. **Open the Wallpaper folder.**

   It's filled with .bmp or .jpg files ready for you to rescue and use on the Mac. See page 288 for instructions on choosing wallpaper for your Mac (or even *self-rotating* wallpaper images).

Note: In Windows 95 or 98, the wallpaper files are in your Program Files→Plus!→Themes folder instead.

Sound Effects

The Mac doesn't let you associate your own sound effects to individual system events, as Windows does (Low Battery Alarm, Maximize, Minimize, and so on). It lets you choose *one* sound effect for all of its attention-getting purposes, using the Sound pane of System Preferences (page 316).

Still, there's nothing to stop you from harvesting all of the fun little sounds from your Windows machine for use as the Mac's error beep.

To find them on the PC, repeat step 1 of the preceding instructions. But in the WINDOWS or WINNT folder, open the Media folder to find the .wav files (standard Windows sound files).

Once you've copied them to your Mac, you can double-click one to listen to it. (It opens up in something called QuickTime Player, which is the equivalent of Windows Media Player. Press the Space bar to listen to the sound.)

To use these sounds as error beeps, follow these steps:

1. **Convert the .wav files to .aiff files.**

   To do this, you need a shareware program like SoundConverter (available from the "Missing CD" page at *www.missingmanuals.com,* for example). Make sure its pop-up menu says AIF, drag the .wav files into its window, and marvel as .aif files appear on your desktop.

   The Mac accepts only *.aiff* files (two F's) as system beeps, though, so you'll have to rename each one, adding the extra F and confirming your choice in the resulting dialog box.

2. **Open your hard drive icon. Open the Library folder. Choose File→New Folder, and create a folder named Sounds (if there isn't one already).**

   This process assumes that you have an *administrator account* (page 267).

3. **Drag the .aiff files into the Sounds folder.**

   Now open System Preferences (by choosing its name from the menu, for example). Click the Sound icon, and then scroll down. There are your new error beeps, reporting for duty.

Web Browser Favorites

Transferring your PC's bookmarks (favorites) list to your Mac's Web browser is a piece of cake.

Just fire up Internet Explorer on your PC, and then choose File→Import and Export. When the Import/Export wizard appears, click Next, Export Favorites, Next, and Next. Choose a location for the exported favorites list (such as My Documents) and then click Next once more. And then Finish. And then OK.

Now you've got a file called *bookmark.html* in your My Documents folder on the PC. Bring it over to the Mac, using any of the techniques in Chapter 5. Rename it *Favorites.html.*

Now drag this file into your Home→Library→Preferences →Explorer folder. When the Mac asks you to confirm, the answer is yes, you do want to replace the existing Favorites file. If you now open Internet Explorer on the Mac, you'll find all of your old PC Favorites in the Favorites menu, ready for action.

Everything Else

See Chapter 6 for details on copying your email, address book, and Outlook calendar information to the Mac.

Document-Conversion Issues

As described in Chapter 4, most big-name programs are sold in both Mac and Windows flavors, and the documents they create are freely interchangeable.

Files in standard exchange formats don't need conversion, either. These formats include JPEG (the photo format used on Web pages), GIF (the cartoon/logo format used on Web pages), HTML (raw Web page documents before they're posted on the Internet), Rich Text Format (a word-processor exchange format that maintains bold, italic, and other formatting), plain text (no formatting at all), QIF (Quicken Interchange Format), MIDI files (for music), and so on.

Part of this blessing stems from the fact that both Windows and Mac OS X use file name extensions to identify documents ("Letter to the Editor.doc" is, of course, a Microsoft Word document).

Moving Data Within the Mac

Most of this chapter concerns the act of moving files between *machines*. Once you've settled in on the Mac, though, you'll frequently want to move data between *documents*.

Fortunately, the Cut, Copy, and Paste commands work almost exactly as they do in Windows. You can't paste a picture into your Web browser, and you can't paste MIDI music information into your word processor. But you can put graphics into your word processor, paste movies into your database, insert text into Photoshop Elements, and combine a surprising variety of seemingly dissimilar kinds of data. All you have to do is get used to the Macintosh keyboard shortcuts, which use the ⌘ key instead of the Ctrl key: ⌘-X for Cut, ⌘-C for Copy, ⌘-V for paste.

You can also drag highlighted text or graphics to another place in the document, into a different window, or into a

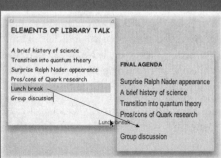

different application, as shown here—a satisfyingly direct feature that works in even more Macintosh programs than Windows programs. Just note that in some Mac OS X programs (*Cocoa* programs; see page 96), you must press the mouse button for half a second before beginning to drag.

You can also drag text, graphics, sounds, and even movie clips out of your document windows and directly onto the *desktop*. Once there, your dragged material generally becomes an icon called a *clipping file*. (In Windows, it's called a Scrap file.)

Later, when you drag a clipping from your desktop *back* into an application window, the material in that clipping reappears. Drag-and-drop, in other words, lets you treat your desktop itself as a giant, computer-wide pasteboard—an area where you can temporarily stash pieces of text or graphics as you work.

For example:

Kind of document	Suffix	Example
Microsoft Word	.doc	Letter to Mom.doc
Excel	.xls	Profit Projection.xls
PowerPoint	.ppt	Slide Show.ppt
FileMaker Pro	.fp5	Recipe file.fp5
JPEG photo	.jpg	Baby Portrait.jpg
GIF graphic	.gif	Logo.gif
Web page	.htm	Index.htm

The beauty of Mac OS X is that most Mac programs add these file name suffixes automatically and invisibly, every time you save a new document, and recognizes files from Windows with equal ease. You and your Windows comrades can freely exchange documents without ever worrying about this former snag in the Macintosh–Windows relationship.

You may, however, encounter snags in the form of documents made by Windows programs that don't exist on the Mac, such as Microsoft Access. Chapter 7 tackles these special cases one by one.

Transferring Email and Contacts

I f you use your PC for email, you won't want to waste any time getting email running on your Mac. Fortunately, switching to a Mac doesn't mean you'll have to reconfigure your email accounts from scratch or manually retype the hundreds of names and addresses tucked away in Microsoft Outlook, Outlook Express, Eudora, or another email program. This chapter covers the secrets of moving your entire email life—messages, addresses, settings, everything—over to the Mac with as little hassle as possible.

As you read this chapter, it's important to keep straight the two leading Windows email programs, which many people don't realize are different programs:

- **Microsoft Outlook.** This program is part of Microsoft Office for Windows. It's a sprawling, network-based email, contact, and calendar program that's ubiquitous in corporate offices. You, or somebody who employs you, paid good money for this software.

- **Outlook Express.** This Windows program is a free, scaled-down version of Outlook. It comes with Microsoft Windows, and is therefore sitting on practically every PC sold. It doesn't have a calendar, a to-do list, or other bells and whistles of Outlook. But it's free.

Unfortunately, each Windows email program—and sometimes each *part* of each Windows program (Outlook's calendar, for example)—requires a different method of exporting its data. And each Macintosh email program requires a different piece of go-between Windows software to ease the transition. There are so many permutations, in fact, that you'd practically need a table to keep them straight. In fact, two tables. They might look something like this:

Ways to Move Your Email

	From Outlook	From Outlook Express	From Eudora
To Apple Mail	Outlook2Mac Netscape 7	Netscape 7	Netscape 7
To Entourage	Outlook2Mac 7 Netscape	Netscape 7	Netscape 7
To Eudora for Mac	Outlook2Mac (soon) Eudora for Windows	Netscape 7 Eudora for Windows	Copy files

Ways to Move Your Address Book

	From Outlook	From Outlook Express	From Eudora
To Mac OS X Address Book	Outlook2Mac Netscape 7	Move2Mac Netscape 7	Netscape 7
To Entourage	Paul Berkowitz scripts Outlook Express ConvertOutlookContacts	Outlook Express	Outlook Express
To Eudora for Mac	Outlook2Mac (soon) Eudora for Windows	Eudora for Windows	Copy files

It's a complex matrix, but if you know what program you've been using on the PC, and which one you want to use on the Mac, you'll find the steps you need somewhere in this chapter.

Transferring Your Outlook Mail

If Microsoft Outlook has been your Windows address book/email program, you're in luck; the world is full of programs designed as moving vans for your online correspondence. Here are the best, in order of simplicity.

All of these methods bring over your entire backlog of existing email—the contents of your Inbox, Sent items, archived mail and, perhaps, even deleted items that are still in your email program's Trash.

Outlook2Mac Method (Quick; $10)

If you value your time, buy Outlook2Mac (*www.littlemachines.com*)—a $10 utility that streamlines the process of bringing most of your Outlook data to your Mac.

With Outlook2Mac, you're spared the lengthy, sometimes tricky steps required by the free conversion methods described in the following pages. The program takes a wizard-like approach to transferring your Outlook data, stepping you through the process as shown in Figure 6-1. It saves all the exported data into one folder (called My_Outlook_Files), making it simple to move the files you need to your Mac.

Outlook2Mac also provides far more options than you get using other methods. For example, it lets you choose messages from only a specific date range—all your 2002 and 2003 email, for example, but nothing older. It also lets you choose whether or not you want to include attachments with the transferred messages. It can even filter out certain attachments based on type (so that you can filter out, for example, .exe files, which can't run on the Mac OS).

Outlook2Mac's other selling point is that it can handle more than just your email messages. It can also convert calendar entries and your address book, which can be imported directly into iCal, the Mac's Address Book, or, with some limitations, to Entourage (see "Paul Berkowitz Method" on page 143).

As a final perk, the program moves email to and from just about any programs: *from* Outlook 97, 98, 2000, or 2002, *to* Apple Mail, MailSmith, PowerMail, iCal, or Entourage. (LittleMachines plans to add the Mac version of Eudora to this list in an upcoming version.)

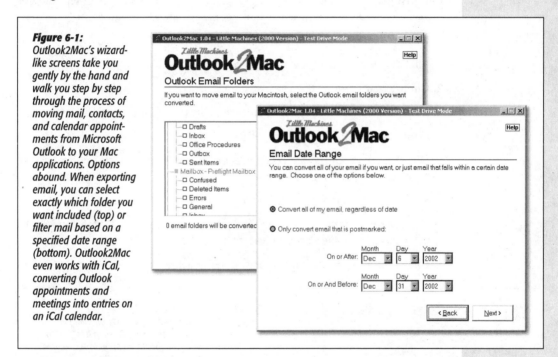

Figure 6-1:
Outlook2Mac's wizardlike screens take you gently by the hand and walk you step by step through the process of moving mail, contacts, and calendar appointments from Microsoft Outlook to your Mac applications. Options abound. When exporting email, you can select exactly which folder you want included (top) or filter mail based on a specified date range (bottom). Outlook2Mac even works with iCal, converting Outlook appointments and meetings into entries on an iCal calendar.

Netscape Method (Time-Consuming; Free)

If you're on a *very* tight budget, too tight for a $10 piece of shareware, you can also transfer your email to the Mac for free. The trick is to import it first into—don't laugh—Netscape 7 for Windows.

But wait, you're thinking, isn't Netscape 7 a *Web browser?* Yes, but it also happens to be a masterful contacts-and-email importer. It even preserves any hierarchical folders you may have set up in programs like Outlook (or Outlook Express) to sort and organize your messages. In other words, your email arrives on your Mac just as well organized as it was when it left your Windows machine.

If you don't have Netscape 7 on your Windows machine—earlier versions won't work—download a free copy from *www.netscape.com.* It requires Windows 98 or later. (If your machine has Windows 95, opt for the Outlook2Mac method described earlier.)

Note: You don't need Netscape on the Mac for this process.

When you've got Netscape 7 installed on the PC, you're ready to follow the three big steps: First, import email into Netscape; next, copy the Netscape mail to your Mac; finally, import the mail into a Mac email program, like Mail or Entourage.

Phase 1: Import to Netscape

Your first job is to bring your existing Outlook mail into Netscape 7. (This method also works for Outlook Express or Eudora mail.) Here's how you do it:

1. **Open Netscape. Open the Mail & Newsgroups window.**

   The Mail & Newsgroups window appears.

2. **Choose Mail→Import.**

   A dialog box opens, allowing you to select the type of information you want.

3. **Choose Mail. Click Next.**

   Don't worry about the Address Books or Settings options at this point. You can move those items over separately.

4. **Select the program from which you want to import messages.**

   Netscape can handle email from Outlook, Outlook Express, Eudora, and earlier versions of Netscape Communicator.

5. **Click Next to start the import process—and be patient.**

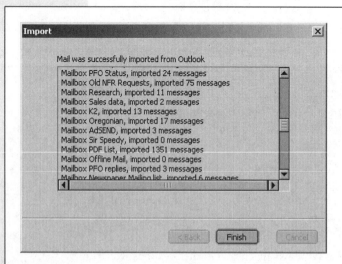

Figure 6-2:
This is Netscape's way of telling you that everything went OK when it imported all your mailboxes and messages. Review this list before forging ahead with your Mac migration to make sure Netscape grabbed all the mail you want brought over to your Mac.

Netscape now starts sucking every last email message into its own email folder. If you've got a hefty stash of email—thousands of messages organized in lots of nested folders—this will take a while. It may even look as if Netscape has stalled; it hasn't. Wait patiently as the progress bar creeps forward.

When the process is finally over, Netscape displays a dialog box listing all the different mailboxes, folders, and subfolders that it has successfully ingested, as shown in Figure 6-2. Click Finish to wrap things up.

When you return to Netscape's Mail & Newsgroups window, you'll see your imported mailboxes listed in the folder pane on the left. Clicking a mailbox icon displays the corresponding messages in the main window.

Phase 2: Copy to the Mac
Your next task is to transfer Netscape's copy of your mail to your Mac.

1. **Open your Application Data folder.**

   The steps depend on your version of Windows. For example:

   Windows 98 or 98SE: Open the My Computer→your hard drive icon→Win98→ Application Data folder.

   Windows Me: Open the My Computer→your hard drive icon→WINDOWS→ Application Data folder.

   Windows 2000: Open the My Computer→your hard drive icon→Documents and Settings→[your name]→Application Data folder, where [your name] is your Windows user account name (the name you use to log into Windows at startup).

   Windows XP: Microsoft's assumption is that you, the lowly, technically ignorant PC user, have no businesses mucking around in the important operating-system folders—and so Windows hides them from you. To expose the hidden files, follow the steps shown in Figure 6-3.

   Once that's done, open the My Computer→your hard drive icon→Documents and Settings→[your name]→Application Data folder.

2. **Once you've opened the Application Data folder, open your Mozilla→Profile folder. Finally, open the folder that corresponds with the profile name you chose when you started running Netscape. (If you didn't bother to set up a profile, it's just called "default.")**

   Inside that folder, you'll find a randomly named subfolder, something like "h4m2ny3s.slt" or "6lihjgy3.slt." Inside *that* folder is a folder called Mail. That's the one you want.

3. **Copy the Mail folder to your Mac.**

   Once again, Chapter 5 describes various ways to go about it.

Once the files are on your Mac, you're ready to bring them into the program of your choice. The steps depend on the email program you're using; read on.

Phase 3: Import into Apple Mail

Mail, Mac OS X's free email program, does an elegant job of importing the files generated by Netscape 7. If you plan to use Entourage or Eudora for Macintosh instead, skip to the alternate "Phase 3" writeups on the following pages.

Here are the steps for feeding the mail from your PC to the Mail program:

1. **Open the Mail program.**

   It's in your Applications folder, and its icon is probably on the Dock.

2. **In Mail, choose File→Import Mailboxes.**

   The Import Mailboxes dialog box appears.

3. **Click the Netscape (4.0+) radio button.**

   Notice that you can also import mail from a variety of *Mac* email programs, including Entourage, Outlook Express, and Eudora.

4. **Click the >> button.**

   The dialog box explains that you are now going to be prompted to locate your Netscape profile. Ignore the "typical location" suggestion (which is based on the faulty assumption that you're importing emails from the *Mac* version of Netscape).

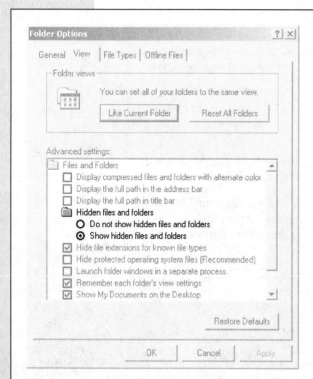

Figure 6-3:
You must uncloak the hidden folders lurking in Windows in order to copy your email files. Here's the trick: In any open folder window, choose Tools→Folder Options. Switch to the View tab, as shown here. In the Advanced settings, turn on "Show hidden files and folders," and then click OK. Now you can see all the previously hidden folders—including the Netscape ones.

5. Click the >> button again. Locate and select the folder containing the Mail folder you brought over from your PC. Click the Choose button.

Mail finds all the Netscape mailboxes it finds within the folder you chose and displays a list of them, as shown in Figure 6-4.

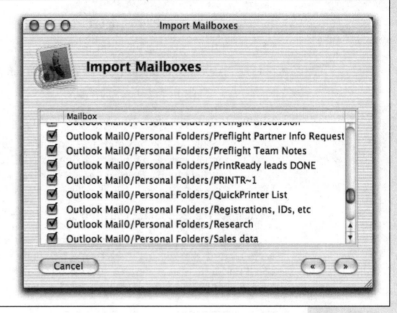

Figure 6-4:
When importing mail messages from Netscape 7, Mail first shows you all the mailboxes it found, ready for import. Turn off the checkboxes next to any folders that you don't want included during the import process.

Import Mailboxes

Import Mailboxes

Mailbox
Outlook Mail0/Personal Folders/Preflight discussion
☑ Outlook Mail0/Personal Folders/Preflight Partner Info Request
☑ Outlook Mail0/Personal Folders/Preflight Team Notes
☑ Outlook Mail0/Personal Folders/PrintReady leads DONE
☑ Outlook Mail0/Personal Folders/PRINTR~1
☑ Outlook Mail0/Personal Folders/QuickPrinter List
☑ Outlook Mail0/Personal Folders/Registrations, IDs, etc
☑ Outlook Mail0/Personal Folders/Research
☑ Outlook Mail0/Personal Folders/Sales data

Cancel   «   »

6. Turn on the checkboxes of the email folders you want to bring into the Mail program.

All the checkboxes start out turned on, meaning that Mail will grab everything you brought over from Netscape. But if you decide at this point that you don't want to include, say, the messages that were in the Trash folder, you can filter them out by turning off the appropriate checkboxes.

Tip: You can use the up and down arrow keys to navigate through a long list of mailboxes and folders in the Import Mail boxes window.

---

7. Click the >> button to start importing.

The import process now begins. Mail shows you the subject line of each message it brings in.

When the process is complete, your imported mailboxes appear under the On My Mac section of the mailbox "drawer." (See Chapter 10 for more on the Mail program.) By selecting an imported mailbox, you can refile its contents into other mailbox folders.

Phase 3: Import into Entourage

If you have Microsoft Office X for Macintosh, you may prefer its more powerful Entourage email program. No problem: You can bring the Netscape files that you brought over from your PC directly into Microsoft Entourage. Note, though, that the process involves a few more steps, because each mailbox and subfolder has to be imported separately.

1. **In Entourage, choose File→Import.**

   The Begin Import dialog box appears.

2. **Choose "Import information from a text file," then click the arrow to proceed.**

   Now you're asked to specify a file type.

3. **Choose "Import messages from an MBOX-format text file." Click the arrow again.**

   The Import Files dialog box appears—and here's where things get tedious. You can't import an entire mailbox in a single step. Each component of the mailbox—Inbox, Sent Items, Deleted Items, and so on—is a separate file. You have to bring these into Entourage one at a time.

4. **Navigate to the Mail folder you brought over from your PC. Open it.**

   Within this folder, you'll find a separate folder with a *.sbd* file name extension for each mailbox that existed in Netscape (see Figure 6-5). Inside the .sbd folder, you'll find a file corresponding to each folder in the mailbox—an Inbox file, a Sent Items file, and so on. These are the files you want to import.

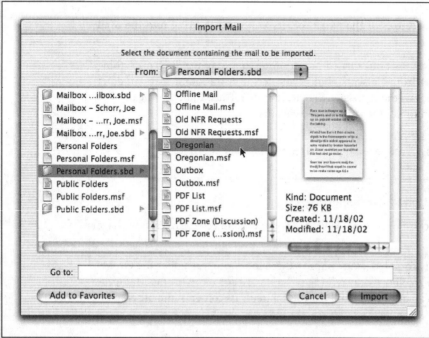

Figure 6-5:
When importing email messages from Netscape 7 into Entourage, look for the files inside the Mail folder without any file name extensions. Those are the ones that are in the MBOX format that Entourage can understand. If you're bringing in multiple folders and subfolders of mail, you have to import each corresponding MBOX file separately.

5. Select the first mail folder you want to import (Inbox, for example), and then click Import.

Once you've selected a file, Entourage begins the import. If the mailbox you're importing is large, be prepared to wait awhile.

Eventually, you'll see a "Ready to Go" message in the Import dialog box, indicating the import is complete.

Note: Alongside each file you need to import is a similarly named file with an .msf file name extension. You can ignore these .msf files; they're not needed for import into Entourage.

---

6. Click Finish.

The mail file you imported should now appear as a folder in Entourage's folder list. Clicking the folder displays the individual messages in the main window.

7. Repeat steps 5 and 6 for each mail folder you want to import.

For example, import your Sent Items, Drafts, and any other personal mail folders you may have originally created.

Phase 3: Import into Eudora for Macintosh

The easiest way to transfer Outlook mail and addresses into Eudora for Macintosh is to use Outlook2Mac, the delightful $10 program described earlier in this chapter—or rather, this *will* be the easiest way. At this writing, the program doesn't yet talk to Eudora for Mac, but it will in the next version. (Check *www.littlemachines.com* for current status.)

If you can't wait, here's a convoluted workaround. Start by importing your Outlook (or Outlook Express) email and addresses into Eudora for *Windows*. (To import from Outlook Express, choose File→Import; to import from Outlook, choose File→ Import and then click Advanced.)

Now that your mail and contacts are in Eudora for Windows (a free download from *www.eudora.com*), see page 150 for getting it all into Eudora for Mac OS X.

Outlook and Exchange

If you run Microsoft Outlook on your office PC, you may be able to transfer the contents of your entire mailbox to your Mac *without* going through any of the import-export pyrotechnics described in this chapter.

On most office networks, Outlook accesses mail through a *Microsoft Exchange Server*—a central computer that stores all the email moving through the network. When you use Outlook in conjunction with Exchange, your mail, appointments, and contacts actually reside on the Exchange server itself—not on your PC's hard drive.

In the summer of 2003, Microsoft plans to release a new version of Entourage for Mac OS X that communicates seamlessly with your office's Exchange Server. You'll be able to see your co-workers' shared calendars, consult the company's address book, and view your email without actually having to download it, just as your comrades on PCs do. Entourage X, in other words, will become an Exchange Server *client.*

If Entourage isn't your thing, you can tap into the same Exchange Server in a slightly less attractive way: by downloading your email from it as though it were a mini-Internet.

Start by interrogating your company's network administrator. Find out, and write down, these pieces of information: the name or IP address of the incoming mail server, plus your email address, user name, and password—the same ones that you use to access your mail on your office network every day.

Then, on the Macintosh, set up a POP or IMAP account in Mail, Eudora, or some other email program, using these same settings. Follow the steps outlined in "Configuring Settings on Your Mac" later in this chapter. (If you're not sure which to use, consult your network administrator. Mention that accessing Outlook with a POP account downloads only the contents of your Outlook *Inbox*; creating an IMAP account gives you access to all your Outlook folders.)

Now you can download the contents of your Outlook folders directly to your Mac without having to manually copy them from machine to machine. (You won't be able to see the Exchange Server's calendar or address book this way.)

Note: If you have a very small, simple email collection, there's yet another way to get your Outlook or Outlook Express email to the Mac. It involves signing up for a $100-per-year .Mac account (page 123), it limits your mail to 5 megabytes' worth, and it obliterates the structure of your email "filing folders." Still interested? At this writing, this method is described at *www.apple.com/switch/howto/mailbox.html.*

From the Outlook Archives

I've got about five years' worth of old Outlook email archived on my hard drive. Is there any way to get the contents of these archives into my Mac's email program?

Absolutely.

When you're in Outlook (on your Windows PC), choose File→Open→Personal Folders File to open any of the Outlook-generated archive files that you want to bring over to your Mac. (Outlook archives have *.pst* file name exten-

sions.) Once you open an archive file, a "mailbox" icon called Archive Folders appears in Outlook's Folder List, allowing you to access any of the individual messages within the archive.

Simply import your Outlook mail into Netscape, as explained earlier in this chapter, *after* opening the archive files. Their contents will be included when you bring the mail into Netscape and when you later transfer your mail folders to your Mac.

Transferring Your Outlook Address Book

The contents of your Contacts list may represent years of typing and compiling. The last thing you want to do is leave that valuable info behind when you move to the Mac or—heaven forbid—manually retype each entry as you set up your Mac email program.

Here are the steps for bringing all those names, phone numbers, email addresses, notes, and other details from Outlook into your favorite Mac contact manager.

Outlook2Mac Method (to Any Program; $10)

If you took the advice on page 134 and bought the Outlook2Mac program, you're already done; this ingenious utility brings over both your email *and* your Outlook addresses to your choice of Mac programs.

Paul Berkowitz Method (to Entourage; $20)

Versatile and useful though it may be, Outlook2Mac can't bring your Outlook calendar, to-do items, or notes into *Entourage*. It brings over email and contact information, but your addresses lose their assigned categories, carriage returns within your notes, and other minor data.

If Entourage is to be the final destination for your Outlook data, you'll probably prefer the software known as Paul Berkowitz's Export-Import Entourage scripts. (You can download them from *www.missingmanuals.com,* among other places.)

This isn't exactly a one-click operation, but the accompanying instructions are careful and detailed. And when it's over, you'll have brought your Outlook addresses, calendar, to-do list, and notes into Entourage, without dropping a single field. After all, you never know when you're going to need the Assistant's Name or one of the other 92 Outlook fields for address information.

Netscape 7 Method (to Address Book; Free)

Once again, Netscape 7 for Windows (page 135) comes to the rescue. Its address book module can extract contact info directly from Outlook, Outlook Express, or Eudora. Better yet, it converts that data into a format that Apple's Address Book understands perfectly (Figure 6-6).

When you've got Netscape 7 installed, you're ready to proceed:

1. **On your PC, open Netscape 7's Address Book.**

   To do so, choose Start→Programs→Netscape 7.0→Address Book. Or, if you've already got Netscape Navigator running, choose Window→Address Book.

2. **Choose Tools→Import.**

   The Netscape Import dialog box appears, introducing a wizard-like series of screens to guide you through the quick import process.

Note: If you don't see an Import command in the Tools menu, make sure you're in Netscape's Address Book window and not the main Navigator window.

3. **Click the Address Books radio button, and then click Next.**

   Now Netscape wants the name of the email program whose addresses you want.

Figure 6-6:
Mac OS X 10.2 comes with a free Address Book program, ready and waiting to receive the contacts you export from Windows programs like Outlook, Outlook Express, or Eudora.

4. **Choose the program from which you want to import addresses (Figure 6-7).**

   You can choose Outlook, Outlook Express, Eudora, or Communicator (an earlier version of the Netscape software).

5. **Click Next.**

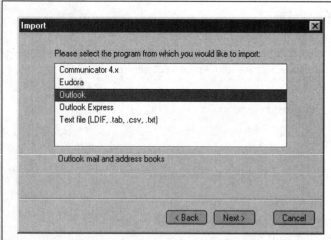

Figure 6-7:
Netscape, the "Swiss Army software," is happy to open the address book of almost any email program, or even a text file containing addresses (such as tab- or comma-delimited text).

Netscape now sniffs out your contacts and pulls all the information into its own Address Book. If all goes well, the Import dialog box displays a message indicating that your contacts were successfully imported.

6. **Click the Finish button to close the dialog box.**

You return to the Address Book window.

Tip: You can confirm that you've successfully imported all your contacts into Netscape by clicking the icon in the Address Books pane of the Netscape window that corresponds with your imported batch of contacts. The name of the icon depends on the program from which you imported the contacts; it may be something like "Contacts" (if from Outlook), "Eudora Nicknames," or "Outlook Express Address Book."

With your contacts safely stored in Netscape, you're halfway home. Next, you need to get these contacts out of Netscape and onto your Mac. To do this, you'll save them into an *LDIF* file. LDIF stands for Lightweight Directory Interchange Format—a text format mostly used by network administrators to synchronize directory information across large networks. It's also a format that Apple's Address Book recognizes.

7. **With your imported contacts displayed in the Netscape Address book, choose Tools→Export.**

The Save dialog box appears.

8. **From the "Save as type" drop-down menu, choose LDIF. Type a name for the file, select a destination, and click Save.**

Netscape writes all your contact data into a single self-contained file with an *.ldif* extension added to the end of its name.

9. **Copy the LDIF file to your Mac.**

You can burn the *.ldif* file to a CD, transfer it via a network, or use any of the techniques described in Chapter 5.

10. **On the Mac, open Address Book (it's in the Applications folder, and its icon is probably on the Dock). Choose File→Import→LDIF.**

The Open dialog box appears.

Figure 6-8:
Apple's Address Book program can slurp up your Windows contacts in one gulp by importing an LDIF file, which you can easily generate using Netscape 7 on Windows.

11. Locate and open the .ldif file you brought over from Windows.

Moments later, all the contacts you brought over from your Windows machine are converted into Address Book entries (see Figure 6-8).

Outlook Express Method (to Entourage; Free)

If your email program of choice on the Mac is Microsoft Entourage, and you can't find the $20 you need to buy Paul Berkowitz's scripts (page 143), don't use the Netscape 7 method to transfer your contacts. Entourage *can't* import LDIF files.

The best way to transfer contacts into Entourage is to import them in *vCard* format. vCard is short for *virtual business card*. More and more email programs send and receive these electronic business cards, which you can easily spot by the *.vcf* extension on their names.

Unfortunately, not all Windows email programs can *export* vCards in a format that Entourage can digest. The vCards dragged out of Outlook Express for Windows work perfectly with Entourage, but those from Outlook are useless. (Eudora doesn't export vCards at all.)

The easiest free route from Outlook to Entourage is to use Outlook Express as a go-between. Here are the steps:

1. **Import your Outlook contacts into Outlook Express on your Windows PC.**

   If Outlook Express isn't already on your PC, you can download it from *www. microsoft.com.*

   To import contacts from Outlook to Outlook Express, choose File→Import→ Messages. Select Microsoft Outlook from the list of programs, and then click OK to accept the default Profile Name. In the Select Folders dialog box, click "Selected folder" and choose Contacts from the list of available folders. Click Next to start the import; click Finish when the process is done.

2. **Click the Outlook Express taskbar button to minimize (hide) the program. Right-click your Windows desktop; from the shortcut menu, choose New→Folder. Name the new folder** *Exported Addresses.*

   You've just created a transfer bucket for the virtual business cards you'll be exporting.

3. **Click the Outlook Express taskbar button to bring the program forward again. On the Outlook Express toolbar, click Addresses.**

   Your list of contacts appears.

4. **Choose Edit→Select All.**

   Every name in your electronic Rolodex should now be highlighted. Position the Outlook Express window so that you can see your Exported Addresses folder on the desktop behind it. (You may have to minimize the main Outlook Express window, not the Addresses window.)

5. **Drag any *one* of the contact names clear out of the Address Book window and onto the Exported Addresses folder on the desktop.**

   All the selected addresses go along for the ride out of Outlook Express. When dragged out of Outlook Express, each contact turns into its own separate little vCard file. If you open the Exported Addresses folder on the desktop, you should see them all neatly nestled.

6. **Copy the Exported Addresses folder to your Mac.**

   You can use any of the transfer techniques described in the previous chapter.

7. **On your Mac, open Entourage. Open the Exported Addresses folder, choose Edit→Select All to highlight all the vCards, and then drag any *one* of them into the Address Book window.**

   All the other vCards go along for the ride. Each now becomes an entry in Entourage. Your work is done here.

ConvertOutlookContacts Method (from Outlook 2000 Only; Free)

If you're using Outlook 2000, Microsoft is way ahead of you. It offers a free conversion program called ConvertOutlookContacts that slurps in your exported contacts list into Entourage (part of Office for Mac OS X). Close the door, unplug the phone, and begin:

1. **Download Microsoft's little ConvertOutlookContacts program.**

   It's actually an AppleScript (page 328); it's available from the "Missing CDs" page of *www.missingmanuals.com*.

2. **In Outlook 2000, choose File→Import and Export.**

   The "Choose an action to perform box" appears.

3. **Click "Export to a file," and then click Next.**

   The "Create a file of type" box pops up.

4. **Click Tab Separated Values (Windows), and then click Next.**

   (You may be asked to insert your original Microsoft Office CD at this point—something Outlook needs to install the necessary translator file.)

   In the following dialog box, you're shown a list of the folders in Outlook.

5. **Click the Contacts folder you want to export, and then click Next. Specify a name (like *Exported Contacts*) and location for the file, click Next, and then click Finish.**

   You've just exported your Outlook address book into a file.

6. **Transfer the Exported Contacts file to the Mac.**

   Use any of the techniques described in Chapter 5.

7. **On the Macintosh, drag the Exported Contacts file onto the icon of the ConvertOutlookContacts program you downloaded in step 1.**

   The program converts the address book into a format that Entourage understands, and then asks you to choose a name and folder location for the resulting file.

8. **Name the file (or accept the proposed *New Outlook Contacts*), and then save it onto your desktop.**

   The resulting file is ready to import to Entourage.

   Before you proceed, look in the folder you downloaded in step 1. In addition to the ConvertOutlookContacts icon, there's a file called Outlook2000Mapping. Your job is to put this file into the right Mac folder. You'll be glad you did: It will make sure that the right fields (Name, Work Phone, and so on) go into the correct Entourage fields.

9. **Drag the Outlook2000Mapping file into your Home→Documents→Microsoft User Data→Import Mappings folder.**

   Now you're ready to open the Entourage program.

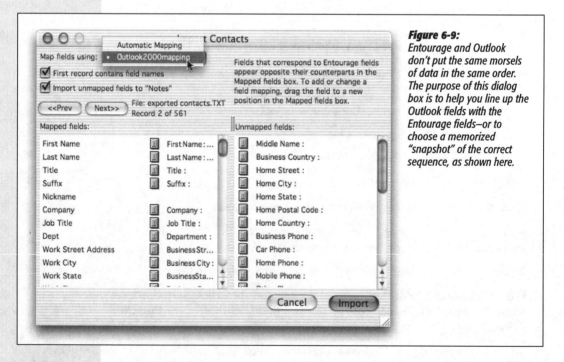

Figure 6-9:
*Entourage and Outlook
don't put the same morsels
of data in the same order.
The purpose of this dialog
box is to help you line up the
Outlook fields with the
Entourage fields—or to
choose a memorized
"snapshot" of the correct
sequence, as shown here.*

10. In Entourage, choose File→Import.

    An Assistant (a wizard) appears.

11. On successive screens, click "Import information from a text file", and then "Import contacts from a tab- or comma-delimited text file," clicking the right-arrow button each time. Locate and double-click the file you made in step 8.

    Now the Import Contacts dialog box appears (Figure 6-9).

12. From the "Map fields using:" pop-up menu, choose Outlook2000Mapping (Figure 6-9). Then click Import.

    In just 13 easy steps, you've imported your Outlook 2000 address book into Entourage!

Eudora Method (Free)

If your aim is to get your contacts into Eudora for Macintosh, see "Phase 3: Import into Eudora for Macintosh" on page 141. The instructions there work to transfer your address book exactly the same way they transfer your messages.

Transferring From Outlook Express

If you've been using Outlook Express on the Windows PC, you'll have very little trouble moving into any of the Mac's email programs.

Moving Your Address Book

You have three alternatives at your disposal:

- **The do-it-yourself method.** You can use free Windows software as a go-between—but which Mac address book you've adopted will determine which to use.

  To import your Outlook Express addresses into Apple's *Address Book,* follow the instructions in "Netscape 7 Method (to Address Book; Free)" on page 143.

  To import them into *Microsoft Entourage* instead, see either "Outlook Express Method (to Entourage; Free)" on page 146, or "Paul Berkowitz Method (to Entourage; $20)" on page 143.

- **The Move2Mac method.** The Move2Mac kit is described on page 112 (and discounted at the back of this book). It does a good job of transferring contacts from Outlook Express on your PC to the Mac's Address Book program.

  Those are, however, the only email programs it handles. Move2Mac won't import the addresses into Entourage instead of Address Book.

Moving Your Mail

Outlook Express is also a pleasant partner when it comes to moving the messages themselves over to the Mac. Here again, you use Netscape as a translator. Follow the steps under "Netscape Method (Time-Consuming; Free)," beginning on page 135.

To Eudora for Mac

Getting your mail and addresses from Outlook Express (Windows) into Eudora (Macintosh) involves moving it first into Eudora for Windows, and then into Eudora for Macintosh. See "Phase 3: Import into Eudora for Macintosh" on page 141 for instructions; they cover moving both your messages and addresses out of Outlook Express.

Transferring Your Eudora Mail

Eudora, an email program written at the University of Illinois in the eighties, used to be wildly popular because it was free and full-featured. Today, this venerable email client, now sold by Qualcomm, is available for both Windows and Mac OS X.

Moving Email into Entourage or Mac OS X Mail

If you'd like your mail to wind up in a Mac email program like Entourage or Mail, it's good old Netscape 7 to the rescue. Once again, follow the steps in "Netscape Method (Time-Consuming; Free)," beginning on page 135.

Moving Email to Eudora for the Mac

If you use Eudora on Windows and want to move your existing messages into the Mac version of Eudora, you can copy them straight over to your Mac. All you need to know is where to find the necessary files and how to set them up on your Mac.

Here's the most direct path for converting your Eudora mailboxes from Windows to Mac:

1. **Find the Eudora .MBX files on your PC.**

   The folder names depend on your version of Windows, but here's the gist:

   Windows 98 or 98SE: Open the My Computer→your hard drive's icon→Win98→ Application Data→Eudora folder.

   Windows Me: Open the My Computer→your hard drive's icon→WINDOWS→ Application Data→Eudora folder.

   Windows 2000, Windows XP: Turn on the hidden files, as shown in Figure 6-6. Then open the My Computer→your hard drive's icon→Documents and Settings→[your name]→Application Data→Eudora.

   All versions: In the Eudora folder, you'll find several files that end with the file name extension .mbx: IN.MBX, OUT.MBX, and TRASH.MBX, as shown in Figure 6-10. These are the files you want.

Note: Can't find an Application Data folder inside your user folder? That's because Application Data is a hidden folder and you have the "Do not show hidden files and folders" option turned on in Windows. See Figure 6-3 to learn how to change this setting.

---

2. **Copy the .mbx files to your Mac.**

    Don't worry about all the other stuff in the Eudora folder. The .mbx files contain all your messages, so they're the only ones you need to convert.

Figure 6-10:
Drill down into the your PC's Applications Data folder to find the Eudora folder, where your Eudora mailbox (.mbx) files live. The trash.mbx file contains messages you've already thrown into Eudora's trash can. There's no need to copy that file over to your Mac unless you want to preserve those trashed messages.

3. **Fix the carriage returns in the .mbx files.**

    Here's where things get a little bit ugly. While these .mbx files are really just text files containing your email messages, Windows handles *line breaks*—the invisible "this is the end of a line!" symbol—differently than the Mac. In order for the Mac version of Eudora to read the files correctly, you have to convert the *hard returns* in the text files into *line breaks*. You can accomplish this by doing a simple find-and-replace in a program like Microsoft Word, as shown in Figure 6-11.

    Tip: If you don't have Microsoft Word, you can also run the .mbx files through a shareware conversion program like CRLF, which is available on the "Missing CD" page at *www.missingmanuals.com,* among other places.

    ---

4. **Remove the .mbx extension from the file names.**

    On the Mac side, Eudora expects the file to be called In, not In.mbx. Remove the extension from each of the mailbox files you've brought over.

5. **Drop the converted .mbx files into Eudora's Mail Folder folder on your Mac.**

Starting from your Home folder, go to Documents→Eudora→Mail Folder, and replace the existing mailbox files with the ones you copied and converted from your PC.

Note: If you don't see a folder called "Mail Folder" inside the Eudora folder, it's probably because you're looking in the Eudora application folder (in the *Applications* folder) instead of the Eudora folder inside your *Documents* folder.

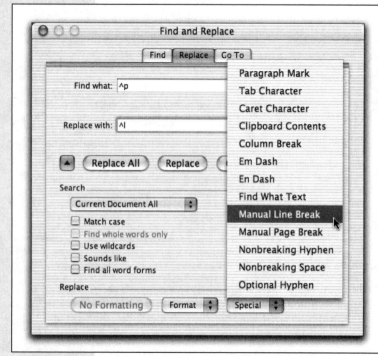

Figure 6-11:
Here's how you'd use Word to convert Eudora mailbox (.mbx) files from Windows to Mac format: Open an .mbx file and choose Edit→Replace. Search for all paragraph marks and replace them all with manual line breaks—or, to be precise, search for ^p and replace with ^l. (You can also choose these symbols by name from the Special menu, as shown here.) Click Replace All to run the conversion, which may take some time; then save the modified text file.

6. **Launch Eudora and read your mail.**

When you launch Eudora, your converted mail should now be accessible. Unfortunately, the status of each message (read, unread, forwarded, and so on) is not preserved, nor are any labels you may have applied to organize the messages within Eudora.

Transferring Your Eudora Address Book

Once again, the steps here depend on which program you'll be using as your Mac address book.

Moving Contacts into Address Book

Fortunately, this one's easy. The "Swiss Army converter" known as Netscape 7 can convert your Eudora address book into a Mac-compatible format; see "Netscape 7 Method (to Address Book; Free)" on page 143.

Moving Contacts into Entourage

As noted earlier in this chapter, the Netscape method won't work if the landing site for your contacts is Microsoft Entourage. In that case, you should use Outlook Express for Windows as a go-between. See "Outlook Express Method (to Entourage; Free)" on page 146.

Moving Contacts into Eudora on the Mac

If you use Eudora on your PC and want to bring your Address Book into the Mac OS X version of Eudora, you can do it—but the process is messy.

First of all, Eudora won't be able to read your Address Book file if any of the nicknames you've assigned your contacts have spaces in them. So, before you do anything else, you have to sift through the nicknames in the Address Book and get rid of any spaces. Turn *Molly Kaufman* into *Molly_Kaufman*, for example.

Next, you have to find the file called nndbase.txt file in your PC's Eudora folder, which is buried inside the Application Data folder. See "Moving Email to Eudora for the Mac" on page 150 for details on locating this sometimes-hidden folder.

Copy the nndbase.txt file to your Mac. If you've created multiple address books in Eudora, you'll also see a subfolder called Nickname in the Eudora directory. Grab any .txt files you find in that folder, too.

After you've copied the nndbase.txt file (and any other .txt files you found in the Nickname folder) over to your Mac, you have to convert all the carriage returns (hard returns) in the files into line breaks (soft returns) so that the Mac version of Eudora can read them correctly. (See Figure 6-11 for directions.)

Finally, change the name of the nndbase.txt file to Eudora Nicknames and drop it into your Mac's Home→Documents→Eudora folder. Put the other converted Nickname files into Documents→Eudora folder→Nicknames folder. You're ready to roll.

Remember, you don't have to mess with that nndbase.txt file at all if you want to bring your Eudora address book into Apple's Address book program or into Microsoft Entourage. All this is necessary only if you're going from Eudora to Eudora.

Email Settings

Chapter 9 guides you through the painless process of plugging your Internet settings—whether by dial-up connection, cable modem, DSL, or network connection—from the PC to your Mac.

But even after you've done that, you can't start sending and receiving email on your Mac until you've transferred some vital email account *settings* from your PC.

Fortunately, there's only a handful of settings you need to grab—and hunting these down and moving them to your Mac is pretty quick work. Here's all the information you need to gather in order to get yourself set up:

- **Account name (or user name).** This is the name you use when you log into your email account, such as *Joe63* or *kjackson*.

- **Password.** The password that you have to enter along with your account name to get into your email account. Passwords usually can't be copied and pasted or directly exported, so you'll need to remember this password and type it in when configuring your Mac email software.

- **Account type.** There are two main kinds of email server protocols—*POP* (which stands for post-office protocol—by far most common) and IMAP (Internet Message Access Protocol). You'll need to know which type you've been using on your PC, so that you can set up accounts on your Mac the same way.

- **Incoming and outgoing mail servers.** The names of the computers that route email to and from you, such as *mail.earthlink.net* or *mailserve.photorabbit.com*. (The incoming and outgoing servers usually have the same address, but they can be two different servers with different names.)

Finding the Settings on Windows

Each of the popular Windows email programs stores these nuggets of email account info differently. Here's how to find the items you need:

WORKAROUND WORKSHOP

Netscape to Netscape

The email programs for Mac OS X are so clean, effortless, and powerful, it's hard to imagine that you might want to commit your email life to Netscape for Mac OS X.

But if you're a dyed-in-the-wool Netscape fiend from way back, it turns out that bringing your addresses over from the Windows version to the Mac version is easy. Both Mac and Windows versions read LDIF files (page 145), so you can use the Tools→Import command in Netscape to open and import the LDIF file you exported from the Windows version of Netscape.

Transferring mail is more complicated. The Mac version of Netscape imports messages only from Eudora or earlier Mac versions of Netscape Communicator.

So the best route for bringing in your mail is, believe it or not, this:

1. In Windows, import your Netscape Mail from Netscape into *Eudora*. (Download it, if you have to; it's free from *www.eudora.com*.) In Eudora for Windows, choose File→Import, and then click Advanced, to bring in your Netscape messages.

2. Transfer your mail into Eudora for Macintosh, following the instructions on page 150. (Again, you can download a free copy of Eudora for Macintosh for this purpose if necessary.)

3. Open Netscape 7 on your Mac. Use the Tools→ Import command to import the mail from the Mac version of Eudora.

It's ridiculously convoluted, but it works.

Outlook Express

Choose Tools→Accounts to open the dialog box containing the list of your current email accounts. Select the name of the account you want, then click the Properties button. In the Properties dialog box, click the Servers tab to reveal the Server Information panel, where you'll find all the info you need, as shown in Figure 6-12.

Tip: If you're using Move2Mac (see the box on page 112), you can transfer Outlook Express's email settings directly from your PC to Apple's Mail program on your Mac. Move2Mac saves you the trouble of having to retype these settings (for these particular email programs).

Figure 6-12:
Here's where Outlook Express for Windows keeps all the settings you need to harvest in order to configure your Mac email. Note that you can't copy the contents of the password field—that's prohibited for security reasons. You'll have to type your password in again when moving to your new machines.

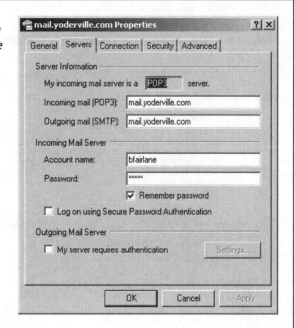

Outlook

If you're connected to a Microsoft Exchange Server computer—and you probably are, if you're running Outlook in a corporate workplace—your user name and password are exactly the same as the ones you use to log into the network when you start up your computer. You'll have to check with your network administrator to get the name of the mail servers being used on the network.

If you're running Outlook in any other situation—at home, for example—choose Tools→E-mail Accounts. Click "View or change existing e-mail accounts," click Next, click your account's name on the E-mail Accounts page, and then click Change. You'll find your name, email address, incoming and outgoing servers, and other key settings staring you in the face. (Click Cancel after you've finished copying it down.)

Eudora

Choose Tools→Options. Click the Getting Started icon (if it's not already selected_ to find your incoming and outgoing mail server names. Then click the Incoming Mail icon to display the Server configuration setting—either POP or IMAP—at the top of the window.

Netscape 7

Choose File→Mail & Newsgroups Account Settings. Each email account you use is listed in the scrolling field on the left side of the window. Click the Server Settings header under the email account you want to look up. In the Server Settings panel, you'll find the type of account, server name, and account name (called the User Name).

Configuring the Settings on Your Mac

Once you've found and copied the email settings on your PC, you can plug them into the appropriate places in your Mac email programs:

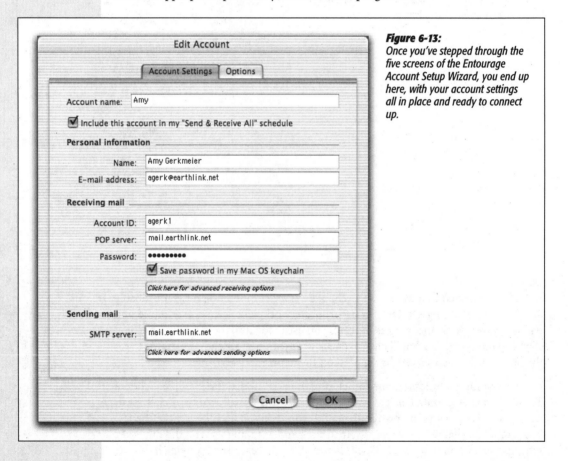

Figure 6-13:
Once you've stepped through the five screens of the Entourage Account Setup Wizard, you end up here, with your account settings all in place and ready to connect up.

Apple Mail

Once you've opened Mail (it's in the Applications folder), choose Mail→Preferences. If the Account panel isn't already visible, click the Accounts icon in the toolbar of the Preferences window. Click the Add Account button. In the Account Information panel, set the Account Type (POP or IMAP), and fill in your email address, name, and incoming and outgoing mail servers. You also need to enter the user name and password for your email account.

Microsoft Entourage

Choose Tools→Accounts. Click the New button in the Accounts window to start the Account Setup Wizard. Follow the screen-by-screen directions to fill in the user name, password, and server information, as shown in Figure 6-13.

Eudora for Macintosh

Choose Special→Settings and click the Getting Started icon. In the Account/Server Information box, enter your user name and mail server information, and then click the Checking Mail icon to set the account type (called Mail Protocol, in this case).

Special Software, Special Problems

As noted in Chapter 4, the beauty of waiting until now to switch to the Mac is that you have so little relearning to do. All the big-name programs look and work almost exactly the same on the Mac as they do on the PC. Once you've mastered the basic differences between the Mac and Windows (keyboard shortcuts, the menu bar, and so on), you'll find that programs from Microsoft, Adobe, Macromedia, and other major software companies feel distinctly familiar in their Mac incarnations. In fact, the documents that they create are even in the same format and generally need no conversion.

But no matter what you think of Windows, one fact is unassailable: There are more software programs available for Windows than there are for the Mac. Sooner or later, you'll probably run into a familiar Windows program for which there's no equivalent on the Mac.

The purpose of this chapter is to make that discovery less painful: to identify the Mac equivalents of the most popular Windows programs, to suggest replacements when no precise equivalents are available, and to guide you in bringing over your settings from Windows to the Mac whenever possible.

ACDSee

As digital photography becomes more popular, so do programs like ACDSee, a popular Windows program that serves as a digital shoebox and basic retouching program for digital photos.

Your Mac, of course, stands ready to run a far more elegant equivalent: iPhoto 2, described on page 343. It's one of the world's most pleasant photo-organizing programs.

iPhoto has only a few photo-editing tools, however. If you need more editing power, consider Photoshop Elements 2, a program that's available for both Mac and Windows and has won rave reviews on both platforms.

Fortunately, ACDSee doesn't have any documents of its own—it does all its work on your existing digital photos, wherever you keep them on your hard drive. All you have to do is move the photos themselves to the Mac, using any of the techniques described in Chapter 5. From there, drag them into the iPhoto 2 window to import and organize them.

Acrobat Reader

Acrobat Reader, which lets you read Acrobat (PDF) files, works precisely the same on the Mac as it does in Windows, except that it looks a little bit nicer. In fact, it's already on your Mac (in the Applications folder).

Tip: When you double-click a PDF file on a fresh copy of Mac OS X, the file does not, in fact, open in Acrobat Reader. Instead, it generally opens in Preview, a little utility program described on page 350. Preview is simpler and opens faster than Acrobat Reader, but Reader scrolls faster and offers searching functions.

If you'd rather have PDF files open in Acrobat Reader instead, see page 86 for instructions on reassigning .pdf files to a different program.

ACT

No Mac version of this address book/calendar program is available, but don't let that stop you. Export and Import commands are the bread and butter of address and calendar programs. Your ACT life can find a happy home in any of several Mac address books:

- Mac OS X's free, built-in Address Book

- Palm Desktop for Mac OS X (a free address book/calendar/to-do program from *www.palm.com,* which works with—but doesn't require—an actual Palm organizer)

- Microsoft Entourage (part of Microsoft Office for Mac OS X)

- Now Contact *(www.nowsoftware.com),* which is networkable. That is, if you have more than one computer in the house, you can check your Rolodex from any machine on the network.

In any case, here are the instructions for transferring your addresses from ACT version 5 or 6 to the Mac:

1. In ACT for Windows, start by choosing File→Data Exchange→Export.

   The Export Wizard dialog box appears.

2. From the "File type" drop-down list, choose Text-Delimited. Specify a folder location and name for your exported file (call it *Exported Contacts,* for example). Click Next, and click Next on the next screen, too.

   Now you're asked "Which contact or group records do you want to export?"

3. Click "All records," and then click Next.

   Now you see a list of the *fields* (information tidbits like City, State, and Zip) that ACT is prepared to export. You can save yourself time later if you take a moment now to remove the ones you don't need (click its name and then click Remove Field).

4. Click Finish.

   If you plan to import your addresses into a commercial program like Now Contact, transfer the Exported Contacts file to the Mac (see Chapter 5), and then import them into Now Contact. The tricky part is making sure that the order of the fields appears in the order Now Contact expects, which may entail some trial, error, and returning to the ACT Export Wizard screen described in step 3 (where you can rearrange the field order).

   If your aim is to import the addresses into Microsoft Entourage on the Mac, or Mac OS X's own Address Book program, though, read on.

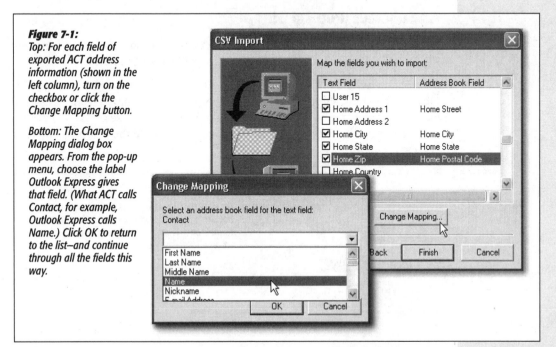

Figure 7-1:
Top: For each field of exported ACT address information (shown in the left column), turn on the checkbox or click the Change Mapping button.

Bottom: The Change Mapping dialog box appears. From the pop-up menu, choose the label Outlook Express gives that field. (What ACT calls Contact, for example, Outlook Express calls Name.) Click OK to return to the list—and continue through all the fields this way.

5. **Open Outlook Express.**

Yes, Outlook Express for Windows, the free program that comes on every PC (and is a free download from Microsoft's Web site). You'll use it as a glorified converter program.

6. **Choose File→Import→Other Address Book. In the "Select the program or file type" dialog box, choose Text File (Comma Separated Values). Click Import.**

Now the "Choose a file to import" box appears.

7. **Click Browse; choose "Text Files (*.txt)" from the "Files of type" drop-down list; find and open your exported file. Click Next.**

Now you're asked to match up the exported fields (Name, Address, and so on) with the fields in Outlook Express. See Figure 7-1.

You've successfully imported your ACT contacts into Outlook Express. From here, you can transfer them into almost any Mac address book program by exporting them as *vCard* files—virtual business cards. To bring them into Entourage for Mac OS X, for example, follow the instructions beginning with step 2 on page 146.

To bring them into the Mac's built-in Address Book program instead, follow steps 2–6 that begin on page 146. Instead of step 7, though, open Address Book, choose File→Import→vCards; in the "Select vCards to import" dialog box, find and click *one* of the vCards you've brought over; press ⌘-A to highlight *all* of them; and then click Open. In a flash, the old ACT addresses now pop into Address Book.

Ad Subtract (Pop-up Stopper)

Nothing quite spoils the fun of the Web like pop-ups—those annoying miniature windows that sprout in front of the Web page you're trying to read.

One quick way to avoid these nuisances is to switch Web browsers. These days, Internet Explorer is about the only Web browser that *doesn't* have a feature designed for eliminating pop-up ads. If you use a Mac OS X browser like Opera, OmniWeb, Chimera, or Apple's Safari (page 261), you can opt to have these pop-ups blocked (see Figure 7-2).

Figure 7-2:
It's easy to stop pop-up ads—as long as you're not using Internet Explorer on the Mac. Safari, Apple's own Web browser, makes pop-up stopping extremely easy.

If you have never tried out one of these other browsers—especially Safari—you owe it to yourself to experiment. But if you're married to Internet Explorer, you can use a shareware program like Pop-up Zapper (which you can download from the "Missing CD" page of *www.missingmanuals.com*) to kill off the pop-ups.

Adobe [your favorite program here]

If anyone has jumped onto the Mac OS X bandwagon, it's Adobe, which reflects the massive size of its customers in the graphic arts business. Most of its bestsellers are available in Mac OS X versions, including Photoshop, Photoshop Elements, After Effects, Illustrator, InDesign, GoLive, Acrobat, Premiere, LiveMotion, and so on. Some of them, in fact, come on the same CD with the Windows version.

Better yet, you generally don't have to do any document conversion. A Windows Photoshop document is exactly the same thing as a Macintosh Photoshop document.

America Online

America Online is available for both Windows and Mac OS X; in fact, the Mac OS X version probably came preinstalled on your Mac. (Look in the Applications folder.) If not, you can download it from *www.aol.com* (scroll to the bottom of the page and look for the Download AOL link). When you use the Macintosh version of the software for the first time, just plug in your existing screen name and password.

The beauty of AOL is that the current Mac and Windows versions store your mail, address book, buddy list, and favorites *online.* You can check your email one day at the office on a PC and the following night at home on the Mac, and you'll always see the same messages there. It makes no difference if you connect to the service using a Windows PC, a Macintosh, or a kerosene-powered abacus.

Tip: Your Favorites (bookmarks) are stored online only if you use AOL for Windows version 8 and later. If you've been using an earlier version on your PC, your Favorites won't be waiting for you when you switch the Mac.

If your PC meets the system requirements, you'd be wise to upgrade its copy of America Online to version 8 before switching to the Macintosh. (This is a free upgrade; you can download the software at *www.aol.com*.) If you do so, you'll find the Favorites waiting for you in AOL for Mac OS X.

This is all really good news, of course, but you may have one headache in performing the switch: your Personal Filing Cabinet. If you've been saving email messages into this virtual filing drawer, the news isn't quite as good: these messages are saved on the PC, not online. So when you switch to the Macintosh, your Personal Filing Cabinet will be empty.

Here are your options at this point:

- Be content with only the last 30 days' worth of old mail, and the last week's worth of new mail. This is what lives on the America Online computers, no matter what computer you use to access it. When you move to the Mac, that much email will immediately appear the first time you use AOL.

- Fire up your old PC and open each message in your Personal Filing Cabinet. Click the Forward button, and type in your own AOL address. You're basically emailing each message to yourself.

   Once the messages have arrived on the Mac, you can save them into its Personal Filing Cabinet. Of course, you were the sender, so you can no longer click Reply to send a response to whoever originally wrote you. (If that's ever necessary, you can always copy and paste the sender's address into your reply.)

- Wait. America Online says that it's working on a utility program, scheduled for completion sometime during 2003, designed explicitly to help you migrate your Windows Filing Cabinet to the Mac.

AIM (AOL Instant Messenger)

If you are an online chat junkie, switching to the Mac involves very little disruption to your routine. AIM is available for the Mac, too, and it awaits your download at *www.aim.com*. Better yet, the minute you fire it up, you'll discover that your entire Windows-version buddy list is intact and ready to use. (That's because it actually lives on the America Online computers, not on your Windows PC.)

Tip: Before you sink fully into the Mac version of AIM, give iChat a try, too. It's a free Mac OS X chat program that's compatible with the whole AIM network, and it's described on page 250.

Children's Software

Thanks to the vast number of Macs in schools, a huge percentage of educational software programs is available in both Mac and Windows versions, often on the same CD. That includes almost everything from The Learning Company (including the Arthur, Carmen Sandiego, Dr. Seuss, Little Bear, and Reader Rabbit series), Broderbund (Kid Pix, Mavis Beacon, The Print Shop, and so on), Disney Interactive (Beauty and the Beast, Winnie the Pooh, Little Mermaid, and so on), Humongous Entertainment (series like Blue's Clues, Dora the Explorer, Freddi Fish, Little Critter, Pajama Sam, Putt-Putt, Thomas and Friends, Tonka Trucks, Nickelodeon, Backyard Sports), and other major educational publishers.

Note: Reflecting the computers that are out in the world of education, many of these programs aren't actually Mac OS X programs. They generally all run just fine on current Macs, but they do so in the Classic mode described on page 100.

Earthlink Total Access

If Earthlink is your Internet service provider, and you're a fan of its Total Access software (which provides access to email, blocks pop-up ads, lets you switch to other family members' accounts, and so on), you're in luck. Hie thee to *www.earthlink.net/ home/software/mac* to download the Macintosh version. (And then see Chapter 9 for details on transferring your Windows account settings to the Mac.)

Easy CD Creator

You don't actually need any add-on software at all to burn CDs in Mac OS X. You can just drag files and folders onto the icon of a blank CD, as described on page 194.

If you want fancier features—recording less common disc formats, recording additional *sessions* onto CD-RW disc, and so on—what you need is Toast for the Macintosh. It comes from Roxio *(www.roxio.com)*, the same company that makes Easy CD Creator. Its rival is DiScribe *(www.charismac.com)*. Both programs can create audio CDs, video CDs, data DVDs, and so on. Both come with a program that helps you turn old vinyl records and tapes into digital CDs.

The only disappointment: Neither program can treat a CD as a glorified floppy disk, as Easy CD Creator for Windows can, so that you can add and delete files freely rather than burning the CD all at once.

There's a workaround, though: Copy the contents of a rewriteable CD (a CD-RW disc) to a folder on your desktop; make whatever changes you like to the contents of this folder; and then burn the CD-RW again. (Use the Disk Utility program in your Applications→Utilities folder to erase the disc first.)

Tip: The CD-burning feature of Mac OS X burns the entire CD each time, even if you've only filled a small portion of it. But if you download the handy shareware program called CD Session Burner, you can perform additional "mini-burns" of new data to the CD until all the space is used up. Each such *session* shows up on your desktop with its own icon, as though it's a separate disc. You can download this program from the "Missing CD" page of *www.missingmanuals.com.*

Encarta

Microsoft's best-selling encyclopedia program isn't available for the Macintosh. The World Book Encyclopedia is, however—in fact, it's a true Mac OS X program. (Details at *www2.worldbook.com.*)

Eudora Pro

You want Eudora? You got Eudora! It's available on the Mac, as it is in Windows. Chapter 6 even tells you how to move your mail and address book over to the Mac version.

Games

Nobody switches to the Mac to play games; of the top 250 computer games for Windows, only about 150 are available for the Macintosh.

Still, that number includes the vast majority of the big-name titles, including Civilization III, Quake III, Harry Potter, Spider-Man, Tomb Raider, The Sims, WarCraft III, Jedi Knight II, Soldier of Fortune II, Max Payne, Links Championship Edition, Age of Empires II, Medal of Honor: Allied Assault, Return to Castle Wolfenstein, and dozens of others.

And once you do get these programs going on the Mac, you're likely to be impressed—especially if they are true Mac OS X programs that don't have to run in the Classic mode (page 100). Recent Macs generally come equipped with pleasantly high-horsepower graphics cards—the kind that high-octane computer games crave.

If you're a game nut, you can stay in touch with what's new and upcoming by reading the articles (and watching the game "trailers") at *www.apple.com/games,* not to mention *www.insidemacgames.com, macgamer.com,* and *macgamefiles.com.*

ICQ

If you're a fan of this Internet-wide chat program, look no further than ICQ for Mac or one of its many shareware rivals. To grab them, visit *www.versiontracker.com* and perform a search, on the Mac OS X tab, for *ICQ.*

Internet Explorer

Not only is Internet Explorer, the world's most used Web browser, available on the Mac, many believe that it's a superior version to the one in Windows. Chapter 11 has the details.

Kazaa

Kazaa, of course, is the "new Napster." People use it to swap music and video files online, hard drive to hard drive—illegally, some would say. You know who you are.

If you visit *www.kazaa.com,* you won't find a Macintosh version of the Kazaa program that you need to do file swapping. There are such programs, however, including something called Neo, which you can download (at this writing, anyway) from *web.ics.purdue.edu/~mthole/neo.* Or, for faster service and simpler software, try Limewire, described next. Happy downloading!

Limewire

Limewire is the same idea as Kazaa (see above), but it runs on something called the Gnutella network—and there's a nice Mac version of the downloading program. You can get it at *www.limewire.com.*

Macromedia [your favorite program here]

Here's another company that knows who its customers are, and therefore has created Mac OS X versions of its best-known programs: Dreamweaver, Director, Flash, Fireworks, FreeHand, and so on. The documents are freely interchangeable between the Mac and Windows—no conversion is necessary.

MacAfee VirusScan

The Mac version is called MacAfee Virex *(www.mcaffee.com)*—but read the box on page 167 first to see whether or not you even need a virus program for Mac OS X.

Microsoft Access

Microsoft has never been much interested in creating a Macintosh equivalent of its flagship database program (which it includes with the higher-priced versions of Microsoft Office for Windows). FileMaker, a much easier-to-use database program, towers over the Macintosh database market like the Jolly Green Giant (and is close to Access in popularity on the Windows side, too). Resistance, Microsoft apparently assumes, is futile.

It's easy enough to get your data out of Microsoft Access; just choose File→Export. In the resulting dialog box, you can choose from a number of common export formats that can serve as intermediaries between the Windows and Mac worlds (see Figure 7-3).

UP TO SPEED

Viruses in Mac OS X (Not!)

One of the greatest perks of moving to Macintosh is that viruses are practically nonexistent. There have been a handful over the last fifteen years, but only a handful, and they were generally of the "I'll display a funny message on December 13th" variety, rather than the "I'll eat all your files and make you wish you were never born" type.

More important, viruses that run in Mac OS X are even less common. At this writing, in fact, not a *single virus* for Mac OS X has been reported.

The one kind of virus that manages to sneak into Mac OS X are Microsoft Word macro viruses that hide in ordinary Word files sent to you by your Windows friends. First, though, on the Mac version of Word, most of these either don't run at all or don't run the way they were intended. Second, whenever you try to open a document that contains macros that you didn't create yourself, you see the error message shown here. All you have to do is click Disable Macros. The file opens normally, 100 percent virus free.

> **Warning**
>
> The document you are opening contains macros or customizations. Some macros may contain viruses that could harm your computer.
>
> If you are sure this document is from a trusted source, click Enable Macros. If you are not sure and want to prevent any macros from running, click Disable Macros.   [Tell Me More]
>
> ☑ Always ask before opening documents with macros or customizations
>
> [Enable Macros]   [Do Not Open]   [Disable Macros]

Among them is Microsoft Excel—that is, you can turn your database into a spreadsheet. The beauty here is that FileMaker on the Macintosh can turn Excel documents into FileMaker databases without even batting an eye. You just drag the exported Excel document onto the FileMaker icon, and FileMaker does the rest.

Tip: If you don't need such a full-fledged database program on the Mac—for example, if you're just managing a mailing list you've exported from Access—you might be perfectly happy with AppleWorks, a Swiss Army knife program with word processor, graphics, and database tools all built-in. AppleWorks comes with every iMac and iBook computer; you can equip other Mac models with it for about $80. In this case, you'll want to export your data from Access as a tab-delimited text file, as shown in Figure 7-3.

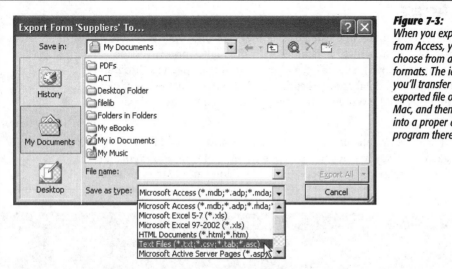

Figure 7-3:
When you export your data from Access, you can choose from any of several formats. The idea is that you'll transfer the resulting exported file onto your Mac, and then import it into a proper database program there.

Unfortunately, there's more to an Access database than just its data. Your database may well have fancy forms (layouts), complete with letterhead and other graphic elements, not to mention relational links between database files. In these situations, the situation isn't quite so hopeful—there's no way to export layouts and relational links to the Macintosh.

In this situation, your best bet might be to run Microsoft Access itself on the Macintosh using Virtual PC, which is described on page 179.

Microsoft FrontPage

There's no Mac version of FrontPage, the Web page-design program that comes with some versions of Office for Windows. But if it's Web-design programs you want, you've come to the right place; according to one recent study, 60 percent of all Web pages are designed on Macs.

The professionals use high-powered, capable-of-anything programs like Adobe GoLive and Macromedia Dreamweaver MX. If you'd prefer something simpler and less expensive, consider Freeway *(www.softpress.com)* and Netscape Composer (part of the free Netscape package at *www.netscape.com)*. Of course, you can also export your Microsoft Word and AppleWorks documents as Web pages, too. And you can build Web pages online in a matter of minutes if you have a .Mac account (page 123).

Microsoft Money

Microsoft doesn't make Money for the Macintosh (although it certainly makes money *from* the Macintosh). If you're looking for a home-finances program for Mac OS X, though, look no further than Quicken *(www.intuit.com)*.

You can even export your Money data into Quicken, although not every scrap of information comes through alive. You'll lose your Money abbreviations, comments, and Lifetime Planner information. Fortunately, the important stuff—your accounts and the transactions in them, including categories, classes, and stocks that you've set up—come through in one piece.

Unfortunately, you have to export one account at a time. Furthermore, you'll be creating something called a QIF (Quicken Interchange Format) file as an intermediary between Windows and the Mac.

Ready? Fire up Money on your Windows PC and then proceed like this:

1. **Choose File→Export.**

   The Export dialog box appears. It wants to know if you are exporting your information to another version of Money ("Loose QIF") or to some other, rival financial program that shall, as far as Microsoft is concerned, remain nameless.

2. **In the resulting dialog box (Figure 7-4), choose Strict QIF, and then click OK.**

Figure 7-4:
Use the Strict QIF option. It lops off category names longer than fifteen characters, but you can't have everything.

To avoid this problem, take a moment, before you begin, either to shorten your category names, or to make a note of which ones might get truncated in the transfer.

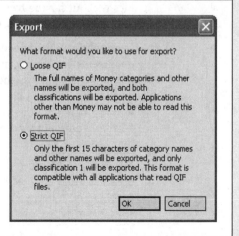

In the resulting dialog box, you're supposed to name and save the exported file. Make sure you give each account a descriptive name (like Citibank Savings).

3. **Specify a name and folder on your PC for the exported file, and then click OK.**

Repeat these three steps for each of your Money accounts.

4. **Transfer the exported files to the Mac.**

You can do it via network, burned CD, or any of the other techniques described in Chapter 5. Then move to the Macintosh, open Quicken 2003 (or whatever later version you have), and create a new file (see the Quicken instructions). Then, once you've got an empty "check register" before you, continue like this:

5. **Choose File→Import QIF. In the "Select a QIF file" dialog box, navigate to, and open, the first exported account file.**

If all goes well, you should see a progress bar appear and then disappear. When the dust settles, you'll see your Money transactions safely ensconced in Quicken. (If you see a message that some transactions couldn't be completed, don't worry; it's just telling you that some of your category names were longer than fifteen characters. and have been marked with asterisks to make them easier for you to find and correct.)

If you have more than one account, choose File→New Account to set it up, and then repeat step 5 to bring in your other Money accounts.

Microsoft Office

Microsoft Office is available for the Mac in what many critics have declared to be a more attractive, less frustrating version than the Windows incarnation. It's called Office v.X for Macintosh.

As noted earlier in this book, the beauty of Word, Excel, and PowerPoint documents is that their format is the same on both Mac and Windows. You can freely exchange files without having to go through any conversion. (As an alternative, Apple's elegant $100 Keynote presentation program opens and saves PowerPoint files, too.)

In heavily formatted documents, you may occasionally see some strange differences: documents containing many numbered paragraphs sometimes become confused when switched across the platform divide, for example. And if the Mac and the originating PC don't have the fonts installed, you'll see different fonts, too. Otherwise, though, documents look identical despite having been shuttled through the ether to a different kind of computer.

Tip: For under $100 (or free with an iMac or iBook), Apple's own AppleWorks suite may be all the Office-type software you'll ever need. It has a word processor, spreadsheet, presentation program, database, and graphics editor. Its feature list isn't as long as Microsoft's—what else is new?—but this program is much easier to learn and, some would say, far better designed. It even opens and saves Office files.

Microsoft Publisher

Microsoft Publisher is a comprehensive page-layout program, complete with canned designs, clip art, and so on.

There's no Mac version of it, but you can perform most of the same tasks using AppleWorks 6. This program comes preinstalled on each iBook, eMac, and iMac model, and costs $80 otherwise.

When it comes to page layout, AppleWorks isn't as comprehensive as Microsoft Publisher; it doesn't offer nearly as many templates, wizards, layouts, and clip art pieces. It does, however, offer several dozen ready-to-go designs and thousands of pieces of art—not to mention a full-fledged database, spreadsheet, word processor, and slide show program.

There are also plenty of stand-alone page-design programs—this is the Mac, after all—from MacPublisher Pro for beginners *(www.metisinternational.com)* to professional powerhouses like Adobe InDesign and QuarkXPress.

Microsoft Visio

If flow charts, org charts, network diagrams, family trees, office layouts, and similar diagrams are part of your workflow, you're in luck—at least some luck. Microsoft Visio isn't available in a Macintosh version, but you'll probably find that OmniGraffle for Mac OS X is a satisfactory, even delightful, replacement (see Figure 7-5).

Figure 7-5:
OmniGraffle comes preinstalled in the Applications folders of many new Mac models, or you can download the latest version from www.omnigroup.com. The current version can't import Visio files, alas, but the company says that the next version (which may even be available as you read this) will.

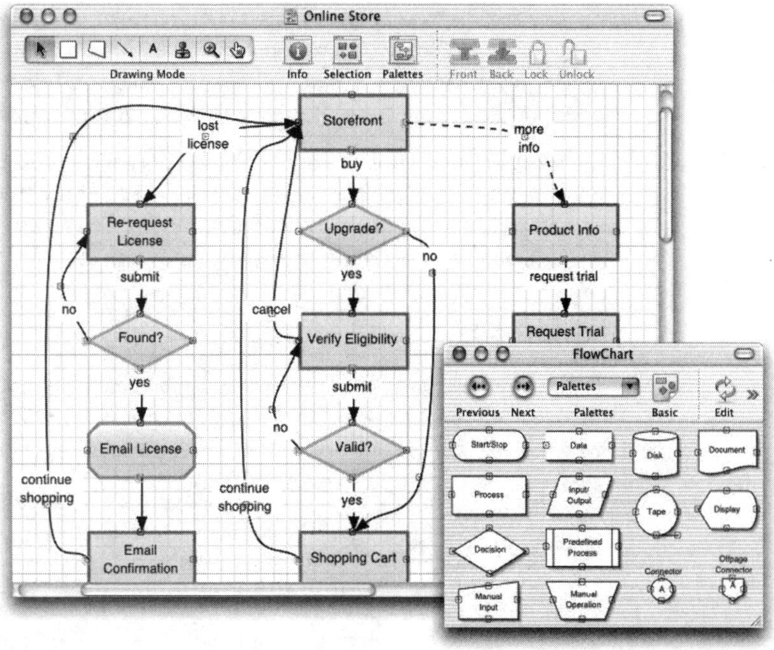

MSN Messenger

Online chat-aholics have nothing to worry about on the Mac. MSN Messenger, the instant-messaging program, is alive and well in a Mac OS X version that you can download from *www.microsoft.com/mac*. Exactly as with AOL Instant Messenger described earlier in this chapter, you don't even have to worry about your carefully assembled Buddy list. From the instant you start up MSN Messenger for Mac OS X, you'll see your Buddy list in place (because the list is actually stored on the Internet, not on your computer).

MSN (Service)

Microsoft is dead serious about challenging America Online for dominance in the easy-to-use online service market. MSN 8 is proving a hit with Windows users: in one single, attractive program, it brings together Web browsing, email (junk mail filters) and multimedia features, plus links to useful Web sites. A key feature for families: The software can email parents a list of what Web sites their kids have visited, and how much time they've spent in chat rooms.

MSN for Mac OS X costs the same as the Windows version: $23 per month with Internet service, or $10 per month if you already have an Internet service provider. And if you've already got an MSN subscription on your PC, then there's nothing to it: You can log in using your Mac using the same name and password.

Naturally Speaking

Speech-recognition programs are far more advanced in Windows than they are on the Macintosh. Windows programs like ScanSoft NaturallySpeaking transcribe your dictated text with almost Star Trek–like accuracy, and even let you make corrections and manipulate the computer itself using all voice commands.

On the Mac, your choices are IBM ViaVoice *(www-3.ibm.com/software/speech/mac)* and iListen *(www.macspeech.com)*. If you just can't use the keyboard, or don't want to, you can get by with either program. But neither, alas, offers anything close to the speed, stability, or accuracy of their Windows rivals.

Netscape

Both Netscape Navigator (the Web browser) and Netscape Messenger are available in Mac OS X versions—and they're free, of course, from *www.netscape.com*. (Mozilla, which is like a Netscape cousin without all the AOL promotional material, is also available for, and popular on, the Mac.)

Newsgroup Readers

If you're a fan of the online bulletin boards known as *newsgroups,* you've come to the right place: The Mac is crawling with newsgroup-reading programs. Netscape for Macintosh has one built in, and so does Microsoft Entourage. In the shareware world (search *www.versiontracker.com*), you can take your pick of MT-NewsWatcher X, NewsBaker, NewsHunter, and NewsWatcher-X, to name a few.

Norton AntiVirus

You can buy Norton Antivirus for the Macintosh, no problem *(www.symantec.com)*. The question is, should you? See the box on page 167.

Norton Utilities

This program, too, is available in a Mac OS X version. It does the same kinds of things it does in Windows: defragments your hard drive, helps recover files in case of disaster, and repairs disk problems.

In times of trouble, though, you may actually prefer Disk Warrior, a similar (and, many experts feel, superior) program that you can buy from *www.alsoft.com*.

Notepad

If you're an aficionado of this beloved note-taking tool in the standard Windows Start menu, you're in luck. Mac OS X's Stickies program (page 354) is even more powerful, because it offers formatting and even graphics. Or, for more of a word processor effect, check out TextEdit (page 357).

Outlook Express

Mac OS X's built-in Mail program is very similar to Outlook Express for Windows, not to mention more powerful (and a lot better-looking). It's described in Chapter 10.

Paint Shop Pro

If your goal is to retouch and edit digital photos, the closest you can come to Paint Shop on the Mac is probably Photoshop Elements 2, a sensational Mac OS X program (about $80) that belongs on the hard drive of any digital camera owner. (Any digital camera owner who doesn't also own the full-blown Photoshop program, of course.)

If your goal is to organize and *use* your photos, rather than paint on them, remember that iPhoto 2 is either already on your hard drive or a quick download away (from *www.apple.com/iphoto*).

Finally, if opening and converting graphics to other formats is your main concern, try Preview (page 350), whose Export command is surprisingly powerful. You may also want to investigate the beloved shareware program GraphicConverter (find and download it at *www.versiontracker.com*), which may be the last graphics editing/ converting program you'll ever need.

Palm Desktop

The CD that came with your Palm organizer included both Mac and Windows versions of this calendar/address book/to-do list/notepad program. Put another way, if you have a Palm, you probably already have Palm Desktop for Mac OS X.

But you don't have to buy a Palm to enjoy its power, good looks, and amazing variety of printing options. You're welcome to use it as a standalone information manager; it's a free download from *www.palm.com/support/macintosh.*)

Pocket PC

The world of palmtop computers falls into two broad camps: Palm compatibles (from Palm, Sony, Handspring, and others) and Pocket PC (from Dell, HP, ViewSonic, Compaq, and others). Pocket PC machines have terrific screens, tend to be a better value than Palm devices, and are loaded with useful features. Unfortunately, they also run a tiny (but still confusing) version of Windows—and they can't exchange information with a Macintosh.

Or at least they can't right out of the box. Once you've added the $70 program called PocketMac *(www.pocketmac.net)*, though, you can synchronize your Pocket PC with the appointments, calendar, and to-do list from any of the popular Mac OS X programs that handle this kind of information: Microsoft Entourage, Address Book, and iCal. You can even load up the pocket PC with files from Word and Excel for viewing and editing on the road, and MP3 files for music listening in transit.

PowerPoint

See "Microsoft Office" in this chapter. Remember, too, that Apple's own Keynote presentation program ($100) is the same idea as PowerPoint, but with much more spectacular graphic effects.

QuickBooks

If you've been happily using QuickBooks for Windows to manage your small business—to prepare estimates and invoices, track bills, maintain lists of inventory and customers, and so on—there's good news and bad news. The good news is that QuickBooks is available on the Mac, and, at least at this writing, comes free with many new Mac models.

The bad news is that the software, by itself, doesn't let you transfer your old QuickBooks data to the Mac version. Intuit will, however, perform this service for a fee, beginning mid-2003.

Quicken

If you've been keeping track of your personal finances in Quicken on your PC, you'll feel right at home when you move to the Mac. Quicken 2003 and later versions are available for Mac OS X.

In general, switching over is quick and painless. You can import into the Mac version of Quicken all of the actual transaction information, including the accounts therein, the categories and classes you've used to group them, and stock holdings. Certain kinds of Windows Quicken information—like schedule transactions, QuickFill transactions, online account information, stock histories, and loan information—don't make it, however.

Here's how to transfer your financial life to the Mac:

1. **Open up your Quicken file on the PC and choose List→Account List. Click Options, and then turn on the View Hidden Accounts checkbox. (Edit your account names, if necessary, so that none is longer than fifteen letters and spaces long.)**

    That's a limit imposed by the Quicken Interchange Format, which you're going to use to transfer the data.

2. **Choose List→Security. Make sure that your stock symbols appear in ALL CAPITAL letters.**

    If you've been using Quicken to track your investments, Intuit advises that you take a few minutes to edit those transactions in some fairly technical and tweaky ways. Full instructions appear (at least at this writing) on the Quicken help Web site: *www.intuit.com/support/quicken/2003/mac/2159.html*.

3. **Clean up your file before exporting.**

    "Clean up" means accepting all online transactions into the register, clearing up any outstanding transactions in the Online Center and Compare to Register windows, and deleting any pending payments.

4. **Export your data to a QIF file.**

    To do so, choose File→Export. Choose QIF File as the format. You'll also be asked what range of dates you want to include, as well as which accounts and which lists (categories, accounts, securities, and so on). Choose a location and name for the file you're about to export (such as *Quicken Windows Export*), and then click OK.

5. **Transfer your Quicken Windows Export file to the Mac.**

    Chapter 5 describes a number of ways you can go about it.

6. **On the Macintosh, fire up Quicken. Choose File→New. Create and save a new document.**

    When the Accounts window appears, click Cancel.

7. **Choose File→Import QIF. Find and double-click your Quicken Windows Export document.**

If the technology gods are smiling, the Mac version of Quicken should take a moment to import all of your Windows data, which now appears neatly in your Register windows, ready to use. Make sure the final balances match the final balances in Quicken for Windows. (If they don't, scan your Mac registers for duplicate or missing transactions.)

RealPlayer

Want to listen to Internet music and watch Internet video in Real format, just as you did on your PC? No sweat. Visit *www.real.com* and download RealPlayer for Mac OS X, either in the free basic edition (which appears in tiny type on the Web page) or the fancy, paid version.

SnagIt

If you prepare instructions for using any kind of computer or software—computer books, magazine articles, or how-to materials of any kind—you may already be familiar with this amazing screen-capture program. It captures any window, menu, or area of the Windows screen and saves it as a graphics file that you can print or pop into a layout program.

In Mac OS X, this feature is built right in. Here's how to capture:

- **The whole screen.** Press Shift-⌘-3 to create a picture file on your desktop, in PDF (Acrobat) format, that depicts the entire screen image. A satisfying camera-shutter sound tells you that you were successful.

    The file is called *Picture 1*. Each time you press Shift-⌘-3, you get another file, called Picture 2, Picture 3, and so on. You can open these files into Preview, AppleWorks, or another graphics program, in readiness for editing or printing.

- **One section of the screen.** You can capture only a rectangular *region* of the screen by pressing Shift-⌘-4. When you drag and release the mouse, you hear the camera-click sound, and the Picture 1 file appears on your desktop as usual.

- **One menu, window, icon (with its name), or dialog box.** Once you've got your menu or window open onscreen, or the icon visible (even if it's on the Dock), press Shift-⌘-4. But instead of dragging diagonally, press the Space bar.

    Now your cursor turns into a tiny camera. Move it so that the misty highlighting fills the window or menu you want to capture—and then click. The resulting Picture file snips the window or menu neatly from its background. (Press the Space bar a second time to exit "snip one screen element" mode and return to "drag across an area" mode.)

Tip: If you hold down the Control key as you click or drag (using any of the techniques described above), you copy the screenshot to your *clipboard,* ready for pasting, rather than saving it as a new graphics file on your desktop.

Mac OS X also offers another way to create screenshots: a program called Grab, which offers a timer option that lets you set up the screen before it takes the shot. It's in your Applications→Utilities folder.

But if you're really serious about capturing screenshots, you should opt instead for Snapz Pro X *(www.ambrosiasw.com),* which can capture virtually anything on the screen—even movies of onscreen procedures, along with your narration—and save it in your choice of graphics format.

Solitaire

Ah yes, Solitaire: possibly the most often used Windows software in the world.

The Mac doesn't come with a preinstalled copy of Solitaire, but the Web is crawling with free and shareware solitaire games for the Mac. Here's a quick way to unearth the most popular 20 or so: On the Web, visit *www.versiontracker.com* (one of most popular sources for freeware and shareware Mac programs). Click the Mac OS X tab, and then, in the Search box, type *solitaire.*

When you click Go or press Enter, you'll see a substantial list of solitaire games, ready to download: Free Cell, MacSolitaire, Klondike, and so on.

Street Atlas USA

This popular mapping and routing software is also available for the Macintosh, although its features aren't quite as complete as they are in the Windows version.

And if it's Europe you want, it's Route 66 (for Mac OS X) you need *(http://rs108.66.com/route66).*

Tip: If you're looking for driving directions and maps, don't forget about *www.mapquest.com.* It's fast, it's convenient, it works the same on both Mac and Windows, and it's free.

Don't forget about the Yellow Pages feature of Sherlock 3, either (page 248). It's sitting right there on your Dock, ready to print directions and draw maps.

TaxCut, TurboTax

Both of these popular tax programs are available for the Mac, just as they are in Windows. You can even buy state versions for the 45 states that require income tax returns. You can buy them wherever fine Mac programs are sold: *www.macmall.com, www.macwarehouse.com, www.macconnection.com,* and so on.

WinAmp, MusicMatch

When it comes to playing MP3 files, creating MP3 files, burning music CDs, and otherwise organizing your music library, you'd be hard-pressed to beat iTunes, the free Mac OS X program that's either already on your Mac or a free download from *www.apple.com/itunes.*

WinAmp *is* available in a Mac version, though, called MacAmp. You can download it, and your choice of several other players, from *www.shareware.com.* But you may well find that iTunes is all the music player you'll ever want.

Windows Media Player

The Macintosh equivalent for Windows Media Player is, of course, QuickTime Player. It handily plays and shows almost any kind of movie, picture, or sound (although you'll want to use iTunes for most music playback).

There are a few entertainment sources that work only with Windows Media Player, though—certain Internet radio stations, for example. Fortunately, Microsoft has gone to the trouble of creating a Macintosh version of Windows Media Player (never mind the irony of its name). You can download from *www.microsoft.com/mac.*

WinZip

You won't encounter .zip files very often on the Mac. Instead, the equivalent program for compressing files (to make them smaller and more convenient to transmit online) is called StuffIt. The files it creates have the file name extension *.sit.*

The program that you need to open .sit files—and, fortunately, .zip files sent to you from Windows machines—is called StuffIt Expander, and it's already sitting in your Applications→Utilities folder. This is the program that, behind the scenes, automatically decompresses files that you download from the Internet (page 105).

To *create* this kind of file, you need either ZipIt (shareware), StuffIt Standard Edition (shareware), or StuffIt Deluxe (which you pay for). Links to all three appear on the "Missing CDs" page of *www.missingmanuals.com.*

Word

See "Microsoft Office" in this chapter.

WordPerfect

Unfortunately, WordPerfect lost the battle with Microsoft Word on the Mac side pretty much the same way it did on the Windows side. In the end, before discontinuing WordPerfect for the Mac completely, Corel made it a free download—in something called WordPerfect 3.5e, which you can still find floating around the Web if you look hard enough.

Even that version, however, is not a true Mac OS X program, and instead runs in Classic mode (page 100). If you're a diehard WordPerfect fan, your best bet might be to invest in Microsoft Word and capitalize on its keystroke-customizing features to turn it into a living simulation of WordPerfect.

Yahoo Messenger

The equivalent chat program on the Mac is, of course, Yahoo Messenger for Mac OS X. It's a free download from *http://messenger.yahoo.com*.

VirtualPC: When All Else Fails

The substitutes and look-alikes described in this chapter ought to fulfill most people's software cravings most of the time. But there may still be one last sticking point, one final Windows program that you just can't live without, with no Macintosh equivalent. Maybe it's a dental-office management program, a DOS-based specialty application that's important to your work, or Microsoft Access.

For many people, the solution is Virtual PC, a Windows simulator for Mac OS X. It comes in various Windows flavors: XP Home, XP Pro, 2000, Me, or 98. (You can find information at either *www.connectix.com* or, once Microsoft's 2003 buyout of the program is complete, eventually at *www.microsoft.com*).

Figure 7-1:
Virtual PC is a perfect solution for the Windows refugee who still has a program or two that simply has no Macintosh equivalent. You even get a Start menu in the Dock for instant access to the Windows side of your split-personality machine.

This unique program gives you a Windows PC in a Macintosh window. You can install and run Windows programs, copy and paste between Windows and Macintosh programs, drag files between the two worlds, access PC-based network file servers, and print on networked PC printers—all while seated comfortably at your gorgeous Mac (Figure 7-6).

Of course, if Virtual PC were flawless, why would anyone buy a Windows PC? Why not just buy a Mac, with its sleek looks and rock-solid operating system, and run Windows software on it in Virtual PC?

The answer is speed. The current version is much faster than earlier versions, but it's not as fast as a real PC. Virtual PC is plenty fast for word processing, number crunching, Web design, databases, and so on. Speech-recognition programs and many 3-D action games, on the other hand, don't run at all.

Still, if there are one or two Windows programs that you can't do without, and they're not too greedy for speed, Virtual PC could be a virtually ideal solution.

Hardware on the Mac

M ost of the discussion in this book so far has covered *software*—not only the Mac OS X operating system that may be new to you, but also the programs and documents you'll be using on it. But there's more to life with a computer than software. This chapter covers the finer points of using Macintosh-compatible printers, cameras, disks, monitors, and keyboards.

Printers and Printing

Today's Mac OS X comes preinstalled with hundreds of printer drivers, including those for all current printer models from Epson, HP, Canon, and Lexmark. All you have to do is connect your printer and start printing, without installing a single piece of printer software. Now *that's* plug and play.

WORKAROUND WORKSHOP

Parallel-Printer Hell

If you have a parallel printer, of course, you might assume that you're out of luck; the Mac has no parallel port.

The technically oriented can make old parallel printers work, though, by buying a cheap component called a *network print server*; plugging it into the Ethernet network; and using CUPS and Gimp-Print to print to that printer. (See the tip on page 186 for more on CUPS.)

All this effort isn't worth the trouble if the old printer is an inkjet printer. Then again, new inkjets are so cheap these days, they practically fall out of specially marked boxes of Frosted Mini-Wheats.

But if it's a parallel printer that lacks Ethernet, or some specialty printer that's supposedly Mac-incompatible (like a dot-matrix printer that you need for printing carbon-paper forms), this is a great solution.

The situation is trickier if you have an older printer—the one you've been using with Windows, for example—that you'd like to make work with your new Mac. If it connects via a cable that the Mac recognizes (USB, for example, or Ethernet if it's an office laser printer), you can probably find Mac OS X–compatible driver software for it in one of these locations:

- *http://gimp-print.sourceforge.net.* That's the Web site for Gimp-Print. It may have an unappetizing name but it is, in fact, a collection of Mac OS X printer drivers for hundreds of older Mac and Windows printers.

- The printer company's Web site.

Introducing the Printer

When you're ready to hook up your printer, follow this guide:

1. **Connect the printer to the Mac, and then turn the printer on.**

   Inkjet printers usually connect to your USB jack. Laser printers generally hook up to your Ethernet connector. (If you're on an office network, the laser printer may already be connected somewhere else on the network, saving you this step. If you're hooking the printer straight into your Mac's Ethernet jack, you'll need an Ethernet *crossover cable* to connect it, rather than a standard Ethernet cable.)

Note: Some Ethernet- or network-connected laser printers communicate with your Mac using a language called AppleTalk. If you have such a printer, here is step 1.5: Open the Network pane of System Preferences. Click the AppleTalk tab. Turn on Make AppleTalk Active, and then click Apply Now. (If you omit this step, Print Center will nag you about it in step 5.)

Further note: If you connect to the Internet using a DSL connection (PPPoE), you may not be allowed to turn on AppleTalk. In that case, open the Show pop-up menu, choose Network Port Configurations, and click New. You'll be allowed to turn on AppleTalk in the new port setup.

---

2. **Open Print Center.**

   Print Center is Mac OS X's printing program. You'll find it in your Applications→Utilities folder. If you haven't already set up a printer, you see the dialog box shown in Figure 8-1.

3. **Click Add.**

   Now a strange little window called Directory Services appears. If you have one of the many inkjet printers that Mac OS X recognizes, and it's turned on and connected to your USB port, you see its name here. Skip to step 5.

   But if you find the Directory Services window empty, you need to tell Print Center where to look to find its new printer.

4. **From the upper pop-up menu, choose the kind of printer you intend to use: USB, AppleTalk, or whatever.**

In other words, tell Print Center how the printer is connected to the Mac. Your selection here should mirror your actions in step 2. For example, choose USB if you've connected an inkjet printer to your USB port (or EPSON USB if it's an Epson printer). Choose AppleTalk if you've hooked up a laser printer through your Ethernet jack.

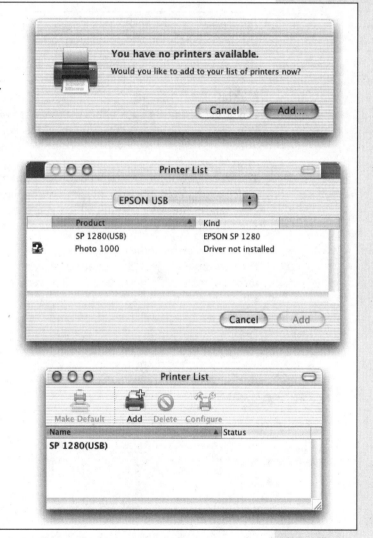

Figure 8-1:
Top: If you've never before hooked up a printer to your Mac, Print Center shows you this message. (If you're trying to hook up an additional printer, on the other hand, begin by choosing Printers→Add Printer.)

Middle: If you choose the right connection method from the pop-up menu, your Mac should automatically "see" any printers that are hooked up and turned on. If you have some oddball printer whose driver doesn't come built into Mac OS X, this is where you find out (see the "Driver not installed" message). Find the driver, if it exists, on the printer's CD or Web site.

Bottom: If you've set up more than one printer in this way, you'll see all of them listed in the Printer List. The one whose name appears in bold is the one currently selected—the one destined to produce your next printout.

After a moment, the names of any printers that are turned on and connected appear in the printer list (Figure 8-1, bottom). For most people, that means just one printer—but one's enough.

5. **Click the name of the printer you want to use, and then click Add.**

   After a moment, you return to the main printer list window, where your printer now appears (Figure 8-1, bottom). You're ready to print.

If you're lucky enough to own several printers, repeat the steps above for each one. Whenever you want to switch from one printer to the other, you *can* return to Print Center and click the new printer's name. There's a much easier way, however: Use the Printer pop-up menu that appears in the Print dialog box (Figure 8-2).

Tip: The printer listed in bold denotes the *default* printer–the one that the Mac will use unless you explicitly choose a different one for a particular printout. To specify a different default printer, click its name in Print Center and then choose Printers→Make Default (⌘-D).

Making the Printout

You print documents from within the programs you use to create them, exactly as in Windows. The options for printing should feel distinctly familiar.

Page Setup

The experience of printing depends on the printer you're using—laser printer, color inkjet, or whatever. In every case, however, all the printing options hide behind two commands: File→Page Setup, which you need to adjust only occasionally, and File→Print, which you generally use every time you print.

The pop-up menu at the top of the Page Setup dialog box offers a command called Page Attributes. Here, for example, are the Orientation commands (to print a document "the long way"), the Scale control (to reduce or enlarge your document), choose a paper size, and so on.

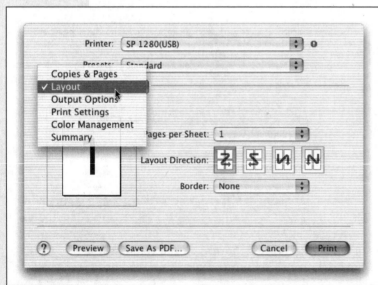

Figure 8-2:
By asking the Mac to print several pages per sheet of paper, you can compare various designs, preview an overall newsletter layout, and so on. Using the Border pop-up menu, you can also request a fine border around each miniature page. Some printers even offer a Print on Both Sides option here, ideal for printing little booklets.

The remaining choices vary. The Page Setup options for an Epson inkjet, for example, differ dramatically from those for a laser printer. Only your printer's user manual can tell you exactly what these choices do.

Tip: You can (and must) configure the Page Setup settings independently in each program you use.

The Print command

Although you can grow to a ripe old age without ever seeing the Page Setup dialog box, you can't miss the Print dialog box. It appears, like it or not, whenever you choose File→Print in one of your programs.

As in Windows, the options you encounter depend on the printer you're using. But here's what you may find on the main screen—that is, when the pop-up menu says Copies & Pages:

- **Printer.** One cool thing about Mac OS X is that if you have more than one printer connected to your Mac, you can indicate which you want to use for a particular printout just by choosing its name from this pop-up menu.

- **Presets.** Here's a way to preserve—and call up again with one click—your favorite print settings. Once you've proceeded through this dialog box, specifying the number of copies, which printer trays you want the paper taken from, and so on, you can choose Save As from the Presets pop-up menu (Figure 8-2), and then assign your settings set a name (like "Borderless, 2 copies"). Thereafter, you'll be able to re-create that elaborate suite of settings just by choosing its name from this pop-up menu.

- **Copies.** Type the number of copies you want printed. The Collated checkbox controls the printing order for the various pages. For example, if you print two copies of a three-page document, the Mac will generally print the pages in this order: 1, 2, 3, 1, 2, 3. If you turn off Collated, on the other hand, it'll print in this order: 1, 1, 2, 2, 3, 3.

- **Pages.** You don't have to print an entire document—you can print, say, only pages 2 through 15. Use commas and hyphens to spell out exactly the pages you want. Typing *1, 3-6, 9* will produce pages 1, 3, 4, 5, 6, and 9.

- **Preview.** This button provides a print-preview function to every Mac OS X program on earth, which, in the course of your life, could save huge swaths of the Brazilian rain forest and a swimming pool's worth of ink in wasted printouts.

Technically, the Preview button sends your printout to the Mac OS X program called Preview (which sits in your Applications folder). When you're satisfied with how it looks, you can either print it (File→Print), cancel it (File→Close), or turn it into an Acrobat file (File→Save as PDF). This final option, which is a very big deal, is described next.

- **Save As PDF.** Clicking this delightful button, of course, turns your document into a *PDF* file instead of printing it. PDF means an Adobe Acrobat document— a file that any Mac, Windows, Linux, or Unix user can view, read, and print using the free Acrobat Reader program included with every Mac and PC. (Much more on PDF files on page 186.)

If you examine the unnamed pop-up menu just below the Presets pop-up menu, you'll find dozens of additional options. They depend on your printer model and the program you're using at the moment, but typically offer control over the layout, paper feed (which tray the paper comes from), print settings (inkjet quality and paper type), and so on.

Tip: Here's one for the technically inclined. If you have a networked printer, open your Web browser and enter this address: *http://127.0.0.1:631.* You find yourself at a secret "front end" for CUPS (Common Unix Printing System), the new underlying printing technology for Mac OS X 10.2—and one that lets your Mac communicate with a huge array of older printers that don't yet have Mac OS X drivers. Using this administration screen, you can manage your networked printers and print jobs—a very slick trick.

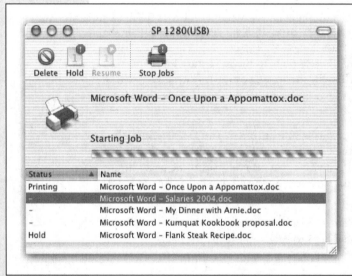

Figure 8-3:
Waiting printouts appear in this Print Center window. You can manipulate this window exactly as you would any Finder list view. For example, you can sort the list by clicking the column headings Name, Status, and so on; make the columns wider or narrower by dragging the column-heading dividers horizontally; or reverse the sorting order by clicking the column name a second time.

When all of your settings look good, click Print (or press Enter) to send your print-out to the printer. Background printing lets you use your Mac while the printing takes place, so feel free to set about working in other programs (or in the same program) while the printing is still going on.

Managing Printouts

The real fun of printing begins only after you've used the Print command. At this point, you can manage the printouts-in-waiting in a number of ways—ways that are useful primarily for people who do a lot of printing, have connections to a lot of printers, or share printers with many other people.

Start by opening Print Center. In the list of printers, the Status column shows you which printers are busy. Double-click a printer's name to see something like Figure 8-3; namely, the printouts that will soon be sliding out of your printer appear in a tidy list. You can delete them, pause them, and sort them, although you can't rearrange printouts by dragging them up or down in the queue lists.

Scanning

In theory, you should be able to use your old Windows scanner with your new Mac—if it connects with USB, FireWire (IEEE 1394), or some other connection the Mac understands.

But in practice, scanning is still a store spot for Mac OS X fans. Most *current* scanner models (Epson, Canon, Agfa, Nikon, Microtek, Umax) work with Mac OS X, but hundreds of older ones still don't have Mac OS X drivers.

If your scanner model isn't one of the lucky ones, hie thee to *www.hamrick.com* to download VueScan. It's a $40 shareware program that makes dozens of scanners work with Mac OS X, including:

- **SCSI models** including *all* SCSI scanners from Apple, Epson, Canon, HP, Microtek, UMAX, LinoType-Hell, Acer, and AGFA.

- **USB models** including all scanners from Epson and many from Canon, HP, Microtek, Umax, and others.

- **FireWire models** including *all* scanners from Epson, Microtek, UMAX, and LinoType-Hell.

If your scanner model isn't on the VueScan list, it may be on the list of SilverFast *(www.silverfast.com),* which restores to life 150 older SCSI and USB scanners from Acer, AGFA, EPSON, Linotype, Microtek, PFU, Polaroid, Quato, and UMAX.

Don't waste any more time pondering the irony that Apple, a company that counts graphics professionals among its core audiences, has ignored the scanning problem for so long. Just download VueScan or SilverFast and rejoice.

PDF Files

Even before your switch from Windows, you probably ran into PDF (portable document format) files at some point. Many a software manual, Read Me file, and downloadable "white paper" come in this format. And no wonder: When you distribute PDF files to other people, they see precisely the same fonts, colors, page design, and other elements that you did in your original document—even if they don't own the fonts or programs used to create the PDF file. Better yet, the same PDF file opens identically on the Mac, in Windows, and even on Unix/Linux machines.

In Windows, you need the free program called Acrobat Reader (page 160) if you hoped to open or print these files. But PDF files are one of Mac OS X's common forms of currency. You can turn *any document* (in any program with a Print command) into a PDF file—a trick that once required the $250 program called Adobe Acrobat Distiller.

> **Note:** All right, that joke about a free copy of Acrobat Distiller is an exaggeration. Mac OS X alone creates *screen-optimized* PDF files: compact, easy-to-email files that look good on the screen but don't have the high resolution for professional printing. For high-end purposes and more optimization for specific uses (Web, fancy press machines, and so on), you still need a program like Adobe Acrobat Distiller.

Opening PDF files

There's nothing to opening up a PDF file on the Mac: Just double-click it. Either Preview or Acrobat Reader takes over from there, and opens the PDF file on your screen.

Creating PDF files

Opening, schmopening—what's really exciting in Mac OS X is the ability to create your *own* PDF files. You can do so in any of several ways.

- **The File→Save as PDF method.** Not all programs offer a File→Save as PDF command. But the ones that do provide by far the easiest method of creating a PDF file. A Save dialog box appears (see page 91). All you have to do is type a name for the file and save it. It's then ready for distribution, backing up, or whatever.

- **The Save As PDF button.** The standard Print dialog box offers a Save As PDF button (Figure 8-2). When you click it, Mac OS X saves your printout-to-be to the disk instead of printing it.

- **The Save as File method.** If that business of clicking a simple Save As PDF button strikes you as too straightforward, you can also choose File→Print. In the Print dialog box (Figure 8-2), choose Output Options from the unnamed pop-up menu. Turn on Save as File, and choose PDF from the Format menu. Finally, click Save.

Fonts in Mac OS X

Only always-smooth font formats work in Mac OS X: namely, TrueType, PostScript Type 1, and OpenType. In other words, Mac OS X type is *all smooth, all the time*. Fonts always look smooth onscreen, no matter what the point size, and always look smooth in printouts, no matter what kind of printer you use.

Where fonts live

If you're used to Windows, one of the most confusing changes is that there is no longer one single Fonts folder for your computer. There are now *five* Fonts folders. The fonts you actually see listed in the Fonts menus of your programs are combinations of these Fonts folders' contents. They include:

• **Your private fonts (your Home folder→Library→Fonts).** You're free to add your own custom fonts to this folder (Figure 8-4). Go wild—it's your font collection and yours alone. Nobody else who uses the Mac will be able to use these fonts, and will never even know that you have them.

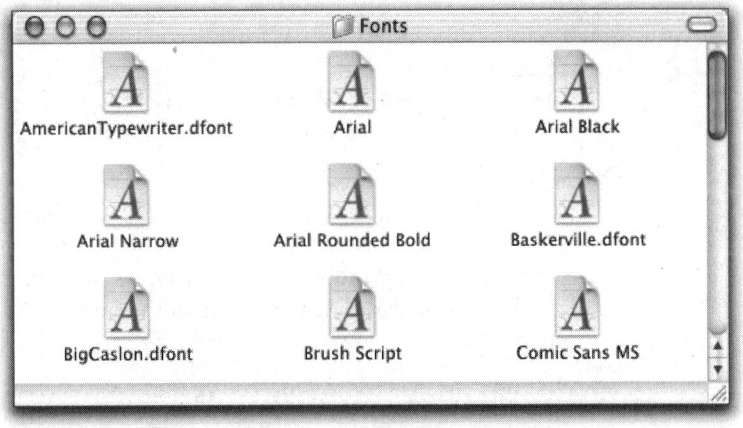

Figure 8-4:
Apple giveth, and Apple taketh away. In Mac OS X, all kinds of fonts are represented by a single icon apiece—a single font suitcase. PostScript fonts no longer require separate files for printer display and screen display. On the other hand, you can no longer double-click a font suitcase to see a preview of what its characters look like, as you can in Windows.

• **Main font collection (Library→Fonts).** This, for all intents and purposes, is the equivalent of the traditional Fonts folder. Any fonts in this folder are available to everyone to use in every program. (As with most features that affect everybody who shares your Macintosh, however, only people with Administrator accounts are allowed to change the contents of this folder.)

• **Network fonts (Network→Library→Fonts).** In certain corporations, a network administrator may have set up a central font collection on another computer on the network, to which your Mac and others can "subscribe." The beauty of this system, of course, is that everybody on the network will be able to rely on a consistent set of fonts.

• **Essential system fonts (System→Library→Fonts).** This folder contains the fonts that the Mac itself needs: the typefaces you see in your menus, dialog boxes, icons, and so on. You can open this folder to *see* these font suitcases, but you can't do anything with them, such as opening, moving, or adding to them.

• **Classic fonts (Mac OS 9 System Folder→Fonts).** Mac OS X automatically notices and incorporates any fonts in the System Folder that you've designated for use by the Classic environment (page100). This folder is also, of course, the source of fonts that appear in the Font menus of your Classic programs.

Note: Suppose you have two slightly different fonts, both called Optima, in different Fonts folders on your system. Which font will you actually get when you use it in your documents?

The scheme is actually fairly simple: Mac OS X proceeds down the list of Fonts folders in the order shown above, beginning with your own home Fonts folder. It only acknowledges the existence of the *first* duplicated font it finds.

Installing fonts

One of the biggest perks of Mac OS X is its preinstalled collection of over 50 great-looking fonts—"over $1000 worth," according to Apple, which licensed them from type companies.

Better yet, you can use most of your old Windows fonts on the Mac, too, since most use the same file format. (The Mac accepts the TrueType and OpenType fonts from your PC, but not Windows PostScript Type 1. You can find out a font's type by right-clicking its icon in the Windows Fonts folder and choosing Properties from the short-cut menu.)

To find your PC's fonts, proceed like this:

- **Windows XP, Windows Me, Windows 2000.** Open My Computer→[your hard drive]→the Windows (or WINNT)→Fonts folder.

- **Windows 95, 98.** Choose Start→Settings→Control Panel→Fonts.

Copy the font files, using any of the techniques described in Chapter 5, into the corresponding Fonts folder on your Mac as described above. (Most of the time, the Library→Fonts folder is the best place for them.)

Note: Newly installed fonts don't appear in the Font menus of programs that are already open. You have to quit and reopen them.)

FREQUENTLY ASKED QUESTION

The Faxing Situation

Hey, how do I send faxes out of Mac OS X?

Using the Mac as a fax machine is a terrific idea, for a lot of reasons. For one thing, it eliminates the silly and costly ritual of printing out something just so that you can feed it into a fax machine. For another, because your fax originates directly from the heart of Mac OS X instead of being scanned by a crummy 200-dpi fax-machine scanner, it blesses your recipient with a spectacular-looking document.

Apple does not, itself, make fax software. But it does provide the bizarrely named FaxSTF, a basic fax sending-and-receiving program included with certain Mac models.

If an inspection of your Applications folder reveals that you don't have FaxSTF, you can always install PageSender. It's a shareware program (available from *www.smilesoft ware.com*) that gives Mac OS X the faxing feature it always hoped for.

To *remove* a certain font on the Mac, you (or an administrator) must drag its corresponding icon out of *all five* Fonts folders. You don't have to quit your open programs first, although you may find it confusing that the font's name remains, now orphaned, in their Font menus.

Digital Cameras

Just like Windows XP, Mac OS X is extremely camera-friendly. The simple act of connecting a digital camera to its USB cable stirs Mac OS X into action—namely, it opens iPhoto, Apple's digital photo shoebox program. See page 343 for a crash course.

Disks

Floppy drives disappeared from Macs beginning in 1997—and in fact, some Windows-PC manufacturers are starting to eliminate them, too.

If you miss having a floppy drive, you can always buy a USB floppy drive for your Mac. In the meantime, there are all kinds of other disks you can connect to a Mac these days: Zips, Peerless cartridges, external DVD burners, FireWire (IEEE 1394) external hard drives (or the iPod music player, which is itself an external FireWire hard drive), and so on.

When you insert any kind of disk, its icon shows up on the right side of the screen; there's no My Computer icon to open when you want to find the inserted disk's icon. Conversely, *no icon* for a drive appears if there's no disc in it. If you've used only Windows, this behavior may throw you at first.

Note: You *can* use Mac OS X like Windows if you choose. To open a single window containing icons of all currently inserted disks, choose Go→Computer. To complete the illusion that you're running Windows, you can even tell Mac OS X not to put disk icons on the desktop at all. Just choose Finder→Preferences and turn off the three top checkboxes—"Hard disks," "Removable media (such as CDs)," and "Connected servers." They'll no longer appear on the desktop—only in your Computer window.

To remove a disk from of your Mac, use one of these methods:

- **Drag its icon onto the Trash icon.** For years, this technique has confused and frightened first-time Mac users. Their typical reaction: Doesn't the *Trash* mean *delete?* Yes, but only when you drag document or folder icons there—not disk icons. Dragging disk icons onto the Trash (at the right end of the Dock) makes the Mac spit them out.

  Actually, all you can really do is *intend* to drag it onto the Trash can. The instant you begin dragging a disk icon, the Trash icon on the Dock changes form, as though to reassure the novice that it will merely eject a disk icon not erase it. As you drag, the wastebasket icon turns into a giant-sized Eject logo (which matches the symbol on the upper-rightmost key of current Mac keyboards).

• **Press the Eject/F12 key on your keyboard.** Recent Mac keyboards, both on laptops and desktops, have a special Eject key in the upper-right corner; on older Macs, you use the F12 key instead. Either way, hold it down for a moment to make a CD or DVD pop out. (If it's any other kind of disk, highlight the icon first.)

• **Highlight the disk icon, and then choose File→Eject (⌘-E).** The disk now pops out.

• **Control-click the disk icon.** Choose Eject from the contextual menu.

Startup Disks

When you turn the Mac on, it hunts for a *startup disk*—that is, a disk containing a copy of Mac OS X. And, as you know, a computer without an operating system is like a machine that's had a lobotomy.

Note: By installing the Mac OS onto a disk—be it a hard drive or rewritable CD or DVD—you can create a startup disk. Not all disks are capable of starting up the Mac, however (RAM disks, older external FireWire disks), and not all older Macs can start up from external FireWire drives.

Selecting a startup disk

It's perfectly possible to have more than one startup disk simultaneously attached to your Mac. Some veteran Mac fans deliberately create other startup disks—on burnable CDs, for example—so that they can easily start the Mac up from a backup startup disk, or a different version of the OS.

FREQUENTLY ASKED QUESTION

The Eject Button That Doesn't

When I push the Eject button on my keyboard (or on my CD-ROM drawer), how come the CD doesn't come out?

There might be two things going on. First of all, to prevent accidental pushings, the Eject key on the modern Mac keyboard is designed to work only when you hold it down steadily for a second or two. Just tapping it doesn't work.

Second, remember that once you've inserted a CD, DVD, or Zip disk, the Mac won't let go unless you eject it in one of the official ways. On Mac models with a CD tray, pushing the button *on the CD-ROM door* opens the drawer only when it's *empty*. If there's a disc in it, you can push that button till doomsday, but the Mac will simply ignore you.

That behavior especially confuses people who are used to working with Windows. (On a Windows PC, pushing the

CD button does indeed eject the disc.) But on the Mac, pushing the CD-door button ejects an inserted disc only when the disc wasn't seated properly (or when the disk drive's driver software isn't installed), and the disc's icon never did appear onscreen.

The Eject key on the modern Mac keyboard, however, isn't so fussy. It pops out whatever CD or DVD is in the drive.

Finally, if a CD or DVD won't come out at all (and its icon doesn't show up on the desktop), restart the Mac. When it "comes to," it will either recognize the disc now or generate an error message containing an Eject button. (Most drives also feature a tiny pinhole in or around the slot. Inserting a straightened paper clip, slowly and firmly, will also make the disc pop out.) Keeping the mouse button pressed as the Mac restarts also makes the disc pop out.)

Only one System folder can be operational at a time. So how does the Mac know which to use as its startup disk? You make your selection in the Startup Disk panel of System Preferences (Figure 8-5). Use it to specify which disk you want the Mac to start up from the next time it starts up.

Tip: If you're in a hurry to start the machine up from a different disk, just click the disk icon and then click Restart in the System Preferences window. You don't have to close the window first.

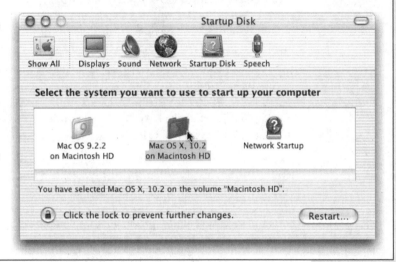

Figure 8-5:
In the Startup Disk panel of System Preferences, the currently selected disk—the one that will be "in force" the next time the machine starts up—is always highlighted. You see the Mac OS X version number and the name of the drive it's on, but not its actual name—until you point to an icon without clicking.

Erasing, Formatting, and Initializing

When you want to erase a disk (such as a CD-RW disc) in Mac OS X, you use Disk Utility, which is located in your Applications→Utilities folder.

Mac OS Extended Formatting

Whether you use Disk Utility to erase a disk (or when you first install Mac OS X and elect to erase the hard drive in the process), you'll be confronted with a choice between formatting options called *Mac OS Extended* and *UNIX File System (UFS)*. (When you erase a floppy disk, you also get an option to create a DOS-formatted disk for use in Windows machines.)

Mac OS Extended refers to the HFS Plus filing system, a disk format that has been proudly maximizing disk space for Mac fans since Mac OS 8.1.

Mac OS X still accepts disks that were prepared using the older, *Mac OS Standard* formatting—the ancient HFS (hierarchical filing system) format—but you can't use one as your startup disk.

As for the UNIX File System option, you generally find it on computers that run Unix (the pure variety, not the dressed-up version that is Mac OS X). Mac OS X recognizes UFS drives, and can even start up from one. But unless you're a Unix/Linux hound, stick with Mac OS Extended format.

You can use this program to erase, repair, or subdivide (*partition*) a hard drive. You can also use it to *lock* a hard drive or cartridge so that it behaves like a CD-ROM. In other words, people can look at what's on it, but they can't store anything new on it.

To erase a CD-RW or DVD-RW disc, launch Disk Utility, click the Erase tab, click the name of the CD (in the left-side list), and click the Erase button.

Burning CDs and DVDs

If your Mac contains a CD-RW drive or an Apple SuperDrive (a drive that plays and burns CDs *and* DVDs), you've got yourself the world's most convenient and elegant backup system. It's like having a rugged floppy disk that holds at least 450 times as many files, or (if it's DVD) 3,350 times as many!

You can buy blank CDs very inexpensively in bulk ($20 for 100 discs, for example) via the Web. (To find the best prices, visit *www.shopper.com* or *www.buy.com* and search for *blank CD-R*.) Blank DVDs are more expensive, but not ridiculously so considering their capacity. At this writing, the Apple Web site, for example, sells them at $15 for five—and prices are sure to come down.

To use one for backup, transporting files, or mailing files, insert a blank CD-R, CD-RW, or DVD-R disc into your Mac. (If you have a slot-loading Mac, simply slip the disc into the slot. If your Mac has a sliding CD/DVD tray instead, open it first by pressing the button on the tray, or—if you have an Eject key in the upper-right corner of your keyboard—pressing it for about one second.)

Tip: Once you've inserted a CD or DVD into your tray, you can close it either by pushing gently on the tray or—if your keyboard has an Eject key—by pressing the key again.

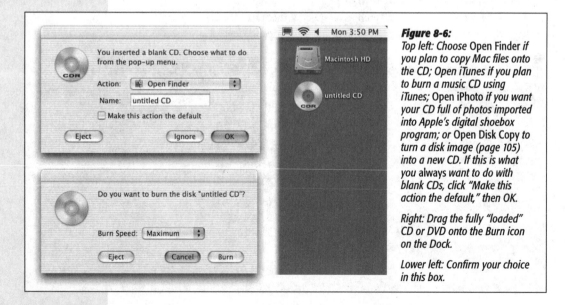

Figure 8-6:
Top left: Choose Open Finder *if you plan to copy Mac files onto the CD;* Open iTunes *if you plan to burn a music CD using* iTunes; Open iPhoto *if you want your CD full of photos imported into Apple's digital shoebox program; or* Open Disk Copy *to turn a disk image (page 105) into a new CD. If this is what you* always *want to do with blank CDs, click "Make this action the default," then OK.*

Right: Drag the fully "loaded" CD or DVD onto the Burn icon on the Dock.

Lower left: Confirm your choice in this box.

After a moment, the Mac notices the blank disc and displays a dialog box asking, in effect, what you want to do with this blank CD. See Figure 8-6 for instructions.

If you choose Open Finder, you'll see the disc's icon appear on the desktop after a moment. At this point, you can begin dragging files and folders onto it, exactly as though it were a particularly well-endowed floppy disk. You can add, remove, reorganize, and rename the files on it just as you would in any standard Finder window. You can even rename the CD or DVD itself just as you would a file or folder (page 48).

Tip: Behind the scenes, the Mac is creating a *disk image* of the CD (or DVD)-to-be, as described on page 105. If your hard drive is very full—too full to set aside a 650-megabyte, 700-megabyte, or 4.7-gigabyte loading area for your files, that is—you'll get an error message.

When the disk contains the files and folders you want to immortalize, do one of these things:

• Choose File→Burn Disc.

• Drag the disc's icon toward the Trash icon on the Dock. As soon as you begin to drag, the Trash icon turns into what looks like a bright yellow fallout-shelter logo. Drop the disc's icon onto it.

• Control-click the disc's icon on the Dock and choose Burn Disc from the contextual menu that appears.

Tip: If you do a lot of CD burning, consider adding a Burn button to your Finder toolbar. It's one of the canned options described on page 72.

In any case, the dialog box shown at bottom left in Figure 8-6 now appears. Click Burn. The Mac's laser proceeds to record the CD or DVD, which can take some time. Fortunately, because this is Mac OS X, you're free to switch into another program and continue using your Mac.

When the recording process is over, you'll have yourself a newly minted DVD or CD that you can insert into any other Mac (or PC, for that matter). It will show up on that computer complete with all the files and folders you put onto it.

Here are a few final notes on burning CDs and DVDs at the desktop:

• Not sure whether your Mac even *has* a CD-burning drive? Open the Apple System Profiler program (located in your Applications→Utilities folder). Click the Devices and Volumes tab. Near the bottom of the display—next to a gray "Bus" triangle—you'll see an indication of the kind of drive your Mac has. It might say "DVD," for example (meaning you can't record anything), or "CD-RW/DVD-R" (meaning you can burn CDs *and* DVDs—therefore, you have a SuperDrive).

• You can only do the most basic recording right in the Finder—convenient as all get-out, but very basic. For example, you can only record an entire CD at once.

You can't add any more files or folders to it once it's been burned (unless it's a CD-RW, in which case you must erase the entire disc and then rerecord the whole thing).

If you'd like to add more to a previously recorded CD-R or CD-RW (technically, to create a *multisession* disc), you'll need either a shareware program like CD Session Burner (available from the "Missing CD" page of *www.missing manuals.com*) or a full-fledged CD-burning program like Toast Titanium *(www.roxio.com)*. Toast can also burn video CDs and a wide variety of other disc formats.

• When you insert a CD-*RW* disc that you've previously recorded, the box shown at top left in Figure 8-6 doesn't appear. Instead, the disc's icon simply appears on the desktop as though it's an ordinary CD. Before you can copy new files onto it, you must erase it using Disk Utility as described in the previous section.

• The CDs that the Mac burns work equally well on Macs and Windows (or Linux) PCs. If you plan to insert a CD into a PC, however, remember that Windows doesn't permit any of these symbols in a file name—\ / : * ? " < > |—and you'll run into trouble if any of your files contain these symbols. In fact, you won't be able to open any folders on your CD that contain illegally named files.

iTunes: The CD and MP3 Jukebox

iTunes, in your Applications folder, is the ultimate software jukebox (Figure 8-7). It can play music CDs, tune in to Internet radio stations, load up your iPod music player, and play back *MP3 files* (sound files in a popular format that stores CD-

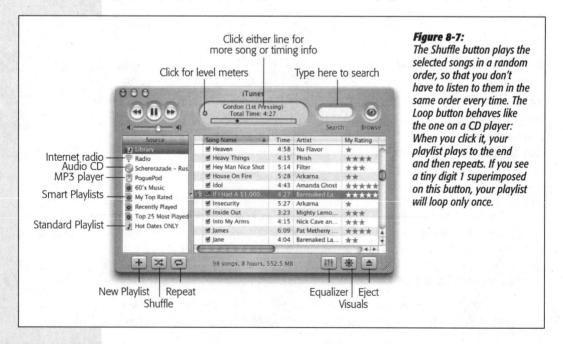

Figure 8-7:
The Shuffle button plays the selected songs in a random order, so that you don't have to listen to them in the same order every time. The Loop button behaves like the one on a CD player: When you click it, your playlist plays to the end and then repeats. If you see a tiny digit 1 superimposed on this button, your playlist will loop only once.

quality music in remarkably small files) and other popular audio formats. It can also turn selected tracks from your music CDs *into* MP3 files, so that you can store favorite songs on your hard drive to play back anytime—without having to dig up the original CDs. In fact, iTunes can even load your MP3 files onto certain portable MP3 players. And if your Mac can burn CDs, iTunes even lets you burn your own custom audio CDs that contain only the good songs.

iTunes can also burn *MP3 CDs:* music CDs that fit much more than the usual 74 minutes of music onto a disc (because they store songs in MP3 format instead of AIFF). Not all CD players can play MP3 discs, however, and the sound quality is slightly lower than standard CDs.

MP3 Files and Company

The iTunes screen itself is set up to be a list—a database—of every song you've got in MP3, AIFF, WAV, or AC3 format. iTunes automatically finds, recognizes, and lists all such files in your Home folder→Documents→iTunes Music folder.

Tip: You can instruct iTunes to display the contents of other folders, too, by choosing File→Add to Library. It promptly copies any sound files from the folder you "show" it into your Home folder→Music→iTunes folder.

Audio CDs

If you're not into collecting MP3 files, you can also populate the main list here simply by inserting a music CD. The songs on it immediately show up in the list.

At first, they may appear with the exciting names "Track 01," "Track 02," and so on. Similarly, the CD itself shows up in the list at the left side of the window with the uninspiring name "Audio CD."

Fortunately, iTunes immediately attempts to connect to the Internet and compare your CD with the listings at *www.cddb.com,* a global database of music CDs and their contents. If it finds a match among the thousands of CDs there, it copies the

FREQUENTLY ASKED QUESTION

Auto-Playing Music CDs

How do I make my Mac play music CDs automatically when they're inserted?

First, make sure iTunes is slated to open automatically when you insert a music CD. You do that on the CDs & DVDs panel of System Preferences (use the "When you insert a music CD" pop-up menu).

Then all you have to do is make sure iTunes knows to begin playing automatically once it launches. Choose iTunes→Preferences, click the General icon, and from the "On CD Insert" pop-up menu, choose Begin Playing, and click OK.

From now on, whenever you insert a music CD, iTunes will launch automatically and begin playing.

album and song names right into iTunes, where they reappear every time you use
this particular music CD.

Tip: If you connect an iTunes-compatible portable MP3 player to your Mac, its name, too, shows up in the
left-side Source list. This is your opportunity to make your Mac the "hub for the digital lifestyle," exactly as
Apple advertises: You can add or remove songs on your player (by dragging them onto its icon), rename
or reorder them, and so on.

Playing Music

To turn your Mac into a music player, click iTunes' triangular Play button (or press
the Space bar). The Mac immediately begins to play the songs whose names have
checkmarks in the main list. Check Figure 8-7 to see what the various onscreen
buttons do.

As music plays, you can control and manipulate the music and the visuals of your
Mac in all kinds of interesting ways. For example, *visuals* is the iTunes term for an
onscreen laser-light show that pulses, beats, and dances in perfect sync to the music
you're listening to. The effect is hypnotic and wild. (For real party fun, invite some
people who grew up in the sixties to your house to watch.)

To summon this psychedelic display, click the flower-power icon in the lower-right
corner of the window (Figure 8-7). The show begins immediately—although it's
much more fun if you choose Visuals→Full Screen so that the movie takes over your
whole monitor. True, you won't get a lot of work done, but when it comes to stress
relief, visuals are a lot cheaper than a hot tub.

Copying (Ripping) CD Songs to Your Hard Drive

iTunes lets you convert your favorite songs from audio CDs into MP3 files on your
hard drive. Once they've been transferred to your Mac, you can play them whenever
you like, without inserting the original CD. (You can also sync them with your iPod
music player, if you have one.)

To *rip* a CD in this way, make sure that only the songs you want to capture have
checkmarks in the main list. (The bottom of the window shows you how many
songs are on the CD, their total playback time, and how many megabytes of disk
space it would take to copy them to your hard drive.) Then click the Import button
at the upper-right corner of the window (Figure 8-8).

When it's all over, you'll find the imported songs listed in your Library (click the
Library icon in the left-side Source list). From there, you can drag them into any
other "folder" (playlist), as described next.

Playlists—and Smart Playlists

When you click the Library icon in the left-side Source list, the main part of the
screen displays every MP3 file iTunes knows about. It's organized much like a Finder
window, with columns indicating the song length, singer or band, album, and so on.

As always, you can rearrange these columns by dragging their headings, sort your list by one of these criteria by clicking its heading, reverse the sorting order by clicking the heading a second time, and so on. And here's the best part: To find a particular song, just type a few letters into the Search blank above the list. iTunes hides all but the ones that match.

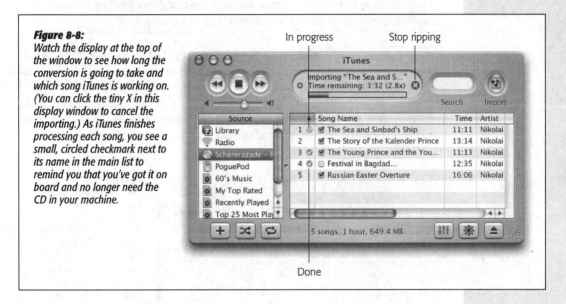

Figure 8-8:
Watch the display at the top of the window to see how long the conversion is going to take and which song iTunes is working on. (You can click the tiny X in this display window to cancel the importing.) As iTunes finishes processing each song, you see a small, circled checkmark next to its name in the main list to remind you that you've got it on board and no longer need the CD in your machine.

In progress   Stop ripping

Done

Apple recognizes that you may not want to listen to *all* your songs every time you need some tunes. That's why iTunes lets you create *playlists*—folders in the Source list that contain only certain songs, like albums of your own devising. You might create one called Party Tunes, another called Blind Date Music, and so on.

Creating playlists

To create a new playlist, click the New Playlist button in the lower-left corner of the window, or choose File→New Playlist (⌘-N). A new playlist appears as an icon in the list at the left side of the screen. You can rename one by clicking, and add songs to one by dragging them out of the main list.

Playing with criteria

iTunes 3's *Smart Playlists* constantly rebuild themselves according to criteria you specify. You might tell one Smart Playlist to assemble 45 minutes' worth of songs that you've rated higher than four stars but rarely listen to, and another to play your most-often-played songs from the eighties. Later, you can listen to these playlists with a turn of the iPod's control dial, uninterrupted and commercial-free.

Tip: iTunes automatically tracks how many times you've played each song, the band name, and other criteria. The rating, however, is one Smart Playlist criterion you have to input yourself.

To rate a song, make the window wide enough that you can see the My Rating column. Then just click in the My Rating column for a selected song. The appropriate number of stars appears (one, two, three, four, or five) depending on the position of your click. You can change a song's rating as many times as you like—a good thing, considering the short shelf life of many a pop hit these days.

To make a smart playlist, choose File→New Smart Playlist (Option-⌘-N). The dialog box shown in Figure 8-9 appears. The controls here are something like a music-only version of the Find command in the Finder; in essence, they're designed to set up a search of your music database. Figure 8-9, for example, illustrates how you'd find 74 minutes' worth of Beatles tunes released between 1965 and 1968—that you've rated three stars or higher and haven't listened to more than a couple of times.

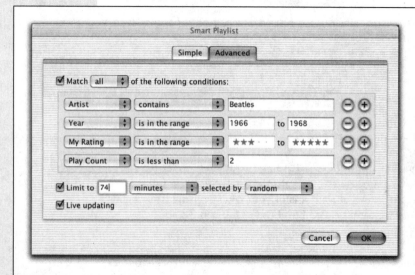

Figure 8-9:
The Smart Playlist dialog box is really a powerful search command (because iTunes is really a powerful database). You can set up certain criteria, like the hunt for particular Beatles tunes illustrated here. Then, provided the "Live updating" checkbox is turned on, iTunes will always keep this playlist updated as your collection changes, as you change your ratings, as your Play Count changes, and so on.

When you click OK, your Smart Playlist is ready to show off. When you click its name in the Source list, the main song list updates itself according to your criteria and any changes in your music collection. (Smart Playlists get transferred to your iPod, but don't continue to update themselves there.)

iTunes: Burning Music CDs

If your Mac has a CD burner, Mac OS X can serve as your own private record label. iTunes can record selected sets of songs, no matter what the original sources, onto a blank CD. When it's all over, you can play the burned CD on any standard CD player, just like the ones from Tower Records—but this time, you hear only the songs you like, in the order you like, with all of the annoying ones eliminated.

Tip: Use CD-R discs. CD-RW discs are not only more expensive, but may not work in standard CD players. (Not all players recognize CD-R discs either, but the odds are better.)

Start by creating a playlist for the CD you're about to make. Drag the songs you want onto its "folder icon" (out of your Library list, for example). Click its icon in the left-side Source list to see the list you've built. Take a moment to drag them up or down in the list to reflect their playback order. Keep an eye on the readout at the bottom of the list, which tells you how much time the songs will take. (About 74 minutes of AIFF audio files fit on one CD. But if you make an MP3 CD instead, as described in the following tip, you can hold ten times as much, or more. Note, though, that MP3 CDs don't play on all CD players—only those advertised with this feature.)

Tip: You can control how many seconds of silence iTunes leaves between tracks on your custom CD. Choose iTunes→Preferences, click the Burn icon, and make a selection from the Gap Between Tracks pop-up menu. This is also where you specify whether you want to make a standard audio CD or a CD in the newer, less compatible MP3 CD format (which holds much more music per disc).

When everything is set up, click the Burn CD button in the playlist window. Insert a blank CD into the Mac and then click Burn CD again.

The burning process takes some time. You can always cancel by clicking the tiny X button in the progress bar, but feel free to work in other programs while iTunes chugs away.

Tip: iTunes can burn CDs using any built-in CD burner or those from most major manufacturers. If your drive isn't on Apple's list, you'll need the help of a program like Toast Titanium *(www.roxio.com)*. Launch Toast and prepare to burn a new CD, choosing Audio CD as the Format. Then drag and drop selections from an iTunes playlist directly to the Toast window and click Burn. Toast burns your custom CD using the files you encoded, organized, and ordered in iTunes.

Playing DVD Movies

If your Mac has a drive that can play DVD's, watching movies couldn't be simpler: Just insert the DVD. The Mac automatically detects that it's a video DVD (as opposed to, say, one that's just filled with files) and launches the DVD Player program. (If DVD Player doesn't start up automatically when you insert a DVD movie, you can open it yourself. It's sitting there in your Applications folder.)

Note: DVD Player doesn't work (and doesn't even get installed) on certain older Macs, including bronze-keyboard PowerBook G3 (Lombard) laptops and early blue-and-white Power Macs.

If DVD Player starts out playing your movie in a window, your first act should be to choose Video→Enter Full Screen (⌘-0). At this point, the movie screen fills your entire monitor—even the menu bar disappears. (To make it reappear, just move your cursor near the top of the screen.)

At this point, you're ready to play the movie. By far the easiest way is to just press the Space bar—once to start, again to pause, again to start again. You can also use the onscreen remote control. Use the commands in the Controls menu to choose a vertical or horizontal orientation for it.

Tip: Watching a movie while sitting in front of your iMac or Power Mac is not exactly the great American movie-watching dream. But remember that you can connect the video-output jacks of your Mac (most models) to your TV for a much more comfortable movie-watching experience.

Just be sure to connect the cables from the Mac's video-output jacks *directly* to the TV. If you connect them to your VCR instead, you'll get a horrible, murky, color-shifting picture–the result of the built-in copy-protection circuitry of every VCR.

Figure 8-10:
Choose DVD Player→ Preferences. Now, if you turn on Enable Viewer Resizing In Full Screen, you'll be able to use the Video menu to change the size of the "screen" on your screen even while you're in full-screen mode. (Remember to move the mouse near the top of the monitor to make the menu bar reappear.)

Keyboard

Switching to the Mac entails switching your brain, especially when it comes to the old keyboard shortcuts. All of those Ctrl-key sequences become, on the Mac, ⌘-key sequences. (Check your Macintosh keyboard: the ⌘ key is right next to the Space bar, usually on both sides.)

But plenty of other Mac keys may seem unfamiliar. For your reassurance pleasure, here's a rundown of what they do:

- **F1, F2, F3...** These function keys do pretty much the same thing they do in most Windows programs: Nothing.

  There are exceptions, though. For example, they work in Microsoft Office programs (F1 means Save, F2 means Undo, and so on). And F12 serves as a CD eject button.

  You can also buy programs like QuicKeys X that let you attach these keys to your favorite programs, so that pressing F5 opens up AppleWorks, F6 launches your Web browser, and so on.

  On current Macs, designated F-keys also correspond to the Dimmer/Brighter controls for your screen, and the Mute, Softer, and Louder commands for your built-in speaker. (You'll know if your keyboard offers these functions by the presence of little sunshine icons for brightness, and little speaker icons for sound.)

- **⏏**. This is the Eject key; it spits out whatever disc is in your drive. (If *nothing* is in your drive, it doesn't do anything—unless you have a tray-loading Mac, in which case holding it down for about a second makes the CD/DVD tray slide open.) When there *is* a disc in there, press the key once to make the computer spit it out.

- **Home, End.** In a desktop (Finder) window, "Home" and "End" are ways of saying "jump to the top or bottom of the window." If you're word processing, the Home and End keys are supposed to jump to the first word or last word of the file, although some programs require you to press Ctrl or ⌘ too, as described on the following pages.

- **Pg Up, Pg Down:** These keys scroll the current window up or down by one screenful, just as on Windows. Once again, the idea is to let you scroll through word-processing documents, Web pages, and lists without having to use the mouse.

- **NumLock, Clear:** Clear means "get rid of this text I've highlighted, but don't put a copy on the invisible Clipboard, as the Cut command would do."

  The NumLock key is just as much of an oddball on the Mac as it is on the PC. In Microsoft Word, the NumLock key works like a Forward Delete key, erasing the next character *after* the insertion point. In Microsoft Excel, the NumLock key actually does something obscure, but you're free to nuzzle up to the online help for that.

- **Esc:** *Esc* stands for *Escape*, and means "Click the Cancel button," such as the one found in most dialog boxes. In other words: same as in Windows.

- **Delete:** This is the backspace key.

- **Del:** This is your Forward Delete key; it erases whatever letter is just *after* the insertion point in text. (If your keyboard lacks a Del key—for example, if you have a laptop—then you produce the Forward Delete function by pressing the *regular* Delete key along with the Fn key in the lower-left corner of the keyboard.)

- **Return and Enter:** In general, these keys do the same thing: wrap your typing to the next line. Be careful, though: Some programs distinguish between the two. In AppleWorks, for example, Return begins a new paragraph, but Enter makes a *page break*, forcing the next typing to begin on a fresh page.

- **Command (⌘):** This key triggers keyboard shortcuts for menu items, as described in Chapter 1.

- **Control, Option:** The Control key triggers contextual menus (like shortcut menus), as described in Chapter 1; the Option key lets you type special symbols and access secret features.

- **Help:** This key opens the online help screens (at least in some programs).

Text-Navigation Keystrokes

In Windows, you may have grown accustomed to certain common keystrokes for navigating text—key combinations that make the insertion point jump to the beginning or end of a word, line, or document, for example.

Mac OS X programs offer similar navigation keystrokes, as you can see here:

Function	Windows keys	Mac keys
Move to previous/next word	Ctrl+arrow keys	Option-arrow keys
Move to beginning/end of line	Home/End	Home/End*
Move to previous/next paragraph	Ctrl+up/down arrows*	Option-up/down arrows*
Move to top/bottom of window	Home/End	Home/End (but see below)
Select all text	Ctrl+A	⌘-A
Select text, one letter at a time	Shift+arrow keys	Shift+arrow keys
Select text, one word at a time	Ctrl+Shift+arrow keys	Option+Shift+arrow keys
Undo	Ctrl+Z	⌘-Z
Cut, Copy, Paste	Ctrl+Z, C, P	⌘+Z, C, P
Close window	Alt+F4	⌘-W
Switch open programs	Alt+Tab	⌘-Tab
Minimize all windows	Windows key+D	Option-⌘-click Finder icon on Dock

* in some programs

Incidentally, the keystroke for jumping to the *top or bottom* of a window varies widely on the Mac. You need ⌘-Home/End in Microsoft Word, ⌘-up/down arrow in TextEdit and Stickies, and Home/End in iPhoto 2 and Finder list windows.

As a consolation prize, though, here's a bit of good news: all *Cocoa* programs (page 96)—TextEdit, Stickies, iPhoto, iDVD, Safari, Keynote, iChat, iCal, Mail, Address Book, and so on—offer an amazing quantity of consistent, Unix-based navigation keystrokes that should last you the rest of your life. Here they are:

- **Control-A.** Moves your insertion point to the beginning of the paragraph. (*Mnemonic:* A = beginning of the alphabet.)

- **Control-E.** Deposits your insertion point at the end of the paragraph. (*Mnemonic:* E = *E*nd.)

- **Control-D.** Forward delete (deletes the letter to the *right* of the insertion point).

- **Control-K.** Instantly deletes all text from the insertion point to the right end of the line. (*Mnemonic:* K = *K*ills the rest of the line.)

- **Control-O.** Inserts a paragraph break, much like Return, but leaves the insertion point where it was, above the break. This is the ideal trick for breaking a paragraph in half when you've just thought of a better ending for the first part.

- **Control-T.** Moves the insertion point one letter to the right—and along with it, drags whichever letter was to its left. (*Mnemonic:* T = Transpose letters.)

- **Option-Delete.** Deletes the entire word to the left of the insertion point. When you're typing along in a hurry, and you discover that you've just made a typo, this is the keystroke you want. It's much faster to nuke the previous word and retype it than to fiddle around with the mouse and the insertion point just to fix one letter.

Four additional keystrokes duplicate the functions of the arrow keys. Still, as long as you've got your pinky on that Control key…

- **Control-B, Control-F.** Moves the insertion point one character to the left or right, just like the left and right arrow keys. (*Mnemonic: B*ack, *F*orward).

- **Control-N, Control-P.** Moves the insertion point one row down or up, like the down and up arrow keys. (*Mnemonic: N*ext, *P*revious).

Monitors

Your Mac can use standard VGA monitors of the type found in the Windows world. Every Macintosh can drive *multiple* screens at the same time, too—so can use your old PC screen either as your Mac's main monitor (if it's a Power Mac or Cube) or as a second, external screen (if it's a laptop or any other model).

If one of those arrangements appeals to you, the only complication might be the connector. Most PC screens, of course, have a standard VGA connector (or a more modern DVI connector) at the tip of their tails. Your Mac may or may not have a place to plug in that VGA or DVI cable:

- Flat-panel iMacs and recent Mac laptops come with a six-inch adapter cable. One end clicks into the laptop; the other end mates with your PC monitor's VGA cable.

- If you have a Power Mac, you may have both a proprietary Apple monitor connector *and* a VGA connector. (If not, you can always buy a second graphics card.)

- Modern Mac models come with an ADC connector (a proprietary Apple monitor connector), but you can buy an ADC-to-DVI converter for use with any DVI-connected monitor. (For example, you can buy the $35 DVI Extractor adapter from *www.drbott.com.*)

In any case, all recent Mac models let you choose either *mirror mode* (where both screens show the same thing—a handy setup in classroom situations) or *desktop extension mode* (where one screen acts as additional real estate, an annex to the first). You specify which mode you want using the Displays panel of System Preferences.

3

Part Three:
Making Connections

Getting Online

Most people connect to the Internet using a modem that dials out over ordinary phone lines. But a rapidly growing minority connects over higher-speed wires, using so-called *broadband* connections that are always on: cable modems, DSL, or corporate networks. This chapter explains how to set up each one (and how to use each with a wireless AirPort system).

Connecting by Dial-up Modem

If you're used to connecting to the Internet via ordinary phone lines, courtesy of your PC's modem and an Internet service provider (ISP) like Earthlink or AT&T, you'll have to transfer your PC's connection settings to the Mac. Set aside—oh, a good six minutes for this task.

Note: You don't have to fool with any settings at all if you use America Online. When you first run AOL for Mac OS X, it will guide you through the setup process automatically. Ditto if MSN is your service provider; the Mac OS X version is slated to appear in mid-2003.

Phase 1: The TCP/IP Tab

Start by opening System Preferences and clicking the Network icon. When you choose Internal Modem from the Show pop-up menu, you see a Configure pop-up menu and two text boxes. Your main mission here is to fill in the Domain Name Server numbers provided by your Internet service provider (ISP).

You can get these numbers either from your ISP or by consulting your old PC, assuming it's still set up to go online.

- **Windows XP.** Choose Start→Control Panel, then open Network Connections. Right-click the icon for your dial-up connection and, from the shortcut menu, choose Properties. Double-click the row that says "Internet Protocol (TCP/IP)." The numbers you want appear in the "Use the following DNS server addresses." (If "Obtain DNS server address automatically" is selected instead, then you don't have to put *anything* into the Domain Name Server boxes on the Mac.)

- **Windows 2000.** Choose Start→Settings→Network and Dial-up Connections. Right-click the icon for your Internet connection; from the shortcut menu, choose Properties. Click the Networking tab. Double-click the row that says "Internet Protocol (TCP/IP)." Once again, copy the numbers that show up in the "Use the following DNS server addresses." (And once again, don't put anything into the Domain Name Server boxes on the Mac if "Obtain DNS server address automatically" is selected instead.)

- **Windows 98, Windows Me.** Choose Start→Settings→Control Panel. In the Control Panel window, double-click Network. Double-click the "TCP/IP→Dial-Up Adapter" row. You'll see your DNS numbers on the DNS Configuration tab.

Now then, back to the Mac: If "Using PPP" is selected in the Configure pop-up menu, then move on to Phase 2. (Later, if you find yourself unable to get online, contact your ISP on the off chance that some unusual settings are required here.)

Phase 2: The PPP Tab

Now click the PPP tab (Figure 9-1). Your job here is to fill in the blanks—but how are you supposed to know what to fill?

Here's a listing of the blanks you find here, and where, on your old Windows machine, to find the necessary information (assuming you were able to get online with *that* machine).

Service Provider

This is the name of your ISP, and it doesn't have to be exact (*EarthLink*, for example).

Account Name, Password, Telephone Number

These are the three key pieces of account information that your Mac needs to dial up. They're easy enough to find in Windows:

- **Windows XP.** Choose Start→Control Panel. Open Network Connections. Double-click the icon for your dial-up connection.

- **Windows 2000.** Choose Start→Settings→Network and Dial-up Connections. Double-click the icon for your Internet connection.

- **Windows Me.** Choose Start→Settings→Dial-Up Networking. In the Control Panel, double-click the icon for your dial-up connection.

- **Windows 98.** Open My Computer→Dial-Up Networking. Double-click the icon for your Internet connection.

In each case, the Connect dialog box appears, with connection information staring you in the face. Copy this information into the corresponding boxes on the PPP tab on the Mac, as shown in Figure 9-1. When you're finished making your settings, either close the window or click Apply Now.

Note: Only an administrator can make changes to the Internet dial-up settings. To make a change, you may have to click the little padlock in the lower-left corner of the dialog box to type in an administrator's name and password.

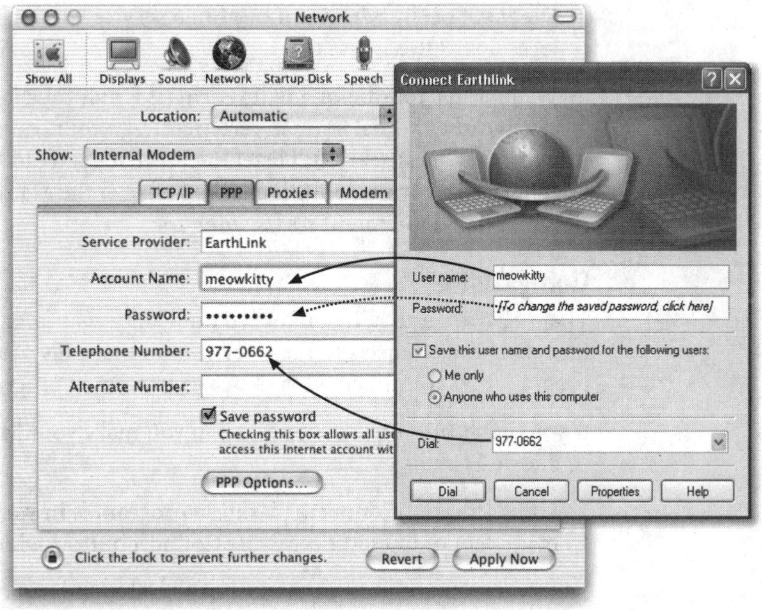

Figure 9-1:
As you copy your ISP details from Windows (XP, shown at right) to the Mac (left), note that your password is blanked out to prevent evildoers from copying it. You'll have to either remember it or throw yourself on the ISP's mercy, because there's no way to copy it out of Windows.

Incidentally, if you click PPP Options in the Network dialog box, you bring up a special Options box, filled with checkboxes that control your online sessions. Here, for example, you can specify how long the Mac waits before hanging up the phone line after your last online activity, and how many times the Mac should dial if the ISP phone number is busy.

One checkbox here that you'll almost certainly want to turn on is "Connect automatically when needed." It makes your Mac dial the Internet automatically whenever you check your email or open your Web browser. (Otherwise, you'd have to establish the Internet call manually, using the Internet Connect program described on page 343. Only then could you check your email or open your Web browser.)

Phase 3: The Modem Tab

This is where you specify the kind of modem you have. Most Mac OS X–compatible Macs have built-in Apple modems, which is why the pop-up menu already says "Apple Internal 56K Modem (v.90)." If you, the heretic, have some other kind of modem, choose its name from the pop-up menu.

Some of the other settings that can be handy include:

• **Sound.** By clicking Off, you make your Mac dial the Internet silently, sparing sleeping family members or dorm roommates from having to listen to your modem shriek as it connects.

• **Dialing.** Specify what kind of phone service you have—Tone or, in a few rural locations, Pulse.

• **Wait for dial tone before dialing.** This is for all you North American laptop owners. Because the dial tones in certain foreign countries sound weird to the Mac, it won't dial because it's still listening for that good old North American dial tone. In that case, turning off this checkbox makes the Mac dial bravely even though it hasn't heard the sound it's listening for.

Going Online

That's all there is to it. If you turned on "Connect automatically when needed," your Mac dials and connects to the Internet automatically whenever an Internet-related program tries to connect (a Web browser or email program, for example).

If you didn't turn on that option, then you make your Mac dial the Internet in one of these ways:

• **Using Internet Connect.** This little program is in your Applications folder. The main item of interest here is the Connect button, which makes the Mac dial.

If you're smart, however, you'll turn on the "Show modem status on menu bar" checkbox found here. It adds a tiny telephone icon—the Modem Status menulet—to the upper-right corner of your screen, which lets you completely bypass Internet Connect the next time you want to go online (Figure 9-2).

• **Use the menu-bar icon.** Just click the Modem Status menulet and choose Connect from the pop-up menu. Your Mac dials without even blocking your desktop picture with a dialog box.

Disconnecting

The Mac automatically drops the phone line 15 minutes after your last activity online (or whatever interval you specified in the PPP Options dialog box). In fact, if other people have accounts on your Mac, the Mac doesn't even hang up when you log out. It maintains the connection so that the next person can Net-surf without redialing.

Of course, if other people in your household are screaming for you to get off the line so that they can make a call, you can also disconnect manually. Either choose Disconnect from the Modem Status menulet or click Disconnect in the Internet Connect window (both shown in Figure 9-2).

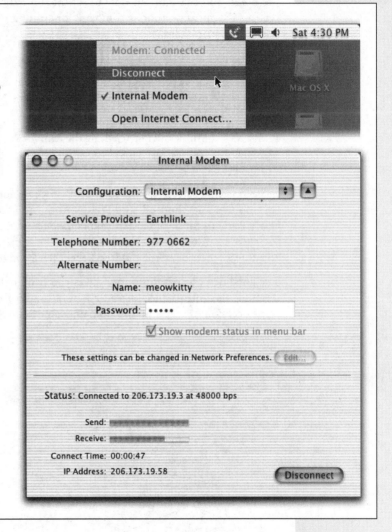

Figure 9-2:
Going online automatically (by launching an Internet program) is by far the most convenient method, but you can also go online on demand, in one of two ways.

Top: The quick way is to choose Connect from this menulet (which doesn't appear until you turn on "Show modem status on menu bar" on the Internet Connect screen).

Bottom: You can also go online manually the long way (using Internet Connect, shown here in its expanded form).

Broadband Connections

If you get online via cable modem, DSL, or office network, you're one of the lucky ones. You have a high-speed connection to the Internet that's always available, always on. You never have to wait to dial, disconnect, or download—everything happens fast.

You set up your account on the Mac like this: Open System Preferences; click the Network icon; from the Show pop-up menu, choose either AirPort or Built-in Ethernet, depending on how your Mac is connected to the broadband modem.

The next step is to make a selection from the Configure pop-up menu—and fill in the boxes. You can find out how to set this up either from your service provider (cable TV company or phone company, for example) or by checking your Windows configuration, as follows:

Settings from Windows XP, Windows 2000

If you have Windows XP, choose Start→Control Panel. Open Network Connections. If you have Windows 2000, choose Start→Settings→Network and Dial-up Connections.

Either way, continue by right-clicking the icon for your broadband connection and, from the shortcut menu, choose Properties. Double-click the row that says "Internet Protocol (TCP/IP)."

If the resulting screen says "Obtain an IP address automatically" (see Figure 9-3), then you should choose Using DHCP from the Mac's Configure pop-up menu. (DHCP stands for *dynamic host configuration protocol,* with the operative word being *dynamic.* Your service provider, behind the scenes, assigns your Mac a different IP address [that is, Internet address] every time you turn on the machine.)

The good news is that this option saves you from having to fill in any of the other boxes in this control panel. Instead, all the settings will come to you over the Internet. (One occasional exception: the Domain Name Servers box.)

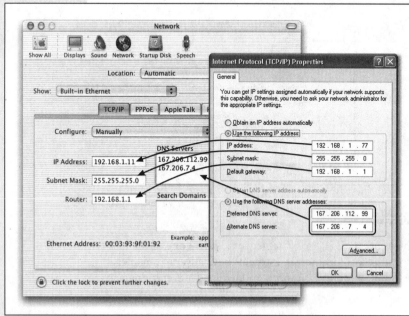

Figure 9-3:
Don't be alarmed by the morass of numbers and periods—it's all in good fun. (If you find TCP/IP fun, that is.) In this illustration, you see the setup for a cable-modem account with a static IP address, which means you have to type in all of these numbers yourself, as guided by the cable company. The alternative is a DHCP server account, which fills most of it in automatically.

If the Windows screen says, "Use the following IP address" instead, copy the numbers into the Mac's Network panel like this (see Figure 9-3):

Copy this Windows setting:	Into this Mac text box:
IP address	IP Address
Subnet mask	Subnet Mask
Default gateway	Router

Similarly, if the Internet Protocol (TCP/IP Properties) dialog box says, "Use the following DNS server addresses," type the numbers in the "Preferred DNS server" and "Alternate DNS server" boxes into the Mac's DNS Servers text box. (Press Return to make a new line for the second number.)

Settings from Windows 98, Windows Me

Choose Start→Settings→Control Panel. In the Control Panel window, double-click Network. Double-click the TCP/IP row that identifies how your PC is connected to the broadband modem. (It may say "TCP/IP→3Com Ethernet Adapter," for example.)

Click the IP Address tab. If "Obtain an IP address automatically" is selected, then you should choose Using DHCP from the Mac's Configure pop-up menu.

If it says "Specify an IP address" instead, copy the IP address and Subnet mask numbers into the same ones on the Mac's Network panel. Then click the Gateway tab, and copy the "Installed gateway" number into the Mac's Router box.

Finally, click the DNS Configuration tab. Copy the strings of numbers you see here into the Mac's DNS Servers text box. (Press Return to make a new line for the second number.)

That's the entire setup—click Apply Now. If your settings are correct, you're online, now and forever. You never have to worry about connecting or disconnecting.

Tip: Your Mac and your PC can share a single cable modem or DSL box, no matter what your phone or cable company tells you. See page 219.

POWER USERS' CLINIC

PPPoE and DSL

If you have DSL service, you may be directed to click the PPPoE tab (which is also in the Network pane of System Preferences). It stands for *PPP over Ethernet,* meaning that although your DSL "modem" is connected to your Ethernet port, you still have to make and break your Internet connections manually, as though you had a dial-up modem. In other words, you're not online full-time.

Fill in the PPPoE tab as directed by your ISP (usually just your account name and password). From here on in, you start and end your Internet connections exactly as though you had a dial-up modem, as described on page 212 (except that the menu-bar pop-up menu is the PPPoE Status menulet, not the Modem Status menulet).

The Jaguar Firewall

If you have a broadband, always-on connection, you're connected to the Internet 24 hours a day. It's theoretically—though remotely—possible for some cretin to use automated hacking software to flood you with email or take control of your machine.

If your Mac is connected to a router, as described above, its *firewall* circuitry is probably protecting you. If not, Mac OS X's firewall *software* can put up a simpler, but effective, barrier.

To turn it on, open the Sharing panel of System Preferences. Click the Firewall tab (Figure 9-4), and then click Start. That's almost all there is to it: you're protected.

Note: If you're using Mac OS X's Internet connection-sharing feature (page 219), turn on the firewall only for the *first* Mac—the one that's the gateway to the Internet. Leave the firewall turned off on all the Macs "downstream" from it.

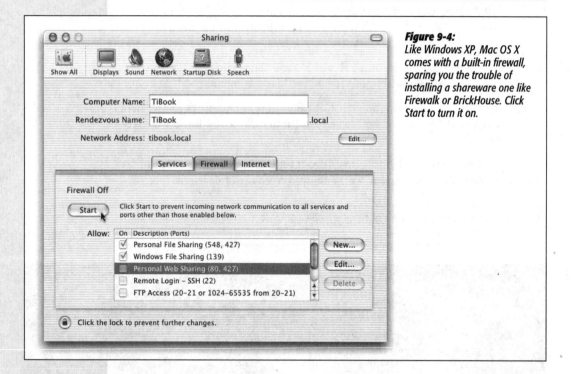

Figure 9-4:
Like Windows XP, Mac OS X comes with a built-in firewall, sparing you the trouble of installing a shareware one like Firewalk or BrickHouse. Click Start to turn it on.

Switching Locations

If you travel with a laptop, you may wind up connecting to the Internet differently in each location: Ethernet at the office, dial-up in the hotel room. Or maybe you simply visit the branch office from time to time, and you're getting tired of having to change the local access number for your ISP each time you leave home (and return home again).

The simple solution is the ⌘→Location submenu. As Figure 9-5 illustrates, all you have to do is tell it where you are. Mac OS X handles the details of switching to the correct Internet connection and phone number.

Figure 9-5:
The Location feature lets you switch from one "location" to another just by choosing its name—either from the ⌘ menu (top) or from this pop-up menu in System Preferences (bottom). The Automatic location just means "the standard, default one you originally set up." (Don't be fooled: Despite its name, Automatic isn't the only location that offers multihoming, which is described later in this chapter.)

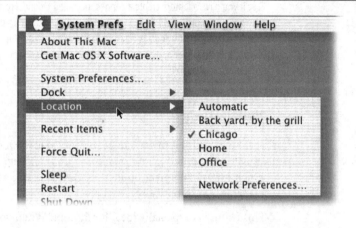

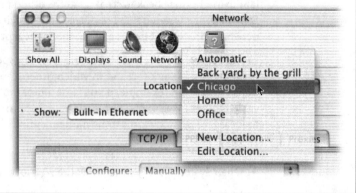

Creating a New Location

To create a *Location*, which is nothing more than a set of memorized settings, open System Preferences, click Network, and choose New Location from the Location pop-up menu. You'll be asked to provide a name for your new location, such as *Chicago Office* or *Dining Room Floor*.

When you click OK, you return to the Network panel, which is now blank. Take this opportunity to set up the kind of Internet connection you use at the corresponding location, just as described on the first pages of this chapter. If you travel regularly, in fact, you can use Location Manager to build a long list of city locations, each of which "knows" the local phone number for your Internet access company (because you've entered it on the PPP tab).

Making the Switch

Once you've set up your various locations, you can switch among them using either the Location pop-up menu (in System Preferences→Network) or the ♦→Location submenu, as shown in Figure 9-5. As soon as you do so, your Mac is automatically set to connect using the new phone number or whatever method you specified.

Tip: If you have a laptop, create a connection called Offline. From the Show pop-up menu, choose Active Network Ports; turn off *all* the connection methods you see in the list. When you're finished, you've got yourself a laptop that will *never* attempt to go online. This setup will save you the occasional interruption of a program that tries to dial but takes three minutes to discover you're on Flight 800 to Miami and have no phone line available.

Multihoming

Speaking of different ways to get online, Mac OS X offers one of the coolest features known to Internet-loving mankind: *multihoming*. That's the ability to auto-detect which Internet connection methods are available and then switch to the fastest one available—automatically.

This feature is especially ideal for laptops. When you open your Web browser, your laptop might first check to see if it's at the office, plugged into a cable modem via the Ethernet—the fastest possible connection. If not, it automatically looks for an AirPort network. Finally, if it draws a blank there, the laptop reluctantly dials the modem.

In short, for each location you create, you can specify which network connections the Mac should look for, and in which order. You can even turn off some connections entirely. For example, if you have a desktop Mac that's always connected to a cable modem, you may never want your Mac to dial using its built-in modem. In that case, you could turn off the modem entirely.

Here's how to go about using this multihoming feature:

1. **Open System Preferences. Click the Network icon.**

   Make sure the appropriate location is selected in the Location pop-up menu.

2. **From the Show pop-up menu, choose Network Port Configurations.**

   Now you see the display shown in Figure 9-6. It lists all the different ways your Mac knows how to get online, or onto an office network.

3. **Drag the items up and down in the list into priority order.**

   If you have a cable modem, DSL, or office network connection, for example, you might want to drag Built-in Ethernet to the top of the list, since that's almost always the fastest way to get online.

   At this point, you can also *turn off* any connections you don't want your Mac to use when it's in this location—the internal modem, for example.

---

4. Click Apply Now.

That's all there is to it. Your Mac will actually switch connections—not just each time you go online, but even in real time, during a single Internet session.

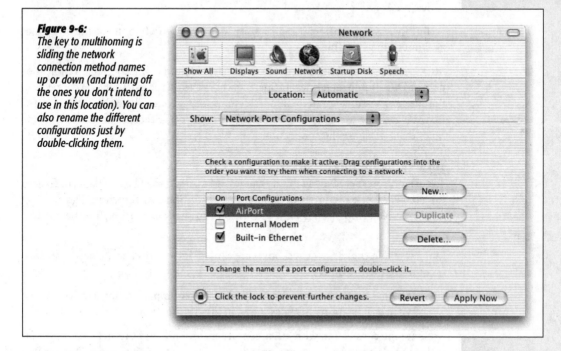

Figure 9-6:
The key to multihoming is sliding the network connection method names up or down (and turning off the ones you don't intend to use in this location). You can also rename the different configurations just by double-clicking them.

Internet Sharing

If you have cable modem or DSL service, you're a very lucky individual. Not only do you benefit from spectacular speed when surfing the Web or processing email, but your connection is on full-time. You never have to wait for some modem to dial (screeching all the way), and wait again for it to disconnect. It's just too bad that only one computer in your household or office can enjoy these luxuries.

Fortunately, it doesn't have to be that way. You can spread the joy of high-speed Internet to every computer on your network in any of these ways:

• **Buy a router.** A *router* is a little box, costing about $80, that connects directly to the cable modem or DSL box. In most cases, it doubles as a hub, providing multiple Internet jacks into which you can plug your Macs and PCs. As a bonus, a router provides excellent security, serving as a firewall to keep out unsolicited visits from Internet hackers. (If you use one, *turn off* Mac OS X's own firewall, as described earlier in this chapter.)

• **Buy an AirPort base station.** Apple's wireless 802.11b (AirPort) base station has a router built in.

• **Use Internet Sharing.** Internet Sharing is the software version of a router, in that it distributes a single Internet signal to every computer on the network. But unlike a router, it's free. You just fire it up on the *one* Mac that's connected directly to the Internet—the *gateway* computer. (Windows Me and XP offer a similar feature.)

But there's a downside: If the gateway Mac is turned off, none of the other machines can get online.

Most people use Internet Sharing to share a broadband connection like a cable modem or DSL. But in fact, Internet Sharing works even if the gateway Mac connects to the Internet via dial-up modem or Bluetooth cell phone. The only requirement is that the gateway Mac *also* has a network connection (Ethernet or AirPort) to the Macs that will share the connection.

Turning on Internet Sharing

To turn on Internet Sharing on the gateway Mac, open the Sharing panel of System Preferences. Click the Internet tab and then click Start, as shown in Figure 9-7 at top. (In most setups, you'll want to turn on Internet Sharing *only* on the gateway Mac.)

Make sure that the correct checkboxes are turned on, to reflect how the gateway Mac is connected to the others:

• **Share your Internet connection with AirPort-equipped computers.** This is the software base-station effect described in the next section.

• **Share the connection with other computers on Built-in Ethernet.** This option is for *wired* networks. In other words, it gives Internet access to other Macs or PCs on the same Ethernet network as the gateway Mac. (That could mean a group of them all connected to the same Ethernet *hub,* or a single other Mac connected to the gateway machine with an Ethernet *crossover cable.*)

Note: Which checkboxes appear here depends on which kinds of Internet connections are turned on in the Network panel of System Preferences. For example, if the gateway Mac doesn't have an AirPort card installed or if AirPort is turned off in the current configuration, the AirPort option doesn't appear.

Now visit each of the other Macs on the same network. Open the Network panel of System Preferences. Using the Show pop-up menu, choose AirPort or Built-in Ethernet—whichever reflects how each Mac is connected to your network. Then, from the Configure pop-up menu, choose Using DHCP. Leave everything else blank, as shown in Figure 9-7. Finally, click Apply Now.

As long as the gateway Mac remains turned on, you should find that both it and your other Macs can get onto the Internet simultaneously, all at high speed. (Even Windows PCs on the same network can get online, as long as you set them up to use DHCP just as you did your "downstream" Macs.)

Note: You may wonder how you can plug in both the cable modem and the local network, if your gateway Mac only has one Ethernet port.

One approach is to install a second Ethernet card. The more economical approach: Connect the cable modem to the *Uplink* or *WAN* jack on your Ethernet hub. Your gateway Mac plugs into the hub as usual.

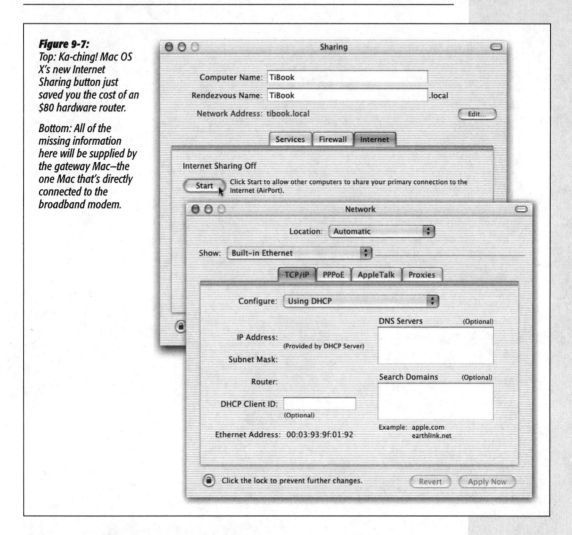

Figure 9-7:
Top: Ka-ching! Mac OS X's new Internet Sharing button just saved you the cost of an $80 hardware router.

Bottom: All of the missing information here will be supplied by the gateway Mac—the one Mac that's directly connected to the broadband modem.

The Software Base Station Effect

If the gateway Mac has an AirPort card, turning on Internet Sharing (and "Share your Internet connection with AirPort-equipped computers") has another profound effect: It creates a *software* base station. The Mac itself is now the transmitter for Internet signals to and from any other wirelessly equipped Macs or PCs within range. You just saved yourself the $200 cost of a physical, flying saucer Apple base station!

As long as the gateway Mac remains turned on, you should find that both it and your PCs or other Macs can get onto the Internet simultaneously—all at high speed.

Mail and Address Book

E very copy of Windows comes with Outlook Express, a basic, free email program; and every copy of Mac OS X comes with Mail, a slightly fancier, free email program. It's a surprisingly complete, refreshingly attractive program, filled with shortcuts and surprises. Together with the high-octane address book program included with Mac OS X 10.2, you may never pine for your Windows setup again.

This chapter assumes that you've already transferred your email, addresses, and email account settings to Mail and the Address Book, as described in Chapter 6.

Checking Your Mail

You get new mail and send mail you've written in any of several ways:

- Click Get Mail on the toolbar.

- Choose Mailbox→Get New Mail. (If you have several accounts, you can check only one of them by choosing from the Mailbox→Get New Mail In Account submenu.)

- Press Shift-⌘-N.

- Wait. Mail comes set to check your email automatically every few minutes. To adjust its timing or turn it off completely, choose Mail→Preferences, then choose a time interval from the "Check for new mail" pop-up menu.

Now Mail contacts the mail servers listed in the account list, retrieving new messages and downloading any files attached to those messages. It also *sends* any outgoing messages and their attachments.

Tip: The Activity window gives you a Stop button, progress bars, and other useful information. Summon it by choosing Window→Show Activity Viewer, or by clicking the little rotating wagon-wheel logo that appears in the upper-right corner of the Mail window when the program is checking for new messages.

The Mailbox Drawer

Mail organizes your email into folders that Apple calls *mailboxes* at one side of the screen, in a sliding pane that looks and acts like a drawer (Figure 10-1). The Mailbox icon on the toolbar opens and closes it. Your mail folders are probably listed under the heading Personal Mailboxes; if you have a Mac.com address (page 123), it gets a heading of its own called .Mac. Under these headings, sometimes hidden by the "flippy triangles," the folders that await are the usual suspects: In, Out, Sent, Drafts, and so on. Only a few may be new to you:

- **Junk** appears automatically when you turn on the Automatic mode for Mail's spam filter, as described later in this chapter.

- **On My Mac** is a "folder" where you can file messages, within subfolders, from a standard ISP account (Earthlink, for example).

POWER USERS' CLINIC

The Mighty Morphing Interface

You don't have to be content with the factory-installed design of the Mail screen. You can control almost every aspect of its look and layout.

For example, you can control the main window's information columns exactly as you would in a Windows email program—make a column narrower or wider by dragging the right edge of its column heading, rearrange the columns by dragging their titles, and so on. You can also control which columns appear using the Hide and Show commands in the View menu. Similarly, you can *sort* your email by clicking these column headings (click a second time to reverse the sorting).

The various panels of the main window are also under your control. For example, you can drag the divider bar—between the list of messages and the Preview pane—to adjust the relative proportions, as shown here. In fact, you can get rid of the Preview pane altogether just by double-clicking the divider line, double-clicking just above the vertical scroll bar, or dragging the divider line's handle all the

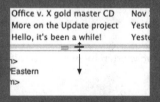

way to the bottom of the screen. (Bring it back by dragging the divider line back up from the bottom.)

You can also control the mailbox's drawer. Drag its outer edge inward or outward to make the drawer wider or narrower, for example. You can even make the drawer disappear or reappear completely by clicking the Mailbox icon on the toolbar.

If you'd like to swap the drawer to the other side of the main window, drag a *message* in the main message list horizontally toward the side where you want the drawer to appear.

Finally, you have full control over the toolbar, which works much like the Finder toolbar. You can rearrange or remove icon buttons (by ⌘-dragging them); add interesting new buttons to the toolbar (choose View→Customize Toolbar); change its display to show *just* text labels or *just* icons—either large or small (by repeatedly ⌘-clicking the white, oval, upper-right toolbar button); or hide the toolbar entirely (by clicking that white button or using the View→Hide Toolbar command).

- **.Mac** lists the subfolders you've created for filing messages from your .Mac account.

- **Trash** works a lot like the Trash on your desktop, in that messages you put there don't actually disappear. They remain in the Trash folder, awaiting rescue on the day you decide that you'd like to retrieve them.

To see what's in one of these folders, click it once. The list of its messages appears in the top half of the main window. When you click a message name, the message itself appears in the bottom half of the main window.

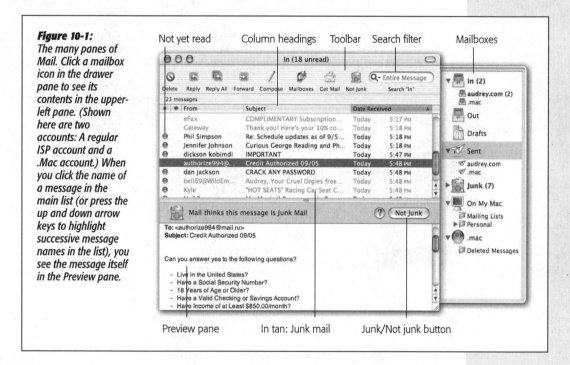

Figure 10-1:
The many panes of Mail. Click a mailbox icon in the drawer pane to see its contents in the upper-left pane. (Shown here are two accounts: A regular ISP account and a .Mac account.) When you click the name of a message in the main list (or press the up and down arrow keys to highlight successive message names in the list), you see the message itself in the Preview pane.

Writing Messages

To send email to a recipient, click the Compose icon on the toolbar. The New Message form, shown in Figure 10-2, opens so you can begin creating the message. If you've ever sent email from a Windows PC, this should all feel familiar. Here are a few notes:

- If you want to send this message to more than one person, separate their addresses in the "To:" box with commas: *bob@earthlink.net, billg@microsoft.com, steve@apple.com.*

- Mail offers auto-complete. If somebody is in your address book (page 239), just type the first couple letters of his name; Mail automatically completes the address. (If the first guess is wrong, just type another letter or two until Mail revises its proposal.)

- As in most dialog boxes, you can jump from blank to blank (from the "To:" field to the "Cc:" field, for example) by pressing the Tab key.

- There are two kinds of email: *plain text* and *formatted* (HTML or, in Mail's case, what Apple calls Rich Text). Plain text messages are faster to send and open, they're universally compatible with the world's email programs, and they're greatly preferred by many veteran computer fans. And even though the message is plain, you can still attach pictures and other files.

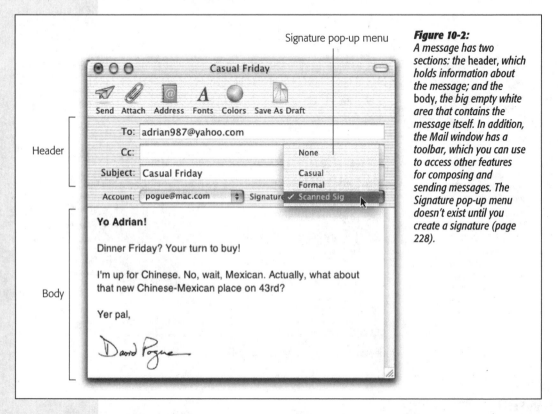

Figure 10-2:
A message has two sections: the header, *which holds information about the message; and the* body, *the big empty white area that contains the message itself. In addition, the Mail window has a toolbar, which you can use to access other features for composing and sending messages. The Signature pop-up menu doesn't exist until you create a signature (page 228).*

By contrast, formatted messages (see Figure 10-3) sometimes open slowly, and in some email programs the formatting doesn't come through at all.

To control which kind of mail you send on a message-by-message basis, choose, from the Format menu, either Make Plain Text or Make Rich Text. To change the factory setting for new outgoing messages, choose Mail→Preferences, click the Composing icon, and choose from the Format pop-up menu.

- As you type your message, Mail checks your spelling, using a dotted underline to mark questionable words (also shown in Figure 10-3). To check for alternative spellings for a suspect word, Control-click the underlined word; a list of suggestions appears in the contextual menu. Click the word you really intended, or choose Learn Spelling to add the word to the Mac OS X dictionary.

(To turn off automatic spell check, choose Edit→Spelling→Check Spelling As You Type so that the checkmark disappears. If you want to spell-check a message all at once, choose Edit→Spelling→Check Spelling [⌘-;] after composing it.)

Figure 10-3:
If you really want to use formatting, click the Fonts icon on the toolbar to open the Font panel described on page 96, or the Colors icon to open the standard Color Picker dialog box. The Format menu (in the menu bar) contains even more controls—paragraph alignment (left, right, or justify), and even Copy and Paste Style commands that let you transfer formatting from one block of text to another.

- When you click Send (or press Shift-⌘-D), your Mac connects to the Internet and sends the message.

If you'd rather have Mail place each message you write in the Outbox folder, quietly collecting them, instead of connecting to the Net the moment you click Send, choose Mailbox→Go Offline. While you're offline, Mail will refrain from trying to connect, which is a great feature when you're working on a laptop at 39,000 feet. (Choose Mailbox→Go Online to reverse the procedure.)

Attaching Files to Messages

Sending little text messages is fine, but it's not much help when you want to send somebody a photograph, a sound, or a Word document. To attach a file to a message you've written, use one of these methods:

- Drag the icons you want to attach directly off the desktop (or out of a folder window) into the New Message window. There your attachments appear with their own hyperlinked icons (Figure 10-3), meaning that your recipient can simply click to open them.

- Click the Attach icon on the New Message toolbar, choose Edit→Attach File, or press Shift-⌘-A. The standard Open File dialog box now appears, so that you can navigate to and select the files you want to include.

Tip: You can choose multiple files simultaneously in this dialog box. Just ⌘-click the individual files you want.

Once you've selected them, click Open (or press Enter). You return to the New Message window, where the attachments' icons appear, ready to ride along when you send the message.

To remove an attachment, drag across its icon to highlight it, and then press the Delete key. You can also drag an attachment icon clear out of the window onto your Dock's Trash, or choose Edit→Remove Attachments.

If you have a high-speed connection like a cable modem, by the way, have pity on your recipient. A big picture or movie file might take you only seconds to send, but tie up your correspondent's modem for hours.

Note: Mail automatically uses the MIME/Base64 encoding scheme for sending attachments. As a result, your Mac- and Windows-using correspondents will generally have no problem opening files you send.

Unfortunately, Mail offers no way to choose a different encoding scheme. Nor does Mail offer automatic compression (using StuffIt, whose .sit files are the Macintosh equivalent of .zip files). If you want to compress your files before sending them, do so using DropStuff, which you can download as part of the shareware StuffIt Lite package from *www.aladdinsys.com*.

Signatures

Signatures are bits of text that get stamped at the bottom of your outgoing email messages. A signature may contain a name, postal address, a pithy quote, or even a scan of your *real* signature.

To create a signature, choose Mail→Preferences, and then click the Signatures icon (Figure 10-4). You can create any number of signatures by clicking the Add Signature button, which opens an editing window in which you can type your new signature and assign a name to it.

Once you've created a signature or two, you can tack one of them onto your outgoing mail either always or on a message-by-message basis.

- **Always append a signature.** On the Signatures preference screen (Figure 10-4, top), use the Select Signature pop-up menu to choose the signature that you'd like to have at the bottom of every email message. (You can always override this choice on a message-by-message basis.)

- **Message by message.** On the Signatures preference screen, turn on "Show signature menu on compose window." From now on, a Signature pop-up menu appears just above the message-body area on every outgoing email note. When you choose from it, Mail pastes the signature at the bottom of the message.

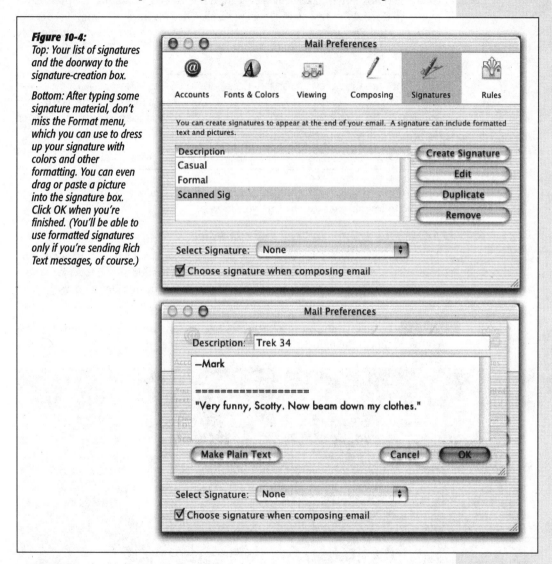

Figure 10-4:
Top: Your list of signatures and the doorway to the signature-creation box.

Bottom: After typing some signature material, don't miss the Format menu, which you can use to dress up your signature with colors and other formatting. You can even drag or paste a picture into the signature box. Click OK when you're finished. (You'll be able to use formatted signatures only if you're sending Rich Text messages, of course.)

Reading Email

Mail puts all the email you get into your Inbox. The statistic in parentheses after the word *Inbox* lets you know how many of its messages you haven't yet read. These new messages are also denoted by colorful, liquidy dots in the main list.

Click the Inbox folder to see a list of received messages. If it's a long list, press Control-Page Up and Control-Page Down to scroll. Click the name of a message once to read it in the Preview pane or double-click a message to open it into a separate window.

Tip: Instead of reading your mail, you might prefer to have Mac OS X read it *to* you, as you sit back in your chair and sip your strawberry daiquiri. Just Control-click inside the Preview pane and choose Speech→Start Speaking from the contextual menu. You'll hear the message read aloud, in the voice you've selected on the Speech pane of System Preferences (Chapter 13).

To stop the insanity, choose Speech→Stop Speaking from the same contextual menu.

Once you've viewed a message, you can respond to it, delete it, print it, file it, and so on. The following pages should get you started.

Adding the Sender to Your Address Book

The Message→Add Sender To Address Book command is a handy timesaving feature. Whenever you choose it, Mail memorizes the email address of the person whose message is on the screen. In fact, you can highlight a huge number of messages and add them all simultaneously using this technique.

Thereafter, you'll be able to write new messages to somebody just by typing the first couple letters of the name.

GEM IN THE ROUGH

All the Little Symbols

The first column of the main email list shows little symbols that let you know at a glance how you've processed certain messages. The most common one is, of course, the gelatinous blue dot (●), which means "new message." (After reading a message, you can mark it once again as an *unread* message by choosing Message→Mark As Unread—or Control-clicking the message's name and choosing Mark As Unread from the contextual menu.)

You might also see these symbols, which represent messages that you've replied to (↩), forwarded (⇥), redirected (⇲), or flagged (⚑).

Incidentally, you may have noticed that, by default, Mail marks a message as having been read the moment you click it. You can change it back to unread, of course, by Control-clicking it—but there's also a more permanent workaround. Just double-click the divider bar above the Preview pane, which hides the Preview pane itself. Once the Preview pane is gone, Mail no longer marks messages "read" just because you clicked one in the list. (You can bring back the Preview pane by double-clicking just above the vertical scroll bar, or by dragging the divider bar back up from the bottom.)

Opening Attachments

Just as you can attach files to a message, people often send files to you in the same way. Sometimes they don't even bother to type a message; you wind up receiving an empty email message with a file attached. Only the presence of the file's icon in the message body tells you that there's something attached.

Tip: Mail doesn't ordinarily indicate the presence of attachments in the main mail list. It can do so, however. Just choose View→Columns→Attachments. A new column appears in the email list—at the far right—where you'll see a paper clip icon and the number of file attachments listed for each message.

Like Outlook Express for Windows, Mail doesn't store downloaded files as normal file icons on your hard drive. They're actually encoded right into the *.mbox* mailbox databases described on page 238. To extract an attached file from this mass of software, you must proceed in one of these ways:

- Drag the attachment icon out of the message window and onto any visible portion of your desktop, as shown in Figure 10-5.

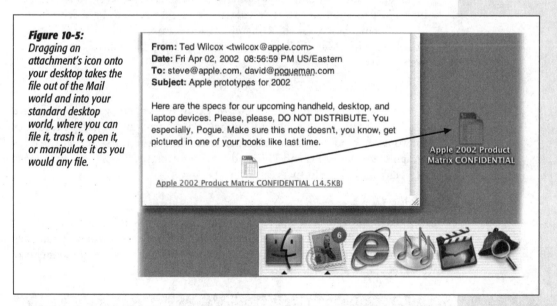

Figure 10-5:
Dragging an attachment's icon onto your desktop takes the file out of the Mail world and into your standard desktop world, where you can file it, trash it, open it, or manipulate it as you would any file.

From: Ted Wilcox <twilcox@apple.com>
Date: Fri Apr 02, 2002 08:56:59 PM US/Eastern
To: steve@apple.com, david@pogueman.com
Subject: Apple prototypes for 2002

Here are the specs for our upcoming handheld, desktop, and laptop devices. Please, please, DO NOT DISTRIBUTE. You especially, Pogue. Make sure this note doesn't, you know, get pictured in one of your books like last time.

Apple 2002 Product Matrix CONFIDENTIAL (14.5KB)

Apple 2002 Product Matrix CONFIDENTIAL

- Double-click the attachment's icon in the message. If you were sent a document (such as a photo, Word file, Excel file, and so on), it now opens in the corresponding program (Preview, Word, Excel, or whatever).

Warning: After the attachment is open, use the *File→Save As* command to save the file into a folder of your choice. Otherwise, any changes you make won't be visible in the file except when you open it from within Mail.

When attachments don't open

Several factors may be at work if you're unable to open a file attachment. For start-ers, your correspondent's email program may have *compressed* or *encoded* the file to make it take less time to send. If you're having trouble getting a file to open, there-fore, your first step should be to drag the attachment's icon onto that of StuffIt Expander, which is in your Applications→Utilities folder. This little program can gracefully re-expand just about any geeky Internet file. (Real Mac OS X masters simplify their lives by parking Expander on the Dock for easy drag-and-drop access.)

If the file still won't open, then you may be dealing with a Windows file that requires a little more effort to open. For example:

- **.exe.** These files, of course, are Windows programs. Without the aid of Virtual PC (page 179), your Mac can't run Windows programs, just as Windows computers can't run Macintosh programs.

- **.html.** A file whose name ends in .html or .htm is a Web page. In the beginning, Web pages hung out only on the Internet. These days, however, you're increas-ingly likely to find that you've downloaded one to your Mac's hard drive (it may be a software manual for some shareware, for example). You can open it just by double-clicking; Mac OS X comes set to open all .htm and .html files into your Web browser.

- **.vcf.** A "business-card" file; see page 146.

If you were sent a file with a three-letter code not listed here, you may well have yourself a file that can be opened only by a Windows program. You might consider asking your correspondent to resend it in one of the more universal formats, such as the graphics formats JPEG and TIFF, and the text formats RTF, TXT, and PDF. (Mac OS X opens all of these formats easily.)

Replying to a Message

To answer a message, click the Reply button on the message toolbar (or choose Message→Reply To Sender, or just press ⌘-R). If the message was originally ad-dressed to multiple recipients, you can send your reply to everyone simultaneously by clicking the Reply to All button instead.

FREQUENTLY ASKED QUESTION

The Resend Command

Hey, what happened to the Resend command? What if I want to resend a message, or send it to somebody new after I've already sent it once?

No problem. Just Option-double-click the message in your Sent mailbox. Mail dutifully opens up a brand-new dupli-cate, ready for you to edit, readdress if you like, and then send again.

(The prescribed Apple route is to highlight the message and then choose File→Open As New Message, but that's a lot more trouble.)

A new message window opens, already addressed. As a courtesy to your correspondent, Mail places the original message at the bottom of the window, denoted by brackets or a vertical bar, as shown in Figure 10-6.

Tip: If you highlight some text before clicking Reply, Mail pastes only that portion of the original message into your reply. That's a great convenience to your correspondent, who now knows exactly which part of the message you're responding to.

At this point, you can add or delete recipients, edit the Subject line or the original message, attach a file, and so on.

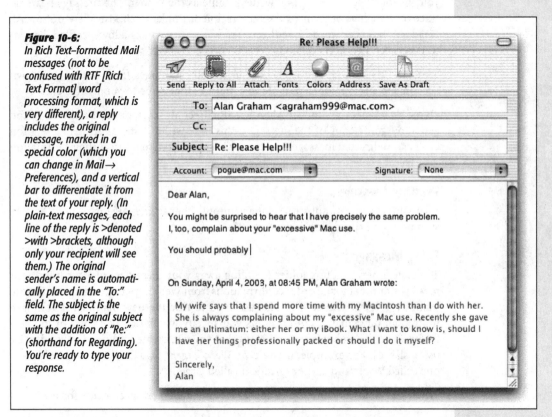

Figure 10-6:
In Rich Text–formatted Mail messages (not to be confused with RTF [Rich Text Format] word processing format, which is very different), a reply includes the original message, marked in a special color (which you can change in Mail→ Preferences), and a vertical bar to differentiate it from the text of your reply. (In plain-text messages, each line of the reply is >denoted >with >brackets, although only your recipient will see them.) The original sender's name is automatically placed in the "To:" field. The subject is the same as the original subject with the addition of "Re:" (shorthand for Regarding). You're ready to type your response.

When you're finished, click Send. (If you click Reply to All in the message window's toolbar, your message goes to everyone who received the original note, *even* if you began the reply process by clicking Reply. Mac OS X, in other words, gives you a second chance to address your reply to everyone.)

Forwarding Messages

To pass on the note to a third person, click the Forward toolbar button (or choose Message→Forward Message, or press Shift-⌘-F). A new message opens, looking a lot like the one that appears when you reply. You may wish to precede the original message with a comment of your own, along the lines of, "Frank: I thought you'd be interested in this joke about Congress."

Finally, address it as you would any outgoing piece of mail.

Redirecting Messages

Here's a handy feature you probably never encountered in Windows: *redirecting* a message.

It's similar to forwarding message, with one extremely useful difference. When you *forward* a message, your recipient sees that it came from you. When you *redirect* it, your recipient sees the *original* writer's name as the sender. The message bears no trace of your involvement (unless the recipient thinks to choose View→Show All Headers). In other words, a redirected message uses you as a low-profile relay station between two other people.

Treasure this feature. You can use it to transfer messages from one of your own accounts to another, or to pass along a message that came to you by mistake.

To redirect a message, choose Message→Redirect Message, or press Shift-⌘-E. You get an outgoing copy of the message—this time without any quoting marks. (You can't *edit* redirected messages, since they're supposed to end up at their destination intact.)

Printing Messages

Sometimes there's no substitute for a printout. Choose File→Print, or press ⌘-P to summon the Print dialog box (page 185).

Filing Messages

To create a new mailbox folder for filing away your messages (one for important messages, another for all order confirmations from Web shopping, and so on), choose Mailbox→New Mailbox. The Mac asks you to title the new mailbox. If you have more than one email account, it lets you specify which one will contain the new folder. (The dialog box also points out that you can create folders *inside* folders by using slashes. For example, if you type *Work/Urgent,* you'll get two new folders—one called Work, and another inside it called Urgent.)

When you click OK, a new icon appears in the mailbox drawer, ready for use.

Tip: The Mailbox menu also contains the commands you need to rename or delete an existing mailbox. You can also drag the mailbox icons up and down in the drawer to place one inside of another.

You can move a message (or group of messages) into a mailbox in any of three ways:

- Drag it out of the list pane onto the mailbox icon (Figure 10-7).

- Highlight one or more messages in the list pane and then choose from the Message→Transfer submenu, which lists all your mailboxes.

- Control-click a message (or one of several that you've highlighted). From the resulting contextual menu, choose Transfer, and then choose the mailbox you want from the submenu.

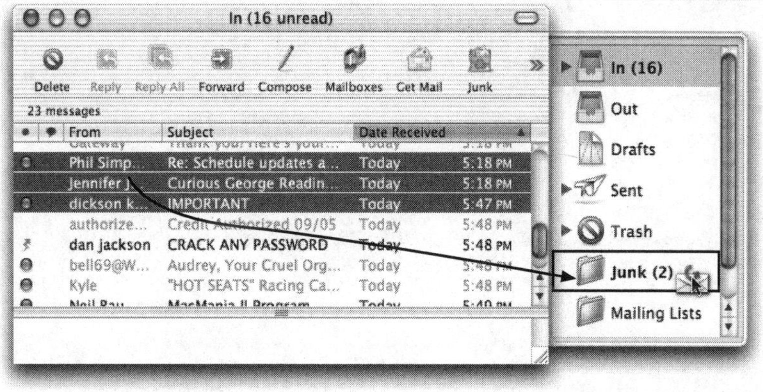

Figure 10-7:
You can use any part of a message's "row" in the list as a handle; the little envelope cursor tells you that Mail knows what's happening. You can also drag messages en masse onto a folder. If you Option-drag a message into a folder, you make a copy, leaving the original message where it was.

Flagging Messages

Sometimes you'll receive email that prompts you to some sort of action, but you may not have the time (or the fortitude) to face the task at the moment. ("Hi there… it's me, your accountant. Would you mind rounding up your expenses for 1993 through 2002 and sending me a list by email?")

That's why Mail lets you *flag* a message, summoning a little flag icon in a new column next to a message's name. These indicators can mean anything you like—they simply call attention to certain messages. You can sort your mail list so that all your flagged messages are listed first (click the flag at the top of the column heading), for example.

To flag a message in this way, select the message (or several messages) and choose Message→Mark As Flagged, or press Option-⌘-G, or Control-click the message's name in the list and choose Mark As Flagged from the contextual menu. (To clear the flags, repeat the procedure, but use the Mark As Unflagged commands instead.)

Finding Messages

See the little text box in the upper-right corner of your main mail window? You can use it to hide all but certain messages, as shown in Figure 10-8.

Tip: You can also set up Mail to show you only certain messages that you've *manually* selected, hiding all others in the list. To do so, highlight the messages you want (Shift-click the first and the last message of a block to make contiguous selections, or ⌘-click to make noncontiguous selections). Then choose View→Focus On Selected Messages. (To see all of them again, choose View→Show All Messages.)

You can also search for certain text within a single message. Choose Edit→Find (or press ⌘-F) to bring up the Find panel shown in Figure 10-9.

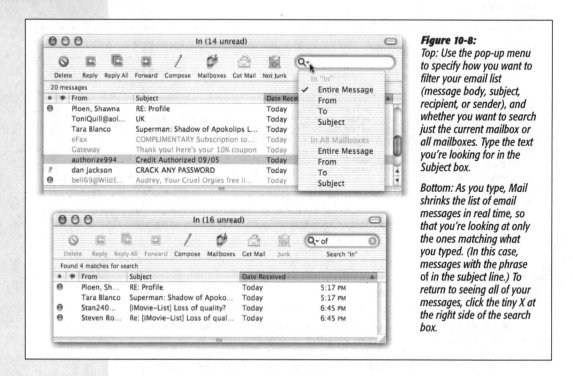

Figure 10-8:
Top: Use the pop-up menu to specify how you want to filter your email list (message body, subject, recipient, or sender), and whether you want to search just the current mailbox or all mailboxes. Type the text you're looking for in the Subject box.

Bottom: As you type, Mail shrinks the list of email messages in real time, so that you're looking at only the ones matching what you typed. (In this case, messages with the phrase of in the subject line.) To return to seeing all of your messages, click the tiny X at the right side of the search box.

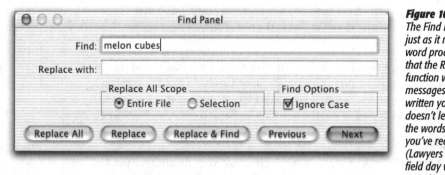

Figure 10-9:
The Find Panel works just as it might in a word processor, except that the Replace function works only on messages that you have written yourself—Mail doesn't let you change the words of mail you've received. (Lawyers would have a field day with that in court.)

Deleting Messages

Sometimes it's junk mail. Sometimes you're just done with it. Either way, it's a snap to delete a selected message, several selected messages, or a message that's currently before you on the screen. Use any of these methods:

- Press the Delete key.

- Click the Delete button on the toolbar.

- Choose Message→Delete.

- Drag a message (or several selected messages) out of the list window and into your Trash mailbox—or even onto the Dock's Trash icon.

Tip: If you delete a message by accident, the Undo command (Edit→Undo or ⌘-Z) restores it.

All of these commands move the messages to the Trash folder. If you like, you can click its icon to view a list of the messages you've deleted. You can even rescue messages by dragging them into any other mailbox (such as right back into the In box).

Method 1: Emptying the Trash folder

Mail doesn't vaporize messages in the Trash folder until you "empty the trash." You can empty it in any of several ways:

- Click a message, or a folder, within the Trash folder list and then click the Delete icon on the toolbar (or press the Delete key). Now it's really gone.

- Choose Mailbox→Erase Deleted Message (⌘-K).

- Control-click the Trash mailbox icon and choose Erase Deleted Messages from the contextual menu.

- Wait. Mail will permanently delete these messages automatically after a week.

  If a week is too long (or not long enough), you can change this interval. Choose Mail→Preferences, double-click the account name, click Special Mailboxes, and set the "Erase deleted messages when" pop-up menu. It offers choices like "Never," "One day old," "One week old," "One month old," and "Quitting Mail" (which makes the program delete your deleted messages every time you quit the program).

Method 2: Deleted mail turns invisible

Mail offers a second—and kind of weird—method of deleting messages that doesn't involve the Trash folder at all. Using this method, pressing the Delete key (or clicking the Delete toolbar button) simply hides the selected message in the list. Hidden messages remain hidden, but don't go away for good until you highlight the mailbox that contain them and then choose Mailbox→Rebuild Mailbox.

If this arrangement sounds useful, choose Mail→Preferences, double-click the account name, click Special Mailboxes, and turn off the checkbox called "Move deleted mail to a separate folder" or "Move deleted messages to the Trash mailbox," depending on what kind of email account you have. From now on, messages you delete simply vanish from the list.

They're not really gone, however. You can bring them back, at least in ghostly form, by choosing View→Show Deleted Messages (or pressing ⌘-L). Figure 10-10 shows the idea.

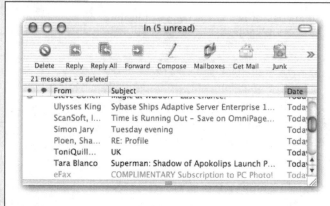

Figure 10-10:
The grayish type indicates deleted messages. (It may be difficult, in this gray scale illustration, to see the difference between colored junk mail and gray deleted mail, but you'll see it on your screen.) You can bring any of them back from the world of the dead by selecting them and then choosing Message→ Undelete (or just pressing Shift-⌘-U), or choosing the same command from the contextual menu. The gray type turns to black, and the message is alive and well once again.

Using this system, in other words, you never truly delete messages; you just hide them. Almost everyone, sooner or later, wishes they could resurrect one deleted message or another—maybe months later, maybe years later. Using the hidden-deleted-message system, your old messages are always around for reference.

When you do want to purge these messages for good, you can always return to the Special Mailboxes dialog box and turn the "Move deleted mail to a separate folder" checkbox back on.

TROUBLESHOOTING MOMENT

Secrets of the Mbox Files

As noted earlier in this chapter, Mail keeps your messages in a series of mailbox database files in your Home→ Library→Mail→Mailboxes folder, inside folders named for your accounts. (The files within—Outbox, Sent Messages, and so on—are *packages*, as described on page 107. To see the actual .mbox files inside of one, Control-click its icon and choose Show Package Contents.)

Knowing this permits you to perform a number of interesting tricks. First of all, now you know what files to back up for safekeeping.

Second, you now have yourself a beautiful monthly archiving system. Each month, create a new mailbox folder in Mail, named for a certain month ("June2002.mbox," for example). Drag into it all the mail you want to archive, and then back up just that mailbox file from your hard drive— instant archiving system! (If you ever want to work with these messages again, just drag that. mbox file back into your Home→Library→Mail folder before opening Mail.)

Third, now you know which files to copy to your laptop to maintain email continuity when you travel.

The Spam Filter

You'll see the effects of Mail's junk-message filter the first time you check your messages: A certain swath of message titles appears in tan lettering. These are the messages that Mail considers junk.

During your first couple of weeks with Mail, your job is to supervise Mail's coloring job. That is, if you get spam that Mail misses, click the message and then click the Junk button at the top of its window (identified in Figure 10-1), or the Junk icon on the toolbar. On the other hand, if Mail flags legitimate mail as spam, swat it gently on the nose and click the Not Junk button. Over time, Mail should get better and better at filtering your mail.

The only trouble with this so-called Training mode is that you're still left with the task of trashing the spam yourself. But once Mail has perfected its filtering skills to your satisfaction, choose Mail→Junk Mail→Automatic. From now on, Mail automatically files what it deems junk into a Junk mail box, where it's much easier to scan and delete the messages en masse.

Tip: Don't miss the Message→Bounce to Sender command. This juicy Mail bonus sends a junk message back to the sender, coded as though it had reached a nonworking email address. Not only are the spammers inconvenienced, but they may take your name off their list.

Address Book

Address Book is Mac OS X's little-black-book program—an electronic Rolodex where you can conveniently stash the names, job titles, addresses, phone numbers, email addresses, and Internet chat screen names of all the people in your life (Figure 10-11). Of course, Address Book can hold other contact information too, such as birthdays and anniversaries, or any other scraps and tidbits of personal data you'd like to keep at your fingertips.

Once you make Address Book the central repository of all your personal contact information, you can search for and access this information in a number of convenient ways:

• You can launch Address Book and search for any contact information by typing just a few letters in the Search box.

• Address Book works seamlessly with Mac OS X's Mail program to fill in email addresses for you when you're composing and addressing messages.

• When you use iChat to exchange instant messages with people whose identities are stored in Address Book, the pictures you've assigned them in Address Book automatically appear in chat windows.

• If you have a Bluetooth cell phone, Address Book can exchange information with the phone and even dial it for you. Using the same wireless connection, you can also exchange contact info between Address Book and some Palm-compatible handhelds.

- If you're a .Mac member (page 123), your Mac can even *synchronize* your address book with the one on another machine, using the Internet as an intermediary, so that (for example) your home and work machines always have the same, updated Rolodex.

You can find the program in your Applications folder, or you can open it from within Mail by choosing Window→Address Book.

Tip: See Chapter 6 for details on importing addresses from other programs into Address Book.

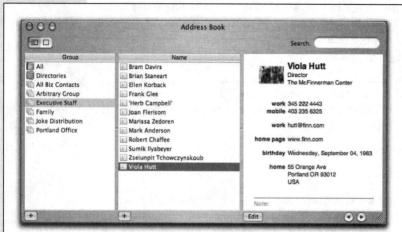

Figure 10-11:
The big question: Why isn't this program named iContact? With its three-paned view, soft rounded buttons and brushed-aluminum style windows, it certainly looks like a close cousin of iPhoto and iTunes.

Creating Address Cards

To add a new person to your collection of contacts, choose File→New Card (or press ⌘-N), then type in the contact information, pressing the Tab key to move from field to field. If one of your contacts happens to have three office phone extensions, a pager number, two home phone lines, a cell phone and a couple of fax machines, no problem; click the little round + buttons when editing a card to add more phone, email, chat name, and address fields.

Each card also contains a free-form Notes field at the bottom, where you can type any other random crumbs of information you'd like to store about the person (a spouse's name, embarrassing nicknames, favorite Chinese restaurant, and so on).

Editing an address

When you create a new address card, you're automatically in Edit mode, which means you can add and remove fields and change the information on the card. As soon as you perform a search or select another address card, however, Address Book flips into Browse Mode—where you can view and copy contact information, but you can't change it. To return to Edit mode, choose Edit→Edit Card, or click the Edit button at the bottom of the Address Book window. You can flip back and forth between Edit and Browse modes by pressing ⌘-L.

Adding Pictures

You can dress up each Address Book entry not only with textual information, but also with a photo. Whenever you're editing somebody's address book card, just drag a digital photo—preferably 64 pixels square—into the "picture well" just to the left of the person's name. Or click the picture well and browse to the picture that you want to use via a standard Open dialog box.

Note: The pictures you add to Address Cards have to be in JPEG, GIF, TIFF, PNG, or PDF format.

You don't necessarily need an actual photo, of course. You can add any graphic that you want to represent someone, even if it's a Bart Simpson face or skull and crossbones.

From now on, if you receive an email from that person, the photo shows up right in the email message. (Well, *usually;* this feature has a reputation for flakiness.) And in iChat (page 250), the photo appears next to each utterance of that person.

Setting Up Groups

A *group* is collection of related address cards, saved under a single descriptive name. When addressing an outgoing message using Mail, you can type this group name instead of having to painstakingly fill in the addresses of everybody who's supposed to get, say, your newsletter.

To make a group, click the + button at the bottom of the Group column in the Address Book window, or choose File→New Group, or press ⌘-Shift-N. Name the newly spawned group icon that appears in the Group column and then populate it with address cards by dragging entries from the Names list into the Group. Clicking on a group name automatically locates and displays in the Names column all the names that are a part of that group—and hides any that aren't.

Tip: To turn a set of address cards into a group very quickly, select multiple entries from the Names column—by either Shift-clicking the names (to make contiguous selections) or ⌘-clicking (for noncontiguous selections)—then choose File→New Group From Selection. You end up with a new group containing all the selected names.

Removing someone from a group

To take someone out of a group, first click the group name in the Group column, then click the person's name in the Name column and press the Delete key.

Note: Be careful with that Delete key! Deleting a name when a group is selected in the Groups column simply removes the entry from the group list. But pressing Delete when All is selected in the Group column actually *removes* the record from the Address Book completely. You have one chance to get it back: Use the Edit→Undo Delete command (⌘-Z) immediately.

Finding an Address

Search for an Address Book entry by simply typing a few letters of a name, address, or any other snippet of contact information into the capsule-shaped Search box on the toolbar (see Figure 10-12).

Tip: No need to click in the search field to start doing a search; just press ⌘-F to jump directly to the search field and start typing.

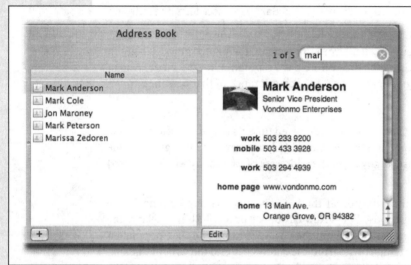

Figure 10-12:
With each letter you type, Address Book filters through all your entries and displays the number of matching address cards just to the left of the search field. The matching records themselves appear in the Name column, with the first of the matching card entries displayed in the main window.

Once you've found the card you're looking for, Address Book lets you perform some interesting stunts. If you click the label of a phone number, for example, you see the Large Type option. Address Book displays the phone number in an absurdly gigantic font that fills the entire width of your screen, making it all-but-impossible to misread the number as you reach for the phone and start dialing. You can also click the label of an email address to create a preaddressed email message, or click a home page label to launch your Web browser and go to a contact's site. Clicking on an address label gives you the option of getting a map of the address via your Web browser.

You can also simply copy and paste address card info, drag it into another program, or convert it into a Sticky Note, as shown in Figure 10-13 (bottom).

Address Book and Bluetooth

Address Book can do far more than just store, retrieve, and display phone numbers. It can actually *dial* them using your cell phone, thanks to the Bluetooth wireless technology.

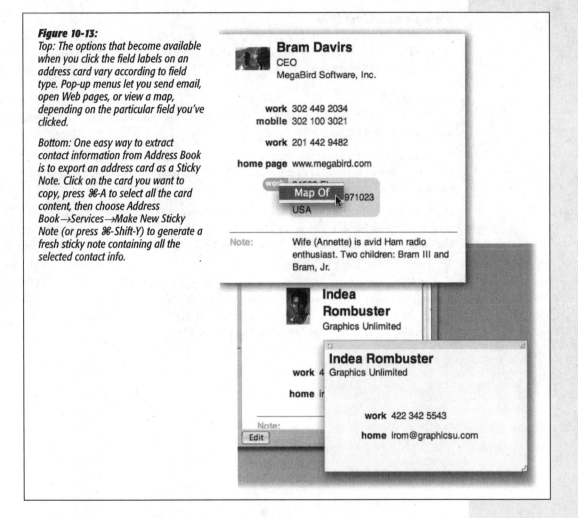

Figure 10-13:
Top: The options that become available when you click the field labels on an address card vary according to field type. Pop-up menus let you send email, open Web pages, or view a map, depending on the particular field you've clicked.

Bottom: One easy way to extract contact information from Address Book is to export an address card as a Sticky Note. Click on the card you want to copy, press ⌘-A to select all the card content, then choose Address Book→Services→Make New Sticky Note (or press ⌘-Shift-Y) to generate a fresh sticky note containing all the selected contact info.

Getting Bluetooth-enabled

To make Address Book talk to the outside world in this way, you have to *pair* it with a Bluetooth-enabled cell phone. (And your Mac, of course, must have a Bluetooth adapter—a built-in option for many models, or an external $50 module for any USB Mac.) Once you've plugged in and turned on all the hardware, your cell phone and Mac have to "find" each other on the wireless network—a task managed by the Bluetooth pane of System Preferences.

Once you've got your computer and phone connected, launch Address Book; you'll see a Bluetooth logo in the Address Book window, letting you know that your phone and computer "see" each other and that you can now make calls and send cell phone messages from your computer.

Dialing with Address Book

To make a phone call, click any phone number field label on an address card and choose Dial from the pop-up menu. Then pick up your cell phone and wait for the person you're calling to answer.

Receiving calls

Once your cell phone and Mac have met, Address Book can notify you of *incoming* calls, too. It's free Caller ID!

When a call comes in, a window opens, showing the caller's number in jumbo type (assuming Address Book is open, that is). If it's somebody in your Address Book, you even see the caller's name.

If you click Answer and then pick up your cell phone, you can begin your conversation. If you click Send to Voicemail instead, your phone stops ringing and you dump the caller into your cell service's answer machine, just as though you'd pressed the Voicemail button on the phone.

Sometimes, you may prefer to send the caller to voice mail *and* create a new SMS message to reply; in that case, click Send SMS Reply. This way, you shut up the ringing phone while your spouse is sleeping, but still manage to type out a reply (like "It's 3:35 AM, for God's sake! What are you doing?!").

Web and Chat Programs

A pple is unabashedly intrigued by the possibilities of the Internet. With each new release of Mac OS X, more clever tendrils reach out from the Mac to the world's biggest network. If you're new to the Mac, or if you've been away for some time, three of these special Internet programs may come as something of a surprise: Sherlock 3, a sort of built-in super-specialized Web bloodhound; iChat, an America Online–compatible instant messenger program; and Safari, a Web browser that puts Internet Explorer's speed to shame.

This chapter tackles this motley crew, plus Internet Explorer for the Macintosh, one by one.

Sherlock 3

Sherlock is like a Web browser that's specifically fine-tuned to bring you the most popular kinds of Web info, without the waiting, without the navigation hassle—and without the ads.

The Sherlock *channels* (icons on its toolbar) bring Web information directly to your Sherlock window, formatted for maximum impact: graphs when you search for stock prices, QuickTime previews when you search for movies, maps when you search for flights, and so on.

Here's how the channels work.

Internet

The Internet channel simply means, "search the Web." You type what you're looking for into the "Topic or Description" box, and then press Enter (or click the green magnifying glass button). After a moment, you see a tidy list of Web sites that match what you looked for, sorted, at the outset, by relevance (see Figure 11-1).

Tip: Sherlock generally sends your search request to *all* of the search services listed at the bottom of the window (About.com, Looksmart.com, Lycos, and so on). But if you click one of these search pages' logos, your Web browser opens up to that search site so that you can confine your quest to it.

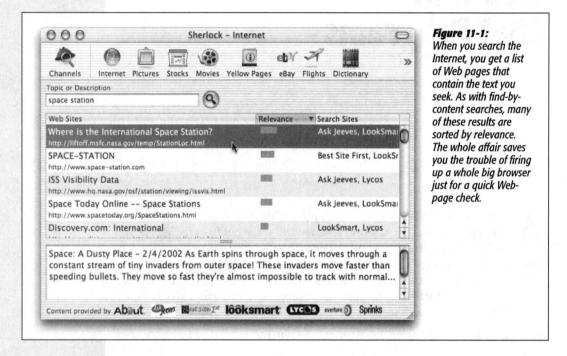

Figure 11-1:
When you search the Internet, you get a list of Web pages that contain the text you seek. As with find-by-content searches, many of these results are sorted by relevance. The whole affair saves you the trouble of firing up a whole big browser just for a quick Web-page check.

Here's what you can do with one of these results:

- **Read the first paragraph.** Click one of the Web pages listed in the search results. As shown in Figure 11-1, Sherlock displays the first paragraph or so of text that appears on that Web page. This blurb is a very useful preview, one that can save you the effort of opening that Web page only to find that it's not what you were looking for.

- **Go to the Web page.** Double-click one of the listings to launch your Web browser and visit the corresponding page.

- **Create an Internet location file.** If you think you might like to visit one of these Web sites later, drag it out of the list and onto your desktop, where it becomes an *Internet location file* (which is a lot like an Internet shortcut in Windows). You can also drag it directly into the Favorites list of Internet Explorer or the Book-marks panel of Safari, where it becomes a bookmark for that browser.

Pictures

Need a photo of something? Type in whatever you're looking for into this channel's "Picture Topic or Description" box—*Santa Claus, October squash, Keanu Reeves*—and then press Enter. In a flash, you see thumbnails of photographs from commercial stock-photo companies all over the Web that match your search. Double-click one to view its Web page in your browser, so that you can download it—and pay for it.

Tip: For noncommercial use, the Image Search tab of Google.com is far more powerful. It finds far more pictures on the topic you're seeking, because it grabs them from *thousands* of everyday Web pages, rather than limiting its search to stock-photo companies. (Yes, you should ask permission from one of the Web sites whose pictures appear before you use it for some other purpose.)

Stocks

This one is amazing. Type the name or stock symbol of a company into the box, and then press Enter. In a moment, you're shown not only the current stock price and accompanying statistics, but also headlines relating to the company and a graph of its stock performance.

Here's some of the fun you can have with this module:

- Double-click the row of stock information to go to the company's Lycos financial-information page in your Web browser. Much more statistical detail appears here.

- Click one of the headlines to view the full article in the area at the bottom of the window. You can select this text and copy it.

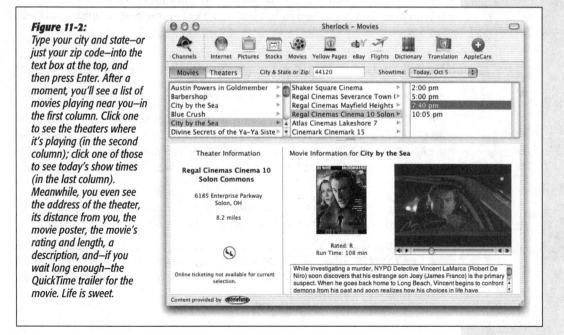

Figure 11-2:
Type your city and state—or just your zip code—into the text box at the top, and then press Enter. After a moment, you'll see a list of movies playing near you—in the first column. Click one to see the theaters where it's playing (in the second column); click one of those to see today's show times (in the last column). Meanwhile, you even see the address of the theater, its distance from you, the movie poster, the movie's rating and length, a description, and—if you wait long enough—the QuickTime trailer for the movie. Life is sweet.

- From the Chart pop-up menu, choose Week, Year, or Intraday (meaning "just today so far") to change the graph.

- Each time you add a stock name, your list of stocks grows. To remove one, just click its row and then press the Delete key.

Movies

For the movie fan, this single feature of Sherlock might be worth the entire price of Mac OS X right there. It makes finding a movie or theater in your neighborhood so easy and efficient, Moviefone.com looks positively antique by comparison. It's an instantaneously updated database of movies and show times for your neighborhood (Figure 11-2).

The only thing stopping this module from becoming an international smash hit is that, in fact, it doesn't work internationally. At the moment, it knows only about movie theaters in the U.S.

Yellow Pages

A Yellow Pages of every business and organization in the entire United States would probably occupy your entire living room, but think of the convenience! It would be so useful to find out where the closest Chinese restaurant, hospital, or all-night drugstore is, especially if you're a laptop-carrying road warrior in a strange city.

Well, now you have one. Into the Business Name box, type whatever it is you're looking for, exactly as though it's a heading in the Yellow Pages business directory. You could type *drug store, cleaning service, health club, tailor, library,* or whatever. When you press Enter, Sherlock not only shows you a list of businesses and organizations that meet your criteria, but it also shows you the phone number, address, and even a map.

Tip: Sherlock will find you a list of local *drug stores,* but it doesn't know anything about *drugstores.* The point is to try a couple of different search terms until you find some "hits."

Sherlock is even happy to provide you with *driving directions* to the selected business—but first you have to tell it where you live. Choose Sherlock→Preferences. On the Locations tab, click Home. Type your address information into the appropriate boxes, then quit and reopen Sherlock. From now on, you'll get turn-by-turn driving directions.

By clicking Add, you can even insert additional locations, so that as you travel, telling Sherlock where you are is only a couple of clicks away.

Tip: If you choose File→Print, Sherlock does the right thing. It creates a beautifully formatted page that identifies the currently highlighted business, its address and phone number, driving directions, and the map—all ready to print and take with you.

---

eBay

This one is for you, auction freaks. Into the Item Title box, type whatever it is you're looking for—*ceramic angel, Babe Ruth baseball card, PowerBook G4,* or whatever. When you press Enter, Sherlock displays a list of all matching items from the eBay Web site currently on auction, complete with description, number of bids, remaining time for the auction, and more. Use the pop-up menus on this screen to further narrow the listing, by specifying price ranges, categories, geographical regions, and so on.

Using the pop-up menu to the right of the "priced between" boxes, you can specify that the items appear listed by price, by time remaining in the auction, and so on. Or you can click the column headings (Price, Bids, Ins, or Title).

Flights

The Flights module is actually two modules in one.

• **Flight Finder.** If you're planning a trip, Sherlock can show you a list of flights that match your itinerary. Just type the arrival and departure cities into the appropriate boxes—or use the pop-up menus provided—and then press Enter.

In this mode, Sherlock is not, by any means, a comprehensive travel Web site like Expedia, Orbitz, or Travelocity. For example, it primarily shows you direct flights only, and just those in the next 24 hours or so. On the other hand, this is the tool to use when a friend or relative is flying in, and you're unsure of the flight number or airline.

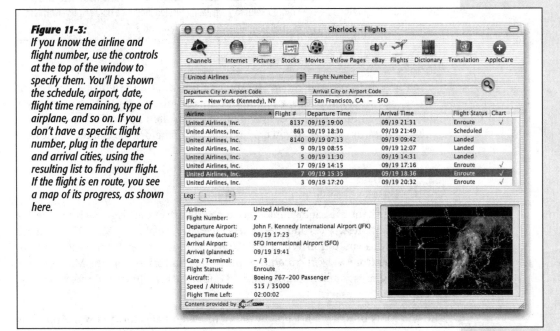

Figure 11-3:
If you know the airline and flight number, use the controls at the top of the window to specify them. You'll be shown the schedule, airport, date, flight time remaining, type of airplane, and so on. If you don't have a specific flight number, plug in the departure and arrival cities, using the resulting list to find your flight. If the flight is en route, you see a map of its progress, as shown here.

- **Flight Tracker.** If you already know a flight number, Sherlock can tell you whether or not it's going to be on time, which airport terminal to go to, and even where, on the map, the flight is at the moment (Figure 11-3).

Dictionary

You have a powerful electronic dictionary built right into your operating system. Just type a word into the Word to Define box and then press Enter.

In seconds, you see what looks like a photocopy of the relevant page from the *American Heritage Dictionary*, complete with phonetic spelling, syllabication, every conceivable word-form variant of the word, and (at the lower half of the window) even synonyms, if there are any.

Translation

This module translates your utterances—or those of the natives—to and from about seventeen languages. Type the sentence or paragraph into the Original Text box, choose the language direction you want from the central pop-up menu, and then press Enter. In a flash, the bottom of the window shows the translation.

Of course, these translations are performed by automated software robots on the Web. As a result, they're not nearly as accurate as what you'd get from a paid professional. On the other hand, when you're standing in the middle of a strange city and you don't know the language—and you desperately need to express yourself—what Sherlock provides may just be good enough.

Tip: You may find this module even more useful for translating foreign language paragraphs—from email or Web pages, for example—into your *own* language so that you can read it.

AppleCare

This module gives you a direct line to Apple's Knowledge Base, a huge collection of answers, troubleshooting tips, and feature explanations for every Mac model ever made. It's based on the same technical library consulted by Apple's tech-support representatives, by the way, so you may as well check it before you call the Apple help line.

iChat

If you're an instant-messaging junkie, good news: Both of the biggies, AIM (America Online Instant Messenger) and MSN Messenger are available for Mac OS X. You use them exactly as you did in Windows. (Download the former from *www.aim.com*, and the latter from *www.microsoft.com/mac*. Once you start using the Mac versions of these programs, you'll find that your old buddy lists are intact and ready to use—no importing necessary.)

AIM and MSN Messenger are not, however, the only chat games in town. Apple has created its own take on instant messaging—something called iChat.

Of course, Apple would be nuts to create a third, mutually incompatible network standard (at the moment, AIM and MSN members can't chat with each other). Fortunately, it wasn't quite that crazy: iChat is AIM-compatible, so you can type back and forth with any of AIM's 150 million members. But iChat's visual design is pure Apple, complete with comic strip–style word balloons and a candy-coated interface.

If you've used any chat program before, you'll find that iChat has some interesting quirks and perks.

Two Chat Networks

iChat lets you reach out to fellow chat partners on two different networks:

- **The Internet.** If you've signed up for a free .Mac account or a free AOL Instant Messenger account, you can chat with anyone in the 150-million-member AOL Instant Messenger network.

- **Your own local network.** Thanks to an automatic network-recognition system called Rendezvous, you can communicate with other Macs on your office network without signing up for anything at all—and without even being connected to the Internet. This is a terrific feature when you're sitting around a conference table, idly chatting with colleagues using your wireless laptop (and the boss thinks you're taking notes).

These two kinds of chats operate in parallel. Each network (AIM and Rendezvous) has its own separate Buddy List window, as described below, and its own chat window. The File menu offers separate commands for connecting to each network ("Log In to AIM" and "Log In to Rendezvous").

Otherwise, however, chatting works identically on both networks. Keep that in mind as you read the following pages.

Signing Up

When you first launch iChat, you see the "Welcome To iChat" window (Figure 11-4). To use iChat via the Internet, you need an *account*. Fortunately, these accounts are free, and there are a couple different ways to acquire one.

If you're already a member of Apple's .Mac service (Chapter 9), your .Mac user name and password appear here automatically. If not, you can access iChat in either of two ways: via a *free* .Mac account or with a free AIM account.

A free .Mac account

Although Apple charges $100 for an annual .Mac subscription, you can get an iChat-only account for free. The trick is to sign up for a "trial" subscription to .Mac. (Click the "Sign up for .Mac" button in the Welcome To iChat window. Your Web browser takes you to Apple's .Mac Web site, where you can sign up for the trial account. This doesn't involve providing a credit card number.) Enter the account name and password you've assigned yourself in the Welcome To iChat window and click OK. (When your trial period ends, you'll lose access to all of the other stuff that .Mac provides, but you'll get to keep your iChat name.)

Note: The one drawback to using a .Mac account on iChat is that people who use very old versions of AOL-compatible instant-messaging programs may have trouble "seeing" you on the network. (Suggest to such people that they upgrade to the latest version of their free instant-messaging software.)

Also, note that if your .Mac name is *missingmanualguy,* you'll actually appear to everyone else as *missingmanualguy@mac.com.* The software tacks on the "@mac.com" suffix automatically, which adds a certain unwieldiness to your "handle."

Figure 11-4:
Nobody can use iChat without an account name and password. It can be your .Mac user name, AOL screen name, or any screen name that's a part of the big AOL/Netscape online conglomeration.

An AIM account

You don't have to have a .Mac name to use iChat; you can use an AOL Instant Messenger (AIM) name instead.

From the Account Type pop-up menu on the Welcome to iChat screen, choose AIM Account. From here, choose the category that fits you:

- **You're a paying AOL member.** You're now all set. Just enter your AOL screen name and password, and click OK.

- **You've used AOL Instant Messenger (AIM) before.** You can use your AIM screen name and password here.

- **You've never used AOL or AIM.** You may still have a valid chat name if you've ever created a screen name at Netscape.com or one of the Time Warner Web sites (*People, Time,* and *Sports Illustrated* magazines, plus CNN.com), all of which are owned by AOL.

- **None of the above.** If you've racked your brain and can't come up with an AOL account name and password, don't worry—you can get one for free. Open your Web browser and go to *my.screenname.aol.com.* Click "Get a Screen Name" to make up an AOL screen name. (You'll have to be creative to come up with a unique name; consider mixing numbers and letters. Remember that 150 million people before you have already claimed the obvious names.)

Once you've signed up, you can enter your new name and password in the Welcome to iChat screen. You're almost ready to go!

When you click OK after entering your screen name, a dialog box asks, "Do you want to turn on Rendezvous messaging?" As noted above, that refers to chats with other people in your building, on your network. Your answer here doesn't really matter; if you decline, you can always choose iChat→Log Into Rendezvous later.

Tip: If you turn on "Enable local network messaging" in the iChat→Preferences dialog box, Rendezvous will always turn on when you use iChat.

The Buddy List

Once you've entered your account information, you're technically ready to start chatting. But you can't chat by yourself. You need a chatting companion, or what's sweetly called a *buddy* in instant-messaging circles. Fortunately, iChat comes complete with a Buddy List window in which you can house the chat "addresses" for all your friends, relatives, and colleagues out there on the Internet.

Note: There's a very similar list for chatting on your office network, by the way: the Rendezvous list. The following discussion deals mainly with the Buddy List window, though, because *you* can't put any names into your Rendezvous list. Anyone who's on the network (and running iChat) appears automatically in the Rendezvous list, courtesy of the Rendezvous technology.

Figure 11-5:
The Buddy List is where you store the names of everyone you know who uses iChat or AOL Instant Messenger. Click the + button to add a new buddy, either by connecting your buddy to the name of someone in your address book or by adding a brand-new buddy from scratch.

Making a list

When you start iChat, your Buddy List automatically appears (Figure 11-5). (If you don't see it, choose Window→Buddy List.)

Adding a buddy to this list entails knowing that person's account name, whether it's on AIM or .Mac. Once you have it, you can either choose Buddies→Add a Buddy (Shift-⌘-A) or click the + button at the bottom-left corner of the Buddy List window.

Out slides a sheet attached to the Buddy List window, offering a window into the Mac OS X Address Book program (Chapter 10). It displays the names of everyone in your Address Book. Just scroll through the list until you find the name you want (or enter the first few letters into the Search box), click the name, and then click Select Buddy.

If your chat companion isn't already in your Address Book, click New Person and proceed as shown in Figure 11-6. If you've got a picture of him on hand, by the way, you can save time by dragging it into the box above the words "Buddy Icon." That way, when you see him online, you'll his mug shot too.

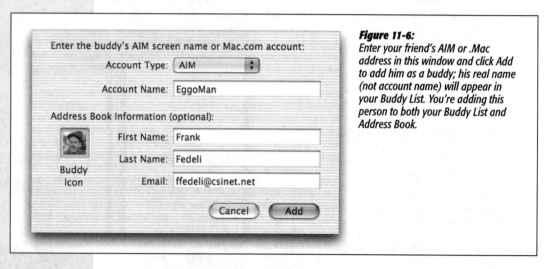

Figure 11-6:
Enter your friend's AIM or .Mac address in this window and click Add to add him as a buddy; his real name (not account name) will appear in your Buddy List. You're adding this person to both your Buddy List and Address Book.

Mysteriously self-appearing names

If you've used AIM before, you may find that you've already got buddies in your list. That's because AIM accounts store their buddy lists on AOL's computers, so that you can keep your buddies even if you switch computers. Likewise, if you add buddies to your AIM account's buddy list using iChat, they'll appear in your Buddy List when you use the AIM chat program itself.

Tip: As you accumulate buddies, your Buddy List may become crowded. But if you click the lower-left icon in your Buddy List window and, from its pop-up menu, turn off "Show Offline Buddies," you'll only see your *currently online* buddies in the Buddy List—a much more meaningful list for the temporarily lonely.

Let the Chat Begin

As with any conversation, somebody has to talk first. In chat circles, that's called *inviting* someone to a chat.

They invite you

To "turn on your pager" so that you'll be notified when someone wants to chat with you, run iChat. Hide its windows, if you like, by pressing ⌘-H.

When someone tries to "page" you for a chat, iChat will come forward automatically and show you the invitation message like the one in Figure 11-7. If the person initiating a chat isn't already in your Buddy List, you'll simply see a note that says "Message from *[name of the person]*."

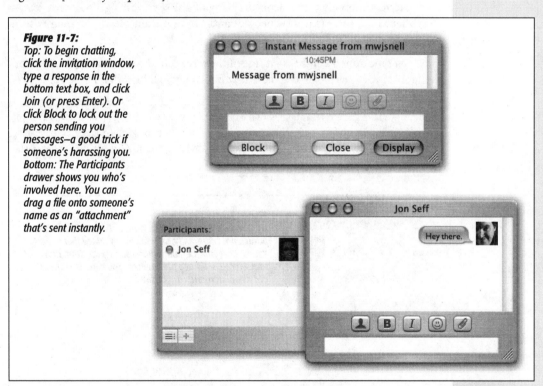

Figure 11-7:
Top: To begin chatting, click the invitation window, type a response in the bottom text box, and click Join (or press Enter). Or click Block to lock out the person sending you messages—a good trick if someone's harassing you. Bottom: The Participants drawer shows you who's involved here. You can drag a file onto someone's name as an "attachment" that's sent instantly.

You invite them

To invite somebody in your Buddy List to chat, just double-click the name, type a quick invite ("You there?"), and press Enter.

Or, to initiate a chat with someone who *isn't* in the Buddy List, choose File→New Chat With Person. Once you type the account name of the person and click OK, iChat will invite that person to chat with you.

The chat begins

A chat works like this: Each time you or your chat partner types something and then presses Enter, the text appears on *both* your screens, as shown in Figure 11-8. iChat displays each typed comment in the chat window next to an icon, which can be any of these three things:

- **A picture you added.** If you've added a picture of your buddy to the Buddy List or Address Book, you see it here next to each utterance by that person.

- **A picture they added.** If the buddy added her *own* picture—to her own copy of iChat or AOL Instant Messenger—it will be transmitted to you, appearing automatically in the chat window. Cool!

- **Generic.** If nobody's done icon-dragging of any sort, you'll get a generic icon—either a blue globe (for .Mac people) or the AOL Instant Messenger man-with-a-word-balloon (for AIM people).

Text *you* type appears at the *right* side of the screen, in the same cartoon-style word balloon. If you haven't yet created a custom icon, you'll look like a blue globe.

Tip: Being a blue globe is really boring. Find a picture of yourself and drag it into the box next to your name in the Buddy List. If you're the shy type who doesn't like to be photographed, find some other image that you like—a TV star, cartoon character, even your cat—and drag *that* in. iChat works much better when someone can connect you with a visual representation.

Figure 11-8:
As you chat, iChat colors the word balloons of various chat participants differently, so you can easily tell them apart. You can set your default balloon shade, text font, and much more in iChat's preferences. You can also turn off all of this balloon-and-icon business.

In-chat fun

Typing back and forth isn't the only thing you can do during a chat. You can also perform any of these productivity stunts:

- **Get Info on someone.** If you click the name of someone in your Buddy list and then choose Buddies→Get Info, you get a little Info window about your buddy, where you can edit her name, address, and picture.

  If you choose Actions from the Show pop-up menu, meanwhile, you can make iChat react when this buddy logs in, logs out, or changes status—for example, by playing a sound or saying, "He's here! He's here!"

- **Send an Instant Message.** Not everything in a chat session has to be "heard" by all participants. If you choose Buddies→Send an Instant Message, you'll get a *private* chat window, where you can whisper something directly to a special someone behind the other chatters' backs.

- **Send Direct Message.** A Direct Message is exactly like an Instant Message except that it's exclusively for sending notes to other people using iChat. It sends a message Mac to Mac, rather than via AOL's central server (which is what happens during an Instant Message session).

- **Send Email.** If someone messages you, "Hey, will you email me directions?" you can do so on the spot by choosing Buddies→Send Email. Your Mail program opens up automatically so that you can send the note along.

- **Send a File.** Via this command, you can quickly send a file to one of your buddies. Click the command, and then pick the file you want to send. iChat sends it directly to your buddy.

Tip: Better yet, just drag the file's icon from the Finder into the box where you normally type. It's also a *great* way to transfer a file that would be too big to send by email. A chat window never gets "full."

Note, though, that this option isn't available in old versions of the AOL Instant Messenger program—only new versions and iChat users. Note, too, that if you don't want *all* participants to get the file, you can drag its icon from the Finder directly onto a buddy's name in the Participants "drawer."

The Chat toolbar

iChat's message windows contain a five-button toolbar, whose buttons provide quick access to some widely disparate but very useful iChat features. Here's a rundown, from left to right:

- **Show or hide participants.** Click this button to hide or show the "drawer" that lists every person participating in your current chat, as shown in Figure 11-7 at bottom. To invite somebody new to the current chat, click the + button at the bottom of the drawer (and choose from the resulting pop-up menu), or drag the person's icon out of the Buddy List window and into this drawer. Either way, iChat sends an invitation to chat.

Tip: You can drag files from the Finder onto individual participants' names in this drawer to send files directly to them.

- **Bold, Italic.** Makes your next typed utterance bold or italic. (You can also press ⌘-B or ⌘-I.)

- **Insert a smiley.** When you choose a face (Undecided, Angry, Frown, and so on), iChat inserts it into the typed response you're about to send.

  If you remember which characters make up an old-fashioned smiley—where :) means a smiling face, for example—you can save time by typing them instead of using the pop-up menu. iChat converts them into graphic smiley icons on the fly.

- **Send a file.** Clicking this icon lets you send a file to *all* the participants of your chat. You can also just drag a file from the Finder into your chat window. (Contrast this with dragging an icon onto an *individual* name in the Participants drawer, which sends a file privately.) Keep in mind that not all versions of AOL Instant Messenger can accept file transfers.

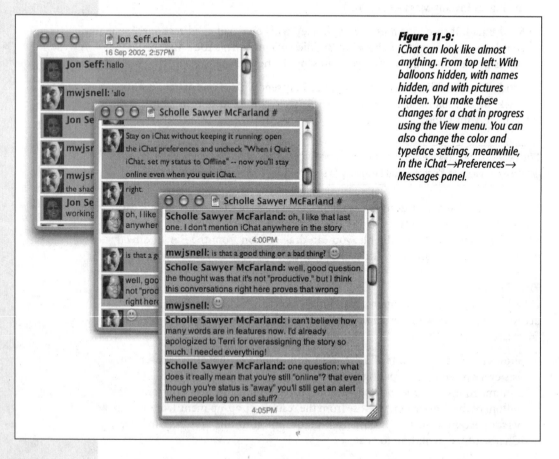

Figure 11-9:
iChat can look like almost anything. From top left: With balloons hidden, with names hidden, and with pictures hidden. You make these changes for a chat in progress using the View menu. You can also change the color and typeface settings, meanwhile, in the iChat→Preferences→ Messages panel.

Tip: When you minimize the iChat message window, its Dock icon displays the icon of the person you're chatting with—a handy reminder that they're still there, awaiting your return.

Popping the Balloons

While a chat is going on, you can change the look of your chat easily using the View menu. For example:

- **Kill the balloons.** Choose View→Show as Text. Now your message window is a series of colored rectangles—iChat user icons on the left side, chat text next to them. Choose View→Show as Balloons to return to the Peanuts look.

- **Kill the icons.** Choose View→Show Names to ditch the icons entirely, replacing them with plain old names.

- **Change the background.** If you tire of iChat's white background, you can change it to any image using View→Set Chat Background. Better yet, find a picture you like and drag it into your chat window—iChat will immediately make that image the background of your chat. To get rid of the background and revert to soothing white, just chose View→Clear Chat Background.

Tip: Ordinarily, messages you type aren't "broadcast" until you actually press Enter. But if you prefer the adrenaline rush of a live, watch-my-letters-appear-as-I-type-them effect, choose iChat→Preferences. Turn on "Send text as I type." (As noted in the dialog box, this feature works only in Rendezvous chats within your building.)

Internet Explorer

Your Mac came with Internet Explorer, the familiar Web browser, preinstalled; just click the lowercase *e* logo on the Dock. It works almost exactly like the Windows version you're probably used to—but here are a few pointers:

- On the Mac, you can leave off the "http://www." and ".com" from the Web site's name when you type it into the Address bar. When you type any common Web site name—*amazon, fedex, nytimes, dilbert, missingmanuals,* whatever—and then press Return or Enter, the Mac fills in the rest of the address automatically.

  And even if the address you want doesn't end with *.com,* you can still save yourself some typing. Just type *nasa.gov* instead of *http://www.nasa.gov,* for example.

- For keyboard-shortcut lovers only: Instead of clicking in the Address bar before typing a Web page's address, press ⌘-L to highlight it. Over your entire career, you could accumulate a savings of literally *minutes* using this timesaver.

- In Internet Explorer for the Mac, you ⌘-click a link on a Web page to open the link in a new, separate Web-browser window. (It's the same thing Shift-click does in Windows.)

- On the Mac, you set your preferences—your preferred Web-page font, starting (home) page, whether or not you want to see graphics—by choosing Internet Explorer→Preferences.

- Your History list (list of recently visited Web sites) is easy to get to on the Mac: It's the Go menu.

The Explorer Bar

The Mac version of Internet Explorer offers a few handy goodies in the skinny bar along the left side of the window. By clicking one of the tabs here, you unveil a secret panel like the one shown in Figure 11-10.

The first three choices are Favorites (same as the Favorites menu), your History list (same as the Go menu), and Search (a search function that's not nearly as good as Google.com).

The next two options, though, are far more interesting. The Scrapbook, for example, is a way to capture snapshots of Web pages, saving them to your own Mac, where you'll still be able to call them up even if the original Web page moves on to the great Internet in the sky. It's an absolutely great feature for preserving order confirmations, online sales receipts, "unsubscribe" instructions, and other online paperwork.

The final tab is called Page Holder; this, too, is extremely handy. Suppose you've just performed a Google search for, say, reviews of a certain digital camera. Open the Page Holder panel and click the Add button at the top. Instantly, your page of search results is committed to the left side of the screen. Figure 11-10 shows how much fun you can have at this point.

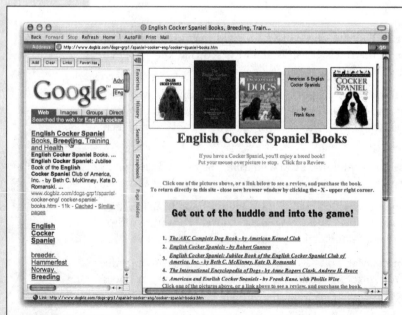

Figure 11-10:
Now you can blithely click away on the links in those search results, watching the main browser window update itself each time. You don't have to click a link, discover it's not what you wanted, hit Back, click the next link, and so on; your search results serve as a fixed table of contents.

Safari

Internet Explorer isn't the only Web browser game in town on the Mac, as it is in Windows. Netscape, Chimera, Opera, iCab, OmniWeb, and other browsers all have their devotees on the Mac.

The most recent development in the browser world, though, is Apple's introduction of its own browser: Safari. If it's not already in your Applications folder, you can download it from *www.apple.com/safari.*

It's certainly worth a try. Safari offers some delicious features, the three most noticeable of which are speed, speed, and speed. It also comes with:

- A built-in search bar that uses Google as its bloodhound.

- An extremely easy-to-understand bookmarks list.

- A delightful neat-freak tendency to clean up after itself when downloading files. You wind up with the fully decompressed file, not a collection of .bin or .gz files strewn across your desktop.

- A command that blocks pop-up windows.

- A button called Snapback, which takes you instantly back to the Web page whose address you last typed (or whose bookmark you last clicked). The point here is that, after burrowing from one link to another in pursuit of some Google result or Amazon listing, you can return to your starting point without having to mash the Back button over and over again.

Otherwise, Safari's operation is a lot like Internet Explorer's, right down to its keyboard shortcuts:

- ⌘-L highlights the Address bar.

- You can omit the "http://www." and ".com" from the Web site's name when you type it.

- Press the Space bar or the Page Down key to scroll down the page; press Shift-Space or the Page UP key to scroll up the page. (Or roll your mouse's scroll wheel, if it has one.)

There are some key differences, though:

- The Bookmarks menu doesn't actually list your bookmarks. To see your bookmarks, click the book icon at the left end of the toolbar. A Bookmark window opens, much like the Organize Favorites window in Windows. To return to browsing, either double-click one of the bookmarks or just click the Back button on the toolbar.

- There's no Home page icon on the toolbar. Whenever you want to return to your Home page (which, by the way, you can specify in the Safari→Preferences dialog box), choose History→Home, or press Shift-⌘-H.

- Safari shows more respect to your screen real estate than just about any browser you can name. It offers a tiny, compact toolbar and no bottom-edge strips at all, so that as much of its window as possible is dedicated to bringing you all the goodness of the Web.

Part Four:
Putting Down Roots

4

Accounts

L ike the Unix under its skin (and also like Windows XP and Windows 2000), Mac OS X is designed from the ground up to be a multiple-user operating system. A Mac OS X machine can be configured so that everyone must *log in*—click or type your name and type in a password—when the computer turns on. And upon doing so, you discover the Macintosh universe just as you left it, including these elements:

• Your icons on the desktop and in the Dock.

• Your desktop picture, screen saver, and language settings.

• Your Dock settings (small or large icons, bottom or side of the screen, and so on).

• Your Web browser bookmarks, Web browser preferred home page, and email account.

• Your personally installed programs and even fonts.

• Your choice of programs that launch automatically at startup.

If you're the only person who uses your Mac, you can safely skip this chapter. You *will* be using one of these accounts, whether you realize it or not—it's just that there won't be any other accounts on your Mac, so it'll appear as though you're using a Mac just as you always have. The Mac will never ask you for the name and password you made up when you installed Mac OS X, because Apple's installer automatically turns on something called *automatic login* (page 274).

Even so, when you're stuck in line at the Department of Motor Vehicles, you may find the concepts presented here worth skimming, as certain elements of this multiple-user operating system may intrude upon your solo activities—and the discussions in this book—from time to time.

Tip: Even if you don't share your Mac with anyone and don't create any other accounts, you might still be tempted to learn about this feature because of its ability to password-protect the entire computer. All you have to do is to turn *off* the automatic login feature described on page 274. Thereafter, your Mac is protected from unauthorized fiddling when you're away from your desk or when your laptop is stolen. (There is a backdoor or two—pre-2003 Macs can be started up from a Mac OS 9 disk, for example—but this step is better than nothing.)

Introducing User Accounts

The first time you turn on a Mac OS X Mac (or install Mac OS X), the screen asks you for a name and password. You may not have realized it at the time, but you were creating the first *user account* on your Macintosh. Since that fateful day, you may have made a number of changes to your desktop—adjusted the Dock settings, set up your folders and desktop the way you like them, added some favorites to your Web browser, and so on—without realizing that you were actually making these changes only to *your account.*

Figure 12-1:
When you set up several accounts, you don't turn on the Mac so much as sign into it. A command in the menu called Log Out also summons this sign-in screen. Click your own name, and type your password, to get past this box and into your own stuff.

You've probably been saving your documents into your own Home folder, which is the cornerstone of your account. This folder, named after you and stashed in the Users folder on your hard drive, stores not only work, but also the preference settings for all the programs you use, special fonts that you've installed, programs you've installed for your own use, and so on.

Now then: If you create an account for a second person, when she turns on the computer and signs in, she'll find the desktop exactly the way it was factory-installed by Apple—blue swirling desktop picture, Dock along the bottom, the default Web browser home page, and so on. She can make the same kinds of changes to the Mac that you've made, but nothing she does will affect your environment the next time you log in. You'll still find the Mac desktop the way you left it: Your desktop picture fills the screen, the Web browser lists your bookmarks, the Dock lists your favorite documents, and so on.

In other words, the multiple-accounts feature has two components: first, a convenience element that hides everyone else's junk; and second, a security element that protects both the Mac's system software and other people's work.

All of this works much the same way it does in Windows 2000 and Windows XP. There are just a few differences, as explained on the following pages.

Setting Up Accounts

If you like the idea of this multiple-accounts business, begin by opening System Preferences. In the System Preferences window, click Accounts.

The screen shown in Figure 12-2 appears, showing you the list of everyone who has an account. If you're new at this, there's probably just one account listed here—yours. This is the account that Mac OS X created when you first installed it.

Administrator Accounts

It's important to understand the phrase you see in the Kind column. On your own personal Mac, it probably says *Admin* next to your name. This, as you could probably guess, stands for Administrator.

Because you're the person who installed Mac OS X to begin with, the Mac assumes that you are its administrator—the technical wizard who's in charge of it. Only an administrator is allowed to:

- Install new programs into the Applications folder.

- Add fonts (to the Library folder) that everybody can use.

- Make changes to certain System Preferences panels (including Network, Date & Time, Energy Saver, Login, and Startup Disk).

- Use the NetInfo Manager and Disk Utility programs.

- Create new folders outside of your Home folder.

• Decide who gets to have accounts on the Mac.

• Open, change, or delete anyone else's files.

The notion of administrators is an important one. For one thing, you'll find certain settings all over Mac OS X that you can change *only* if you're an administrator—including those in the Accounts panel itself (see Figure 12-2). For another thing, whether or not you're an administrator plays an enormous role when you want to network your Mac to other kinds of computers.

As you create accounts for other people who'll use this Mac, you'll be offered the opportunity to make each one an administrator just like you. Needless to say, use discretion. Bestow these powers only upon people as responsible and technically masterful as you.

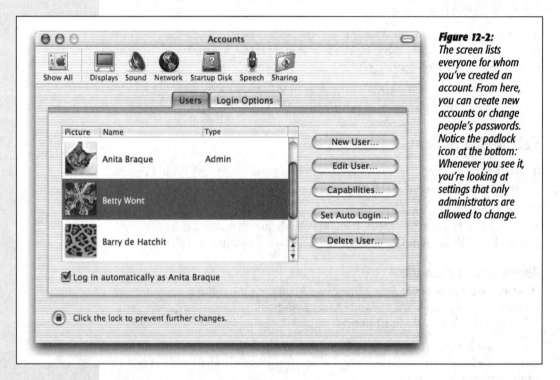

Figure 12-2:
The screen lists everyone for whom you've created an account. From here, you can create new accounts or change people's passwords. Notice the padlock icon at the bottom: Whenever you see it, you're looking at settings that only administrators are allowed to change.

Normal Accounts

Anyone who isn't an administrator will probably just be an ordinary, everyday Normal account holder. In Figure 12-2, that includes anyone whose account *doesn't* say Admin.

These people will have everyday access to their own Home folders and to some of the System Preferences, but most other areas of the Mac will be off-limits. Mac OS X won't even let them create new folders on the main hard drive, except inside their own Home folders (or in the Shared folder described later).

A few of the System Preferences panels contain a padlock icon like the one in Figure 12-2. If you're a Normal account holder, you can't make changes to these settings without the assistance of an administrator. Fortunately, you aren't required to log out so that an administrator can log in and make changes. You can just call the administrator over, click the padlock icon, and let him type in his name and password—if, indeed, he feels comfortable with you making the changes you're about to make.

Adding an Account

To create a new account, click New User. The dialog box shown in Figure 12-3 appears. This is where you fill in certain information about the new account holder.

- **Name.** If it's just the family, this could be Chris or Robin. If it's a corporation or school, you'll probably want to use both first and last names.

- **Short Name.** Particularly if your name is, say, Alexandra Stephanopoulos, you'll quickly discover the value of having a short name—an abbreviation of your actual name. When you sign into your Mac in person, you can use either your long or short name. But when you access this Mac by dialing into it or connecting from across the network (as described in the next chapter), the short variation is all you need.

  As soon as you tab into this field, the Mac proposes a short name for you. You can replace the suggestion with whatever you like, as long as it's fewer than eight characters and all lowercase letters.

- **Password, Verify.** If you click the Password tab of the dialog box, you'll see where you're supposed to type this new user's password (Figure 12-3). In fact, you're supposed to type it twice, to make sure you didn't introduce a typo the first time. The Mac displays only dots as you type, to guard against the possibility that somebody is watching over your shoulder.

Tip: Mac OS X 10.2 doesn't limit your password length. Oddly, though, only the first eight characters *matter*—Mac OS X ignores whatever you type after that. Capitalization does matter, though.

The usual computer book takes this opportunity to stress the importance of a long, complex password—a phrase that isn't in the dictionary, something made up of mixed letters and numbers. This is excellent advice if you create sensitive documents and work in a big corporation.

But if you share the Mac only with a spouse or a few trusted colleagues in a small office, for example, there's no particular urgency to the mission of thwarting the world's hackers with a convoluted password. In fact, you may want to consider setting up *no* password—leaving both password blanks empty. Later, whenever you're asked for your password, just leave the Password box blank. You'll be able to log in that much faster each day.

- **Password Hint.** If you gave yourself a password, you can leave yourself a hint in this box. Later, if you ever forget your password, the Mac will show you this cue to jog your memory (if you've left this option turned on, as described on page 274).

- **Login Picture.** The usual Mac OS X sign-in screen (Figure 12-1) displays each account holder's name, accompanied by a little picture.

  You can choose a little graphic for yourself using any of several methods. If you like the selections that Apple has provided along the bottom of the window, just click one to select it. If there's another graphics file somewhere on the hard drive that you prefer—a digital photo of your own head, for example—you can click the Choose Another button. You'll be shown a list of what's on your hard drive so that you can select it.

Tip: You can also click out of this window, find the graphics file you want (in almost any conceivable graphics format) in whatever window contains it, and drag the graphic itself onto the Login Picture box, as shown in Figure 12-3.

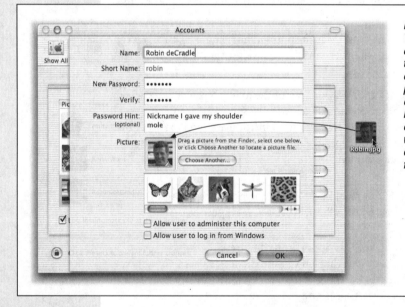

Figure 12-3:
You can drag a graphic out of a Finder window right onto the Login Picture box. This is also where you specify a password for your new user, designate whether or not this lucky individual will be an administrator, and determine whether or not he can connect via a Windows PC from the network.

- **Allow user to administer this computer.** This is the big one: the master switch that turns this ordinary, unsuspecting computer user into an administrator, as described previously.

- **Allow user to log in from Windows.** Here's one of the most important new features in Mac OS X 10.2: the option that lets you connect to your Mac from across a network while seated at a Windows PC (page 116).

When you're finished with the settings, click Save (or press Enter). After a moment, you return to the Users list, where the new person's name joins the names that were already there.

The Capabilities Screen

Once you're back at the list of accounts, you have the opportunity to shield your Mac—or its very young, very fearful, or very mischievous operator—from confusion and harm. This is a great feature to remember when you're setting up accounts for students, young children, or easily intimidated adults.

Clicking the name of any Normal account and then clicking Capabilities reveals a broad array of muzzles you can place over the usual Mac OS X design:

- **Simple Finder.** This bizarre feature strips away most of the menus and icons from the Finder, presenting only an almost frighteningly bare, goof-proof screen. The lucky recipients of this rubber-walls treatment can't move anything, change views, or do much of anything besides single-clicking program icons that you've selected for them, and saving documents into their own Home folders.

- **Limited access.** By tinkering with the checkboxes here, you can declare certain programs off-limits to this account holder, or turn off his ability to remove Dock icons, burn CDs, and so on.

In both cases, you'll be offered the opportunity to specify exactly which programs this person is allowed to use; the rest are off-limits.

Editing Name, Password, and Picture

Administrators have all the fun, but even peon Normal users are permitted to change their passwords and startup pictures. In fact, Mac OS X 10.2 provides two different paths to these controls: one that lets you change your *own* account settings, and another that lets administrators change *anyone's* settings.

- **To change your own account.** Open System Preferences. Click the My Account icon.

- **To change someone else's account.** Be an administrator. Open System Preferences. Click the Accounts icon. Changing the settings is very easy: Just double-click somebody's name in the Users list. (Or, if it's a slow day at work, click the name and then click Edit User.)

Either way, a variation of the dialog box shown in Figure 12-3 appears; this is where you can change whatever settings you like. (Well, *almost* any settings: Only administrators can change an account's name—and even they can't change an account's *short* name once the account has been created.)

Setting Up Your Startup Items

There's one additional System Preferences setting pertaining to accounts, one that the account holders can take care of themselves. Each user can decide which programs or documents open automatically upon login, creating an effect that's much like the Startup program group in Windows (see Figure 12-4). You can even turn on the Hide checkbox for each one, so that the program is running in the background at login time, waiting to be called into service with a quick click, rather than constantly being in your face.

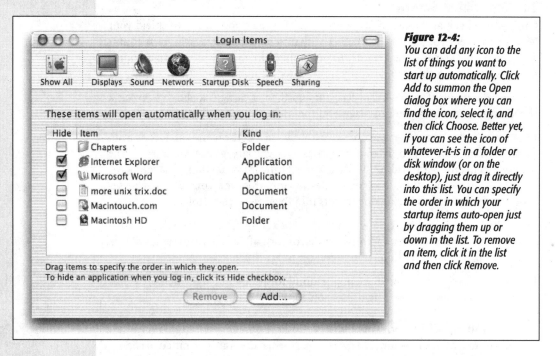

Figure 12-4:
You can add any icon to the list of things you want to start up automatically. Click Add to summon the Open dialog box where you can find the icon, select it, and then click Choose. Better yet, if you can see the icon of whatever-it-is in a folder or disk window (or on the desktop), just drag it directly into this list. You can specify the order in which your startup items auto-open just by dragging them up or down in the list. To remove an item, click it in the list and then click Remove.

Don't feel obligated to limit this list to programs and documents, by the way. You can make startup items out of disks, folders, servers on the network, and other fun icons. Used judiciously, this feature can save you a huge amount of time each morning.

Deleting User Accounts

Hey, it happens: Somebody graduates, somebody gets fired, somebody dumps you. Sooner or later, you may need to delete a user account from your Mac.

Deleting somebody's account doesn't delete all of the corresponding documents, settings, and so on. All of the former account's folders remain on the Mac—but in a tidy digital envelope that doesn't clutter your hard drive and can be reopened in case of emergency.

To delete a user account, click the appropriate name in the Accounts list (Figure 12-2) and then click Delete User. Mac OS X now provides a capsule summary of what's about to happen, as described in the following paragraphs. Click OK, and then read on.

Once you, an administrator, have deleted somebody's account, its name no longer appears in the Accounts list. Yet its files and settings live on—in the Users→Deleted Users folder. Inside is a folder named for the dearly departed, and inside *that* is a disk image file (.dmg) like the ones described on page 105. If you double-click it, you'll find a new, virtual disk icon on your desktop named for the deleted account. You can open folders and root through the stuff in this "disk," just as if it were a living, working Home folder.

If fate ever brings that person back into your life, you can use this disk-image business to reinstate the deleted person's account. Start by creating a brand-new account. Then copy the contents of the folders in the mounted disk image (Documents, Pictures, Desktop, and so on) into the corresponding folders of the new Home folder.

Setting Up the Login/Logout Process

Once you've set up more than one account, the dialog box shown in Figure 12-1 appears whenever you turn on the Mac (or whenever you relinquish your turn at the Mac by choosing →Log Out). But a few extra controls let you, an administrator, set up either more or less security at the Login screen—or, put another way, build in less or more convenience.

Login Options

Open System Preferences, click Accounts, and then click the Login Options tab (see Figure 12-5).

Here are some of the ways you can shape the login experience:

- **Display Login Window as.** If you're especially worried about security, you might turn on "Name and password." Now each person who signs in must *type* his name (into a blank that appears), rather than just clicking his name in a list—a very inconvenient, but secure, arrangement.

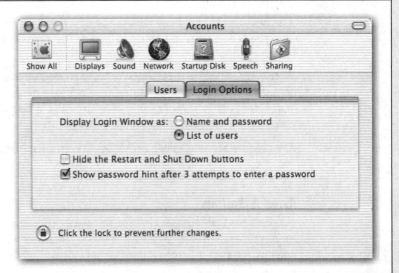

Figure 12-5:
These options make it easier or harder for people to sign in, offering various degrees of security.

- **Hide the Restart and Shut Down buttons.** The dirty little secret of the Mac OS X security system is that it's easy to bypass. Truly devoted evildoers can bypass the standard Login screen in a number of different, fairly technical ways: restart in Mac OS 9 (on pre-2003 models), restart in FireWire Disk Mode, restart at the Unix Terminal, and so on. Suddenly, these no-goodniks have full access to every document on the machine, blowing right past all of the safeguards you've so carefully established.

  One way to thwart them is to turn on this checkbox. Now nobody can restart the Mac, period. That's plenty of protection in most homes, schools, and workplaces; after all, Mac people tend to be *nice* people.

- **Show password hint after 3 attempts to enter a password.** Remember the password hint you created on page 270? If you haven't been at work for a while, and you're fumbling to sign in, unable to remember your password, you'll be glad you left this option turned on. It reveals your hint after three attempts to sign in with the wrong password.

Automatic Login

You can tailor the login process in one final, extremely handy way: by eliminating the need to sign in at all. It's a timesaving, hassle-free arrangement if only one person uses the Mac, or if one person uses it most of the time.

This option awaits on the Users tab (of the Accounts panel of System Preferences). If you click the Set Auto Login button, as shown in Figure 12-2, you're prompted for the name and password of the lucky person who's receiving this express ticket. Click OK.

From now on, the dialog box shown in Figure 12-1 won't appear *at all* at startup time. After turning on the machine, you, the specified account holder, will zoom straight to your desktop.

Of course, only one lucky person can enjoy this streamlined entrance experience. Everybody else must still enter their names and passwords.

Note: Automatic login can be extremely frustrating to the people who *don't* have the magic ticket. If you think about it, they can restart the Mac for hours, trying and trying to sign into their own accounts—but can't, because you, Mr. or Ms. Bigshot, have set up the Mac so that only *your* account signs on automatically.

The solution is to remember that automatic login kicks in only when you *turn on or restart* the Mac. When you choose →Log Out, the usual Login screen appears.

Logout Options

As you'll read later in this chapter, the usual procedure for finishing up a work session is for each person to choose →Log Out. After you confirm your intention to log out, the sign-in screen appears, ready for the next victim.

But sometimes people forget. You might wander off to the bathroom for a minute, run into a colleague there who breathlessly begins describing last night's date and proposes finishing the conversation over pizza. The next thing you know, you've left your Mac unattended but logged in, with all your life's secrets accessible to anyone who walks by your desk.

Fortunately, Mac OS X offers a simple but effective form of protection against this phenomenon: a password-protected screen saver that locks your Mac after a few minutes of inactivity.

In System Preferences, click Screen Effects (described more completely on page 304). Click the Activation tab. Here you'll find a slider that lets you control how much time the Mac waits before password-protecting your screen. Turn on "Use my user account password" to seal the deal. Now, whenever somebody tries to wake up your Mac after the screen saver has appeared, the "Enter your password" dialog box will appear. No password? No access.

Signing In

Once somebody has set up your account, here's what it's like getting into, and out of, a Mac OS X machine. (For the purposes of this discussion, "you" are no longer the administrator—you're one of the students, employees, or family members for whom an account has been set up.)

Identifying Yourself

When you first turn on the Mac—or when the person who last used this computer chooses ⌘→Log Out—the Login screen shown in Figure 12-1 appears. At this point, you restart the Mac, shut it down, or log in by clicking your name in the list (or by typing the first couple letters of your name and then pressing Return or Enter).

Figure 12-6:
If your account was set up with a password, you now encounter the Password box. You can try as many times as you want to type the password in. With each incorrect guess, the entire dialog box shudders violently from side to side, as though shaking its head "No." If you try unsuccessfully three times, your hint appears—if you've set one up.

Your World

Once you're in, the world of the Mac looks just the way you left it (or the way an administrator set it up for you). Mac OS X keeps almost everything in your Mac world separate from anybody else who uses this Mac. A few examples are especially worth noting:

- **Fonts.** You can install your own preferred fonts into your Home folder→ Library→Fonts folder. Only you will be able to see them and use them in your programs.

- **Programs.** Unless you're an administrator, you'll quickly discover that you're not allowed to install any new programs (or indeed, to put anything at all) into the Applications folder. That folder, after all, is a central software repository for everybody who uses the Mac, and all such universally shared folders are off-limits to everyday account holders. (You can drag things out of the Applications folder, but doing so doesn't actually move them—it just copies them.)

  That's not to say that you can't install new programs of your own. You can—but you must put them somewhere in your own Home folder (where you'll be the only person with access to such programs) or in the Shared folder (if you want other people to be able to use them). You may want to create a Programs folder there just for this purpose.

- **Bookmarks.** When you browse the Web, you can freely "bookmark" your favorite Web pages, confident that nobody else who uses your Mac will be able to see where you've been or what you consider your favorite sites.

- **Mail.** Your email collection is yours and yours alone. When other people run the same email program, they'll find *their* email there.

DON'T PANIC

The Case of the Forgotten Password

Help—I forgot my password! And I never told it to anybody, so even the administrator can't help me!

No problem. Your administrator can simply open up System Preferences, click Users, click the name of the person who forgot the password, and then click Edit to reestablish the password.

But you don't understand. I am the administrator! And I'm the only account!

Aha—that's a different story. Insert the Mac OS X CD. Restart the Mac while pressing down the letter C key, which

starts up the Mac from the CD and launches the Mac OS X installer.

On the first installer screen, choose Installer→Reset Password. When the Reset Password screen appears, click the hard drive that contains Mac OS X. From the first pop-up menu, choose the name of your account. Now make up a new password and type it into both boxes. Click Save, close the window, click the installer, and restart.

And next time, be more careful! Write down your password on a Post-it note and affix it to your monitor. (Joke—that's a joke!)

The Shared Folder

If you try to open anybody else's Home folder, you'll see a tiny red "no go here" icon superimposed on almost every folder inside, telling you, "Look, but don't touch." There are exceptions, though. As shown in Figure 12-7, two folders are designed to be distribution points for files your co-workers want you to see: Public and Sites.

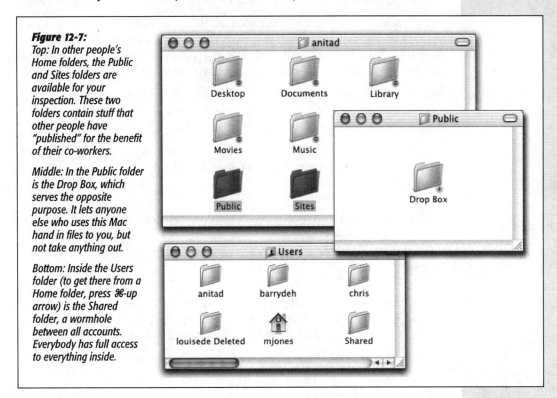

Figure 12-7:
Top: In other people's Home folders, the Public and Sites folders are available for your inspection. These two folders contain stuff that other people have "published" for the benefit of their co-workers.

Middle: In the Public folder is the Drop Box, which serves the opposite purpose. It lets anyone else who uses this Mac hand in files to you, but not take anything out.

Bottom: Inside the Users folder (to get there from a Home folder, press ⌘-up arrow) is the Shared folder, a wormhole between all accounts. Everybody has full access to everything inside.

You, too, have Public and Sites folders in your own Home folder, of course. Here again, anything you put into these folders is available for inspection—although not for changing—by anyone else who uses this Mac.

Sitting in the Users folder is one folder that doesn't correspond to any particular person: Shared. This is the one and only folder that everybody can access, freely inserting and extracting files. It's the common ground among all the account holders. It's Central Park, the farmer's market, and the grocery store bulletin board.

Changing Permissions

A factory-fresh installation of Mac OS X offers one way for you to submit files *to* somebody else (that person's Public folder), one way to accept files *from* other people (your Drop Box folder), and one community folder (the Shared folder).

This arrangement is relatively secure and relatively easy to understand. But maybe you'd like even more security; you'd rather seal off your Public folder so that people can't see what's inside. Or maybe you'd like greater convenience; you'd like to set up some additional drop box folders, or other "public" folders, for your co-workers' use.

The business of changing the permissions, or *access privileges,* for certain folders can be complex and brain-bending, but here's a quick summary of some typical setups:

In each case, you can't make changes unless either (a) you have an Administrator account or (b) it's a folder that you *own* (either it's in your Home folder or you created it). Begin by highlighting the folder in question, choosing File→Get Info, and then expanding the Ownership & Permissions section (see Figure 12-8):

- **Full access by everybody.** If you want to turn one of your folders into one that resembles the Shared folder (full access by anyone with an account), set up its Get Info window like the one shown at left in Figure 12-8.

- **Give, but don't take.** To make another folder work like your Drop Box folder (people can put things in, but can't actually open the folder), set things up as shown at middle in Figure 12-8.

Tip: Remember that people can't put anything into a new Drop Box–type folder if they can't get *to* it. That is, make sure you've turned on "Read" access for whatever folder it's in. (Making a Drop Box folder in your Documents folder, for example, won't work, since nobody is allowed to *open* your Documents folder to begin with.)

- **Look, but don't touch.** You can also turn any of your folders into another Public-type, "bulletin board" folder—that is, people can open or copy files from inside, but they can't put anything in or save any changes they make (Figure 12-8, right).

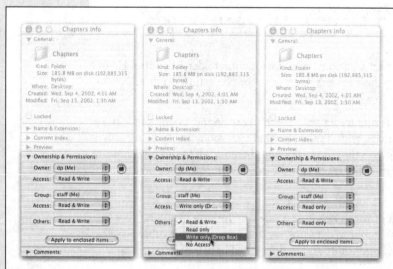

Figure 12-8:
Three typical configurations for folders you've created in your Home folder. Highlight the folder and then choose File→Get Info; open the Ownership & Permissions section. Then set the three pop-up menus as shown for a Shared-type folder (left), a drop-box folder (middle), and the "bulletin board" folder (right). Click the "Apply to enclosed items" button if you want the same settings to apply to all the folders inside this one. Finally, close the Get Info window.

You'll realize the importance of mastering these various access permissions when you get a load of this startling fact: Unless you intervene, everybody else who uses this Mac will be able to peek into everything *in every new folder* you create (unless it's inside a folder that is, itself, off-limits). Technically speaking, every new folder springs into existence with Read-only permissions for Everyone. They're allowed to open or copy anything inside.

The bottom line: As you type the title of a new folder that you suspect might be best kept private (*Salaries 2003* or *My Spicy Dreams Journal,* let's say), remember to use the File→Get Info routine to change the new folder's Everyone and Group settings to None.

(Even so, remember that anyone with an *Administrator* account can blow your intentions to smithereens. Such people can, at any time, override your ownership and permission settings, even making your folders off-limits to *you,* if they so desire. That's what you get for using a Mac that you've allowed somebody else to set up for you. Details on page 267.)

Logging Out

When you're finished using the Mac, choose →Log Out (or press Shift-⌘-Q). A confirmation message appears; if you click Cancel or press Esc, you return to whatever you were doing. If you click Log Out, or press Return, you return to the screen shown in Figure 12-1, and the entire sign-in cycle begins again.

The Root Account

An administrator's account isn't exactly a skeleton key that gives unfettered access to every corner of the Mac. Even an administrator isn't allowed to remove files from the System folder or other files whose removal could hobble the machine.

It turns out that Normal and Administrator aren't the only kinds of accounts. There's one account that wields ultimate power, one person who can do anything to any file anywhere. This person is called the *superuser.*

Unix fans speak of the superuser account—also called the *root* account—in hushed tones, because it offers absolutely unrestricted power. The root account holder can move, delete, rename, or otherwise mangle any file on the machine, no matter what folder it's in. One wrong move—or one Internet hacker who manages to seize the root account—and you've got yourself a $2,500 doorstop. That's why Mac OS X's root account is completely hidden and, in fact, deactivated.

Treat the root account, in other words, as you would one of those "Break glass in case of fire" boxes. If you know what you're doing, and you see no alternative, you might be glad the root account is available.

You turn on the root account like this:

1. **In your Applications→Utilities folder, open the NetInfo Manager program. Click the tiny padlock in the lower-left corner of its screen.**

   A dialog box asks you for an administrator's name and password. After all, you wouldn't want ordinary underlings fooling around with the superuser account.

2. **Type your name and password, and then click OK.**

   You're in.

3. **Choose Security→Enable Root User.**

   If this is the first time you've performed this particular surgery, you'll be told, "The root password is currently blank." You're asked to make up a "non-trivial" (meaning virtually impossible for anyone to guess) password for the newly created root account.

4. **Click OK and then type the password in both of the bottom Password boxes. Click OK two more times.**

   The second dialog box simply tells you that if you intend to make any *more* changes in NetInfo Manager, you'll have to sign in as an administrator *again*. But your work is done here.

5. **Quit NetInfo Manager.**

   You've just brought the dormant root account to life.

6. **Log out. Log back in again as *root*.**

   That is, when the Login screen appears, click Other User (a choice that magically appears once you've turned on the root account). In the first text box, type *root*. In the second, type the password you made up in step 4. Click Log In.

That's it—you arrive at the desktop, where no matter what you do, no error messages regarding access privileges or ownership will interrupt the proceedings. In the words of every movie hero's sidekick: "Be careful out there."

When you're finished going about your business as a root user, immediately log out again. It's important to rule out the possibility that some clueless or malicious person might wander up to the Mac while you're still logged in as the superuser.

In fact, if you don't anticipate needing your superuser powers again soon, consider turning off the root account altogether. (Just repeat steps 1 and 2 above. In step 3, choose Security→Disable Root User.)

System Preferences

Remember the Control Panel on the PC? On the Mac, it's called System Preferences, but it's still the same thing: a collection of little icons that open various preference panels. Some are extremely important, because their settings determine whether or not you can connect to a network or go online to exchange email. Others handle the more cosmetic aspects of customizing Mac OS X. This chapter guides you through the entire System Preferences program, panel by panel.

Tip: Only a system administrator (see page 267) can change settings that affect everyone who shares a certain machine: its Internet settings, Energy Saver settings, and so on.

The tiny padlock in the lower-left corner of a panel (see Figure 13-11, for an example) is the telltale sign. If you, a nonadministrator, would like to edit some settings, call an administrator over to your Mac and ask him to click the lock, input his password, and supervise your tweaks.

The System Preferences Window

You can open System Preferences by choosing its name from the menu, clicking its "light-switch" icon in the Dock, or double-clicking its icon in the Applications folder. At first, the rows of icons are grouped according to function: Personal, Hardware, and so on.

But you can also view them in tidy alphabetical order, as shown at bottom in Figure 13-1. That can spare you the ritual of hunting through various rows just to find a certain panel icon whose name you already know. (This alphabetical arrangement matches the way the various panels are organized in this chapter, too.)

Either way, when you click one of the icons, the corresponding controls appear in the main System Preferences window, and the other icons vanish. To access a different preference pane, you have a number of options:

- *Fast:* Click the Show All icon in the upper-left corner of the window (or press ⌘-L, a shortcut worth learning). Then click the icon of the new panel you want.

- *Faster:* Choose any panel's name from the View menu.

- *Fastest:* Click the icon you want—if it's there—on the System Preferences toolbar. And why shouldn't it be there? By all means, stash the panels you use most frequently up there, as shown in Figure 13-1.

Tip: You can rearrange toolbar icons by dragging horizontally or remove one by dragging it directly away from the toolbar. On the other hand, you can hide the toolbar altogether (to maximize your screen space) by clicking the white oval button in the window's upper-right corner. At that point, you switch among different System Preferences panes by using the View menu.

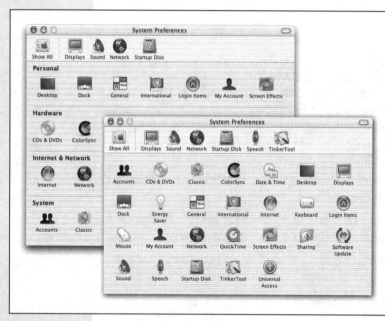

Figure 13-1:
Top: You can hide the toolbar by clicking the upper-right capsule-shaped button. You can also customize this toolbar—and you should—by dragging onto it the icons of the System Preferences panels you use the most.

Bottom: For the first time in Mac OS X, you can view your System Preferences icons alphabetically, rather than in rows of categories; just choose View→Show All Alphabetically. This approach not only saves space, but makes finding a certain panel much easier, because you don't need to worry about which category it's in.

Accounts

This is the master list of people who are allowed to log into your Mac. It's where you can adjust their passwords, startup pictures, and permissions to use various features of the Mac. All of this is described in Chapter 12.

Bluetooth

You have this System Preferences pane only if your Mac has a *Bluetooth transmitter,* either preinstalled or added in the form of Apple's $50 Bluetooth USB adapter.

Bluetooth is a long-delayed, but promising, cable-elimination technology. It's designed to let Bluetooth-equipped gadgets communicate within about 30 feet, using radio signals. Already you can buy Bluetooth adapters—little snap-on cartridges or slide-in cards—for computers, printers, Palm and Pocket PC organizers, certain Sony camcorders, and so on. Even some phones have built-in Bluetooth transmitters.

If your Mac is Bluetooth-equipped, you can sync with a Bluetooth-equipped Palm organizer, or use a Bluetooth cell phone as a modem to get you online. Both of these feats may entail a bit of technical fiddling; search your Mac's Help system for *Bluetooth* instructions. (Be aware that going online via cell phone may require added fees from your cellular company.)

One of the easiest and most immediate benefits of Bluetooth, though, is shooting files across the airwaves to another Bluetooth-equipped computer (Mac *or* PC). It works like this:

1. **In System Preferences, click the Bluetooth icon. Click the Settings tab (Figure 13-2). Turn on Discoverable.**

   Discoverable means, "Other Bluetooth gadgets can see me."

Figure 13-2:
If a device (like your Mac) isn't in "discoverable" mode, then no other Bluetooth gizmos can see it. You get plenty of privacy, but no productivity. While you're at it, by the way, you might want to turn on "Show Bluetooth status in the menu bar." This checkbox produces a menulet in the menu bar, which produces a menu of useful settings.

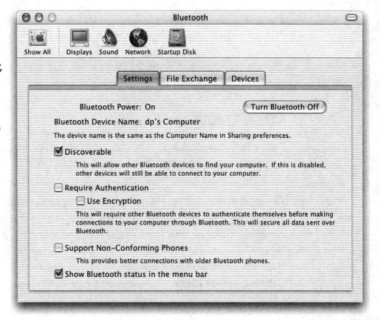

2. **Close System Preferences. Find Bluetooth File Exchange.**

   You'll find it in your Applications→Utilities folder.

3. **Drag the files you want to send onto the Bluetooth File Exchange icon.**

   A dialog box appears.

4. **Click Search.**

   The Bluetooth software scans the airwaves in search of other Bluetooth-equipped computers. At least in the near term, as Bluetooth slowly catches on, you'll probably know perfectly well which ones are in range. (They, too, must be in Discoverable mode.)

5. **In the list of found machines, click the name of the one you want to send your files to, and then click Send.**

   What happens now—on the receiving end—depends on the settings you've made on the File Exchange tab of the Bluetooth System Preferences panel. In most cases, a dialog box tells the receiver that files are arriving; if he clicks Accept, the download proceeds.

Note: When you send files to a Windows PC or some other gadget using this method, security may be tighter. You may be asked to make up a temporary, one-time password that must be typed into both your Mac and the receiving device within, say, one minute, to prove that this transfer is authorized.

Bluetooth isn't especially fast—in fact, it's pretty slow. (You'll get transfer speeds of 30 to 50 K per second, depending on the distance.) But when you consider the time you'd have taken for wiring, passwords, and configuration using any other connection method, you may find that Bluetooth wins—at least in casual, spur-of-the-moment, airport-seat situations.

CDs & DVDs

This panel (Figure 13-3) is practically the mirror image of the dialog box that pops up in Windows XP when you insert a CD or DVD. It specifies what should happen when you insert a certain kind of disc.

For example, when you insert a music CD, you probably want the Mac to open the iTunes program (page 196) automatically so that you can listen to the music. Similarly, when you insert a picture CD (such as a Kodak Photo CD), you probably want iPhoto to open automatically, in readiness to import the pictures from the CD into your photo collection—and when you insert a DVD from Blockbuster, you want the Mac's DVD Player program to open automatically.

Classic

Pre–Mac OS X programs can still run under Mac OS X, thanks to a program called Classic (page 100). This panel lets you start, stop, and restart Classic—and, in the unlikely event that you have more than one Mac OS 9 System Folder installed, it lets you choose which one you want to fire up whenever you open a pre–Mac OS X program.

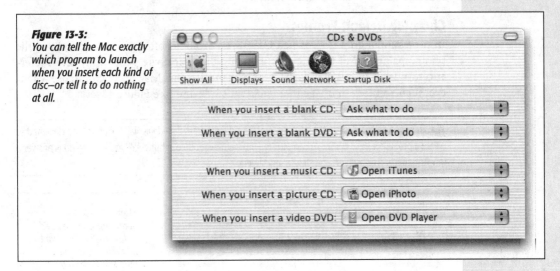

Figure 13-3:
You can tell the Mac exactly which program to launch when you insert each kind of disc—or tell it to do nothing at all.

ColorSync

As you may have discovered through painful experience—computers aren't great with color. Each device you use to create and print digital images "sees" color a little bit differently, which explains why the deep amber captured by your scanner may be rendered as chalky brown on your monitor, yet come out as a fiery orange on your Epson inkjet printer. Since every gadget defines and renders color in its own way, colors are often inconsistent as a print job moves from design to proof to press.

ColorSync attempts to sort out this mess, serving as a translator between all the different pieces of hardware in your workflow. For this to work, each device (scanner, monitor, printer, digital camera, copier, proofer, and so on) has to be calibrated with a unique *ColorSync profile*—a little file that tells your Mac exactly how your particular monitor (or scanner, or printer, or digital camera) defines colors. Armed with the knowledge contained within the profiles, the ColorSync software can make on-the-fly color corrections, compensating for the various quirks of the different devices.

Most of the people who lose sleep over color fidelity are those who do commercial color scanning and printing, where "off" colors are a big deal—after all, a customer might return a product after discovering, for example, that the actual product color doesn't match the photo on a company's Web site.

Getting ColorSync Profiles

ColorSync profiles for most Apple color printers, scanners, and monitors come built into Mac OS X. When you buy equipment or software from, say, Kodak, Agfa, or Pantone, you may get additional profiles. If your equipment didn't come with a ColorSync profile, visit Profile Central (www.chromix.com), where hundreds of model-specific profiles are available for downloading. Put new profiles into the Library→ColorSync→Profiles folder.

Choosing Default Profiles

In professional graphics work, a ColorSync profile is often embedded right in the photo, making all of this automatic. Using the ColorSync panel of System Preferences, you can specify standard ColorSync profiles that Mac OS X should use whenever it encounters an image that *doesn't* include one (see Figure 13-4).

Tip: In your Applications→Utilities folder, you'll find a program called Display Calibrator. It's designed to create a profile for your particular monitor in your particular office lighting—all you have to do is answer a few fun questions onscreen and drag a few sliders.

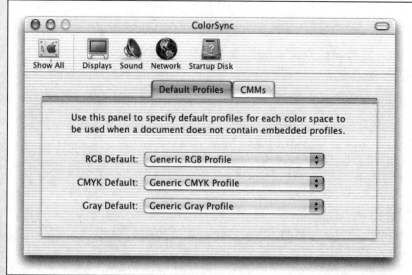

Figure 13-4:
Some programs embed ColorSync profiles right into the documents themselves. If your program doesn't, use the Document Profiles tab of the ColorSync System Preferences panel to specify which color settings your documents should use by default. Clearly, knowing which settings to apply here requires a certain understanding of color spaces (color-description algorithms like RGB and CMYK).

More on ColorSync

If you find yourself wishing you could get deeper into ColorSync, you won't find much in Mac OS X's Help system. Instead, your quest should begin on the Web. At *www.apple.com/colorsync,* for example, you'll find articles, tutorials, and—perhaps most important of all—a link to an email discussion group where you can pose questions and read other people's answers. Going to a search site like *www.google.com* and searching for *ColorSync* is also a fruitful exercise.

Date & Time

Your Mac's conception of what time it is can be very important. Every file you create or save is stamped with this time, and every email you send or receive is marked with this time. As you might expect, setting your Mac's clock is what the Date & Time panel is all about.

Date & Time Tab

Go to the Date & Time pane. Select the correct month and year under Today's Date by clicking the little arrow buttons next to the month and year labels. Then specify the *day* of the month by clicking a date on the mini calendar. Click Save.

Tip: There's no need to set the date, time, or time zone on your Mac manually if you use the Network Time option, described below.

To set your clock, start by clicking one of the numbers in the time field under the Current Time label. Then adjust the corresponding number, either by typing the numbers or by clicking the tiny up or down arrow buttons. To jump to the next number for setting, press the Tab key. Alternatively, you can set the time by *dragging the hands* on the analog clock. Finally, click Save.

Tip: If you're frustrated that the Mac is showing you the 24-hour "military time," go to the International panel of System Preferences. Once there, click the Time tab. There you'll see the "24-hour clock" and "12-hour clock" options.)

Time Zone Tab

You'd be surprised how important it is to set the Time Zone for your Mac. If you don't do so, the email and documents you send out—and the Mac's conception of what documents are older and newer—could be hopelessly skewed. Teach your Mac where it lives using the Time Zone map: First, click a section of the map to select a general region of the world; second, use the pop-up menu to specify your country within that region.

Network Time Tab

With the network time server option turned on, your Mac sets its own clock by consulting a highly accurate scientific clock on the Internet. Turn on the "Use a network time server" checkbox, select one of the time servers listed in the pop-up window, and then click Set Time Now. (No need to worry about Daylight Savings Time, either, as the time servers take that into account.) The Mac immediately connects to the Internet and sets its own clock.

Tip: If you have a full-time Internet connection (cable modem or DSL, for example), you can leave "Use a Network Time server" turned on, so that your Mac's clock is always correct. If you connect to the Internet by modem, however, turn off the checkbox, so that your Mac won't keep trying to dial spontaneously at all hours of the night.

Menu Bar Clock Tab

In the Menu Bar Clock pane, you can specify whether or not you want the current time to appear, at all times, at the top of your screen. If you turn on the "Show the date and time in the menu bar" checkbox, you can choose between two different clock styles from the pop-up menu—digital (Text) or analog (Icon). If you go the View as Text route, you get several other options that govern this digital clock display: whether or not you want to include designations for AM and PM, the display of seconds, the day the week, and a blinking colon.

And by the way, your menu-bar clock always shows the current *time.* When you need to know today's *date,* just click the clock. A menu drops down revealing the complete date. The menu also lets you switch between digital and analog clock types and provides a shortcut to the Date & Time panel in System Preferences.

Desktop

The Desktop panel lets you dress up your Desktop with the background image of your choice. You can choose one of the several dozen background pictures that come with Mac OS X or use your own pictures. In fact, you can even schedule these background pictures to change automatically at regular intervals—an essential feature for the easily bored.

Apple's Canned Picture Collections

Mac OS X comes with four collections of Desktop pictures, ranging from National Geographic–style nature photos to plain solid colors. To install a new background picture, first choose one of the four image categories from the Collections pop-up menu, as shown in Figure 13-5. Your choices include Apple Background Images (muted, soft-focus swishes and swirls), Nature (plants, bugs, water), Abstract (swishes and swirls with wild colors), or Solid Colors (boring grays, blues, and greens).

Now click the thumbnail of any available picture to apply it immediately to the Desktop. (There's no need to remove the previously installed picture; picking a new picture automatically replaces the old one.)

Note: Several of Apple's ready-to-use Desktop pictures come in two sizes. The elongated versions (with the flatter, squashed-down thumbnails) are designed to perfectly fill the extra-wide screens on certain Mac models and unusually wide flat-panel screens.

Your Own Pictures I: A Folder of Your Own

Decorating your Mac desktop is much more fun if you use one of your own pictures. You can use any digital photo, scanned image, or graphic you want in almost any graphics format (JPEG, PICT, GIF, TIFF, PDF, or Photoshop).

One way to find a suitable picture is to open the Collection pop-up menu, which lets you choose Pictures (meaning your Home→Pictures folder), or Choose Folder (so you can choose any folder containing pictures). The menu also lists any picture folders you've recently chosen.

Once you've narrowed things down to a certain folder, you can browse and choose a picture within it, as shown in Figure 13-5.

Figure 13-5:
Using the Collection pop-up menu, you can preview an entire folder of your own images before installing one specific image as your new Desktop picture. Just use the Choose Folder command from the Collection pop-up menu to select a folder in order to view thumbnails of all the images it contains. (That's what was done in this example.) Clicking one of the thumbnails installs the corresponding picture on the desktop.

Your Own Pictures II: Drag a Photo

If there's one certain picture you like, you can easily skip all that folder-choosing business. Just drag the image file itself onto the *well* (the mini desktop displayed in the Desktop panel). A thumbnail of your picture instantly appears in the well and, a moment later, your picture is plastered across your monitor.

Using Your Own Pictures III: Apply from Within iPhoto

If you organize your pictures in Apple's free iPhoto program (and you should), applying a photo to your desktop is as easy as clicking a thumbnail, clicking the Share button at the bottom of the window, and then clicking the Desktop button. The picture appears instantly on your desktop.

Making the Picture Fit

No matter which method you use to choose a photo of your own, you have one more issue to deal with. Unless you've gone to the trouble of editing your chosen photo so that it matches the precise dimensions of your screen (1024 x 768 pixels, for example), it probably isn't exactly the same size as your screen. Fortunately, Mac OS X 10.2 offers a number of solutions to this problem. Try the various settings in the pop-up menu just to the right of the Current Desktop Picture preview (shown in Figure 13-5) until you find a stretch mode that looks good.

Auto-Picture Changing

The novelty of any desktop picture, no matter how interesting, is likely to fade after several months of all-day viewing. That's why the randomizing function is so delightful.

Here's how it works: Create a folder filled with images you'd like to use as desktop pictures. (A group of digital photos works great.) Using the Collections pop-up menu, choose Choose Folder, and then, yes, choose the folder. (You can also choose Pictures Folder from this pop-up menu, which will access all the photos in your Home→Pictures folder.)

Now turn on "Change picture" at the bottom of the dialog box. From the pop-up menu, specify when you want your background picture to change: "every day," "every 15 minutes," or, if you're *really* having trouble staying awake at your Mac, "every 5 seconds." (The option called "when waking from sleep" refers to the *Mac* waking from sleep, not its owner.)

Finally, turn on "Random order," if you like. (If you leave it off, your desktop pictures will change in alphabetical order by file name.)

That's all there is to it. Now, at the intervals you specified, your desktop picture changes automatically, smoothly cross-fading between them like a slide show. You may never want to open another window.

Displays

Displays is the center of operations for all your monitor settings. Here, you set your monitor's *resolution*, determine how many colors are displayed onscreen, and calibrate color balance and brightness. The specific controls you'll see here depend on the kind of monitor you're using, but here are the ones you'll most likely see:

Display Tab

This tab is the main headquarters for your screen controls. It governs these settings:

- **Resolution.** All Mac desktop and laptop screens today can make the screen picture larger or smaller, thus accommodating different kinds of work. You perform this magnification or reduction by switching among different *resolutions* (measurements of the number of dots that compose the screen). The Resolutions list displays the various resolution settings your monitor can accommodate: 800 x 600, 1024 x 768, and so on (Figure 13-6).

Note: Just remember that on any flat-panel screen, including laptop screens, only one resolution setting looks really great: the maximum one. That's what geeks call the *native* resolution of that screen.

That's because on flat-panel screens, every pixel is a fixed size. At lower resolutions, the Mac does what it can to blur together adjacent pixels, but the effect is fuzzy and unsatisfying. (On a traditional bulky monitor, the electron gun can actually make the pixels larger or smaller, so you don't have this problem.)

• **Colors.** The Colors pop-up menu generally offers only two choices: Thousands and Millions, which correspond to the True Color and High Color settings in Windows. There's very little downside to leaving your screen at its maximum depth setting ("Millions" of colors). Photos, in particular, look best when your monitor is set to higher depth settings.

Figure 13-6:
If some of these settings are dimmed, as shown here, turn off "Show modes recommended by display." These "unauthorized" settings now become available; when you choose one, the Mac may ask you to confirm that you can see the effect. If it does something wacky to your screen, on the other hand, the Mac restores the previous setting in fifteen seconds.

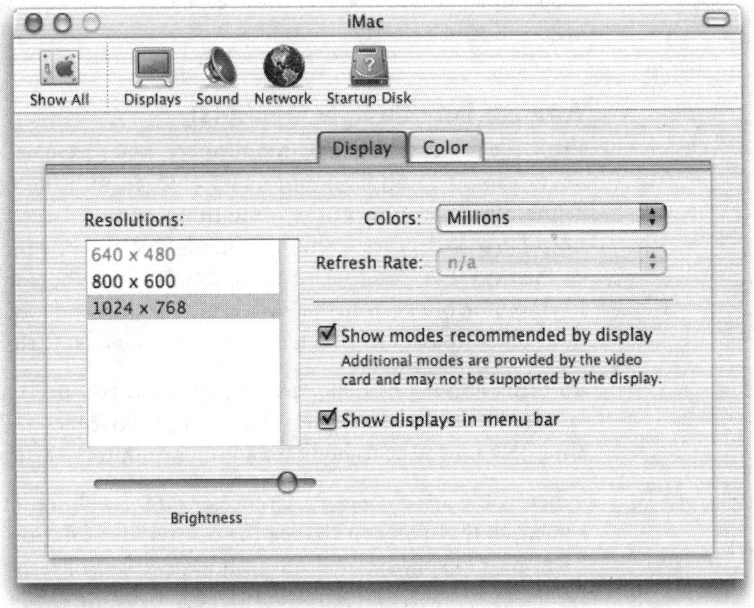

• **Refresh Rate.** If you have a choice here at all, this pop-up menu lets you adjust how many times per second your screen image is repainted by your monitor's electron gun. (You don't see this pop-up menu if you have a flat-panel screen.) Choose a setting that minimizes flicker.

• **Brightness, Contrast.** Use these sliders to make the screen look good in the prevailing lighting conditions. You'll usually want the Contrast control all the way up—if you have it at all (flat-panel screens usually don't)—and Brightness near the middle.

Of course, your keyboard probably has its own dedicated brightness keys on the top row, so these software controls are included just for completeness' sake.

Tip: You can adjust the color depth and resolution of your monitor without having to open System Preferences. Just turn on "Show Displays in menu bar," which adds a Monitors pop-up menu to the right end of your menu bar for quick adjustments.

Geometry Tab

This pane appears only on Macs with built-in, non-flat screens—for the most part, that means eMacs and the older, fruit-colored iMacs. It lets you adjust the position, size, and angle of the screen image on the glass itself—controls that can be useful in counteracting distortion in aging monitors.

Tip: Don't miss the opportunity to eliminate the black borders around your screen perimeter! That's just wasted space. Click the Height/Width button. Then click the "expand vertical" and "expand horizontal" buttons at the lower-right corner of the miniature monitor image until you've eliminated the black borders around the screen.

Arrange Tab (Multiple Monitors)

From the dawn of the color-monitor era, Macs have had a terrific feature: The ability to exploit multiple monitors all plugged into the computer at the same time. Some Macs can project the same thing on both screens (*mirror mode*), which is useful in a classroom. A few lucky models permit one monitor to act as an extension of the next. For example, you might have your Photoshop image window on your big monitor, but keep all the Photoshop controls and tool palettes on a smaller screen. Your cursor passes from one screen to another as it crosses the boundary.

To bring about this delicious arrangement, you need a Mac with a video output jack. (All current Mac laptops have one, as do iMacs and eMacs.) You don't have to shut down the Mac to hook up another monitor—just put it to sleep.

When you open System Preferences, you see a different Displays window on each screen, so that you can change the color and resolution settings independently for each. Your Displays *menulet* also shows two sets of resolutions, one for each screen.

If your Mac can show different images on each screen, your Displays panel offers an Arrange tab, showing a miniature version of each monitor. By dragging these icons around relative to each other, you can specify how you want the second monitor's image "attached" to the first. For the least likelihood of going insane, consider placing the real-world monitor into the corresponding position—to the right of your first monitor, for example.

For committed multiple-monitor fanatics, the fun doesn't stop there. See the microscopic menu bar on the first-monitor icon? You can drag that tiny strip onto a different monitor icon, if you like, to tell Displays where you'd like your menu bar to appear. (And check out how most screen savers correctly show different stuff on each monitor!)

Color Tab

The Color pane lets you calibrate your monitor to create an accurate Color Sync profile for it. See page 285 for details.

Dock

See Chapter 3 for details on the Dock and its System Preferences pane.

Energy Saver

The Energy Saver program is the equivalent of the Power Options control panel in Windows. It helps you and your Mac in a number of ways. By blacking out the screen after a period of inactivity, it prolongs the life of your monitor. By putting the Mac to sleep half an hour after you've stopped using it, Energy Saver cuts down on electricity costs and pollution. And on a laptop, Energy Saver extends the length of the battery charge by controlling the activity of the hard drive and screen.

Sleep Settings

When you first open Energy Saver, you're shown a pair of sliders, one of which starts out dimmed.

Note: If you don't see the sliders, click the Show Details button. (You're probably using a laptop—and on laptops, the sliders are normally hidden.)

The top slider controls when the Mac will automatically go to sleep—anywhere from one minute after your last activity to Never. (Activity can be mouse movement, keyboard action, or Internet data transfer; Energy Saver never turns off your Mac in the middle of a download.)

At that time, the screen goes dark, the hard drive stops spinning, and your processor chip slows to a crawl. Your Mac is now in *sleep* mode, using only a fraction of its usual electricity consumption. To wake it up when you return to your desk, press any key; everything you were working on, including open programs and documents, reappears onscreen, exactly as it was. (To turn off this automatic sleep feature entirely, drag the slider to Never.)

For more control over the sleeping process, activate the second slider by turning on "Use separate time to put the display to sleep," shown in Figure 13-7.

Tip: In Mac OS X, the Mac wakes almost instantly from sleep—one of the great payoffs of Mac OS X.

Laptop Options

When you open Energy Saver on a laptop, it looks quite different, as shown in Figure 13-7. That's because power management is ten times more important on a laptop, where every drop of battery power counts.

The Optimize Energy Settings pop-up menu, for example, offers several canned Energy Saver settings, appropriate for several common laptop situations: Longest Battery Life (puts the laptop to sleep quickly, slows down the processor), DVD Playback (screen on, hard drive off), and so on.

Note, by the way, that the expanded Energy Saver dialog box also offers a pop-up menu called "settings for," which lets you establish independent variations of the

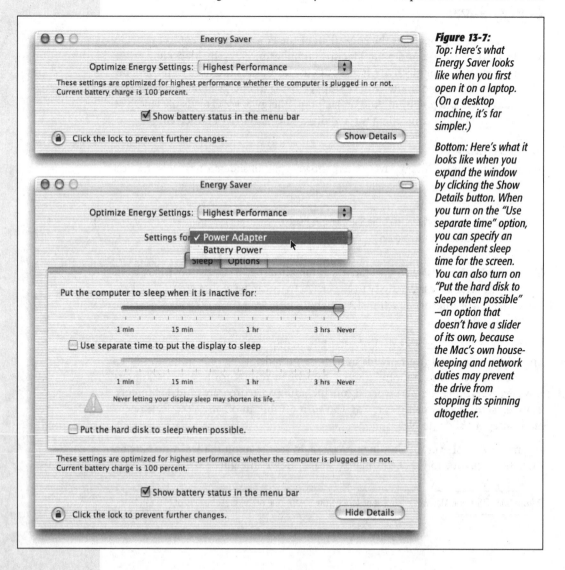

Figure 13-7:
Top: Here's what Energy Saver looks like when you first open it on a laptop. (On a desktop machine, it's far simpler.)

Bottom: Here's what it looks like when you expand the window by clicking the Show Details button. When you turn on the "Use separate time" option, you can specify an independent sleep time for the screen. You can also turn on "Put the hard disk to sleep when possible" —an option that doesn't have a slider of its own, because the Mac's own housekeeping and network duties may prevent the drive from stopping its spinning altogether.

presets for the two times you'll be using your laptop: when plugged in and when running on battery. In other words, you really have two versions of each preset— one DVD Playback for battery, another for AC power; one Presentations setting for battery, another for AC power; and so on.

Tip: Don't miss the checkbox called "Show battery status in the menu bar"–another exclusive for laptops. It puts a handy status indicator in the menu bar–a menulet–that keeps you informed of your battery's life.

It's actually a menu that lets you choose between displaying the actual *number of minutes* left until a battery is depleted and the *percentage* of battery life that remains. (When the laptop is plugged in, these statistics are slightly different. Now you see the number of minutes left *until* the battery is fully recharged, or the percentage of full charge you've achieved so far.)

General

The General panel puts you in control of the look and behavior of windows, menus, buttons, scroll bars, and fonts in Mac OS X. Nothing you find here lets you perform any *radical* surgery—the overall Mac OS X look stays the same—but you can tweak several settings to match your personal style.

Changing Colors

Two pop-up menus let you crank up or tone down Mac OS X's overall colorfulness:

- **Appearance.** Choose between Blue or Graphite. Blue refers to Mac OS X's default bright, candy-colored scroll bar handles, progress bars, menu, and pulsing OK buttons—and those shiny red, yellow, and green buttons in the corner of every window. If you, like some graphics professionals, find all of this circus-poster coloring a bit distracting, then choose Graphite, which renders all of those interface elements in various shades of gray.

- **Highlight color.** When you drag your cursor across text, its background changes color to indicate that you've selected it. Exactly what color the background becomes is up to you—just choose the shade you want using the pop-up menu.

Tweaking the Scroll Bars

These radio buttons control the scroll bar arrow buttons of all your windows. You can keep these arrows together at one end of the scroll bar, or you can split them up, Windows-style: The "up" arrow sits at the top of the scroll bar, and the "down" arrow sits at the bottom. (Horizontal scroll bars are similarly affected.)

Number of Recent Items

Just how many of your recently opened documents and applications do you want the Mac to show using the Recent Items command in the menu? Pick a number from the pop-up menus. (You'll probably find that 5 is too few; 30 is more practical.)

Font-Smoothing Style

The Mac's built in text-smoothing (*antialiasing*) feature is supposed to produce smoother, more commercial-looking text anywhere it appears on your Mac: in word processing documents, email messages, Web pages, and so on.

Using this pop-up menu, you can control *how much* smoothing is performed. For example, Apple suggests Standard for CRT screens (that is, traditional, bulky, television-style screens), and Medium for flat-panel screens like laptops and the iMac. (**Note:** You'll see no effect until the next time you open the program in question. In the Finder, for example, you won't notice the difference until you log out and log back in again.)

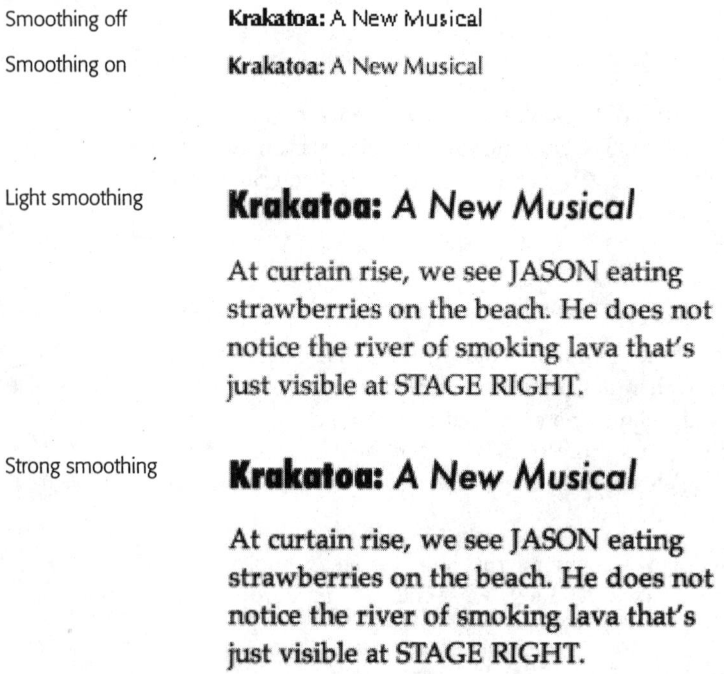

Smoothing off   **Krakatoa:** A New Musical

Smoothing on   **Krakatoa:** A New Musical

Light smoothing

Krakatoa: A New Musical

At curtain rise, we see JASON eating strawberries on the beach. He does not notice the river of smoking lava that's just visible at STAGE RIGHT.

Strong smoothing

Krakatoa: A New Musical

At curtain rise, we see JASON eating strawberries on the beach. He does not notice the river of smoking lava that's just visible at STAGE RIGHT.

Figure 13-8:
Top: The same 12-point type with text smoothing turned off and on.

Bottom: Here's the widest difference in text-smoothing styles: Light smoothing vs. Strong. Standard and Medium, of course, are in between.

Turning Off Smoothing on Tiny Fonts

At smaller type sizes, such as 10-point and smaller, you might find that text is actually *less* readable with font smoothing turned on (Figure 13-8). For that reason, the Size pop-up menu lets you choose a cutoff point for font smoothing. If you choose 12 from this pop-up menu, for example, then 12-point (and smaller) type still appears crisp and sharp; only larger type, such as headlines, displays the graceful edge smoothing. (These settings have no effect on your *printouts*—just on screen display.)

Ink

Much to the bafflement of Mac fans, Apple recycled the handwriting-recognition software from its unsuccessful Newton palmtop for use in Mac OS X 10.2. Now called Inkwell, it does exactly what it used to: turns your handwriting into "typed" text in any program. (Just think of it as a Tablet PC, *YOURS FREE!* with purchase of Mac OS X.)

Note: Inkwell appears in Mac OS X only if you have a compatible graphics tablet, like one of the Wacom stylus-and-pad devices found generally only on the desks of graphic artists.

You turn on handwriting recognition by setting the "Handwriting Recognition is" button to On (Figure 13-9, top). Right away, you'll see a change on your screen: the InkBar toolbar appears (Figure 13-9, bottom).

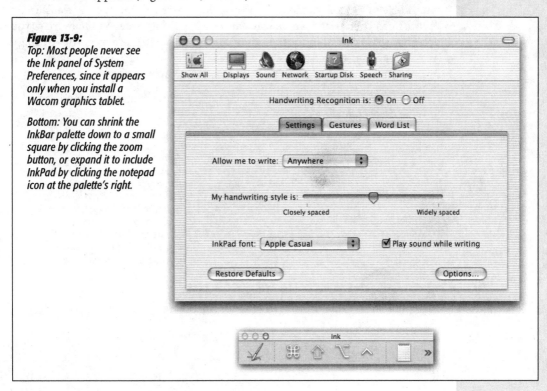

Figure 13-9:
Top: Most people never see the Ink panel of System Preferences, since it appears only when you install a Wacom graphics tablet.

Bottom: You can shrink the InkBar palette down to a small square by clicking the zoom button, or expand it to include InkPad by clicking the notepad icon at the palette's right.

The InkBar Palette

Ink's floating palette lets you "press" the keys for menu commands: ⌘, Shift, Option, or Control. For example, to trigger the Shift-⌘-H keystroke (for Replace) in Microsoft Word, you'd tap the ⌘ button, tap Shift, and then write the letter H.

The icon at the far left of the palette is the on/off switch for handwriting recognition—a handy feature as you move from Photoshop to your email program, for example. When the icon shows an arrow cursor, your pen is just a pointing device, not a writing device. (However, you can write in the InkPad window, described below, even when you're in pointing-only mode.)

Two Ways to Write

Ink can detect what you write in either of two places:

• Anywhere on the screen (Figure 13-10).

• Only in a floating "note pad" window called InkPad.

You can switch back and forth anytime, using the "Allow me to write" pop-up menu on the Ink panel of System Preferences. Either way, you can control how Ink works using the InkBar palette.

If you have a graphics tablet, you can try it right now. Visit a program that accepts typing—TextEdit, for example. Click anyplace where you can type. A translucent, yellow, lined overlay appears as you start writing. Print neatly on the overlay (you don't have to stick within the bounds of the text area in the program you're using). Avoid connecting the letters, as Ink can't read cursive script. Stay on the lines, if you can, and make capital letters distinctly larger than lowercase letters.

A moment after you stop writing, the Mac turns your writing into text and "types" it into the current document.

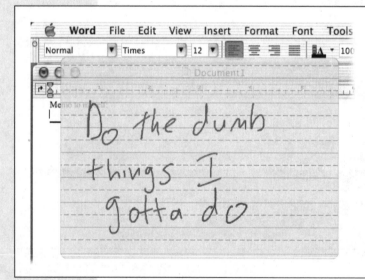

Figure 13-10:
As you begin writing, Ink lays a partially transparent window—which looks like paper from a legal pad—over whatever is on your screen. As you write, your penstrokes appear on screen. They disappear as the Mac recognizes your writing and inserts it at the insertion point.

Using InkPad

If you don't want your pen to transform handwriting into text everywhere on your screen, you can limit the writing area to the built-in InkPad application. That's a useful arrangement when you're working in a graphics program and want the Mac to distinguish between penstrokes that draw and penstrokes that write.

To summon InkPad, click the notepad icon at the far right of the InkBar palette, which expands to become a window that looks remarkably like a lined sheet of paper. When you move your stylus over that area, your cursor turns into a pen. You're ready to write.

At the bottom of the InkPad window, you see two buttons, labeled with the letter A and a star. When the A is highlighted, Mac OS X expects you to write. Afterward, click the Send button to have it "typed" into your document. (You can even perform simple edits before you click Send.)

If you click the star, on the other hand, the InkPad window turns into a sheet of graph paper. At this point, you can draw or write anything you want, but the Mac doesn't recognize it as text; it just remains in graphic form.

Click Clear to completely erase the InkPad. When you click Send, whatever you sketched drops into whatever program you're currently running (assuming it's a program that accepts graphics).

Don't give up if Ink doesn't perfectly recognize your handwriting right away. There are plenty of settings you can modify to improve its chances; click Options on the Ink System Preferences panel to take a look at them.

International

The International panel lets you set up your Mac to work in other languages. If you bought your Mac with a *localized* operating system—a version that already runs in your own language—and you're already using the only language, number format, and keyboard layout you ever plan on using, then you can probably ignore the International panel.

Another Language—Instantly

In Mac OS X, you can shift from language to language in certain programs on the fly, without reinstalling the operating system or even restarting the computer.

Open the International panel. On the Language tab, you see a listing of the fifteen different languages the Mac can switch into—French, German, Spanish, and so on. Just drag one of the languages to the top of the list to select it as the target language, as shown in Figure 13-11. (You can also choose a different *script*—not just a different language, but an entirely different alphabet representation, such as one of the Asian character sets you see listed.)

Now launch Internet Explorer, TextEdit, or Stickies. Every menu, button, and dialog box is now in the new language you selected! If you log out and back in (or restart) at this point, the entire Finder will be in the new language, too.

Dates, Times, Numbers, and Prices

The Date, Time, and Numbers tabs let you set up Mac OS X to display the date, time, currency, and other numbers in a format appropriate for the language. For example, you can set up the European date format, in which 7/4 means "April 7"; the military time format (15:05 instead of 3:05 p.m.); and European punctuation for big numbers (25,600.99, for example, would be written 25 600,99 in France, and 25.600,99 in Spain). The Numbers pane also lets you pick an appropriate currency symbol ($, F, £, and so on) and your preference of metric system (standard or metric).

Figure 13-11:
Feel like working in Dutch? Just drag Nederlands to the top of the Language list, log out and back in, and you're ready to start. Programs like TextEdit and Internet Explorer appear in Dutch. To switch back, simply return to System Preferences→ International, and drag your own language back up to the top of the list. (You have to relaunch any programs that are running to switch them to a different language.)

Input Menu Tab

While the Mac can display many different languages at the same time, *typing* in those languages is another matter. The symbols you use when you're typing Swedish aren't the same as when you're typing English. Apple solved this problem by creating different *keyboard layouts,* one for each language. Each rearranges the letters that appear when you press the keys.

For example, when you use the Swedish layout and press the semicolon key, you don't get a semicolon (;)—you get an ö. (Apple even includes a Dvorak layout—a scientific rearrangement of the standard layout that puts the most common letters directly under your fingertips on the home row. Fans of the Dvorak layout claim greater accuracy, better speed, and less fatigue.)

Use the list in the Keyboard Menu pane to indicate which keyboard layout you want. If you check off more than one keyboard layout, a tiny icon appears to the right of your Help menu—a keyboard *menu* that lets you switch from one layout to another just by choosing its name. (To preview a certain keyboard arrangement, launch the Key Caps program described in the next chapter.)

Internet

The Internet panel has four tabs. For most purposes, you don't need to fill in all of these fields, but filling in a few choice ones can save you a lot of time down the road:

- **.Mac.** This is where you fill in your member name and password for your .Mac account, if you've subscribed. (See page 123 for a discussion of these accounts.)

- **iDisk.** The Disk Space graph indicates how full your electronic iDisk is (page 123). The Public Folder Access controls let you specify whether or not other people are allowed to put new files into your Public folder (a special iDisk folder that requires no password), and whether or not outsiders need a password to see what's in your Public folder.

GEM IN THE ROUGH

The Character Palette

There you are, two-thirds of the way through your local chess-club newsletter, when it hits you: You need an arrow symbol. Right now.

You know there's one in one of your symbol fonts, but you're not about to take two weeks off from work just to hunt through your fonts, typing every single combination of keys until you produce the arrow symbol. You can't help wishing there was an easier way to find those special symbols that hide among your fonts—fancy brackets, math symbols, special stars and asterisks, heart shapes, and so on.

The Key Caps program described in Chapter 14 is one solution. But you won't need it nearly as much, thanks to the new Character Palette.

To make it appear, open System Preferences, click the International icon, click the Input Menu tab, and turn on the

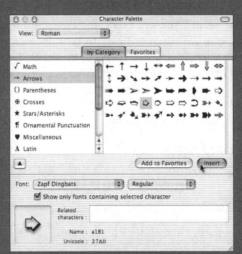

Character Palette checkbox. Now inspect your menu bar: You've just added the keyboard menu.

Next time you're word processing or doing page layout, choose Show Character Palette from this menu. The resulting window rounds up *all* symbols from *all* your fonts at once. To find a particular symbol, click the "by Category" tab, and then click the various category headings: Arrows, Stars/Asterisks, Math, and so on. When you find the symbol you want, double-click it to make it appear in your document.

If you're using a Cocoa program, the correct symbol pops into your document. If not, you may get only the correct character, but not in the correct font. In that case, you'll have to change the font of the inserted character manually. To find out what font it came from, click the black, down-pointing triangle button; you'll see the font name in parentheses.

- **Email.** Fill in all blanks. If you're not sure what to type, contact your Internet access company (or its Web page) for help. The most important setting is the Default Email Reader pop-up menu, which tells the Mac which email program you prefer to use (Mail, Entourage, or whatever). From now on, whenever you click a "Click here to send email" link on a Web page, that program opens automatically.

- **Web.** All of the settings on this panel are important. Fill in the Home Page (the page you want to open when you first launch your Web browser). Next, click Select to specify a Downloads folder—where you want files you download from the Internet to be saved. (Mac OS X proposes the desktop itself, which is a good idea. The point is to eliminate the frustration of not being able to find something that you downloaded.)

  Use the Default Web Browser pop-up menu to indicate which browser you prefer—say, Internet Explorer or Safari. This is the browser that will automatically open whenever you click a link in some other program (like a Word document).

Keyboard

The Keyboard panel lets you do some frivolous keyboard fine-tuning. It also unlocks Mac OS X's strange and remarkable Full Keyboard Access feature, which lets you control your Mac's menus, windows, dialog boxes, buttons, the Dock, and the toolbar—all from the keyboard.

Repeat Rate Tab

On the Mac, as in Windows, *every* key starts spitting out repetitions if you hold it down long enough, making it easy to type, for example, "No WAAAAAAAY!" or "You go, girrrrrrrrrl!" The two sliders in the Repeat Rate pane of the Keyboard panel govern this behavior. On the right: a slider that determines how long you must hold dow n the key before it starts repeating (to prevent triggering repetitions accidentally, in other words). On the left: a slider that governs how fast each key spits out letters once the spitting has begun.

Full Keyboard Access Tab

For a full discussion of the options on this pane, see page 87.

Login Items

This simple panel controls which programs launch automatically at startup time. Details are in Chapter 12.

Mouse

It may surprise you to hear that the cursor on the screen doesn't move five inches when you move the mouse five inches on the desk. Instead, the cursor moves farther when you move the mouse faster.

How *much* farther depends on how you set the first slider in the Mouse panel. The Fast setting is nice if you have an enormous monitor, since you don't need an equally large mouse pad to get from one corner to another. The Very Slow setting, on the other hand, forces you to pick up and put down the mouse frequently as you scoot across the screen. It offers no acceleration at all, but it can be great for highly detailed work like pixel-by-pixel editing in Photoshop.

The Double-Click Speed setting specifies how much time you have to complete a double-click. If you click too slowly—beyond the time you've allotted yourself with this slider—the Mac "hears" two *single* clicks instead.

Trackpad Options

On laptops, the bottom part of the Mouse panel offers some extra controls that affect the trackpad.

Under normal circumstances, you touch a Mac laptop's trackpad exclusively to move the cursor. For clicking and dragging, you're supposed to use the clicking button *beneath* the trackpad.

Many people find, however, that it's more direct to tap and drag directly on the trackpad—using the same finger that's been moving the cursor. That's the purpose of these four checkboxes:

- **Clicking.** When this box is turned on, you can tap the trackpad surface to register a mouse click at the location of the cursor. Double-tap to double-click.

- **Dragging.** Turn on this option if you want to move icons, highlight text, or pull down menus—in other words, to drag, not just click—using the trackpad. Start by tapping twice on the trackpad, then *immediately* after the second tap, begin dragging your finger. You can stroke the trackpad repeatedly to continue your movement, as long as your finger never leaves the trackpad surface for more than about one second. When you finally stop touching the pad, you "let go," and the drag is considered complete.

- **Drag lock.** If the dragging maneuver described above makes you nervous that you're going to "drop" what you're dragging if you stop moving your finger for a fraction of a second, turn on this option instead. Once again, begin your drag by double-clicking, then move your finger immediately after the second click.

  When this option is on, however, you can take your sweet time in continuing the movement. In between strokes of the trackpad, you can take your finger off the laptop for as long as you like. You can take a phone call, a shower, or a vacation; the Mac still thinks that you're in the middle of a drag. Only when you tap *again* does the laptop consider the drag a done deal.

- **Ignore trackpad while typing.** This option addresses a chronic syndrome of laptop owners who turn on the Clicking option: While you're typing along, a finger accidentally brushes the trackpad, sending the insertion point onto a different line of text. Before you even notice, you've typed into some random part of your document.

This ingenious option locks out the click-and-drag trackpad functions when you're actually typing on the keyboard—a sweet and simple solution.

- **Ignore trackpad when mouse is present.** Here's another ingenious advance in laptop technology: When you hook up a mouse to your laptop, the trackpad is deactivated. Obviously, if you're using a mouse, then you probably won't want to use the trackpad—and by turning on this checkbox, you're no longer susceptible to accidentally brushing it.

My Account

This panel, too, is described in Chapter 12. It's where you can change your password, Address Book card, and the picture next to your name on the Welcome screen.

Network

The Network panel is the brain of your Mac's Internet and local networking connections. See Chapter 9 for the settings you need to plug in.

QuickTime

The settings in the QuickTime panel affect the way movies are played back on your Mac, including movies that stream to you from a Web page and movies stored on your own system that you watch using QuickTime Player (Chapter 14).

You don't even have to touch most of these settings, but you should certainly inspect your Connection Speed. Set it to match the actual speed and type of your Internet connection. (Some streaming QuickTime Web sites are set up with multiple versions of the same movie, each saved at a different size and frame rate. Based on your connection speed setting here, the QuickTime plug-in can automatically request the appropriately sized version of a movie for the best possible playback.)

Screen Effects

In previous versions of Mac OS X, this panel was called Screen Saver. Why did Apple change the name? Very simple: This feature doesn't actually save your screen. In fact, flat-panel screens can't burn in at all, and even traditional CRT screens wouldn't burn an image into the screen unless you left them on continuously—unused, with the same image on the screen—for two straight years. It's just not going to happen.

No, screen savers are mostly about entertainment, pure and simple—and Mac OS X's built-in screen saver is certainly entertaining.

In the Screen Saver panel, you can choose from nine different screen saver modules—most of them beautifully designed. For example:

- **Computer Name.** This display shows nothing more than the Apple logo and the computer's name, faintly displayed on the monitor. (These two elements do actually shift position every few minutes—it just isn't very fast.) Apple probably imagined that this feature would let corporate supervisors glance over at the screens of unattended Macs to find out exactly who away from their desks.

- **Flurry.** You get flaming, colorful, undulating arms of fire, which resemble a cross between an octopus and somebody arc welding in the dark.

- **Abstract, Beach, Cosmos, Forest.** These are photographic screen savers, featuring gorgeous pictures that slowly zoom and softly crossfade into each other. Abstract features psychedelic swirls of modern art. In the Beach, Cosmos, and Forest screen savers, you see a series of tropical ocean scenes, deep space objects, and lush rain forests.

  Each creates an amazingly dramatic, almost cinematic experience, worthy of setting up to "play" during dinner parties like the lava lamps of the seventies.

For any of these options, you can click the Configure button to see a dialog box like the one shown in Figure 13-12.

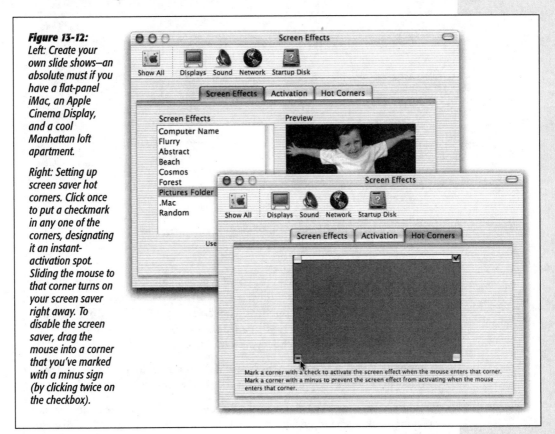

Figure 13-12:
Left: Create your own slide shows—an absolute must if you have a flat-panel iMac, an Apple Cinema Display, and a cool Manhattan loft apartment.

Right: Setting up screen saver hot corners. Click once to put a checkmark in any one of the corners, designating it an instant-activation spot. Sliding the mouse to that corner turns on your screen saver right away. To disable the screen saver, drag the mouse into a corner that you've marked with a minus sign (by clicking twice on the checkbox).

Tip: Don't forget that·iPhoto (in your Applications folder) lets you organize your photos into *albums* (subfolders). You can turn any album into a custom screen saver with just one click (on the Screen Saver icon at the bottom of the Share panel).

- **Pictures Folder.** This is one of the coolest Screen Effects modules. It lets you transform your *own* collection of pictures into a self-playing slide show.

  If you just click Pictures Folder and walk away, the screen saver will display the digital photos in your Home→Pictures folder, complete with spectacular zooming and dissolving effects.

  But if you click Pictures Folder and then click Configure, you'll see the dial-up box shown in Figure 13-13.

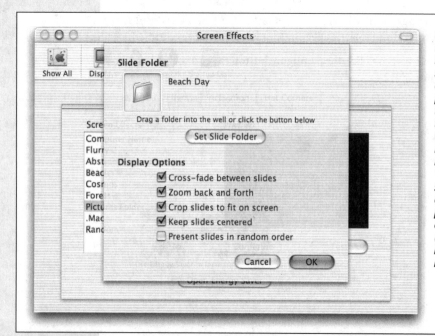

Figure 13-13:
Here, you can instruct Mac OS X to create a screen saver out of any folder full of pictures. Either drag the folder itself into the little Slide Folder well, or click Set Slide Folder and then navigate to it. The "Crop slides to fit on screen" checkbox ensures that every photo will be nicely centered and sized. (Don't worry: Apple really means "shrink," not "crop.")

- **.Mac.** One of the perks for paying $100 per year for a .Mac membership is the ability to create slide shows online, which can play back either on your own Mac or (if you opted to make it public) on anybody else's. Click the Configure button to open the dialog box where you can specify which member's slide show collection you want to view, and how you want it to appear.

- **Random.** If you can't decide which one of the modules to use, click Random. The Mac will choose a different module each time your screen saver kicks in.

When you click a module's name in the Screen Savers list, you see a mini version of it playing back in the Preview screen. Click Test to give the module a dry run on your full screen.

When you've had enough of the preview, just move the mouse or press any key. You return to the Screen Saver panel.

Activating the Screen Saver

You can control when your screen saver takes over your monitor in a couple of ways:

- In the **Activation** pane, you can set the amount of time that has to pass without keyboard or mouse activity before the screen saver starts.

  You also get the option of requiring you to enter your user password (page 269) in order to disengage the screen saver. If you turn this feature on, you can use the screen saver as a sort of lock for your Mac. You can walk away from your desk at work, knowing that once the screen saver takes over, no one will be able to read the email on your screen or rifle through your files.

- On the **Hot Corners** pane, you can turn each corner of your monitor into a *hot corner* (Figure 13-12). Whenever you roll your cursor into that corner, the screen saver can either turn on instantly (great for those times when you happen to be shopping on eBay at the moment your boss walks by) or stay off permanently (for times when you're reading onscreen or watching a movie).

Sharing

Once you've connected Macs and PCs into a network, you can enjoy *file sharing*. That's when you summon the icon for a folder or disk attached to another computer on the network. It shows up on your screen underneath your own hard drive, as shown in Figure 13-14. At this point, you can drag files back and forth, exactly as though the other computer's folder or disk is a gigantic CD you've inserted into your own machine.

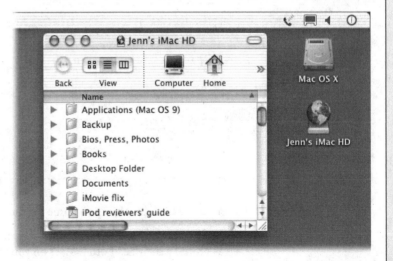

Figure 13-14:
The whole point of file sharing: to bring icons for the hard drives or folders from other Macs and PCs onto your own screen—like the Jenn's iMac HD icon shown here. By dragging icons back and forth, you can transfer your work from your main Mac to your laptop, give copies of your documents to other people, create a "drop box" that collects submissions from various authors for a publication, and so on.

Note: These instructions cover the basics of sharing Macs with other Macs on the network. For instructions on sharing a Mac with a PC on the same network, see page 116.

Phase 1: Setting up the Computers

These instructions assume that you've already wired the network together.

Setting up a Mac OS X machine

Begin by creating an *account*—a name, password, and Home folder—for each person who might want to visit. See Chapter 12 for full instructions. Then you're ready to proceed with preparing the machine for access from elsewhere on the network.

1. **Open System Preferences.**

   You can click its icon on the Dock, for example, or choose ■→System Preferences.

2. **Click the Sharing icon.**

   The Sharing panel appears, as shown at top in Figure 13-15.

Note: Only administrators (page 267) are allowed to fool around with the settings you're about to change. If the little padlock icon in the lower-left corner of the dialog box looks locked, call an administrator over, click the lock, and prove that you have permission to do what you're doing by entering (or asking the administrator to enter) the administrator's name and password.

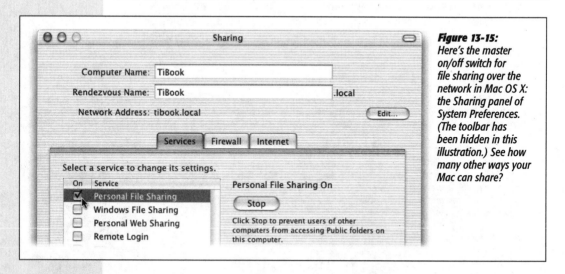

Figure 13-15:
Here's the master on/off switch for file sharing over the network in Mac OS X: the Sharing panel of System Preferences. (The toolbar has been hidden in this illustration.) See how many other ways your Mac can share?

3. **In the Computer Name blank, type a name for the computer, if necessary.**

   Your Mac will appear on the network with this name. Make it nice and descriptive, such as Front Desk iMac. If other Macs on your network run Mac OS X 10.2

or later, you can also edit its *Rendezvous* name (a system of automatic equipment recognition on a network), providing you don't use any spaces or punctuation (except hyphens).

4. **In the list of checkboxes, turn on Personal File Sharing (Figure 13-15).**

   If you want Windows PCs on your network to be able to connect to your Mac too, turn on Windows File Sharing as well.

5. **Close the window, if you like.**

Repeat this process on each Mac OS X machine in your office, giving each one a different computer name.

Phase 2: Connecting to Another Mac from Mac OS X

Suppose you're seated at your Power Mac, but you need a file that's on the 17-inch iMac down the hall. The steps are the same, no matter which version of the Mac operating system the other machine's running (as long as it's later than Mac OS 8.5).

To bring its hard drive icon (or a shared folder's icon) onto your screen, follow these steps on the Mac OS X machine:

1. **Choose Go→Connect to Server (or press ⌘-K).**

   The Connect to Server command opens up the window shown in Figure 13-16.

   If you've done this before, don't miss the "At" pop-up menu at the top of the dialog box. Its commands include a list of Recent Servers—computers you've accessed recently over the network. If you choose one of them from this pop-up menu, you can skip the next two steps.

Figure 13-16:
You may see the names of individual machines in the leftmost column, or on bigger networks, you may see globe icons that indicate further network structures or protocols. These may represent AppleTalk zones, Windows workgroups, or other Mac OS X machines. In any case, click the network cluster (globe) you want, if necessary, and then double-click the name of the actual machine you want in the second column. (Don't be freaked out by the appearance of your own Mac's name. That's all normal.)

2. **In the left-side list, click the correct "limb" of your network tree, if necessary.**

What you see in this list depends on the complexity of your network. For example, if your network is just your Mac and a couple of laptops, you'll see their names listed here, ready for double-clicking. You won't see the globe icons shown in Figure 13-16.

If you *do* see globe icons, however, then your Mac is seeing different network types at once. Here's how to find your way around:

To see a list of Mac OS X machines on the network: Click the Local icon.

To see a list of Windows machines on the network: Click the name of the *workgroup* (computer cluster) that contains the machine you want. In small office networks, it's usually called MSHOME or WORKGROUP.

In the second column, you should now see a list of every Mac for which you turned on File Sharing. (If not, then something's wrong with your network wiring, or you haven't prepared those Macs as described in "Phase 1: Setting up the Computers," above.)

3. **In the second column, double-click the name of the computer you want.**

Alternatively, press the right-arrow key to highlight the second column, press the up or down arrow keys to highlight the Mac you want, and then press Enter or Return to click the Connect button.

Tip: If your network is a real bear to navigate, consider taking this opportunity to click the name of a Mac you plan to access frequently, and then click Add to Favorites at the bottom of the window. For now on, you'll be able to skip steps 2 and 3 by choosing the Mac's name from the At pop-up menu at the top of the window.

Now the "Connect to the file server" box appears (Figure 13-17, top). You're supposed to specify your account name and password, so that you can sign in and access your own files on that other Mac.

Although it may hurt your brain to contemplate, you can even do so *while* somebody else is actually using the Mac in person. The Mac can actually process the work of many people simultaneously. In fact, you, Chris, and Robin can each log into Ellen's Mac from across the network—each of you using your own files on that same machine—even while Ellen is using her *own* account!

4. **Type your short user name (Figure 13-17, top)**

Not sure what your short user name is? Open System Preferences on your home-base Mac, and then click My Account. Your short name appears at the top of the dialog box.

5. Press Tab, and then type your password.

If you work alone or with a small group of trusted people, and you've left your password blank, just skip the password box here.

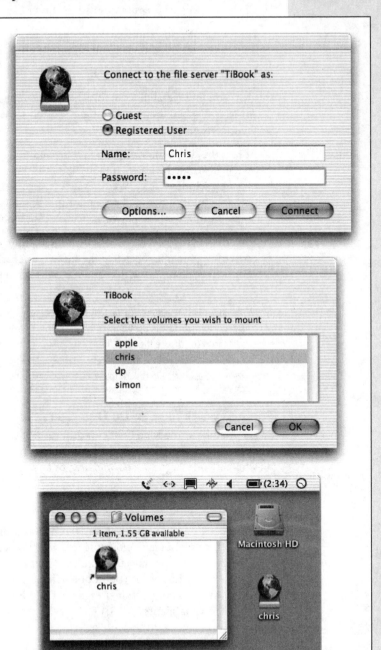

Figure 13-17:
The sequence of connecting to another disk on the network continues. First chose Go→Connect to Server, double-click Local Network, and then double-click the name of the Mac you want (Figure 13-16).

Top: Now you specify your password, or if you didn't require one, leave the password box blank. Click Connect.

Middle: Double-click the name of the shared folder or disk you actually want to open.

Bottom: At long last, you're in. The other Mac's shared disk or folder appears on your desktop just as though it's another hard drive.

Tip: If you click the Options button, you'll be offered a checkbox called Add Password to Keychain. If you turn on this checkbox, you won't have to type your password the next time you connect.

6. **Click Connect, or press the Return or Enter key.**

   Now a list of disks and folders on that Mac that have been *shared* for network access appears (Figure 13-17, middle).

7. **Double-click the name of the disk or folder you want to open.**

   Or, if you see several disks or folders listed here that you'd like to open all at once, you can ⌘-click them to highlight several—and then click OK to bring all of their icons onto your desktop.

   At last, the disk or folder you've connected to appears on the right side of your screen, illustrated with what looks like a tiny hard drive with a globe balanced on it. A new window called Volumes opens, too, listing each partition, shared disk, or shared folder that's accessible to your Mac—including the one you just brought online from across the network (Figure 13-17, bottom).

   You can open its icon (either on the desktop or in the Volumes window) to open, copy, move, rename, or delete the files on it, exactly as though the files were on your own computer—with certain limitations, described next.

Tip: Make an alias of the hard drive icon that you've just pulled onto your screen, or put it onto your Dock, or choose Add to Favorites (in the Connect to Server dialog box). The next time you want to connect to it, just click the icon (or choose the name from the pop-up menu in the Connect to Server window). You'll skip all seven steps of the connection process described above. As long as you've allowed the Keychain to memorize your password, the disk or folder pops open instantly.

Phase 3: What You Can Do Once You're In

When you tap into a Mac OS X machine across the network, you can access only what's in certain designated folders. Precisely which folders are available depends on whether you're a *guest,* a *normal user,* or an *administrator* (see the previous chapter).

If you're a Guest

If you're just a guest—somebody for whom an account hasn't already been set up—you can't do very much. Connecting to a Mac OS X machine as Guest offers you a list of everyone who has an account on it. (This list looks like the center illustration in Figure 13-17.) But when you double-click someone's name, you'll discover that there's nothing inside that folder except a Drop Box folder and sometimes a Public folder, as shown in Figure 13-18. (Technically, the Drop Box folder is actually inside each person's Home→Public folder.)

You can do only two things: Copy files into someone's Drop Box (which you can't open, though), or open anything that people have put into their Public folders. (If you don't see any Public folders, then nobody has put anything into them for you to see.) The rest of the Mac is invisible and off-limits to you.

Figure 13-18:
Top: If you connect as a guest, there's not much to see. You can deposit files into the Drop Box folder of any account holder, but not into the window that holds it—the little slashed-pencil icon in the upper-left corner tells you that it's off-limits.

Bottom: Suppose that Frank has put three files into his Public folder. (Every person's Home folder contains a Public folder.) When you connect to his Mac, you'll see whatever is in his Public folder—in this case, his Drop Box plus those three files. You can't put anything in Frank's window (except in the Drop Box), but you can open the three files he's left there for you to see.

If you're a Normal account holder

If you have a Normal account, you'll enjoy Drop Box access, Public-folder access, *and* the ability to see and manipulate what's inside your own Home folder on the distant Mac. You can do anything you like with the files and folders you find there, just as though you're actually seated in front of that Mac.

All other disks and folders on the Mac, however, including the System and Application folders, are invisible to you.

If you're an Administrator

When you connect to a Mac OS X machine as a guest or a normal user, you never even see the name of the hard drive on that machine. As illustrated at center in

Figure 13-17, you see only the names of the people who have *accounts* on that machine (so that you can use their Drop Boxes and Public folders).

But if you're an *administrator,* you get to see both those user folders *and* the hard drive to which you're connecting. If you, O lucky administrator, open that hard drive, you'll discover that you not only have the same freedoms as a Normal account holder (described above), but also the freedom to see and manipulate the contents of these folders:

- Applications

- Desktop folder

- Library (and the System→Library folder, but nothing else in the System folder)

- Users→Shared folder (page 277)

- The other disks connected to the Mac OS X machine

Note: There's actually one more kind of account: the *root user.* Whoever holds this account has complete freedom to move or delete *any file or folder anywhere,* including critical system files that could disable your Mac. Page 279 has details.

Why aren't Normal and Administrator account holders allowed to see what's in the System folder? Because Mac OS X is extremely protective of its System folder. To make Mac OS X remain as solid and stable as the day you installed it, human beings are not allowed to play with it, whether they're visiting over the network or not.

Normal and Administrator account holders aren't allowed to see what's in other users' Home folders, either. That's part of Mac OS X's security feature. Each person who uses a Mac OS X machine has an individual account to which she alone has access.

Disconnecting Yourself

When you're finished using a shared disk or folder, drag its icon to the Trash (whose icon changes as you drag), highlight its icon and choose File→Eject, or Control-click its icon and choose Eject from the contextual menu. You also disconnect from a shared folder or disk when you shut down your Mac, or if it's a laptop, when you put it to sleep.

Disconnecting Others

In Mac OS X, there's no visual clue to alert you that other people on the network are accessing *your* Mac.

Still, if you're feeling particularly antisocial, you can slam shut the door to your Mac just by turning off the File Sharing feature. (Click System Preferences on the Dock, click the Sharing icon, and turn off the Personal File Sharing or Windows File Sharing checkbox.)

If anybody is, in fact, connected to your Mac at the time (*from* a Mac), you see the dialog box shown in Figure 13-19. If not, your Mac instantly becomes an island once again.

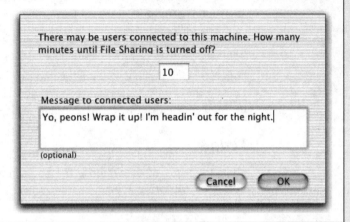

Figure 13-19:
This dialog box asks you how much notice you want to give your co-workers that they're about to be disconnected– 10 minutes to finish up what they're doing, for example. If you're feeling rushed or rude, type a zero. Doing so disconnects that person instantly, without warning. Then click OK. (When you disconnect people by closing your laptop lid, having a system crash, or unplugging the network wires, your co-workers get no notice at all. A message appears on their screens that says, "The server has unexpectedly shut down.")

Software Update

It occurred to both Microsoft and Apple that a software programmer's work is never done. In any project as complex as an operating system, there are always bugs to be fixed, features to be sped up, and enhancements to add. That's why Windows has Automatic Updates—and why Apple has Software Update.

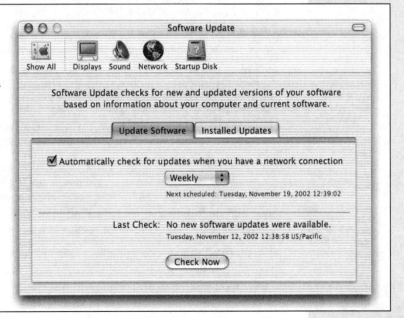

Figure 13-20:
Apple has always created updated and bug-fixing versions of its software components, but they don't do you any good if you don't know about them. You no longer have to scour Mac news Web sites to discover that one of these components has been released and then hunt down the software itself. When Software Update finds an appropriate software morsel, it offers to install it automatically.

Whenever Apple comes up with a new software fix, this program can notify you, download the update, and install it into your System automatically.

Fortunately, Software Update doesn't actually download the new software without asking your permission first and explicitly telling you what it plans to install, as shown in Figure 13-20.

For maximum effortlessness, turn on the Automatically checkbox and then select a frequency from the pop-up menu—daily, weekly, or monthly.

Software Update also keeps a meticulous log of everything it drops into your system. On the Install Updates tab, you see them listed—and you can even reinstall one by double-clicking it here.

Sound

Using the panes of the Sound panel, you can configure the sound system of your Mac in the following ways:

Sound Effects

"Sound effects" means *error beeps*—the sound you hear when the Mac wants your attention, or when you click someplace you shouldn't. Just click the sound of your choice to make it your standard system beep. Most are funny and clever, yet subdued enough to be of practical value as alert sounds.

As for the other controls on the Sound Effects panel, they include:

- **Alert Volume slider.** The *main* volume slider for your Mac is at the bottom of the Sound panel, called "Output volume." The slider on the Alert Sounds panel is *just* for error beeps; Apple was kind enough to let you adjust the volume of these error beeps independently.

- **Play user interface sound effects.** This option produces a few subtle sound effects when you perform certain Finder operations: dragging something off of the Dock, for example, or dropping something into the Trash.

- **Play feedback when volume keys are pressed.** Most Mac keyboards have little speaker icons that, when pressed, adjust the overall volume louder or softer. Each time you press one of these keys, the Mac beeps to help you gauge the current speaker level.

  That's all fine when you're working at home. But more than one person has been humiliated in an important meeting when the Mac made a sudden, inappropriately loud sonic outburst—and then amplified that embarrassment by furiously and repeatedly pressing the down volume key, beeping all the way.

  If you turn off this checkbox, the Mac won't make any sound at all as you adjust its volume. Instead, you'll see only a visual representation of the steadily decreasing (or increasing) volume level.

Tip: This System Preferences panel is another one that offers a "Show in menu bar" option at the bottom. It installs a volume control right in your menu bar, making the volume control instantly accessible from any program.

Output Tab

"Output" means speakers. For 99 percent of the Mac-using community, this panel offers nothing useful except the Balance slider, with which you can set the balance between your Mac's left and right stereo speakers.

Input Tab

This panel lets you specify which microphone you want the Mac to "listen to," if indeed you have more than one connected. It also lets you adjust the sensitivity of that microphone—its "input volume"—by dragging the slider and watching the real-time Input Level meter above it change as you speak.

Speech

The Mac's speech features—both listening and talking back—are far more extensive than what you're probably used to from Windows. Depending on the kind of work you do, these features might give you both a productivity boost and a good giggle along the way.

Speech Recognition

The Apple marketing machine may have been working too hard when it called this feature "speech recognition"—the Mac OS feature called PlainTalk doesn't take dictation, typing out what you say. Instead, PlainTalk is what's known as a *command-and-control* program. It lets you open programs, choose menu commands, trigger keystrokes, and click dialog box buttons and tabs—just by speaking their names.

Truth is, very few people use PlainTalk speech recognition. But if your Mac has a microphone, PlainTalk is worth at least a 15-minute test drive. It may become a part of your work routine forever.

The on/off switch for speech recognition in Mac OS X is the Speech panel of System Preferences. Where you see "Apple Speakable Items is," click On. (The first time you do this, a small instructions window appears. Read it if you like, and then click Continue. If you ever want to see these tips again, click the Helpful Tips button on this pane.)

The Feedback window

Check out the right side of your screen: A small, microphone-ish window now appears (Figure 13-21). The word *Esc* in its center indicates the "listen" key—the key you're supposed to hold down when you want the Mac to respond to your voice. (You wouldn't want the Mac listening all the time—even when you said, for example, "Hey, it's cold in here. *Close the window.*" Therefore, the Mac comes ready to listen only when you're pressing that key.)

You can specify a different key, if you wish, or eliminate the requirement to press a key altogether, as described in the next section.

When you start talking, you'll also see the Mac's interpretation of what you said written out in a yellow balloon just over the Feedback window.

Tip: The Feedback window lacks the standard Close and Minimize buttons. If it's in your way, just double-click it (or say "minimize speech window") to shrink it onto your Dock.

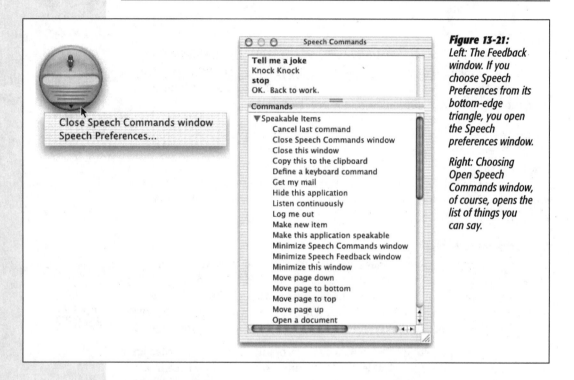

Figure 13-21:
Left: The Feedback window. If you choose Speech Preferences from its bottom-edge triangle, you open the Speech preferences window.

Right: Choosing Open Speech Commands window, of course, opens the list of things you can say.

The Speakable Commands window

The only commands the Mac understands are those listed in the Speakable Commands window, which generally appears automatically when you turn on speech recognition. Keeping your eye on the Speakable Commands window is absolutely essential, because it offers a complete list of everything your Mac understands. As you can see, some of them represent shortcuts that would take several steps if you had to perform them manually.

To open this list if it's not open, click the tiny arrow at the bottom of the Feedback window and choose Open Speech Commands Window from the commands that appear. Here are a few examples of what you'll find in the list at first:

- **Open Sherlock.** Launches the Sherlock file-finding program, as described in Chapter 11, saving you the trouble of using a menu or keystroke to open it.

- **Close this window.** Closes the frontmost window instantly.

- **Switch to AppleWorks.** Brings AppleWorks to the front. (Of course, you can say "switch to" and then the name of *any* running or recently used program.)

- **Quit all applications.** Saves you the trouble of switching into each program and choosing Quit.

- **Open the Speech Commands window** or **Show me what to say.** Opens the Speech Commands window, of course.

- **What day is it?** Tells you the date.

- **Tell me a joke.** Begins a pathetic/funny knock-knock joke. You've got to play along, providing the "who's there?" and "so-and-so *who?*" answers.

Mac OS X *updates* the listing in the Speech Commands window in real time, according to the context. When you switch from one program to another, you see a list of the local commands that work in the new program. You'll discover that when you use the "Tell me a joke" command, for example, you don't necessarily have to say, "Who's there?" You can also say "Stop," "Go away," or "Stop with the jokes!" (It must really be fun to work at Apple.)

Speaking to the Mac

When you're ready to talk to your computer, position the microphone between one and three feet from your mouth. If it's a headset, make sure it's plugged in. If it's built-in, speech recognition may not be as accurate.

In any case, finish up by opening the Speech panel of System Preferences. Click the Listening tab, and use the Microphone pop-up menu to specify which microphone you'll be using (if you have a choice).

Now you're ready to begin. While pressing the Esc key (if that's still the one identified in the Feedback window), begin speaking. Speak normally; don't exaggerate or shout. Try one of the commands in the Speakable Commands list—perhaps "What time is it?" If the Feedback window doesn't display animated sound waves, indicating that the Mac is hearing you, something's wrong with your microphone setup. Open the Speech panel again, and confirm that the correct microphone is selected.

Triggering menus by voice

On the Speech panel of System Preferences, click the Speech Recognition tab, and then click the Commands *mini*-tab on that window. Here you'll find a list of the command categories that Speakable Items can understand. As you turn each checkbox on or off, watch the Speech Commands window. Giant swaths of commands appear or disappear as you fool with these checkboxes, giving you a good indication as to their function. Here's a rundown:

- **General Speakable Items commands.** This is the master list of Speakable Items shown in Figure 13-21.

- **Specific application commands.** Certain Mac OS X programs come with preset lists of commands that work only when you're in that program. For example, whenever you're in the Finder, you can say, "Empty the trash," "Go to my home directory," "Hide the dock," "Minimize all windows," "Make a new folder," and so on. When this checkbox is turned off, the Mac no longer recognizes any of these handy commands.

- **Application switching commands.** This is the command category at the bottom half of the Speech Commands list—"Switch to Address Book," "Switch to AOL," and so on.

- **Front Window commands.** When you turn on this option, a small window may appear, letting you know that you must turn on the master "assistive features" switch on the Universal Access panel of System Preferences. Click the Universal Access button, which takes you to the Universal Access panel described on page 324. Turn on the checkbox called "Enable access for assistive devices." You've just thrown the master switch for Front Window and Menu Bar commands. (Apple's implication is that these command sets are useful only for the disabled, but that's not true at all.)

Right away, in your Speech Commands window, you'll note the appearance of a new category of commands, called Front Window. The idea here is to provide you with quick, speech-recognition access to the most prominent buttons, tabs, and icons in whichever window is before you. Figure 13-22 elaborates on the idea.

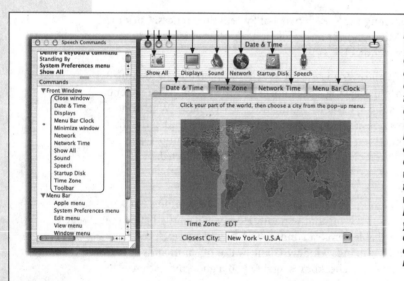

Figure 13-22:
The Front Window commands change automatically to reflect the controls that are in the frontmost window. For example, in the Date & Time panel of System Preferences, you can say anything in the circled area of the Speech Commands window: the name of any tab, toolbar icon, or window control (indicated by the arrows). Whenever you say an item, the Mac clicks it for you. You can also speak the menus' names to open them.

- **Menu Bar commands.** This command lets you open menus (in the menu bar) by speaking their names. You need to turn on the "assistive devices" checkbox (page 324) for this to work.

Once you say its name ("File menu," for example), the menu opens. Now you can say any command in the open menu ("New Playlist," "Save," or whatever). The Menu Bar category of the Speech Commands window changes to remind you of what you can say at any given moment.

You can probably see that the combination of Front Window and Menu Bar commands lets you do quite a bit of work on your Mac without ever needing the mouse or keyboard.

Improving the PlainTalk vocabulary

By putting an alias of the favorite document, folder, disk, or program into the Home→Library→Speakable Items folder, you can teach PlainTalk to recognize its name and open it for you on command. You can name these icons anything you want. You can also rename the starter set that Apple provides. You'll have the best luck with polysyllabic names—"Microsoft Word," not just "Word."

The Mac Talks Back

The conversation doesn't have to be one-way; it's even easier to make the Mac *talk*.

The Mac can read almost anything you like: text that you pass your cursor over, alert messages, menus, and *any text document in any program*. It can speak in your choice of 22 synthesizer voices, ages eight to fifty. The Mac's voice comes out of its speakers, reading with a twangy, charmingly Norwegian accent.

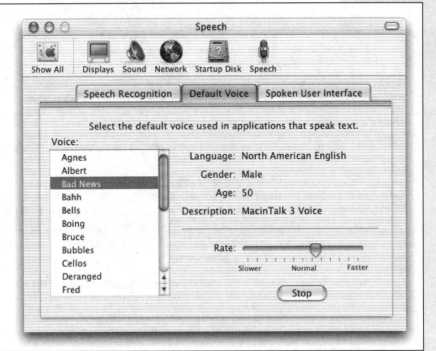

Figure 13-23:
For 15 minutes of hilarious fun, try clicking the Mac's voices in turn (or press the up and down arrow keys) to hear a sample sentence spoken in that voice. Drag the slider to affect how fast he or she speaks. (Clearly, Apple's programmers had some fun with this assignment.)

To configure the way the Mac talks, revisit the Speech panel of System Preferences. Click the Default Voice tab at the top of the window. As you can see in Figure 13-23, you can control which voice your Mac uses, as well as how fast it should speak.

To start your Mac reading aloud, visit the Universal Access panel of System Preferences. Make sure that "Enable access for assistive devices" is turned on.

Now visit the Speech panel of System Preferences. Click the Spoken User Interface tab (Figure 13-24).

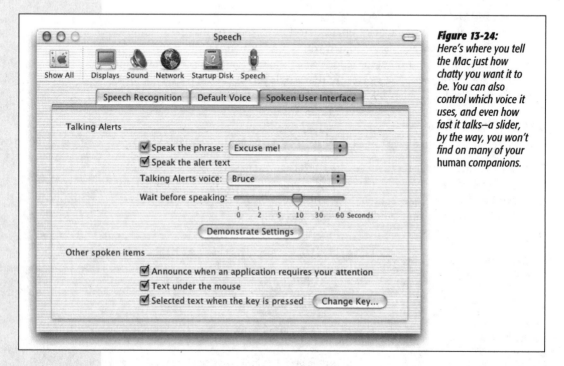

Figure 13-24:
Here's where you tell the Mac just how chatty you want it to be. You can also control which voice it uses, and even how fast it talks—a slider, by the way, you won't find on many of your human companions.

Here are all the different occasions when the Mac can talk to you:

When an alert message appears onscreen
You can make the Mac read aloud error messages and alert messages that may appear on your screen. Using these controls, you can specify an utterance that the Mac should speak before the actual error message—for example, "*Excuse me!* The Trash could not be emptied" or "*Attention!* The document could not be printed." If you don't want any such preamble, turn off the checkbox.

If you choose "Next in the list" or "Random from the list" from this pop-up menu, you'll never hear the same expletive twice. Better yet, choose Edit Phrase List to open a dialog box where you can specify your own words of frustration. (Apple Computer, Inc. is not liable for any trouble you may get into with people in neighboring cubicles.)

When an application requires your attention

A jumping dock icon means that the program is trying to get your attention. It might be Print Center (because your printer is out of paper), or it might be Entourage (because new email has come in). In any case, now the Mac can tell you, in so many words, which program needs some loving care.

When your cursor passes over some text

This feature is, obviously, a spectacular help for anyone who has trouble seeing. Now your cursor can "read" buttons, tabs, dialog box options, desktop icons, the subject lines of messages in your email inbox, and so on.

When a key is pressed

In its own humble way, this option offers the most dramatic possibilities of all. It means that the Mac can read any text in any program. Now you can hear any Web page read to you, any email message, any sticky note—in many cases, this can be a welcome break for sore eyes, and a superb way to proofread something.

The very first time you turn on this checkbox, the Mac prompts you to specify a keystroke. Choose a keystroke that doesn't conflict with the program you're using—Shift-Option-Z, for example.

Now go to the program where you'd like the reading to happen. Highlight some text (or just press ⌘-A to select all of it). Then press the keystroke you specified. The Mac begins reading it aloud immediately. To interrupt the playback, press the same keystroke again, or press ⌘-period.

And be glad you were alive to see the day.

Tip: Your Mac can perform an astonishing feat: It can convert a text file into a *spoken digital recording* in AIFF audio format. If you transfer these files to your iPod or a CD, you can listen to your documents—email, Web pages, reports, manuals, electronic books, or anything else you can type or download—as you commute, work out, or work outside. To pull this off, you need the two sample AppleScript scripts at *www.apple.com/applescript/macosx/text2audio.html*.

Of course, commuters and joggers have been listening to Books on Tape for years, but these products limit your listening to other people's stuff.

Startup Disk

Use this panel to pick the System Folder your Mac will use the next time you start your Mac—swapping between Mac OS X and Mac OS 9.2, for example. Check out the details in Chapter 4.

Universal Access

The Universal Access panel is designed for people who type with one hand, find it difficult to use a mouse, or have trouble seeing or hearing. (These features can also be handy when the mouse is broken or missing.) They closely correspond to the identical features in Windows. For example:

Seeing Tab (Magnifying the Screen)

This feature allows you to enlarge the area surrounding your cursor in any increment—and, if you like, also to invert the colors of the screen so that white is black, blue is yellow, and so on.

To make it work, press ⌘-Option-* (use the asterisk on the numeric keypad, or add Shift-8 to invoke the asterisk on the main keyboard) as you're working. Or, if the Seeing panel is open in front of you, just click the gigantic Turn On Zoom button. That's the master switch.

No zooming actually takes place, however, until you press Option-⌘-plus sign (to zoom in) or Option-⌘-minus sign (to zoom out). Here, you can use either the numeric keypad or the top row of keys on the keyboard.

With each press, the entire screen image gets larger or smaller, creating a virtual monitor that follows your cursor around the screen.

POWER USERS' CLINIC

Direct System Preferences Access from the Dock

Pining for the days of Windows, when all control panels were only a click away (in the menu or Start→Control Panel menu)? Pine no more. Within one minute, you can have yourself a tidy pop-up menu of System Preferences panels right there in your Dock.

Make a new folder (in your Home folder, for example). Name it whatever you want the Dock icon to say—Control Panel, for example.

Now open your System→Library→ PreferencePanes folder, which contains the icons for the various System Preferences panes. Select all of them—or only the ones you actually use.

Drag them into your SysPrefs folder, taking care to press Option-⌘ as you release the mouse. (Option-⌘-dragging makes aliases of them.) If the .prefPane suffix on the aliases bugs you, select all of the aliases, press ⌘-I, open the Name & Extension panel in the Get Info window, and turn on "Hide extension."

Finally, drag the SysPrefs folder onto the right side of your Dock. Now, whenever you want to open a particular panel, just Control-click (or hold the mouse button down on) this SysPrefs Dock icon. You get a handy pop-up list, as shown here. (The icons may look like folders, but they're standard, double-clickable icons that take you directly to the corresponding panel of System Preferences.)

You'll be amazed at just how much you can zoom in. In fact, there's nothing to stop you from zooming in so far, that a *single pixel* fills the entire monitor. (That may not be especially useful for people with limited vision, but it can be handy for graphic designers learning how to reproduce a certain icon, dot by dot.)

While you're at it, pressing Control-Option-⌘-* (asterisk) inverts the colors of the screen, so that text appears white on black—an effect that some people find easier to read.

Hearing Tab (Flashing the Screen)

If you have trouble hearing the Mac's sounds, you may appreciate the "Flash the screen whenever an alert sound occurs" option. Now you'll see a white flash across the entire monitor whenever the Mac would otherwise beep.

Keyboard Tab (Typing Assistance)

This panel offers two clever features designed to help people who have trouble using the keyboard.

- **Sticky Keys** lets you press multiple-key shortcuts (involving keys like Shift, Option, Control, and ⌘) one at a time instead of all together (see Figure 13-25).

  If you press a modifier key *twice*, meanwhile, you lock it down. (Its onscreen symbol gets brighter to let you know.) When a key is locked, you can use it for several commands in a row. For example, if a folder icon is highlighted, you could double-press ⌘ to lock it down—and then type O (to open the folder), look around, and then press W (to close the window). Press the key a third time to "un-press" it.

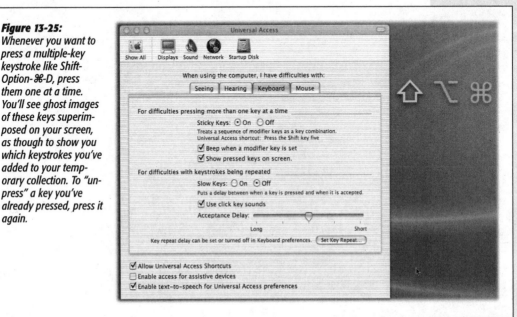

Figure 13-25:
Whenever you want to press a multiple-key keystroke like Shift-Option-⌘-D, press them one at a time. You'll see ghost images of these keys superimposed on your screen, as though to show you which keystrokes you've added to your temporary collection. To "un-press" a key you've already pressed, press it again.

• **Slow Keys,** on the other hand, doesn't register a key press at all until you've held down the key for more than a second or so—a feature designed to screen out accidental key presses.

Mouse Tab (Cursor Control from the Keyboard)

This feature, called Mouse Keys, is designed to help people who can't use the mouse— or who want more precision when working in graphics programs. It lets you click, drag, and otherwise manipulate the cursor by pressing the keys on your numeric keypad. The 5 key acts as the clicker—hold it down for a moment to "click the mouse," do that twice to double-click, and so on. Hold down the 0 key to lock down the mouse button, and the period key to unlock it. (The amount of time you have to hold them down depends on how you've set the Initial Display slider.)

Move the cursor around the screen by pressing the eight keys that surround the 5 key. (For example, hold down the 9 key to move the cursor diagonally up and to the right.) If you hold one of these keys down continuously, the cursor, after a pause, begins to move smoothly in that direction—according to the way you have adjusted the sliders called Initial Delay and Maximum Speed.

The Freebie Programs

R ight out of the box, Mac OS X comes with a healthy assortment of over 30
 freebies: programs for sending email, writing documents, doing math, even
 playing games. Some are dressed-up versions of Mac programs that have
been around for years. Others, though, are new programs that not only show off
some of Mac OS X's most dramatic new technologies, but let you get real work done
without having to invest in additional software.

These programs reside in two important folders on your hard drive: Applications
(in the main hard drive window) and Utilities (within the Applications folder). The
Applications folder houses the productivity programs; Utilities holds a couple of
dozen maintenance programs for setting up printers and network connections, fixing
problems on your hard disk, and so on.

Tip: You can jump straight to the Applications folder in the Finder by pressing Shift-⌘-A, or by clicking the
Applications button in the Finder window toolbar (it's the button that looks like an *A*). You might consider
adding the Application and Utilities folders' icons to the right side of your Dock, too, so that you can access
them no matter what program you're in.

This chapter guides you through every item in your new software library, one program at a time. (Depending on your Mac model, you may find other programs in
your Applications folder; Apple occasionally licenses software from other companies to spice up the collection for, say, iMacs or Power Macs.)

Acrobat Reader 5.0

Just about every computer on earth comes with a copy of the free Adobe program, Acrobat Reader. As its name implies, Acrobat Reader lets you open and read PDF (Portable Document Files) files. This is quite a useful task since, as you've probably noticed, software manuals, product brochures, tax forms, and many other documents are distributed as PDFs these days.

Tip: Here's the most important thing to remember about reading PDF files in Acrobat: *press Enter.* With each press, you "turn the page." If the screen shows only part of a page, the Enter key brings the next portion into view. Press Shift-Enter to go *up* the page (or back a page).

At first glance, the inclusion of Acrobat Reader with Mac OS X may seem a little redundant. After all, Mac OS X comes with its *own* free PDF-reading utility: Preview (described later in this section). Why do you need Acrobat Reader if you already have Preview?

Don't be fooled. Preview can open and display PDFs, but that's about it. Acrobat Reader, on the other hand, offers a full-screen option (press ⌘-L) for a PowerPoint-like presentation mode; a search command; the ability to copy text out of a PDF file (click the T tool on the toolbar); and interactivity (forms for filling in, bookmarks, hyperlinks, and so on).

Adobe has done a surprisingly good job of documenting its additional features within the program itself. Just choose Help→Reader Help in Acrobat (or press ⌘-?) for the details.

Address Book

The Address Book is a database that stores names, addresses, email addresses, phone numbers, and other contact information. Chapter 6 covers Address Book in detail.

AppleScript

AppleScript may be hard for a Windows switcher to grasp right away, because there's simply nothing like it in Windows. It's a programming language that's both very simple and very powerful, in that it lets Mac programs send instructions or data to *each other.*

A simple AppleScript program might perform some simple daily task for you: backing up your Documents folder, for example. A more complex script can be pages long. In professional printing and publishing, where AppleScript enjoys its greatest popularity, a script might connect to a photographer's hard drive elsewhere on the Internet, download a photo from a predetermined folder, color-correct it in Photoshop, import it into a specified page-layout document, print a proof copy, and send a notification email to the editor—automatically.

Ready-made AppleScripts

Mac OS X comes with several dozen prewritten scripts that are genuinely useful—
and all you have to do is choose their names from a menu. "Playing back" an
AppleScript in this way requires about as much technical skill as pressing an eleva-
tor button.

To sample some of these cool starter scripts, you must first bring the Script menu to
your menu bar (a new feature in Mac OS X 10.2). To do so, open your Applications→
AppleScript folder. Inside, double-click the icon called Script Menu.menu (it may
look like a folder).

Now open the newly installed Script menu, whose icon looks like a scroll, to see the
list of prewritten scripts (Figure 14-1).

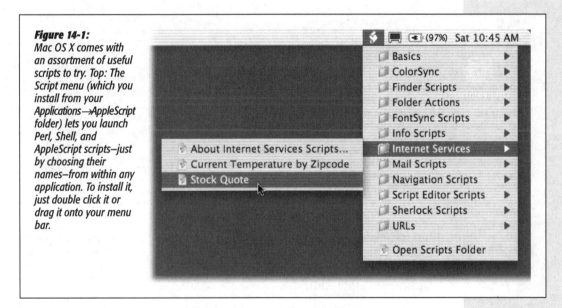

Figure 14-1:
Mac OS X comes with an assortment of useful scripts to try. Top: The Script menu (which you install from your Applications→AppleScript folder) lets you launch Perl, Shell, and AppleScript scripts—just by choosing their names—from within any application. To install it, just double click it or drag it onto your menu bar.

Some of the scripts in this menu operate on familiar components of the Mac OS,
like the Finder; others show off applications or features that are new in Mac OS X.
Here are a few of the best:

- **Basics→Open Script Editor** launches Script Editor, a program that you can use
  to edit and write your own AppleScript programs.

- **Finder→Add to File Names, Finder→Add to Folder Names** tack on a prefix or
  suffix to the name of every file or folder in the frontmost Finder window (or, if
  no windows are open, on the desktop). Now you're starting to see the power of
  AppleScript: You could use this script to add the word *draft* or *final* or *old* to all of
  the files in a certain folder.

- **Finder→Finder Windows – Hide All** minimizes all open Finder windows to the Dock. **Finder Windows – Show All**, of course, brings them back from the Dock.

- **Finder→Replace Text in Item Names** lets you do a search-and-replace of text bits inside file names, folder names, or both. When one publisher rejects your 45-chapter book proposal, you can use this script to change all 45 chapter files from, for example, "A History of Mouse Pads—A Proposal for Random House, Chapter 1" to "A History of Mouse Pads—A Proposal for Simon & Schuster, Chapter 1."

- **Info Scripts→Font Sampler** is designed to show you what all your fonts look like (see Figure 14-2).

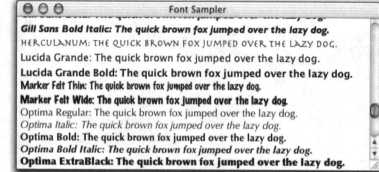

Figure 14-2:
The Font Sampler script launches TextEdit, opens a new document, and fills it with dozens of copies of the classic "What does this font look like?" test sentence: The quick brown fox jumped over the lazy dog. *Then, as you watch, it formats each line with a different font—a good page to print out and keep as a reference.*

- **Internet Services→Stock Quote, Internet Services→Current Temperature by Zipcode** fetch those respective bits of information, popping them into a dialog box without having to use your Web browser, thanks to the power of SOAP (Simple Object Access Protocol).

- **Mail Scripts→Count Messages in All Mailboxes** counts all unread messages in the Mac OS X Mail program (Chapter 6) and displays the result.

- **Mail Scripts→Crazy Message Text** is Apple at its wackiest. When you run it, a dialog box asks you what message you want to send ("Happy Birthday," for example). Mail then creates a colorful, zany, outgoing formatted message in which each letter has a random typeface, style, color, and size. It's ideal for making people think you spent a long time with your Format menu for their entertainment.

- **Mail Scripts→Quick Mail** prompts you for an address and a subject line, launches the Mail application, and sets up a new message for you with those attributes. With a little analysis of this script, you should be able to see how it could save you time in generating canned, regularly scheduled outgoing mail messages.

- URLs→CNN and the other commands in the URLs submenu simply open your browser, connect to the Internet if necessary, and then open the specified Web page. The last script, Download Weather Map, is much cooler. In a flash, it downloads the current U.S. weather-map image and then opens the file in the Preview program for viewing.

Writing Your Own AppleScripts

As programming languages go, AppleScript is easy to understand. It takes only a few weeks, not years, to become comfortable with AppleScript. And the power AppleScript places in your hands is well worth the effort you'll expend learning it.

For example, here's a fragment of actual AppleScript code:

```
open folder "AppleScript" of folder "Applications" of startup
disk
```

You probably don't need a manual to tell you what this line from an AppleScript program does. It opens the Applications→AppleScript folder on your hard drive. (That's the folder that contains Script Editor, the Mac OS X program that lets you write your own AppleScripts, and Script Menu.menu, described on page 329.)

No single chapter—in fact, no entire book—can make you a master AppleScript programmer. Gaining that kind of skill requires weeks of experimentation and study, during which you'll gain a lot of appreciation for what full-time software programmers endure every day. AppleScript, despite its friendly appearance and abundance of normal English words, uses many of the same structures and conventions as more advanced programming languages.

By far the best way to learn AppleScript is to study existing scripts (like those in the Library→Scripts folder) and to take the free online training courses listed at the end of this chapter. And there are thousands of examples available all over the Web. Trying to figure out these scripts—running them after making small changes here and there, and emailing the authors when you get stuck—is one of the best ways to understand AppleScript.

Mac OS X comes with only very general online help for AppleScript, and truth be told, it's pretty lame if what you want to do is get help writing scripts. But at *www.apple.com/applescript/guidebook/sbrt/index.html*, you'll find online AppleScript Guidebook modules with a lot of useful routines that you can use, borrow from, or dissect for the purposes of learning.

Furthermore, few Mac technologies have more ardent fans than AppleScript, and free beginner (and expert) tutorials are available all over the Web. For example:

- **Apple's AppleScript Web site.** At *www.apple.com/AppleScript*, click the Resources link to see links to several useful resources. Links on this page take you to commercial AppleScript training course offerings, technical encyclopedias that describe every single AppleScript command in detail, AppleScript news sites, and so on.

- **Bill Briggs' AppleScript Primers.** Read dozens of articulate, thoughtful tutorials for the beginning scripter.

- **AppleScript mailing lists.** Sign up for one of these free, email-based discussion lists whose members are all AppleScript fans. Apple runs one; the MacScript list is independent. Given the shortage of specific tutorials based on Mac OS X, these lists are possibly the best source of solutions for the new scripter.

Calculator

The Mac OS X Calculator is useful for performing quick arithmetic without having to open a spreadsheet, but it can also act as a scientific calculator for students and scientists, a conversion calculator for metric and U.S. measures, even a currency calculator for world travelers.

Note: If Mac OS X came preinstalled on your new Mac, you might not have the Calculator program. In its place, Apple offers the equally delightful PCalc 2, a popular shareware scientific calculator.

Here's everything you need to know for basic math:

- The calculator has two modes: Basic and Advanced (see Figure 14-3). Switch between them by clicking the appropriate button just underneath the calculator readout.

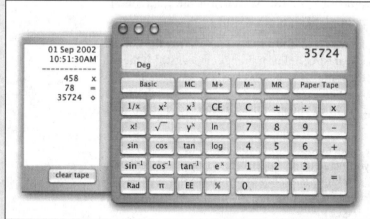

Figure 14-3:
The new Calculator program offers both a four-function Basic mode and a full-blown scientific calculator mode (shown here). Each one offers a "paper tape" feature that lets you correct errors made way back in a calculation. To edit one of these numbers, drag through it, retype, and then press Enter. (You can also print the tape; choose File→Save Tape As, or File→Print Tape.)

- You can operate the calculator by clicking the onscreen buttons, but it's much easier to press the corresponding number and symbol keys on your keyboard.

Tip: If you have a Mac laptop, don't miss the embedded numeric keypad, superimposed on the right side of the keyboard and labeled on the keys in a different color ink. When you press the Fn key in the lower-left corner of the keyboard, typing these keys produces the numbers instead of the letters.

- As you go, you can make your calculator speak each key you press. This is a sensational feature; the Mac's voice ensures that you don't mistype as you keep your eyes on the receipts in front of you, typing by touch.

  Just choose Speech→Speak Button Pressed to turn this feature on or off. (You can choose the voice in the Speech panel of System Preferences.)

- A "paper tape" option shows a scrolling list of your calculations. You can actually edit these numbers, even long after a calculation is over. You can also print or save the paper tape; see Figure 14-3.

- Once you've calculated a result, you can copy it (using File→Copy, or ⌘-C) and paste your answer directly into another program.

Conversions

Calculator is more than a calculator; it's also a conversion program. No matter what units you're trying to convert—meters, grams, inches, miles per hour—the calculator is ready. Proceed like this:

1. **Clear the calculator. Type in the starting measurement.**

   To convert 48 degrees Celsius to Fahrenheit, for example, type *48*.

2. **From the Convert menu, choose the kind of conversion you want.**

   In this case, choose Temperature. When you're done choosing, a little dialog box appears.

3. **Use the pop-up menus to specify which units you want to convert to and from.**

   To convert feet to meters, for example, choose Feet from the first pop-up menu, and Meters from the second.

4. **Click OK.**

   That's it. The calculator displays the result—in degrees Fahrenheit, in this example.

Calculator is especially amazing when it comes to *currency* conversions—from pesos to American dollars, for example—because it actually does its homework. It goes online to download up-to-the-minute currency rates to ensure that the conversion is accurate.

All you have to do is choose Convert→Update Currency Exchange Rates. Then, when you use the Convert→Currency command, your numbers will be the very latest.

Tip: If you Control-click the calculator's results display, the contextual menu offers an option called Large Type—a great way to make sure the peons in the back row can see the answer.

Chess

Mac OS X comes with only one game, but it's a beauty (Figure 14-4). Chess is a traditional chess game played on a gorgeously rendered board with a set of realistic 3-D pieces. The program is actually a 15-year-old Unix-based chess program, Gnu Chess, that Apple packaged up in a new wrapper.

Figure 14-4:
Chess isn't just another computerized chess game; it's also one of the more visually striking programs you get with Mac OS X. You don't have to be terribly exact about grabbing the chess pieces when it's time to make your move. Just click anywhere within a piece's current square to drag it into a new position on the board.

GEM IN THE ROUGH

Talking to Chess

If your friends and co-workers are, for some reason, still unimpressed by Mac OS X and your mastery of it, invite them over to watch you play a game of chess with your Mac—by *talking* to it.

Open the Chess program. Unless you've turned it off (in Chess→Preferences), the game's speech-recognition feature is already turned on. When it's on, the round Feedback window should be visible onscreen.

To learn how to speak commands in a way that Chess will understand, click the small gray triangle at the bottom of the Speech Feedback panel to open the Speech Commands window. As usual, it lists all the commands that Chess can comprehend.

You specify the location of pieces using the grid of num-

bers and letters that appears along the edges of the chessboard. The White King, for example, starts on square e1 because he's in the first row (1) and the fifth column (e). To move the King forward by one square, you'd say: "King e1 to e2."

Although it doesn't seem quite as satisfying (for some reason), you can actually skip the name of the piece you want to move (Pawn, Knight, and so on). It's perfectly OK to call out the square locations only ("g3 to f5").

As the Speech Commands window should make clear, a few other commands are at your disposal. "Take back move" is one of the most useful. When you're ready to close in for the kill, the syntax is, "Pawn e5 takes f6."

And smile when you say that.

When you launch Chess, you're presented with a fresh, new game that's set up in Human vs. Computer mode—meaning that you (the Human, with the white pieces) get to play against the Computer (your Mac, on the black side). Drag the chess piece of your choice into position on the board, and the game is afoot.

Tip: Choose Chess→Preferences to change the difficulty level, change sides, and turn on the Mac's voice-recognition mode, described in the box on the facing page.

Clock

Launching Clock puts a digital or analog clock in a floating window right on your desktop or in the Dock. A visit to Clock→Preferences gives you all sorts of options regarding how you want this clock to look and act: analog or digital, degree of transparency, and so on.

DVD Player

DVD Player, your Mac's built-in movie projector, is described on page 201.

iCal

In many ways, iCal, Mac OS X's calendar program, is not so different from those "Hunks of the Midwest Police Stations" paper calendars we leave hanging on our walls for months past their natural life span. But iCal offers several advantages over paper calendars. For example:

- It can automate the process of entering repeating events, such as weekly staff meetings or gym workout dates.

- iCal can give you a gentle nudge (with a sound, a dialog box, or even an email) when an important appointment is approaching.

- iCal can share information with your Address Book program, with Mail, with your iPod, with other Macs, with "published" calendars on the Internet, or with a Palm organizer. Some of these features require one of those .Mac accounts described in Chapter 5, and some require iSync (described later in this chapter). But iCal also works just fine on a single Mac, even without an Internet connection.

When you open iCal, you see something like Figure 14-5. By clicking one of the View buttons on the bottom edge of the calendar, you can switch among any of the standard calendar-software views: Day, Week, or Month.

Tip: iCal provides a quick way to get to the current day's date–choose Calendar→Go to Today, or press ⌘-T.

Recording Events

You can quickly record an appointment using any of several techniques, listed here in order of decreasing efficiency:

- Double-click the appointed time on the calendar, in any view. A colored box appears, where you type the name for your new appointment.

- When viewing a day or week view, drag vertically through the time slots that represent the appointment's duration, and then type inside the newly created colored box.

- Using the month view, double-click the appropriate date, and then type in the newly created colored bar.

- Choose File→New (or press ⌘-N). A new appointment appears on the currently selected day, regardless of the current view.

Unless you use the drag-over-hours method, a new event believes itself to be one hour long, but you can adjust its duration by dragging the bottom edge vertically. Drag the dark top bar up or down to adjust the start time.

In many cases, that's all there is to it. You have just specified the day, time, and title of the appointment.

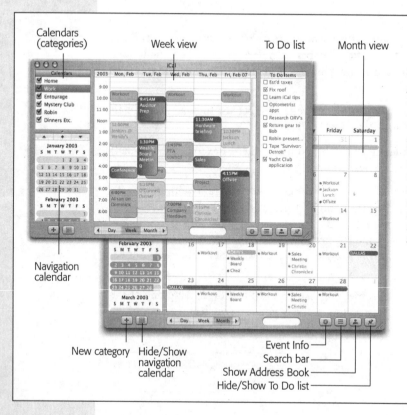

Calendars (categories)

Week view

To Do list

Month view

Navigation calendar

New category

Hide/Show navigation calendar

Event Info
Search bar
Show Address Book
Hide/Show To Do list

Figure 14-5:
The miniature calendar at left provides an overview of adjacent months; you can jump to a different week or day by using the triangle buttons for navigation, and then clicking within the numbers. At right, you can see a big view of the current month, week, or day. If an event has a reminder, a small alarm clock icon appears in the box; if the event is recurring, it shows a little stack-of-papers icon.

But if you double-click an appointment's title bar, or if you double-click a month-view square, you bring up the Event Info window shown in Figure 14-6. Using it, you can create far more specific appointments, decked out with far more bells and whistles. For example:

- **"All-day event"** refers to something that has no specific time of day associated with it: a holiday, a birthday, a book deadline.

Tip: If you turn on "All-day event," the lower Date box becomes un-dimmed so that you can specify a different ending date. This way, you can create *banners* like the one shown in Figure 14-5.

- **The Calendar pop-up menu** specifies which calendar this appointment will belong to.

  A *calendar*, in iCal's confusing terminology, is a subset—a category—into which you can place various appointments. You can create one for yourself, another for family-only events, another for book-club appointments, and so on. Later, you'll be able to hide and show these categories at will, adding or removing them from the calendar with a single click.

  At this point, you may also want to use the Status pop-up menu to classify this appointment as Tentative, Confirmed, or Canceled.

- **The ringing-bell icon** lets you set up a reminder, if you like. iCal can send the three kinds of flags to get your attention: It can display a message on the screen, send you an email, or play a sound.

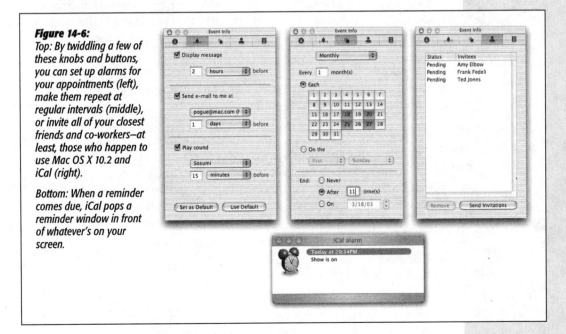

Figure 14-6:
Top: By twiddling a few of these knobs and buttons, you can set up alarms for your appointments (left), make them repeat at regular intervals (middle), or invite all of your closest friends and co-workers—at least, those who happen to use Mac OS X 10.2 and iCal (right).

Bottom: When a reminder comes due, iCal pops a reminder window in front of whatever's on your screen.

- **The recurrence schedule icon** (third at the top of the Event Info window), in conjunction with its pop-up menu (which starts out saying Never), lets you set up recurring events: daily, weekly, monthly, or yearly (Figure 14-6, middle). Once you've made a selection, you get an additional set of controls that let you set up variations like the first Sunday of the month, every Tuesday and Wednesday, and so on.

  The bottom part of the box lets you indicate how many times this event will recur. If you click "Never," you'll be stuck with seeing this event repeating on your calendar until the end of time (a good choice for recording, say, your anniversary, especially if your spouse might be consulting the same calendar). You can also turn on "After___ time(s)," which is a useful option for car and mortgage payments. You can also turn on "On," and specify the date that the repetitions come to an end; use this option to indicate the last day of school, for example.

Your newly scheduled event now shows up on the calendar, complete with the color-coding that corresponds to the calendar category you've assigned.

What to Do with an Appointment

Once you've entrusted your agenda to iCal, you can start putting it to work. iCal is only too pleased to remind you (via pop-up messages) of your events, reschedule them, print them out, and so on. Here are a few of the possibilities:

- **Editing event.** To edit a calendar event's name, just double-click it. To edit any of the appointment's other characteristics, you have to open its Event Info window. To do that in day or week view, double-click the top bar (where its time appears); in month view, double-click the dot before the name. The calendar event pops up in its window, where you can alter any of its settings as you see fit.

Tip: If you simply want to change an appointment's "calendar" category, you can bypass the event dialog box. Instead, just Control-click the appointment's name (or anywhere on its block), and choose the category you want from the resulting contextual menu.

- **Rescheduling.** If an event in your life gets rescheduled, you can drag an appointment vertically in its column to make it later or earlier the same day, or horizontally to another date, using its "time bar" as a handle in day or week view. If something is postponed for, say, a month or two, you have no choice but to double-click its name and then edit the starting and ending dates or times in the Event Info window. (Alas, iCal doesn't let you copy, cut, or paste calendar events.)

- **Lengthening or shortening events.** If a scheduled meeting becomes shorter or your lunch hour becomes a lunch hour-and-a-half (in your dreams), changing the length of the representative calendar event is as easy as dragging the top or bottom border of its block in any column view.

- **Deleting events.** To delete an appointment, just select it and then press the Delete key. In the confirmation dialog box, click Delete (or press Enter).

- **Searching for events.** You should recognize the oval text box at the bottom of the iCal screen immediately: it's almost identical to the one in the Finder toolbar. This search box is designed to let you hide all appointments except those matching what you type into it. Figure 14-7 has the details.

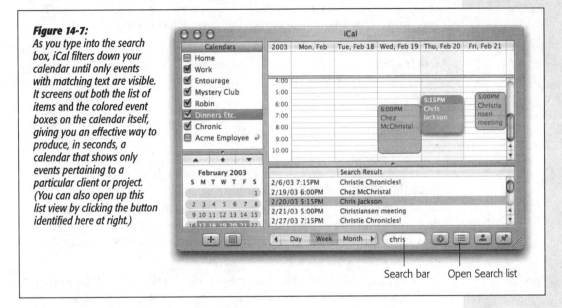

Figure 14-7:
As you type into the search box, iCal filters down your calendar until only events with matching text are visible. It screens out both the list of items and the colored event boxes on the calendar itself, giving you an effective way to produce, in seconds, a calendar that shows only events pertaining to a particular client or project. (You can also open up this list view by clicking the button identified here at right.)

Search bar   Open Search list

The "Calendar" Calendar Concept

Just as iTunes has *playlists* that let you organize songs into subsets, and iPhoto has *albums* that let you organize photos into subsets, iCal has something called *calendars* that let you organize appointments into subsets. One person might have

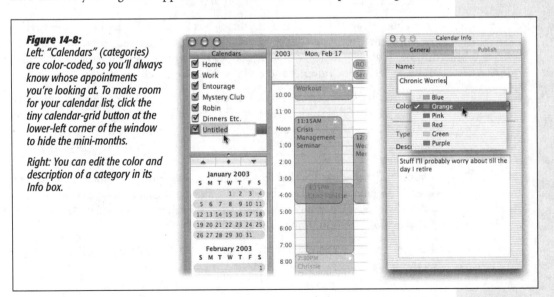

Figure 14-8:
Left: "Calendars" (categories) are color-coded, so you'll always know whose appointments you're looking at. To make room for your calendar list, click the tiny calendar-grid button at the lower-left corner of the window to hide the mini-months.

Right: You can edit the color and description of a category in its Info box.

calendars called Home, Work, and TV Reminders. Another might have Me, Spouse 'n' Me, and Whole Family. A small business could have categories called Deductible Travel, R&D, and R&R. They can be anything you like.

To create a calendar, double-click any white space in the Calendar list (below the others), or click the + button at the lower-left corner of the iCal window. Type a name that defines the category in your mind (see Figure 14-8).

You assign an appointment to one of these categories using the pop-up menu on its Event Info window. After that, you can hide or show an entire category of appointments at once just by turning on or off the appropriate checkbox in the Calendars list.

Tip: Click a calendar name *before* you create an appointment. That way, the appointment will already belong to the correct calendar.

"Publishing" Calendars to the Web

One of iCal's best features is its ability to post your calendar on the Web, so that other people—or you, using a different computer—can subscribe to it, which adds *your* appointments to *their* calendars. If you have a .Mac account, then anyone with a Web browser can also *view* your calendar, right online.

For example, you might use this feature to post the meeting schedule for a group or club that you manage, or to make clear the agenda for a series of financial meetings coming up that all of your co-workers will need to consult.

Publishing

iCal can publish only one "calendar" (category) at a time. Begin, then, by clicking the calendar category you want in the left-side list.

Then choose Calendar→Publish; the dialog box shown in Figure 14-9 appears. Here you customize how your saved calendar is going to look and work. You can even turn on "Publish changes automatically," so that whenever you edit the calendar, iCal connects to the Internet and updates the calendar automatically.

When you click Publish, your Mac connects to the Web and then shows you the Web address (URL) of the finished page, complete with a Send Mail option that lets you fire the URL off to your colleagues.

Subscribing

If somebody else has published a calendar, you subscribe to it by choosing Calendar→Subscribe. In the Subscribe to Calendar dialog box, type in the Internet address you received from the person who published the calendar. Alternatively, click the Subscribe button in any iCal Web page.

When it's all over, you see a new "calendar" category in your left-side list, representing the appointments from the published calendar.

Tip: This feature of iCal is a brilliant solution to the old, "My spouse and I each have a Palm, but we can't see each other's calendars" problem. In conjunction with iSync (described at the end of this chapter), each person can now summon the other's calendar to the screen on demand.

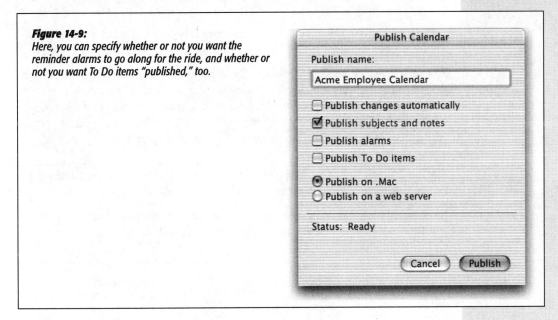

Figure 14-9:
Here, you can specify whether or not you want the reminder alarms to go along for the ride, and whether or not you want To Do items "published," too.

iChat

This instant-messaging program is described in Chapter 11.

iDVD

If your Mac came with a built-in *SuperDrive* (a drive that can burn both CDs and DVDs), then it also came with iDVD, a program that lets you turn your finished iMovie movies into real DVDs. *(iMovie 3 and iDVD: The Missing Manual* tells all.)

Image Capture

This unsung little program is something of an orphan. It was designed to download pictures from a USB digital camera and then process them automatically (turning them into a Web page, scaling them to emailable size, and so on). Of course, since Image Capture's birth, iPhoto came along, blowing its predecessor out of the water.

Even so, Apple still includes Image Capture with Mac OS X for these reasons:

- Image Capture makes it easy to download only *some* pictures from your camera. iPhoto, by contrast, always downloads the *entire* contents of your camera's memory card. (Figure 14-10 shows how to choose individual pictures.)

• iPhoto is great, but it can't hold more than about 2,000 pictures before it starts to feel like quicksand. At that point, most Mac fans shop for a more powerful digital-shoebox program—thus losing iPhoto's photo-downloading features. In those situations, Image Capture is a handy downloading tool. Once it's grabbed shots from the camera, you (or your beefier shoebox program) can take it from there.

• Starting in Mac OS X 10.2, Image Capture can grab images from Mac OS X–compatible scanners, too, not just digital cameras.

To open Image, either double-click its icon in your Applications folder, or set it up to open automatically whenever you connect the camera. (To set up that arrangement, open Image Capture manually. Choose Image Capture→Preferences, and choose Image Capture from the "When a camera is connected, open:" pop-up menu.) In any case, once Image Capture is open, it looks like Figure 14-10.

Tip: Sure, Image Capture *opens* automatically when you plug in your camera. But you still have to click the Download button to transfer the pictures. You call that automatic?

Yes—if you visit Image Capture→Preferences and turn on "Automatically download all items." From now on, just plugging in the camera both opens Image Camera *and* downloads its photos.

Figure 14-10:
Top: You can set up Image Capture to open automatically when you attach a USB camera to your Mac. One click (on Download All) transfers its pictures to the hard drive.

Bottom: If you click Download Some, you get this "slide-sorter" window, where you can choose the individual pictures you want to download, use the buttons at the top to rotate selected shots, or delete shots from the camera. In slide-sorter view, Shift-click or ⌘-click the thumbnails of the pictures you want to rotate, download, or delete en masse.

Here, you can use the pop-up menus to specify a destination folder for downloaded pictures and specify what happens automatically after they arrive ("Build slide show" or "Build Web page," for example).

iMovie 3

iMovie was the world's first video-editing program for nonprofessionals. You just connect a digital camcorder to your Mac with a FireWire cable, import your footage, and arrange the resulting video snippets (*clips*) on a timeline; season with music, credits, and special effects to taste. (*iMovie 3 and iDVD: The Missing Manual* goes into somewhat more detail than this paragraph.)

Internet Connect

If you have a full-time Internet connection (cable modem, DSL, or corporate network, for example), skip this section.

Internet Connect is just for dial-up modems. It shows your current dial-up status and settings (as configured in the Network pane of your System Preferences), and provides a Connect/Disconnect button for opening or closing a connection. Here's what you can accomplish with Internet Connect:

- Click Connect to dial out using your current modem settings.

- Once you're hooked up, check the status display to confirm whether or not your modem successfully connected to your ISP—or if you've been disconnected.

- You can also see your connection *speed*, to find out if you really connected up at 56 K (ha!), or if your modem was only able to negotiate a 28 K connection.

- A timer shows how long you've been connected.

- Internet Connect keeps a neat log of your connection activity (choose Window→Connection Log). Reading this log is about as exciting as reading random entries from the White Pages. Nonetheless, if you're having serious connection problems, it can be a useful troubleshooting tool.

- The "Show modem status in menu bar" checkbox lets you use a menu-bar icon to dial and observe your connections—without using Internet Connect at all.

- Internet Connect is also your gateway to a feature called Virtual Private Networking, which laptop lovers in the corporate world can use to tunnel into their company's network from the road.

Of course, even then, you don't really need Internet Connect to get online. If your dial-up settings are configured correctly (see page 211), your Mac will automatically dial whenever you launch a program that requires one (such as Internet Explorer).

Internet Explorer

See page 259.

iPhoto 2

iPhoto is a rich, flexible, "digital shoebox" for your digital photos. It's a glorious program that could easily be the topic of its own book. In fact, it is a book—*iPhoto 2: The Missing Manual.*

But the basics are easy enough. When you connect a recent-model USB camera and click Import (Figure 14-11), this program automatically sucks the pictures into your Mac.

Editing Photos

Once they're in iPhoto, there's no end to the fun you can have with your pictures.

- **Magnify or shrink them.** Just drag the little slider at the lower-right corner of the window, and watch in amazement as all of the photos grow larger or smaller. You can drag the slider so far to the right that each picture fills the screen—or so far to the left that they become the size of molecules. (Of course, you're not actually changing the photos; just the way they're displayed.)

- **Rotate a picture.** Every now and then, you may have had to turn the camera 90 degrees to take a picture—of, say, a giraffe or a skyscraper. When you import the photos to your iMac, those vertical photos wind up displayed horizontally.

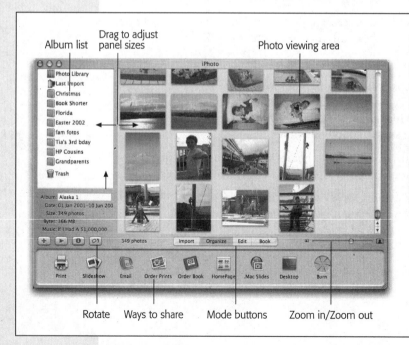

Figure 14-11:
iPhoto 2 at a glance. Once you hit about 2,000 photos, the program begins to slow down a lot; that's a good argument for splitting up your photos into individual libraries that keep the numbers more manageable. You can use the free program called iPhoto Library Manager for this purpose (available at www.missingmanuals.com).

To fix the problem in iPhoto, click the photo and then click the Rotate button, which is identified in Figure 14-11. The photo turns counterclockwise—unless you press the Option key while clicking, which makes it turn the other way.

- **Crop a picture.** Part of the artistry in becoming a shutterbug is learning how to *crop* a picture—to trim away excess background. Most of the time, a picture is more effective when it's a tight shot around the subject.

  To trim out excess background in iPhoto, double-click the picture. It opens into a special mode called Edit. At this point, drag diagonally so that the unwanted background becomes faded.

Tip: If you want to be sure that the photo remains photo-like in its proportions—ruling out the possibility that you'll wind up with a tall, skinny slice of the picture—use the Constrain pop-up menu at the left side of the editing window. Choose one of the standard photo sizes listed there, such as 4 x 6, before you drag across the picture.

Once you've highlighted the portion of the picture you want to keep, click the Crop button on the bottom edge of the window.

Note: *Nothing you do in iPhoto ever changes the original photo;* behind the scenes, iPhoto creates a backup copy of the original whenever you make a change. Even if you crop a picture, for example, you can return to it, months or years later, click it in the iPhoto window, open the File menu, and then choose Revert to Original. iPhoto brings back the picture as it looked the day you first imported from the camera.

- **Adjust brightness, contrast, and redeye.** When you double-click the picture, you also gain access to the Brightness/Contrast sliders (which can improve a photo by making it brighter or bringing out the difference between light and dark), the Enhance button (an amazing, one-click-does-it-all brightness/contrast/color fixer), and the Retouch brush (drag back and forth across a scar, a stray wire, or a freckle to erase it, thus "healing" the photo).

  This is also your opportunity to correct *redeye*—the occasional problem where somebody in a flash photo shows up with reddish pupils. Drag diagonally across the affected area with your cursor, and then click the Redeye button.

Organizing Photos

iPhoto's tendency to keep all of your pictures on one massive, scrolling screen isn't always the most efficient arrangement. You're better off creating little folders—*albums*, as they're called in iPhoto—that contain subsets of these pictures.

The trick is to click the little + button beneath the album list. iPhoto asks you to type in a name for the album you're about to create; do so and then click OK.

Now look in the list at the left side of the window: a new little book icon appears there. Above it in the list, click Photo Library (to see every photo you've ever taken) or Last Import (to see only the pictures from your last importing session).

Your challenge now is to select the pictures that you want to put into the newly created album. Click one picture to select it. ⌘-click additional pictures to select them, as well. To select several pictures in a row, ⌘-click the first one, and then *Shift*-click the last one. You've just highlighted all of the pictures in between, as well. Or drag diagonally across a group of folders to select all of them at once.

In any case, once you've highlighted the pictures, drag any *one* of them on top of the album book icon.

Note that dragging pictures into an album like this doesn't remove them from the main photo library. Instead, you're just creating imaginary duplicates that are *linked* back to the original pictures—something like Windows file shortcuts. Thanks to this quirk, you can put a single photo into as many different albums as you like.

Presenting Your Photos

iPhoto provides a number of different features for bringing your photos to a wider audience (the "Ways to share" buttons identified in Figure 14-11). Click the Organize button beneath the pictures, and then read on.

- **Slide Show.** Click the album icon whose pictures you want to see in the slide show, and then click the Slide Show icon at the bottom of the screen. A dialog box appears, offering you the chance to choose a background song (which iPhoto extracts from your iTunes music library).

  When you click Play Slideshow, you get a spectacular full-screen slide show, with pictures cross-fading into each other, your choice of music playing in the background. At any time, you can press the Space bar to freeze the show on a particular picture for audience scrutiny; press Space again to continue the show. (To re-enter automatic-advance mode, press the Space bar again.)

  To stop the show, click the mouse.

- **Send a picture by email.** Start by selecting one picture, or a few. Then click the Mail button. (Its icon reflects your choice of email program, as you've specified in the iPhoto→Preferences command.)

  iPhoto asks you what size you want to photo to be—an extremely friendly gesture, because sending a *full-size* digital camera picture is grossly overblown for viewing onscreen, and will probably choke your recipient's email account. That's why iPhoto offers to scale the picture down to reasonable size, such as 640 x 480 dots.

  Click Compose. After a moment, an empty piece of email appears, with the file already attached, ready for you to type in the address and any comments you'd like to include.

- **Order prints.** Click this button if you'd like your electronic photos turned into actual glossy prints, courtesy of an Internet-based printing service, at sizes you specify. You'll be offered a complete price list when you click the Order Prints button—and the thrilling opportunity to type in your credit card information.

- **Order Book.** More on this feature in a moment.

- **HomePage.** Highlight some photos, and then click this button to turn them into a bona fide Web page, which iPhoto can actually post on the Internet for billions of people to see. This feature requires that you've signed up for a .Mac account, as described on page 123. You'll be offered a choice of designs for your online gallery, plus the opportunity to type in some captions for them.

- **Desktop.** Click one photo and then click this button. iPhoto instantly fills your desktop background with that photo.

  If you click one *album* and then click this button, you turn that album's contents into a spectacular screen saver feature that fills your screen with animated, gently flowing photographs when your iMac isn't in use.

- **Book.** If you really want to see what your Mac can do, turn your pictures into a *book*: a hardback, linen-covered, acid-free, full-color, professionally published gift book that arrives in a slipcover in about four days. It costs about $30—more if you go beyond ten pages—and creates an unforgettable impact on the recipients.

  To design the book, click the album that contains them. (Make sure you've dragged them into the sequence you'll want for the book when you're in Organize mode.)

  Now click the Book button (to the right of the Edit button). In this miniature book-design program, choose an underlying design for your book, using the Theme pop-up menu. For example, the theme called Classic leaves plenty of margin around your pictures, but Picture Book blows up your photos so that they fill the page edge to edge.

  Next, click each page of the book and design it, using the Page Design pop-up menu to specify how many photos should appear on that page. As you change the number of pictures on a page, the pictures on the pages *following* it slide left or right to take up the slack.

  You can also designate special pages as the cover, introduction, and final pages. You can also rearrange the pages just by dragging them horizontally. Some of the page designs feature text boxes, too, where you can type in captions and descriptions.

  When the whole book looks good, click the Organize-mode button, and then click the Order Book button. The program now offers you the chance to choose the color you want for the cover. It may also warn you that some of the photos' resolutions (quality) are too low to look good in your book. If you proceed without making the photos smaller, they'll look blotchy in the resulting published book.

  How you wrap up your book-publishing process depends on whether or not you've created a "1-click account," a means of ordering stuff from Apple without having to type in your name and address over and over again. And to do *that*, you'll need an *Apple ID*—a name and password that you make up. The software guides you through both of these steps.

Finally, your book design is sent to the Internet, and in a few days, to the address you specified.

iSync

If Apple ever had evidence to back up its "digital hub" hype, iSync is it.

This attractive, simple program is designed to keep the calendars and phone lists on your various computers, Palm organizer, cell phone, and even your iPod in perfect synchronization, sparing you the headache of the modern age: inputting the same information over and over again. (See Figure 14-12.) Here's what it can keep synched:

- **A Bluetooth phone.** Of course, this also requires a Bluetooth adapter for your Mac (some models have it built in, or you can buy an Apple USB Bluetooth module for $50). And it requires a certain amount of technical setup (creating a phone profile, pairing the phone with your Mac, opening iSync and choosing Device→Add Device, and selecting the phone). You'll find detailed instructions in the iSync Help screens.

- **Other Macs.** This part requires a .Mac account, but it can be fantastically useful. It means that you and a colleague, or you and a spouse, or you and yourself at the office, can keep your calendars in sync, using the Internet as an intermediary.

    To set this up, just open iSync and click the .Mac icon. Click Register, type a name for your Mac, and then click Continue.

- **A Palm organizer.** iSync can also keep iCal and Address Book synched with a Palm-compatible organizer. It doesn't do the work itself; it relies, behind the scenes, on Palm's own HotSync software, which must be installed and properly configured beforehand. (You must also install the separate iSync_Palm.pkg software after installing iSync and Palm Desktop.)

    Once that's done, open HotSync Manager in your Palm folder. Choose Hotsync→ Conduit Settings. See where it says Address Book, Date Book, and To Do List? Double-click each one, select Do Nothing, and click Make Default.

    Then double-click iSync Conduit; turn on Synchronize Contacts and Synchronize Calendars; click OK; and quit HotSync Manager. You've just told Palm's own synching software to butt out. From now on, iSync will handle these data types (Address Book, Date Book, and To Do List).

    Finally, in iSync, choose Devices→Add Device to make iSync "see" your Palm, which you've put into its cradle, attached to its cable, or (if it's a Bluetooth Palm) made discoverable. To start the synchronization, press the physical HotSync button on the palmtop's cradle, cable, or HotSync screen. (Clicking iSync's Sync Now button never affects the Palm—only the iPod, phone, and .Mac connections.)

Note: All of this leaves your Palm memos unsynched, because neither Address Book nor iCal has a place for memos. The workaround: Use Palm Desktop to view and edit them.

- **An iPod.** Connect the iPod to the Mac, and help iSync find it using the Devices→ Add Device command. Now it's simple to consult your little black book on your little white block. (The synching is one-way: iSync copies your calendar and phone book to the iPod, but of course you can't use the iPod to add to, edit, or delete any of this information.)

Figure 14-12:
Top: For each gadget, you can specify which iCal calendar categories and which contacts you want synched, and (for a .Mac account) whether or not you want the synching to be automatic.

Bottom: The Safeguard window warns you about exactly how many changes you're about to make. (You can turn off this confirmation box in the iSync→ Preferences dialog box.) You can also revert your setup to the last sync, or back up all your data, using commands in the Devices menu.

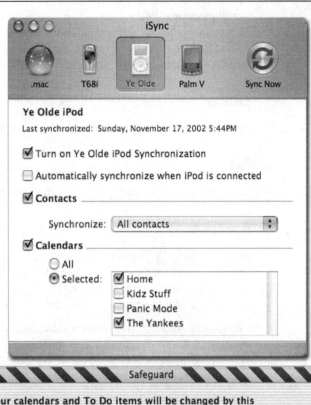

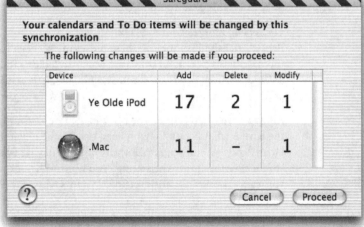

When you open iSync, its toolbar shows the icons of any synchable devices connected to your Mac at the moment. Click the appropriate gadget on the toolbar—your iPod, for example—to see the synching options available. Turn on the checkboxes you want, and then click the Sync Now button. iSync does the deed.

iSync is plenty smart when it comes to resolving conflicts among your gadgets. For example, if you edit somebody's home phone number on your Palm, and your spouse simultaneously edits the same person's office number on the Mac, iSync will smoothly incorporate both changes into all copies of your address book. Unless you and your spouse *both* change the home number in different ways; then iSync will present a Resolve Conflicts button. Click it, and choose which info you believe should prevail.

iTunes

iTunes is Apple's beloved digital music-library program. (Chapter 8 tells all.)

Mail

Mail, the Mac OS X email program, is described in Chapter 10.

Preview

Preview is Mac OS X's built-in graphics viewer. When you double-click the icon of a graphics file whose "parent" the Mac can't identify (maybe something you grabbed from a Web page or imported with your digital camera), Preview takes over. It does the work of opening and displaying the image onscreen.

Preview's hallmark is its surprising versatility. It works with pictures saved in a wide variety of formats, including less commonly used formats like BMP, PNG, SGI, TGA, and MacPaint, as well as the typical JPEG, TIFF, GIF, and PICT images. Preview can even open Photoshop files and multipage PDF documents.

Converting images with Preview

Preview doesn't just open all these file formats—it can also convert between most of them. You can pop open some old Mac PICT files and turn them into BMP files for a Windows user, pry open some SGI files created on a Silicon Graphics workstation and turn them into JPEGs for use on your Web site, and so on.

All you have to do is open the file you want to convert and choose File→Export. In the Save As dialog box that appears, choose the new format for the image using the Format pop-up menu. An Options button may be available for certain formats. If so, click it and choose the settings you want. When exporting to JPEG, for example, you can choose a Quality setting. When saving TIFF files, you can turn built-in compression on or off.

Finally, click OK to dismiss the Options dialog box, and then click Save to export the file.

Note: While Preview understands many of the most common formats, there are a few notable exceptions. You can't open, save, or export EPS files using Preview. And while you can open GIFs, Preview can't convert files in other formats into GIF.

Flipping your view with Preview

Preview isn't Photoshop, but it offers a few basic image manipulation commands. For example, you can rotate an image—even a PDF document—in 90-degree increments and then flip it vertically or horizontally.

The Thumbnails panel

The Thumbnails "drawer" panel slides out from the side of the main Preview window whenever (a) you open a multipage PDF file, or (b) you highlight a bunch of graphics files in the Finder and open them all at once. The idea is that these thumbnails (miniatures) let you navigate pages or graphics without having to open a rat's nest of individual windows. Figure 14-13 expands on the idea.

Tip: You can change the size of these miniatures by choosing Preview→Preferences and adjusting the slider. In the same dialog box, you'll find buttons that govern whether the Thumbnails drawer shows icons, text labels, or both.

Figure 14-13:
To open or close the new Thumbnails drawer (right), click the Thumbnails icon at the left end of the toolbar. Once you've clicked a thumbnail, you can move to the next or previous one by pressing the up or down arrow keys.

Preview and PDF

You can open and read PDF files with Preview, but you won't be able to use any of the interactive features built into some PDF files—bookmarks, hyperlinks, forms, and so on. For those functions, you need to use Acrobat Reader, described earlier in this chapter.

Here's what you *can* do with a PDF file using Preview:

- Save out a single page from a PDF as a TIFF file, so that you can use it in other graphics, word processing, or page layout programs—some of which might not directly support PDF. Use the File→Export command.

- Use ⌘-left arrow and ⌘-right arrow to page through a document. (Page Up and Page Down also work.)

- Zoom in and out using ⌘-up arrow and ⌘-down arrow. You can also fit a page to the size of the window (⌘-=), and display the PDF at actual size (Option-⌘-=).

- Turn *antialiasing* (font smoothing) on or off to improve readability; just choose Preview→Preferences.

Tip: Preview can even open multi page TIFF files, which is a big deal for anyone who's signed up for the free eFax service *(www.efax.com).* (eFax provides you with a private fax number. Whenever a fax is sent to that number, you get the fax by email. As a result, you can get faxes without owning a fax machine or having a fax line, and you can get faxes even when you're traveling.)

Either save your eFax attachments with the .tif extension, or send an email to eFax customer support with a request to have your incoming faxes tagged with the .tif extension automatically.

QuickTime Player

Dozens of Mac OS X programs can open QuickTime movies, play them back, and sometimes even incorporate them into documents: Word, FileMaker, AppleWorks, PowerPoint, Internet Explorer, America Online, and so on.

But the cornerstone of Mac OS X's movie-, sound-, and photo-playback software is QuickTime Player, which sits in your Applications→QuickTime folder (and comes factory-installed on the Dock). It does exactly what it's designed to do: show pictures, play movies, and play sounds. You might think of it as Apple's take on Windows Media Player.

Playing Movies

You can open a movie file by double-clicking it, dragging it onto the QuickTime Player icon, or by launching QuickTime Player and then choosing File→Open Movie in New Player (⌘-N). The most important controls (Figure 14-14) are:

- **Scroll bar.** Drag the diamond (or, in the Pro version described in a moment, the black triangle) to jump to a different spot in the movie.

- **Play/Stop button.** Click once to start, and again to stop. You can also press the Space bar, Return key, or ⌘-right arrow for this purpose. (Or avoid the buttons altogether and double-click the movie itself to start or stop playback.)

Tip: You can make any movie automatically play when opened, so that you avoid clicking the Play button. To do so, choose QuickTime Player→Preferences→Player Preferences, and turn on "Automatically play movies when opened."

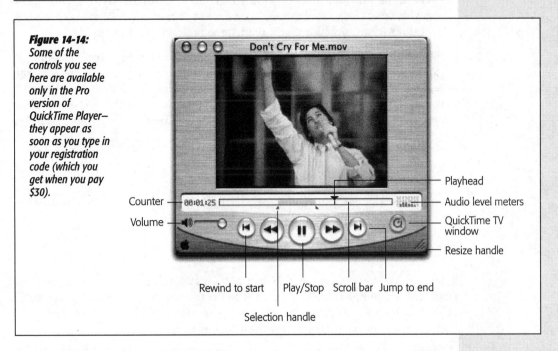

Figure 14-14:
Some of the controls you see here are available only in the Pro version of QuickTime Player— they appear as soon as you type in your registration code (which you get when you pay $30).

Don't Cry For Me.mov

Playhead

Counter — Audio level meters

Volume — QuickTime TV window

Resize handle

Rewind to start   Play/Stop   Scroll bar   Jump to end

Selection handle

- **Selection handles.** These tiny black triangles appear only in the $30 Pro version. You use them to select, or highlight, stretches of footage.

- **Volume.** If you like, you can make the soundtrack louder or softer by dragging this slider with your mouse or clicking in its "track." You may find it easier, however, to press the up or down arrow keys.

Tip: Try minimizing a QuickTime Player window while a movie is playing. It shrinks to the Dock—and *keeps on playing.* Do this enough times, and you'll know what it's like to be Steve Jobs on stage.

QuickTime Player Pro

If you've spent the $30 to upgrade your free copy of QuickTime Player to the Pro version—and to shut up the "Upgrade Now!" advertisement that appears the first time you open QuickTime Player each day—you've unlocked a number of useful features. For example:

- Your Movie menu contains additional playback options, including full-screen playback.

- When you find a QuickTime movie on a Web page, you can usually save it to your hard drive. (Click on the movie; hold down the mouse button until a pop-up menu appears; choose Save Movie to Disk, or the equivalent in your browser.)

- Using the commands in the Edit menu, you can view, turn on and off, add, or delete the individual *tracks* in a particular movie. (Most movies have nothing but a video track and a soundtrack. But a few specialized movies may also contain a text track, an animation track, alternate soundtracks, and so on.)

By far the most powerful feature you gain in the Pro version, however, is its ability to *edit* QuickTime movies. You can rearrange scenes, eliminate others, and save the result as a new movie with its own name. (Even QuickTime Player Pro doesn't let you *create* live-action QuickTime movies with a camcorder. For that, you need iMovie or a more complex editing program like Final Cut Express. QuickTime Player Pro simply lets you edit *existing* movies.)

Sherlock 3

Sherlock is Mac OS X's magnificent Web-information mini-browser, as described in Chapter 11.

Stickies

Stickies lets you create virtual Post-it notes that you can stick anywhere on your screen—a triumphant software answer to the thousands of people who stick notes on the edges of their *actual* monitors. If you're a fan of the Windows Notepad, you might find yourself getting heavily into Stickies instead.

You can use Stickies to type quick notes and to-do items, paste in Web addresses or phone numbers you need to remember, or store any other little scraps and snippets of text you come across. Your electronic Post-its show up whenever the Stickies program is running.

You can use a mix of fonts, text colors, and styles within each note. You can even copy and paste (or drag) *pictures, movies, and sounds* into your notes, producing the world's most elaborate reminders and to-do lists (Figure 14-15). You can even spell-check your notes and search-and-replace text.

Creating Sticky Notes

The first time you launch Stickies, a few sample notes appear automatically, describing some of the program's features. You can quickly dispose of each sample by clicking the close button in the upper-left corner of each note or by choosing File→Close (⌘-W). Each time you close a note, a dialog box asks if you want to save the note. If you click Don't Save, the note disappears permanently.

To create a new note, choose File→New Note (⌘-N) and start typing, pasting, or dragging text (or graphics, movies, or sounds) in from other programs.

Organizing Stickies

Once you start plastering your Mac with notes, it doesn't take long to find yourself plagued with desktop clutter. Fortunately, Stickies includes a few built-in tricks for managing a deskful of notes:

- There's a small resize handle on the lower-right corner of each note. Drag it to make notes larger or smaller on screen.

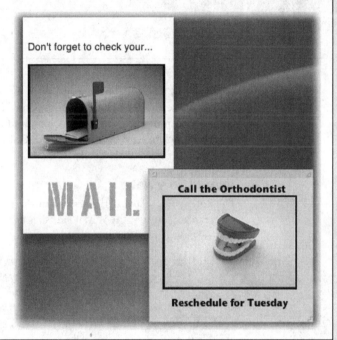

Figure 14-15:
Thanks to full-text formatting features and support for graphics and multimedia, even the humble to-do item can display a certain graphic sophistication in Mac OS X. You've come a long way from Notepad, baby.

- Use the small triangle in the upper-right corner of each note to zoom and shrink note windows with a single click. The first click collapses a note down to a more compact size. Another click pops the note back open to normal size.

- The best option: Double-click anywhere along the dark strip at the top of each note to miniaturize it into a compact one-line mini note, as shown in Figure 14-16. You also can miniaturize a selected note by choosing Window→Miniaturize Window (⌘-M).

- If your notes are scattered randomly across the desktop, you can line them all up in a neatly ordered cascading stack by choosing Window→Arrange in Front.

Tip: The most efficient way to use Stickies is to keep the notes in their miniaturized state, as shown in Figure 14-16. When a note is miniaturized, the first line of text shows up in tiny type right in the collapsed title bar of the note, so you don't have to expand the note to remember what's in it. And since many—if not most—of your notes can probably be summed up in a couple of words ("pick up dry cleaning," "call mom"), it's perfectly possible to keep your sticky notes in their miniaturized state permanently.

Figure 14-16:
If the first line of text gets truncated, as in the third note shown here, you can tug the right corner of the note and drag it wider without de-miniaturizing it.

Formatting Notes

Stickies has several word processor–like commands for creating designer sticky notes, with any combination of fonts, colors, and styles. (You can also choose from six different background colors from the Color menu.) For the full scoop on Mac OS X's Font panel, see page 96.

Saving Sticky Notes

The notes you create in Stickies last only as long as you keep them open. If you close a note to get it out of the way, it vanishes permanently (unless you promptly choose Edit→Undo Close Window, that is).

POWER USERS' CLINIC

The Hidden Stickies Commands

The casual Stickies user may miss some of the program's more interesting commands, which are accessible only through the contextual menus that pop up when you Control-click a sticky note. Here's what you'll find *only* in the contextual pop-up menus:

Check Spelling As You Type. Turning on this spell-check option flags misspelled words the moment you type them. You must turn this option on or off for each individual *note*—not for the Stickies program in general.

Font underlining. For some reason, you can format text with underlining using only the contextual pop-up menu, not the regular Note menu. (Bold and italic, however, are available from *both* menus.)

Speech. Don't just read your notes—*listen* to them. You can use the Mac's Text-to-Speech feature to hear your notes read aloud. Choose Speech→Start Speaking to hear the Mac read a selected portion of a note, or use the command with nothing selected to hear the entire contents of a note. The only way to stop the speech is to Control-click again and choose Speech→Stop Speaking.

(To pick the voice and speed of the reader, go to the Speech pane of System Preferences, as described on page 321).

The Speech commands are available in the Stickies→Services→Speech submenu, too, but the contextual-menu route is far more direct than opening a sub-sub-submenu.

If you want to preserve the information you've stuffed into your notes in a more permanent form, use File→Export Text to save each note as a stand-alone TextEdit document. When you use the Export Text command, you can save the file as a plain text file, RTF (a special format recognized by most word processors), and RTFD (a strange and powerful variant of RTF that can contain *attachments*—graphics, files, and even programs you've dragged into the note).

You can also save a note as Stationery: a template, complete with formatting and even text or graphics, that can serve as the basic formatting for new notes in the future. If you wanted to regularly post a note that had the heading "This Week's Shopping List," you could create a stationery sticky and thus avoid typing those words into a new note each week.

Mac OS X saves Stickies stationery with a *.tpl* file name extension. To use the template, choose File→Import Text, and then choose the .tpl file. You get a fresh, new note containing whatever was in the template. (Unfortunately, a Stickies stationery document stores a note's text and font style, but not its color, size, or shape.)

System Preferences

This program opens the door to the very nerve center of Mac OS X's various user preferences, settings, and options. Chapter 13 covers every option in detail.

TextEdit

TextEdit is a word processor—a basic one, to be sure, closer to WordPad than the Windows Notepad. It's got full formatting, font styles, and even a multiple-level Undo command. If you had to, you could write a novel in TextEdit and it would look pretty decent.

Tip: TextEdit recognizes some of the very same keyboard shortcuts found in Microsoft Word. For example, you can advance through documents one word at a time by pressing Option-left arrow or Option-right arrow. Adding the Shift key to those key combinations lets you *select* one whole word at a time. You can also use the Control or ⌘ key in conjunction with the right and left arrow keys to jump to the beginning or end of a line.

Setting Up TextEdit

To unleash the program's full potential as a word processor, set things up like this:

- **Choose Format→Wrap to Page.** Now you'll see the actual width of your page, with visible margins—just as in a real word processor. (The default Wrap to Window mode is a marginless view in which your text reflows to fill the width of the window.) Wrap to Page view also produces a Zoom menu in the lower-right corner of each window with ten different levels of magnification.

- **Turn on the text ruler.** If you don't see a ruler at the top of the window, choose Format→Text→Show Ruler (⌘-R). Now the ruler appears, complete with all the standard tools for setting margins, indents, tabs, line spacing, and paragraph alignment. It works almost exactly like the rulers you'd find in Microsoft Word or WordPad (Figure 14-17).

- **Fire up the spell-checker.** Check to make sure that the Edit→Spelling→Check Spelling As You Type command is turned on, if you like. This is interactive spell-checking. It works just as it does in Microsoft Word and other word processors; that is, misspelled words get flagged with a dashed red line the moment you type them.

Now you've got something that's starting to look and act like a real word processor.

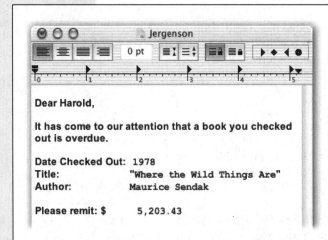

Figure 14-17:
The Text Ruler gives you control over tab stops, line spacing, paragraph justification, and so on. Pressing ⌘-R makes it appear and disappear. The two little padlock icons lock or unlock fixed line spacing, which controls whether or not a pasted graphic or a super-big typed character will be allowed to spread the paragraph lines farther apart.

Formatting Documents in TextEdit

Considering it's a free program that Apple tossed in primarily for opening Read Me files, TextEdit has a surprisingly good selection of real formatting tools:

- The Format→Font submenu holds the standard commands for applying Bold, Italic, and Underline styles to selected text.

- The Font command even offers advanced typographic controls like kerning (for adjusting letter spacing), ligatures (letter pairs, such as fl and ff, that, in fancy typesetting, are often conjoined into special combination characters, as shown here), and baseline control. (The baseline is the imaginary "floor" for text characters in a line of type. You can push text above this line or sink it below the baseline using the Raise and Lower commands in the Baseline submenu.)

- To change a font, or font size, press ⌘-T or choose Format→Font→Font Panel to open up the standard Mac OS X Font Panel (page 96).

- Common paragraph-alignment options—Align Left, Align Right, Center, Justify—are all available in Format→Text submenu.

- You can easily add graphics to a TextEdit file by dragging or pasting pictures directly into a document. The program understands TIFF, PICT, JPG, and GIF formats.

Utilities: The Mac OS X Toolbox

The Utilities folder (inside your Applications folder) is home to another batch of freebies: another couple dozen tools for monitoring, tuning, tweaking, and troubleshooting your Mac.

The truth is, though, that you're likely to use only about six of these utilities. The rest are very specialized gizmos primarily of interest only to network administrators or Unix geeks who are obsessed with knowing what kind of computer-code gibberish is going on behind the scenes.

AirPort Admin Utility

Don't even think about this program unless you've equipped your Mac with the hardware necessary for Apple's wireless AirPort networking technology (page 214).

Even then, you don't use the AirPort Admin Utility to set up AirPort connections for the first time. For that task, use the AirPort Setup Assistant (described below), which takes you gently by the hand and guides you through the steps involved in hooking up a wireless network connection.

After you're set up, you can use AirPort Admin Utility to monitor the connections in an existing AirPort network. (You can also use this utility to set up new connections manually, rather than using the step-by-step approach offered by the Assistant.)

AirPort Setup Assistant

An Assistant, in Apple-ese, is what you'd have called a Wizard in Windows. It presents a series of screens, posing one question at a time.

The AirPort Setup Assistant is the screen-by-screen guide that walks you through the steps needed to set up and use AirPort wireless networking. You'll be asked to name your network, provide a password for accessing it, and so on. When you've followed the steps and answered the questions, your AirPort hardware will be properly configured and ready to use.

Apple System Profiler

Apple System Profiler is the approximate equivalent of the Device Manager in Windows. It's a great tool for learning exactly what's installed on your Mac and what's not—in terms of both hardware and software. It combs through your system software, performing a quick analysis of every piece of hardware plugged into your machine and every program installed, and producing a neat, printable report on what it finds. The people who answer the phones on Apple's tech-support line are particularly fond of Apple System Profiler, since the detailed information it reports can be very useful for troubleshooting nasty problems.

Tip: Instead of burrowing into your Applications→Utilities folder to open System Profiler, it's usually faster to use this trick: Choose →About This Mac. In the resulting dialog box, click the More Info button. Boom—Apple System Profiler opens.

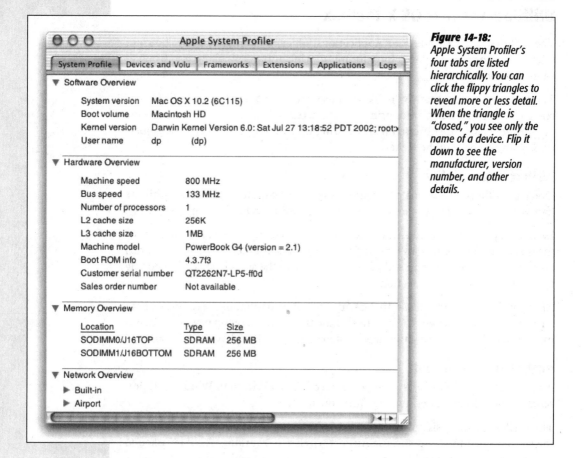

Figure 14-18:
Apple System Profiler's four tabs are listed hierarchically. You can click the flippy triangles to reveal more or less detail. When the triangle is "closed," you see only the name of a device. Flip it down to see the manufacturer, version number, and other details.

Asia Text Extras

Talk about niche markets: The tools in this folder are exclusively for designers of Asian fonts. The Chinese Text Converter utility, for example, converts documents between Simplified Chinese and Traditional Chinese character sets.

These tools aren't of any value to you unless (a) you've turned on the Chinese input method on the International panel of System Preferences, and (b) you have a clue what you're doing.

Audio MIDI Setup

Mac OS X comes with spectacular internal wiring for music, sound, and MIDI (Musical Instrument Digital Interface, a standard "language" for inter-synthesizer communication). Software companies are only gradually writing their programs to capitalize on it.

If you're a Mac musician who owns one of these programs, you'll find this little program worth exploring. The first tab, Audio Devices, is the master control panel for all your various sound inputs and outputs: microphones, line inputs, external speakers, and so on.

The second tab, MIDI Devices, should look familiar to synthesizer fans who have used software like OMS or FreeMIDI to teach the Mac about their studio configurations. By clicking Add Device, you create a new icon that represents one of your pieces of gear. Double-click the icon to specify its make and model. Finally, by dragging lines from the "in" and "out" arrows, you teach your Mac (and its MIDI software) how the various components are wired together.

Bluetooth File Exchange, Bluetooth Serial Utility

One of the luxuries of owning a Bluetooth-equipped Mac is the ability to shoot files (to similarly forward-thinking colleagues) through the air, up to 30 feet away. Bluetooth File Exchange makes it possible, as described on page 127.

ColorSync Utility

This "bet-you'll-never-touch-it" utility performs a fairly esoteric task: repairing ColorSync profiles that may be "broken" because they don't strictly conform to the *ICC profile* specifications. (ICC [International Color Consortium] profiles are part of Apple's ColorSync color management system, as described on page 285.)

Console

Console is a magic window that shows you what's happening under the hood of your Mac as you go about your business. Its function is to record a text log of all the internal status messages being passed between the Mac OS X and other applications as they interact with each other.

Opening the Console log is a bit like stepping into an operating room during a complex surgery; you're exposed to stuff the average person just isn't supposed to see. (Typical Console entries: "kCGErrorCannotComplete" or "doGetDisplay-TransferByTable.") You can adjust the font and word wrapping using Console's Format menu, but the truth is that the phrase "CGXGetWindowType: Invalid window – 1" looks ugly in just about *any* font.

Console isn't useless, however. These messages can be of great value to programmers who are debugging software or troubleshooting a messy problem.

CPU Monitor

CPU Monitor, another techie tool, lets you see how much of your Mac's available processing power is being tapped at any given moment. Think of it as an electrocardiogram for your Mac.

Launch CPU Monitor so that the thermometer-like Monitor window is open. Then go about your usual Mac business: Launch a few programs, drag a playing Quick-Time movie across the screen, or play a game. You'll see the level on the monitor rise and fall, depending on how busy you're keeping the CPU. On multiple-processor Macs, you see a different bar for each chip, enabling you to see how efficiently Mac OS X is distributing the work among them.

CPU Monitor actually offers three different ways of displaying the monitor readout, as explained in Figure 14-19. If you choose CPU Monitor→Preferences, you can customize the various monitor panels in a number of ways, changing their colors and other attributes.

Tip: To keep your eye on your Mac's activity without taking up additional space onscreen, open CPU Monitor→Preferences→Application Icon, and turn on one of the first two radio buttons. This replaces the icon that appears in the Dock when CPU Monitor is running with a live readout showing the CPU load as you work.

Figure 14-19:
Top: The three faces of CPU Monitor. The unobtrusive floating view (left) hovers over your desktop and can be turned semi-transparent in the Preferences window. The Standard view (middle) provides a single level indicator. The Extended view (right) uses different colors to represent different processes and can be stretched to any size.

Bottom: The CPU Monitor icon can be set to display moment-by-moment CPU activity right in the Dock.

DigitalColor Meter

With the DigitalColor Meter, you can grab the exact color value of any pixel on the screen, which can be helpful when matching colors in Web page construction or other design work. After launching the DigitalColor Meter, just point to whichever pixel you want to measure, anywhere on the screen. A magnified view appears in the meter window, and the RGB color value of the pixels appears in the meter window. You can display the color values as RGB percentages or absolute values, or in Hex form (which is how colors are defined in HTML; white is represented as #FFFFFF, for example).

Here are some tips for using the DigitalColor Meter to capture color information from the screen:

- To home in on the exact pixel (and color) you want to measure, drag the Aperture Size slider to the smallest size—one pixel. Then use the *arrow keys* to move the aperture to the precise location you want.

- Press Shift-⌘-C (Color→Copy Color) to put on the Clipboard the numeric value of the color you're pointing to.

- Press Shift-⌘-H (Color→Hold Color) to "freeze" the color meter on the color you're pointing to—a handy stunt when you're comparing two colors onscreen. You can point to one color, hold it using Shift-⌘-H, then move your mouse to the second color. Pressing Shift-⌘-H again releases the hold on the color.

- When the Aperture Size slider is set to view more than one pixel, DigitalColor Meter measures the *average* value of the pixels being examined.

Directory Access

If you use your Mac at home, or if it's not connected to a network, you'll never have to touch Directory Access. Even if you *are* connected to a network, there's only a remote chance you'll ever have to open Directory Access—unless you happen to be a network administrator, that is.

This utility controls the access that each individual Mac on a network has to Mac OS X's *directory services*—special databases that store information about users and servers. Directory Access also governs access to *LDAP directories* (Internet- or intranet-based "white pages" for Internet addresses).

A network administrator can use Directory Access to do things like select *NetInfo domains,* set up *search policies,* and define *attribute mappings.* If those terms don't mean anything to you, just pretend you never read this paragraph and get on with your life.

Disk Copy

This program creates and manages *disk images,* electronic versions of disks or folders that you can send electronically to somebody else.

The world's largest disk-image fan is Apple itself; the company often releases new software in disk-image form. A lot of Mac OS X add-on software arrives from your Web download in disk-image form, too, as described on page 105. Disk images are popular for software distribution for a simple reason: Each file precisely duplicates the original master disk, complete with all the necessary files in all the right places. When a software company sends you a disk image, it ensures that you'll install the software from a disk that *exactly* matches the master disk.

It's important to understand the difference between a *disk-image file* and the *mounted disk* (the one that appears when you double-click the disk image). Figure 14-20 should make the distinction clear.

Tip: After you double-click a disk image, go ahead and click Skip in the verification box that appears. If something truly got scrambled during the download, you'll know about it right away—your file won't decompress correctly, or it'll display the wrong icon, for example.

In fact, you can make Disk Copy *always* skip that verification business, which is a relic from the floppy-disk days. To do so, choose Disk Copy→Preferences, click the Verifying tab, and turn off Verify Checksums.

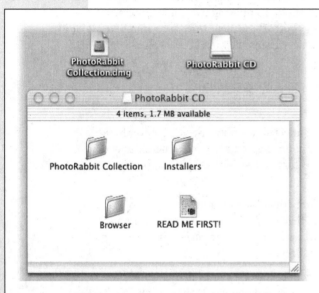

Figure 14-20:
The usual life cycle of a disk-image file: First, you download it from the Internet. The result is an icon whose name usually ends in .img or .dmg (upper left). (Files that end with .smi are also disk images, but self-mounting ones that don't require Disk Copy.) Second, when you double-click this icon, Disk Copy creates an icon that simulates a new disk (upper right). Finally, when you double-click this icon, you see exactly what the original creator of the image wanted you to see (bottom).

Fun with Disk Copy

You may not even be aware that Disk Copy is involved when you double-click a disk image to open it. You may be even less aware that *you* can create disk images, too. Doing so can be very handy in situations like these:

- You want to create a backup of an important CD or (non-copy-protected) DVD. By turning it into a disk-image file on your hard drive, you'll always have a safety copy, ready to burn back onto a *new* CD or DVD. (This is an essential practice for educational CDs to be handled by children.) The procedure for doing this appears below.

- You bought a game that requires its CD to be in the drive at all times. Most programs like these run equally well off of a mounted disk image that you made from the original CD.

- You want to send somebody else a copy of a CD via the Internet. You simply create a disk image, and then send *that*—preferably in compressed form.

To make a disk image, proceed as follows:

1. **Choose File→New→Image from Device.**

   That's how you'd start if you wanted to turn a *disk* into an image—a CD or Zip, for example. To make an image from a folder or a disk partition instead, choose File→New→Image from Folder or Volume.

   Tip: Control-click the Dock icon for Disk Copy (or just hold your mouse down on it and wait) to open a handy pop-up menu of shortcut commands. Choosing New Image from Device this way requires less mouse-gymnastic ability than choosing File→New→Image from Device in this step.

   Either way, the Device Selector dialog box appears. It lists the disks currently in, or attached to, your Mac. Unfortunately, they're listed a tad cryptically. You don't get to see their names—only their Unix ID numbers and types ("hard drive," "CD-ROM," or whatever). Still, you should be able to figure out which one is the disk you want by examining their descriptions and capacity listings ("250 MB" is probably a Zip disk, for example).

2. **Click the disk you want to copy. Click the Image button (or press Enter).**

   In the next dialog box, you're offered some fascinating options.

3. **From the Image Format pop-up menu, choose the format you want to use for your disk image.**

   If you choose "read/write," your disk image file, when double-clicked, will turn into a superb imitation of a hard drive. You'll be able to drag files and folders onto it, drag them off of it, change icons' names on it, and so on.

   If you choose "read/only," however, the result will behave more like a CD. You'll be able to copy things off of it, but not make any changes to it.

   The "compressed" option is best if you intend to send the resulting file by email, for example, or if you'd like to preserve the disk image on some backup disk for a rainy day. It takes a little longer to create a simulated disk when you double-click the disk image file, but it takes up a lot less disk space than an uncompressed version.

   Finally, choose "DVD/CD master" if you're copying a CD or a DVD. The resulting file is a perfect mirror of the original disc, ready for copying onto a blank CD or DVD when the time comes.

4. **If privacy is important, open the Encryption pop-up menu and choose "AES-128 (recommended)."**

   Here's a great way to lock private files away into a vault that nobody else can open. In one of the next steps, you'll be asked to assign a password to your new image file. Nobody will be able to open it without the password—not even you. Furthermore, if you save it into your Keychain (page 370), it won't be such a disaster if you forget the password.

5. Choose a name and location for your new image file.

The name you choose here doesn't need to match the original disk or folder name.

6. Click Save (or press Enter).

If you opted to create an encrypted image, you'll be asked to make up a password at this point.

When you press Enter, Disk Copy creates the image and then *mounts* it—that is, turns the image file into a simulated, yet fully functional, disk icon on your desktop.

When you're finished working with the disk, eject it as you would any disk (Control-click it and choose Eject, for example). Hang onto the .dmg disk image file itself, however. This is the file you'll need to double-click if you ever want to re-create your "simulated disk."

Turning an image into a CD

One of the other most common disk-image tasks is turning an image *back* into a CD or DVD—provided you have a CD or DVD burner on your Mac, of course.

All you have to do is choose File→Burn Image (or choose Burn Image from Disk Copy's Dock icon). In the resulting dialog box, locate the disk-image (.dmg) file you want to turn into a CD or DVD. Insert a blank CD or DVD, and then click Burn.

Disk Utility

Disk Utility is Mac OS X's own little Norton Utilities: a powerful hard-drive administration tool that lets you repair, erase, format, and partition disks. If you make the proper sacrifices to the Technology Gods, you'll rarely need to run Disk Utility. But keep it in mind, just in case you ever find yourself facing a serious disk problem.

Here are some of the tasks you can perform with Disk Utility:

- Get size and type information about any disks attached to your Mac (but with less detail than you get with Apple System Profiler).

- Fix disks that won't mount on your desktop or behave properly.

- Repair folders and files that don't work because you supposedly don't have enough "access privileges."

- Completely erase disks—including rewritable CDs (CD-RW).

- Partition a disk into multiple *volumes* (that is, subdivide a drive so that its segments appear on the desktop with separate disk icons).

- Set up a *RAID array* (a cluster of separate disks that acts as a single volume).

Note: Disk Utility can't verify, repair, erase, or partition your *startup disk*—the disk on which your system software is currently running. That would be like a surgeon performing an appendectomy on himself—not a great idea.

If you want to use Disk Utility to fix or reformat your startup disk, you must start up your Mac from a different system disk, such as the Mac OS X Install CD.

The left Disk Utility panel lists your hard drive and any other disks in your Mac at the moment. On the right is a panel with five tabs, one for each of the main Disk Utility functions:

- **Information.** Click the icon of a disk to read size, type, and partition information.

- **First Aid.** This is the disk-repair part of Disk Utility. You're supposed to click the icon of a disk and then click either Verify (to get a report on the disk's health) or Repair (which fixes whatever problems the program finds). In other words, First Aid attempts to perform the same healing effects on a sick hard drive as, say, a program like Norton Utilities. It does a great job at fixing many disk problems; when you're troubleshooting, Disk Utility should always be your first resort.

  If Disk First Aid reports that it's unable to fix the problem, *then* it's time to invest in Norton Utilities (if a Mac OS X version is available) or its rival, Drive 10 (*www.micromat.com*).

Tip: If Disk First Aid finds nothing wrong with a disk, it reports, "The volume appears to be OK." Don't be alarmed at the wishy-washy, not-very-confident wording of that message—that's the strongest vote of confidence Disk First Aid can give. Even a brand-new, perfectly healthy hard drive only *appears* to be OK to Disk First Aid.

  The Verify and Repair Disk *Permissions* buttons straighten out problems with the invisible Unix *file permissions* that keep you from moving, changing, or deleting files or folders. (The occasional software installer can create problems like this.)

- **Erase.** The Disk Utility program is also the Mac's Erase Disk command. Launch it, click the Erase tab, and blow away the data on the disk of your choice, whether it's a floppy, hard drive, CD-RW, or a DVD-RW.

- **Partition.** With the Partition tools, you can erase a hard drive in such a way that you subdivide its surface. Each chunk is represented on your screen by two (or more) different hard drive icons. (See Figure 14-21.)

  Some people partition very large hard drives because it gives them a psychologically satisfying sense of separation; maybe they like to keep old projects on one partition, and current stuff on another. There are, however, a few good reasons *not* to partition a drive these days: A partitioned hard drive is more difficult to resurrect after a serious crash, requires more navigation when you want to open a particular file, and offers no speed or safety benefits.

• **RAID.** RAID stands for Redundant Array of Independent Disks, and refers to a special formatting scheme in which a group of separate disks are configured to work together as one very large, very fast drive. In a RAID array, multiple disks share the job of storing data—a setup that can improve speed and reliability.

Most Mac users don't use or set up RAID arrays, probably because most Mac users only have one hard drive (and Disk Utility can't make your startup disk part of a RAID array).

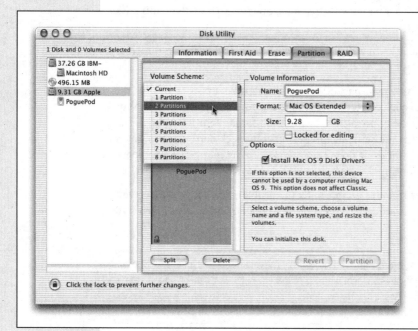

Figure 14-21:
To partition your drive—which involves erasing it completely—launch Disk Utility, switch to the Partition pane, and select the hard drive you want to partition from the list on the left. From the Volume Scheme pop-up menu, choose the number of partitions you want, as shown here. Now drag the horizontal lines in the Volumes map to specify the relative sizes of the partitions you want to create. Assign a name and format for each partition in the Volume Information area, and then click OK.

If you're using multiple external hard disks (SCSI or IDE format), though, you can use Apple RAID to merge them into one giant disk. Just drag the icons of the relevant disks (or disk partitions) from the left-side list of disks into the main list (where it says, "Drag disks here to add to set"). Use the RAID Scheme pop-up menu to specify the RAID format you want to use (Stripe is the most common), name your new mega-disk, and then click Create. The result is a single "disk" icon on your desktop that actually represents the combined capacity of all the RAID disks.

Display Calibrator

The Display Calibrator is another of the Mac's Assistant programs, designed to help you adjust your monitor's color settings. It walks you through a series of six screens, presenting various brightness and color balance settings in each screen so you can pick the settings that look best to you; at the end of the process, you save your moni-tor tweaks as a *ColorSync profile* (page 285) that ColorSync-savvy programs can use to adjust your display for improved color accuracy.

Grab

Grab takes pictures of your Mac's screen, for use when you're writing up instructions, illustrating a computer book, or collecting proof of some secret screen you found buried in a game. You can take pictures of the entire screen (press ⌘-Z, which for once in its life does *not* mean Undo) or capture only the contents of a rectangular selection (press Shift-⌘-A). When you're finished, Grab displays your snapshot in a new window, which you can print, close without saving, or save as a TIFF file, ready for emailing, posting on a Web page, or inserting into a manuscript.

Tip: The Mac also has built-in screen-capture keystrokes, just as Windows does; see page 176 for details.

Installer

You'll never launch this. It's the engine that drives the Mac OS X installer program and other software installers. There's nothing for you to double-click, configure, or set up.

Java Folder

Programmers generally use the Java programming language to create small programs that they sometimes embed into Web pages—animated effects, clocks, calculators, stock tickers, and so on. Your browser automatically downloads and runs such applets (assuming that you have "Enable Java" turned on in your browser), thanks to the Java-related tools in this folder.

Key Caps

Key Caps is a single window containing a tiny onscreen keyboard (Figure 14-22). When you hold down any of the various modifier keys on your keyboard (such as ⌘, Option, Shift, or Control), you can see exactly which keys produce which characters. The point, of course, is to help you learn which keys to press when you need special symbols or non-English characters, such as © or ¢, in each font.

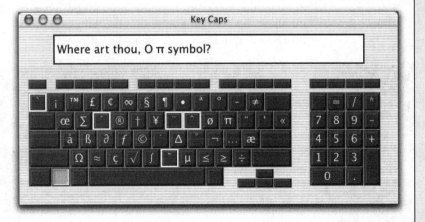

Figure 14-22:
How do you make a π symbol? Key Caps reveals the answer. When you press the Option key, the Key Caps keyboard shows that the pi character (π) is mapped to the P key. Once you've found and typed the character in Key Caps, you can copy and paste it into any other program.

Note: Key Caps shows only the symbols you can produce by typing keystrokes. A font may contain thousands of other characters that can't actually be typed; the Character Palette (page 301) is the only way to access these other symbols.

If you want to see the effect of typing while pressing the modifier keys, either click the onscreen keys or type on your actual keyboard. The corresponding keys on the onscreen keyboard light up as they're pressed.

Change the Key Caps font

Different fonts contain different hidden characters. For example, Palatino contains a character (produced by pressing Shift-Option-K), yet Adobe Garamond does not.

Fortunately, Key Caps lets you see the characters lurking within almost any installed font; just choose a font's name from the Font menu to see all of its modifier-key characters. (You may have to change the keyboard layout to see all symbols in some fonts.) Alas, this feature doesn't work in a few of the fonts where it would be the most useful, notably symbol fonts like Symbol and Zapf Dingbats.

Tip: You're not stuck viewing all characters in 12-point size—a good thing, because some of them are hard to read when displayed that small. Just "zoom" the Key Caps window (by clicking the green gel-button near the top-left corner) to magnify the Key Caps window and its font, as shown in Figure 14-22.

Keychain Access

The information explosion of the computer age may translate into bargains, power, and efficiency, but it carries with it a colossal annoyance: the proliferation of *passwords* we have to memorize. Shared folders on the network, Web sites, your iDisk, FTP sites—each requires another password to remember.

Apple's *Keychain* concept is brilliant: Whenever you log into Mac OS X and type in your password, you've typed the master code that tells the computer, "It's really me. I'm at my computer now." The Mac responds by *automatically* filling in every password blank you encounter in your networking exploits. You can safely forget all of the passwords required for accessing the various other Macs on your network.

UP TO SPEED

Bringing Dead Keys to Life

If you press Option while the Key Caps window is open, you see little white outlines around certain keys (shown in Figure 14-22, for example). These rectangles identify the Mac's five *dead keys*—keys that, when pressed once, type *nothing* onscreen. However, when you type *another* key— a normal letter, for example—it appears with the dead key's displayed marking over it. To type the ñ in *jalapeño*, you must first press Option-N and *then* type an *n*. This same two-step approach lets you type characters like ö and é.

Because it's on all the time and memorizes most passwords automatically, the Keychain winds up being invisible for many people. Just go about your business, tapping into other computers on the network as described earlier in this chapter, connecting to your iDisk, and so on. Behind the scenes, the Mac quietly collects the various passwords so that you don't need to enter them again.

Locking and unlocking the Keychain

When your Keychain is unlocked, you can open your password-protected FTP sites, iDisk, network servers, and so on, without ever having to enter a password. Apple figured: "Hey, you've *already* entered a name and master password—when you logged into the Mac. That's good enough for us." If you work alone, the Keychain therefore becomes automatic, invisible, and generally wonderful.

But if you work in an office where someone else might sit down at your Mac while you're getting a candy bar, you might want to *lock* the Keychain when you wander away. (Locking it requires no password.) Mac OS X will no longer fill in your passwords—until you return to your desk and unlock the Keychain again.

You can lock the Keychain in any of several ways, each of which involves the Keychain Access program:

• **Lock the Keychain manually.** Click the Lock button in the toolbar of the Keychain Access window (see Figure 14-23, top).

• **Lock the Keychain automatically.** In the Keychain Access program, choose Edit→[your name] Settings. As shown in Figure 14-23 at bottom, you can set up the Keychain to lock itself, say, five minutes after the last time you used your Mac, or whenever the Mac goes to sleep. When you return to the Mac, you'll be asked to re-enter your account password in order to unlock the Keychain, restoring your automatic-password feature.

WORKAROUND WORKSHOP

When Keychains Don't Unlock the Web

Unfortunately, when it comes to password proliferation, we're not out of the woods yet. The Keychain can't store passwords in programs that haven't been rewritten to be *Keychain-aware.* Notable among programs that ignore the Keychain is Internet Explorer (version 5.2). In other words, the Keychain doesn't store passwords for secure Web pages, such as those for your bank and online-brokerage accounts, that you type into Internet Explorer. (On the other hand, Internet Explorer has its own built-in password-memorizing feature. It's not as convenient as the master Keychain password, but it's better than nothing.)

The highly regarded Web browser called OmniWeb, however, is Keychain-aware, and *does* memorize many kinds of Web site passwords. This Web browser is available from the software page of *www.missingmanuals.com,* for example.

Note: As noted above, you unlock your Keychain using the same password you used to log into Mac OS X. But that's just a convenience. If you're really worried about security, you can click Change Passphrase (see Figure 14-23) thereby establishing a *different* password for your Keychain. Of course, doing so also turns off the automatic-Keychain-unlocking-when-you-log-in feature.

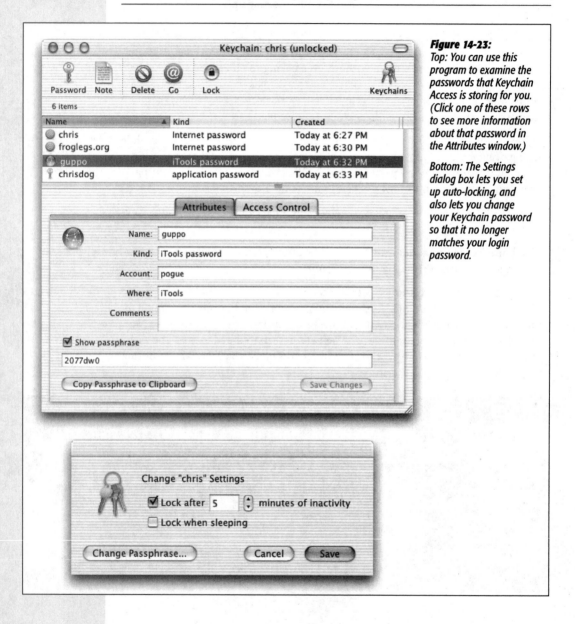

Figure 14-23:

Top: You can use this program to examine the passwords that Keychain Access is storing for you. (Click one of these rows to see more information about that password in the Attributes window.)

Bottom: The Settings dialog box lets you set up auto-locking, and also lets you change your Keychain password so that it no longer matches your login password.

Managing Keychains

To take a look at your Keychain, open the Keychain Access program. By clicking one of the password rows, you get to see its *attributes*—name, kind, account, and so on. At this point, you can turn on "Show Passphrase" to see the actual password it's storing.

Keychain files

Keychains are represented by separate files in your Home folder→Library→Keychains folder. Knowing that can be handy in several circumstances:

- **Deleting a Keychain.** You can delete a Keychain easily enough—just drag a Keychain file out of this folder and into the Trash.

- **Copying a Keychain.** You can copy one of your keychain files into the corresponding location on another computer, such as your laptop. It carries with it all the password information for the networks and Web sites of your life.

NetInfo Manager

NetInfo is the central Mac OS X database that keeps track of user and group accounts, passwords, access privileges, email configurations, printers, computers, and just about anything else network related. NetInfo Manager is where a network administrator (or a technically inclined Mac guru) can go to view and edit these various settings.

While most of NetInfo Manager is of little use to a typical Mac user, a few parts of this utility can be valuable even to a non–system administrator.

To dive into NetInfo Manager, start by clicking the padlock button at the bottom of the main window and enter an administrator's password. Then examine the various parameters in the top-left Directory Browser list. As you'll quickly discover, most of these settings are written in Unix techno-speak.

A few, however, are easy enough to figure out. If you click *users* in the left-side list, you'll see, in the next column, a list of accounts you've created. Click one of the user names there, and you'll see, in the properties pane at the bottom of the screen, some parameters that may come in handy, such as each person's name, password, and password hint. By double-clicking one of these info items, you can edit it, which can come in genuinely handy if someone on your school or office network forgets their password.

Network Utility

The Network Utility gathers information about Web sites and network users. It offers a suite of advanced, industry-standard Internet tools like these:

- Use **WhoIs** to gather an amazing amount of information about the owners of any particular domain (such as *www.apple.com*)—including name and address info, telephone numbers, and administrative contacts—using the technique shown in Figure 14-24.

- Use **Ping** to enter a Web address (such as *www.google.com*), and then "ping" (send out a "sonar" signal to) the server to see how long it takes for it to respond to your request. Network Utility reports the response time in milliseconds—a useful test when you're trying to see if a remote server (a Web site, for example) is up and running.

- **Traceroute** lets you track how many "hops" are required for your Mac to communicate with a certain Web server. Just type in the network address then click Trace. You'll see that your request actually jumps from one *trunk* of the Internet to another, from router to router, as it makes its way to its destination. You'll find that a message sometimes crisscrosses the entire country before it arrives at its destination. You can also see how long each leg of the journey took, in milliseconds.

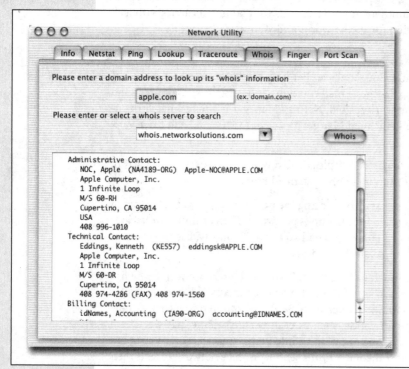

Figure 14-24:
The WhoIs tool is a powerful part of Network Utility. First enter a domain that you want information about, then choose a WhoIs server from the pop-up menu (you might try checking whois.networksolutions.com). When you click the WhoIs button, you'll get a surprisingly revealing report about the owner of the domain, including phone numbers, fax numbers, contact names, and so on.

ODBC Administrator

This program is designed to arbitrate ODBC access requests. Any questions?

If you have no idea what that means, and no corporate system administrator has sat down with you to explain it to you, then your daily work probably doesn't involve working with corporate ODBC (Open Database Connectivity) databases. You can ignore this program or throw it away.

Print Center

This is the hub of your Mac's printing operations. You can use the Print Center to set up and configure new printers, and to check on the status of print jobs, as described in Chapter 8.

Process Viewer

Even when you're only running a program or two on your Mac, dozens of computational tasks *(processes)* are going on in the background. Like the Windows Task Manager, the Mac's Process Viewer lets you see all the different processes—foreground and background—that your Mac is handling at the moment.

If you want to get a peek at just how busy your Mac is, even when you're just staring at the desktop, launch the Process Viewer. Check out how many items appear in the Process Listing Window. Some are easily recognizable programs (such as Finder), while others are background system-level operations you don't normally see. For each item, you can see the percentage of CPU being used, who's using it (either your account name or *root,* meaning the Mac itself), and the percentage of memory it's using.

Tip: When one of your programs freezes or crashes, double-click its name in Process Viewer. You'll be offered the Quit Process dialog box, which you can use to exit the stuck program as safely as possible. This technique often works to jettison the troublemaker when all else fails.

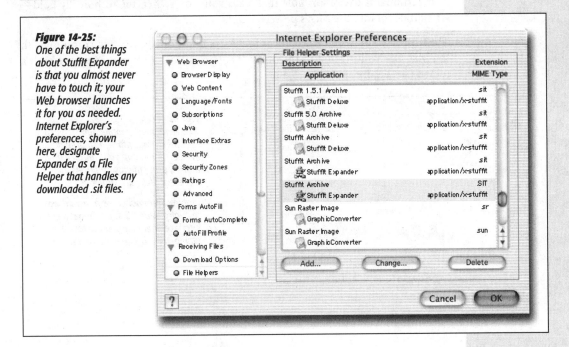

Figure 14-25:
One of the best things about StuffIt Expander is that you almost never have to touch it; your Web browser launches it for you as needed. Internet Explorer's preferences, shown here, designate Expander as a File Helper that handles any downloaded .sit files.

StuffIt Expander

StuffIt Expander, a free program from Aladdin Systems, is an indispensable utility for decompressing and decoding files, especially those that you download from the Internet or receive as email attachments. It automatically restores all kinds of compressed files into usable form, including StuffIt files (whose names end with .sit), Zip files (.zip), BinHex files (.hqx), UUEncoded files (.uu), MIME or Base64 files (.mime), and—especially important in Mac OS X—.tar and .gzip files, which were once found only on Unix machines. (Your Mac *is* a Unix machine.)

Usually, you needn't *do* anything with StuffIt Expander. It just does its thing, automatically and unbidden, whenever you download a compressed file. That's because most Web browsers come configured to treat StuffIt Expander as a *helper application;* the browsers summon Expander the moment they recognize that you've downloaded a compressed file (see Figure 14-25).

If you end up with a .sit or .zip file on your Mac that needs decompressing—and StuffIt Expander hasn't been launched automatically—just drag the file onto the StuffIt Expander icon to expand it.

Terminal

Mac OS X's resemblance to an attractive, mainstream operating system like Windows or the old Mac OS is just an optical illusion; the engine underneath the pretty skin is Unix, one of the oldest and most respected operating systems in use today. And Terminal is the rabbit hole that leads you—or, rather, the technically bold—straight down into the Mac's powerful Unix world.

The first time you see it, you'd swear that Unix has about as much in common with the Mac OS X illustrated in the other chapters of this book as a Jeep does with a melon (see Figure 14-26).

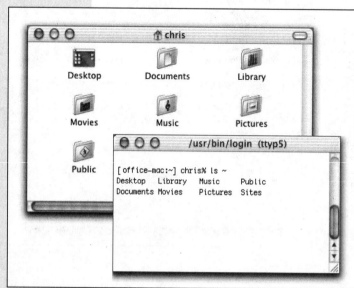

Figure 14-26:
Top: What most people think of when they think "Macintosh" is a graphic interface—one that you control with a mouse, using menus and icons to represent files and commands.

Bottom: Terminal offers a second way to control Mac OS X: a command line interface, meaning you operate it by typing out programming codes.

What the illustration at the bottom of Figure 14-26 shows, of course, is a *command line interface:* a place where you can type out instructions to the computer itself. This is a world without icons, menus, or dialog boxes; even the mouse is almost useless.

Surely you can appreciate the irony: The brilliance of the original 1984 Macintosh was that it *eliminated* the command line interface that was still the ruling party on the computers of the day (like Apple II and DOS machines). Most non-geeks sighed with relief, delighted that they'd never have to memorize commands again. Yet here's Mac OS X, Apple's supposedly ultramodern operating system, complete with a command line! What's going on?

Actually, the command line never went away. At universities and corporations worldwide, professional computer nerds kept right on pounding away at the little *C:* or % prompts, appreciating the efficiency and power such direct computer control afforded them.

Now, you never *have* to use Mac OS X's command line. In fact, Apple has swept it far under the rug, obviously expecting that most people will use the beautiful icons and menus of the regular desktop.

For intermediate or advanced computer fans with a little time and curiosity, however, the command line opens up a world of possibilities. It lets you access corners of Mac OS X that you can't get to from the regular desktop. It lets you perform certain tasks with much greater speed and efficiency than you'd get by clicking and dragging icons. And it gives you a fascinating glimpse into the minds and moods of people who live and breathe computers.

A Terminal crash course

Terminal is named after the terminals (computers that consist of only a monitor and keyboard) that tap into the mainframe computers at universities and corporations. In the same way, Terminal is just a window that passes along messages to and from the Mac's brain.

The first time you open Terminal, you'll notice that there's not much in its window except the date and time of your last login, a welcome message, and the "%" (the command line prompt).

For user-friendliness fans, Terminal doesn't get off to a very good start—this prompt looks about as technical as computers get. It breaks down like this (see Figure 14-27):

- **office-mac:** The prompt begins with the name of your Mac (at least, as Unix thinks of it), as recorded in the Sharing panel of System Preferences.

- **~.** The next part of the prompt indicates what folder you're "in" (see Figure 14-27). It denotes the *working directory*—that is, the current folder. (Remember, there are no icons in Unix.) Essentially, this notation tells you where you are as you navigate the machine.

The very first time you try out Terminal, the working directory is set to the symbol ~, which is shorthand for "your own Home folder." It's what you see the first time you start up Terminal, but you'll soon be seeing the names of other folders here—*[office-mac: /Users]* or *[office-mac: /System/Library]*, for example. (More on this slash notation on the facing page.)

Note: Before Apple came up with the user-friendly term *folder* to represent an electronic holding tank for files, folders were called *directories.* (Yes, they mean the same thing.) But in any discussion of Unix, "directory" is simply the correct term.

- **chris%.** The next part of the prompt begins with your short user name. It reflects whoever's logged into the *shell* (the programming environment), which is usually whoever's logged into the *Mac* at the moment. As for the % sign: think of it as a colon. In fact, think of the whole prompt shown in Figure 14-27 as Unix's way of asking, "OK, Chris, I'm listening. What's your pleasure?"

The insertion point looks like a tall rectangle at the end of the command line. It trots along to the right as you type.

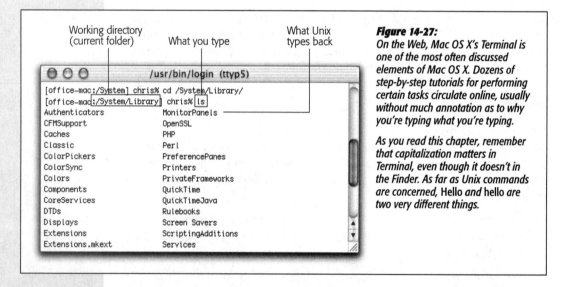

Figure 14-27:
On the Web, Mac OS X's Terminal is one of the most often discussed elements of Mac OS X. Dozens of step-by-step tutorials for performing certain tasks circulate online, usually without much annotation as to why you're typing what you're typing.

As you read this chapter, remember that capitalization matters in Terminal, even though it doesn't in the Finder. As far as Unix commands are concerned, Hello *and* hello *are two very different things.*

Unix programs

Each Unix command generally calls up a single application (or *process,* as geeks call it) that launches, performs a task, and closes. Many of the best-known such applications come with Mac OS X.

Here's a fun one: Just type *uptime* and press Enter. (That's how you run a Unix program: just type its name and press Enter.) On the next line, Terminal shows you how long your Mac has been turned on continuously. It shows you something like: "6:00PM up 8 days, 15:04, 1 user, load averages: 1.24, 1.37, 1.45"—meaning your Mac has been running for 8 days, 15 hours nonstop.

You're finished running the *uptime* program. The % prompt returns, suggesting that Terminal is ready for whatever you throw at it next.

Try this one: Type *cal* at the prompt, and then press Enter. Unix promptly spits out a calendar of the current month.

```
[office-mac:~] chris% cal
     June 2003
 S  M Tu  W Th  F  S
 1  2  3  4  5  6  7
 8  9 10 11 12 13 14
15 16 17 18 19 20 21
22 23 24 25 26 27 28
29 30
[office-mac:~] chris%
```

As you can see, it wraps up the response with "[office-mac:~] chris%"—yet another prompt, meaning that Terminal is ready for your next command.

This time, try typing *cal 11 2003*, *cal -y*, or *cal -yj*. These three commands make Unix generate a calendar of November 2003, a calendar of the current year, and a *Julian* calendar of the current year, respectively.

Navigating in Unix

If you can't see any icons for your files and folders, how are you supposed to work with them?

You use Unix commands like *pwd* (tells you what folder you're looking at), *ls* (lists what's *in* the current folder), and *cd* (changes to a different folder).

UP TO SPEED

Pathnames 101

In many ways, browsing the contents of your hard drive using Terminal is just like doing so with the Finder. You start with a folder, and move down into its subfolders, or up into its parent folders.

In Terminal, you're frequently required to specify a certain file or folder in this tree of folders. But you can't see their icons from the command line. So how are you supposed to identify the file or folder you want?

By typing its *pathname*. The pathname is a string of folder names, something like a map, that takes you from the *root level* to the next nested folder, to the next, and so on. (The root level is, for learning-Unix purposes, the equivalent of your main hard drive window. It's represented in Unix by a single slash. The phrase */Users*, in other words, means "the Users folder in my hard drive window," or, in other terms, "the Users directory at the root level.")

To refer to the Documents folder in your own Home folder, for example, you could type */Users/chris/Documents* (if your name is Chris, that is).

Tip: As you can tell by these examples, Unix commands are very short. They're often just two-letter commands, and an impressive number of those use *alternate hands* (ls, cp, rm, and so on).

The reason has partly to do with conserving the limited memory of early computers and partly to do with efficiency: most programmers would just as soon type as little as possible to get things done. User-friendly it ain't, but as you type these commands repeatedly over the months, you'll eventually be grateful for the keystroke savings.

Getting help

Mac OS X comes with nearly 900 Unix programs. How are you supposed to learn what they all do? Fortunately, almost every Unix program comes with its own little help file. It may not appear within an elegant Mac OS X window—in fact, it's pretty darned plain—but it offers much more material than the regular Mac Help Center.

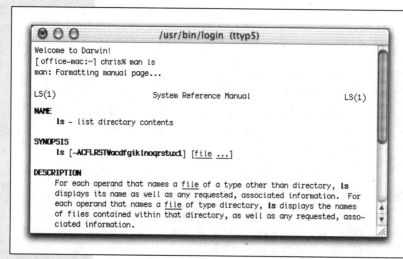

Figure 14-28:
To move on to the next man screen, press the Space bar. To go back, you can either use the Terminal window's scroll bar or press B. To close the manual and return to a prompt, press Q.

These help files are called user-manual pages, or *manpages*, which hold descriptions of virtually every command and program available. Mac OS X, in fact, comes with manpages on about 4,000 topics—about 9,000 printed pages' worth. Unfortunately, manpages rarely have the clarity of writing or the learner-focused approach you'll find in the Mac Help Center. They're generally terse, just-the-facts descriptions. In fact, you'll probably find yourself needing to reread certain sections again and again. The information they contain, however, is invaluable to new and experienced users alike, and the effort spent mining them is usually worthwhile.

To access the manpage for a given command, type *man* followed by the name of the command you're researching. For example, to view the manpage for the *ls* command, enter: *man ls*. Now the manual appears, one screen at a time, as shown in Figure 14-28.

For more information on using *man*, view its *own* manpage by entering—what else?—*man man*.

Tip: The free program ManOpen, available for download from the "Missing CD" page of *www.missingmanuals.com,* is a Cocoa manual-pages reader that provides a nice-looking, easier-to-control window for reading manpages.

Learning more

Unix is, of course, an entire operating system unto itself. If you get bit by the bug, here are some sources of additional Unix info:

- *www.westwind.com/reference/OS-X/commandline.* A command reference of *cd, ls, rm,* and all the other commands you can use in Terminal or the console.

- *www.ee.surrey.ac.uk/Teaching/Unix.* A convenient, free Web-based course in Unix for beginners, focused on the tcsh shell (the Mac OS X dialect).

- *Learning Unix for Mac OS X,* 2nd Edition, by Dave Taylor & Brian Jepson (O'Reilly & Associates). A compact, relatively user-friendly tour of the Mac's Unix base.

Tip: Typing *unix for beginners* into a search page like Google.com nets dozens of superb help, tutorial, and reference Web sites. If possible, stick to those that feature the *tcsh shell.* That way, everything you learn online should be perfectly applicable to navigating Mac OS X via Terminal.

Part Five:
Appendixes

5

Installation and Troubleshooting

If you're lucky, this is a wasted appendix. After all, you'll probably never have to install Mac OS X (assuming it came preinstalled on your Mac), and in the best of all technological worlds, you won't have to do much troubleshooting, either. But here's this appendix, anyway—just in case.

Installing Mac OS X 10.2

If your computer came with Mac OS X 10.2 already installed on it, you can skip this writeup—for now.

But if you're running an earlier version of the Mac OS and want to savor the X experience, this chapter describes how to install the new operating system on your Mac. It also prepares you for the inevitable arrival of Mac OS X 10.3, 10.4, or whatever else comes down the pike.

Four Kinds of Installation

Mac OS X requires a Mac with a G3 or G4 processor, 1.5 gigabytes of free disk space, and (for reasonable speed) 256 megabytes of memory or more. If all of that checks out, then read on.

The Mac OS X installer can perform a number of different installations. For example, it can put a copy of Mac OS X 10.2 onto a hard drive that currently has:

• **Nothing on it.** If you one day have to erase your hard drive completely—because it's completely hosed, or, less drastically, because you've bought a new, empty external hard drive—see "The Basic Installation," below.

- **Mac OS 9 on the hard drive.** See "The Basic Installation," below, for the step-by-step process.

- **Mac OS X 10.0 or 10.1.** The 10.2 installer can turn your older copy of Mac OS X *into* the 10.2 version, in the process retaining all of your older preferences, fonts, documents, accounts, and so on. See "The Upgrade Installation" on page 388.

On the other hand, a substantial body of evidence points to the wisdom of performing a *clean install*, described next, rather than an upgrade installation. You'll still retain all of your documents and accounts, although a few settings may have to be reset. But overall, a clean installation (rather than an upgrade) provides a healthier, more glitch-proof copy of 10.2. See "The Clean Install" on page 388.

- **Mac OS X 10.2.** In times of dire troubleshooting, you can actually give yourself a *fresh copy* of 10.2, even though 10.2 is already on the hard drive. This process is called a *clean install*, and it's an infinitely simpler procedure than the clean install in Windows. Again, see "The Clean Install" on page 388.

The Basic Installation

The installation process takes about an hour, but for the sake of your own psyche, you'll probably want to set aside a whole afternoon. Once the installation is over, you'll want to play around, organize your files, and learn the lay of the land.

Here's how you install Mac OS X 10.2 onto a drive that doesn't have any version of Mac OS X on it already:

1. **Insert the Mac OS X CD (or DVD). In its window, double-click the Install Mac OS X icon. When the Restart button appears, click it.**

   If you're installing a Mac OS X updater and not a fresh copy, you'll be asked for an administrator's password (see Chapter 12). Installing new versions of the operating system is something that only competent people are allowed to do.

   The installer will soon fall into a pattern: Read the instructions, make a couple choices, and click Continue to advance to the next screen.

   As you go, the list on the left side of the screen shows where you are in the overall procedure.

2. **Click your way through the Select Language, Welcome, Important Information, and Software License Agreement screens. On the Select a Destination screen, click the disk or partition on which you want to install Mac OS X.**

   Icons for all of your disks (or partitions) appear on the screen, but ones that are off-limits to Mac OS X (like CDs and USB hard drives) appear dimmed. Click the icon of the drive or partition that will be your new main startup drive.

Note: If a yellow exclamation point triangle logo appears on a drive, it probably has a *newer* version of Mac OS X 10.2 on it. (Click it and read the message at the bottom of the dialog box to find out.) That's the case if you're trying to do a clean install from a 10.2 CD, but you already have 10.2.4 on the hard drive, for example. No problem—you should be reading the "The Clean Install" instructions on page 388 anyway.

3. **Click Continue.**

You arrive at the Easy Install screen. The easiest way to proceed here is to click Install. But you can save a few hundred megabytes of disk space if you take the time to click Customize.

The Installer shows you a list of the various chunks that constitute Mac OS X. A few of them are easily dispensable. For example, if you turn off Fonts for Additional Languages, Additional Asian Fonts, Localized Files (for Japanese, German, and French), and the printer models that you don't own, you save a staggering *890 megabytes*. It's like getting a whole hard drive for free (ka-ching!). Click Install.

Now you're in for a 45-minute wait as the Installer copies software onto your hard drive.

4. **If the first disc pops out, insert Disc 2.**

(Mac OS X comes on a single DVD with some Mac models, two CDs with others.) The installer picks up right from where it left off.

When the installer's finished, you see a message indicating that your Mac will restart in 30 seconds. If you haven't wandered off to watch TV, click the Restart button to end the countdown and get on with it.

Mac OS X is now installed on your Mac—but you're not quite ready to use it yet. Now you're treated to some arty, liquid visual effects, some jazzy music, and an animated stream of Welcome messages in various languages. Once Apple has finished showing off its multimedia prowess, you arrive at a Welcome screen.

Once again, you're in for a click-through-the-screens experience, this time with the aim of setting up your Mac's various settings. After answering the questions on each screen, click Continue. You'll specify your country, preferred keyboard layout, registration info—and you'll create your Administrator account (Figure 15-1).

Most of the steps up to this point have been pretty inconsequential, but this is a big moment. You're about to create your *account*—your Administrator account, in fact, as described in Chapter 12. All you have to do is make up a name, short variation of your name (eight characters or fewer—no spaces), and password (same deal). Choose carefully; you can't easily change your account name later.

Tip: If you're the only one who uses your Mac, it's perfectly OK to leave the password blank empty.

Next, you'll be offered the chance to set up your Internet account (see Chapter 9) or a .Mac account (page 123), and prompted to set the time zone, date, and time.

When you click Continue, the final screen asks you to enjoy your Apple computer—and when you click Done, you wind up at the Mac OS X desktop, just as described in Chapter 2.

The Upgrade Installation

If Mac OS X version 10.0-point-anything or 10.1-point-anything is on your hard drive, the Mac OS X 10.2 installer can neatly nip and tuck its software code, turning it *into* version 10.2. Everything remains just as you had it: your accounts, folders, files, email, network settings, everything-else settings, and so on.

As noted earlier, this sophisticated surgery *occasionally* leaves behind a minor glitch here and there: peculiar cosmetic glitches, a checkbox that doesn't seem to work, and so on. If that possibility concerns you, a clean install is a much safer way to go.

If you're still game to perform the upgrade installation, follow the preceding steps 1 and 2. On the Select a Destination Disk screen, however, click Options.

Now you're offered four variations of the basic installation. The one you want is Upgrade Mac OS X. Click it and then click OK. Proceed with step 3.

The Clean Install

In Windows, the *clean install* is an essential last-ditch troubleshooting technique. It entails installing a second Windows folder—a fresh one, uncontaminated by the detritus left behind by you and your software programs.

But in general, you and your software *can't* invade the Mac OS X System folder. The kind of gradual corruption that could occur in other operating systems is theoretically impossible in Mac OS X, and therefore the need to perform a clean install is almost completely eliminated.

That's the theory, anyway. In fact, somehow or other, things do go wrong with your Mac OS X installation. Maybe you or somebody else has been fiddling around in Terminal (page 376) and wound up deleting or changing some important underlying files. Certain shareware programs can perform deep-seated changes like this, too.

The point is that eventually, you may wish you could just start over with a new, perfect copy of Mac OS X. And now, thanks to the new Clean Install option, you can—without having to erase the hard drive first, as you did in earlier Mac OS X versions.

Tip: You can't perform a clean install "upward" from an earlier version of Mac OS X–only from 10.2. In other words, if you have 10.1 and want a clean, perfect installation of 10.2, perform an Upgrade installation first, as described above. Then perform *another* installation, this one a clean one, as described here.

Start by following steps 1 and 2 of the preceding steps. On the Select a Destination Disk screen, though, click Options.

Now you're offered four kinds of installation. Turn on "Archive and Install" and then "Preserve Users and Network Settings."

This powerful option leaves all of your accounts (Home folders, documents, pictures, movies, Favorites, email, and so on) *untouched.* As the option's name implies, it also leaves your network and Internet settings alone. But it deactivates your old System folder (you'll find it later in a new folder called Previous System Folders) and puts a new one in its place. And that's exactly what you want.

Click OK and then continue with the previous step 3. When it's all over, you'll be confident that your Mac OS X installation is clean, fresh, and ready for action.

Troubleshooting

Mac OS X is far more resilient than its predecessors, but it's still a complex system with the potential for occasional glitches.

It's safe to say that you'll have to do *less* troubleshooting in Mac OS X than in Windows, especially considering that most freaky little glitches go away if you just try these two steps one at a time:

- Quit and restart the wayward program.

- Log out and log back in again.

It's the *other* problems that will drive you batty.

Problems That Aren't Problems

Before you panic, accept the possibility that whatever is frustrating you is a Mac OS X *difference,* not a Mac OS X *problem.* Plenty of "problems" turn out simply to be quirks of the way Mac OS X works. For example:

- **System Preferences controls are dimmed.** As noted in Chapter 12, many of Mac OS X's control panels are off-limits to standard account holders. That is, only people with Administrator accounts are allowed to make changes, as indicated by the padlock icon at the lower-left corner of such panels.

- **"I can't log in! I'm in an endless login loop!"** If the standard Login screen never seems to appear, it's because somebody has turned on the automatic login feature described on page 274. The Login screen won't appear, and therefore give you a chance to sign in with your own account, until somebody either turns off automatic login or chooses →Log Out.

- **Can't move or open a folder.** Like it or not, Mac OS X is Unix, and Unix has a very strict sense of who, among the people who share a Mac over time, *owns* certain files and folders. For starters, people who don't have Administrator accounts (page 267) aren't allowed to move, or even open, certain important folders. Page 393 has much more on this topic.

If whatever problem you're having doesn't fall into one of those categories, then maybe something truly has gone wrong; read on.

Minor Eccentric Behavior

Mac OS X itself is generally extremely stable. It's the *programs* that most often cause you grief.

All kinds of glitches may befall you. Maybe Mail has sprouted new mailboxes, or your Freehand palettes won't stay put, or the Dock leaves remnants of its "puff of smoke" animation on the screen.

When a single program is acting up like this, try the following steps, in this sequence:

First resort: Restart the program

If a program starts acting up, the first and easiest step to take is simply to quit the program and start it up again.

Remember that in Mac OS X, every program lives and dies in solitude, in its own stainless steel memory bubble. Jettisoning a confused program doesn't affect other running programs in the least. Restarting the flaky program lets it load from scratch, having forgotten all about its previous problems.

Second resort: Toss the Prefs file

To test this theory, take this simple test. Log in using a different account (perhaps a dummy account that you create just for testing purposes). Run the problem program. Is the problem gone? If so, then the glitch exists only when *you* are logged in—which means it's a problem with *your* copy of the program's preferences.

Return to your own account. Open your Home folder→Library→Preferences folder, where you'll find neatly labeled preference files for all of the programs you use. Each ends with the file name suffix *.plist*. For example, com.apple.finder.plist is the Finder's preference file, com.apple.dock.plist is the Dock's, and so on.

Put the suspected preference file into the Trash, but don't empty it. The next time you run the recalcitrant program, it will build itself a brand-new preference file that, if you're lucky, lacks whatever corruption was causing your problems.

If not, quit the program. You can reinstate its original .plist file from the Trash, if you'd find that helpful as you pursue your troubleshooting agenda.

Remember, however, that you actually have *three* Preferences folders. In addition to your own Home folder's stash, there's a second one in the Library folder in the main hard drive window (which administrators are allowed to trash), and a third in the System→Library folder in the main hard drive window (which nobody is allowed to trash).

The only way to throw away the .plist files from this most deep-seated source (inside the System folder) is to use one of the security-bypass methods described in the box on page 393.

In any case, the next time you log in, the Mac will create fresh, virginal preference files.

Third resort: Log out
Sometimes you can give Mac OS X or its programs a swift kick by logging out (**⌘**→Log Out) and logging back in again. It's an inconvenient step, but not nearly as time-consuming as restarting the computer.

Fourth resort: Empty the Login Items list
If a program is crashing just after you log in, inspect and clear out your Login Items list (page 271). It may be that you've set up a program to auto-start…that doesn't like auto-starting in Mac OS X 10.2.

Last resort: Trash and reinstall the program
Sometimes reinstalling the problem program clears up whatever the glitch was.

First, however, throw away all traces of it. Just open the Applications folder and drag the program's icon (or its folder) to the Trash. In most cases, the only remaining piece to discard is its .plist file (or files) in your Home→Library→Preferences folder.

Then reinstall the program from its original CD or installer—after first checking the company's Web site to see if there's an updated version, of course.

Frozen Programs (Force Quitting)
The occasional unresponsive application has become such a part of Mac OS X life that, among the Mac cognoscenti online, the dreaded, endless "please wait" cursor has been given its own acronym: SBOD (Spinning Beachball of Death). When the SBOD strikes, no amount of mouse clicking and keyboard pounding will get you out of the recalcitrant program.

Here are the different ways you can go about *force quitting* a stuck program (the equivalent of pressing Ctrl-Alt-Delete in Windows), in increasing order of desperation:

- **Use the Dock.** If you can't use the program's regularly scheduled File→Quit command, try Control-clicking its Dock icon and choosing Quit or (if the program *knows* it's dying) Force Quit from the pop-up menu.

- **Force quit the usual way.** Choose **⌘**→Force Quit to terminate the stuck program, or use one of the other force-quit methods described on page 79.

- **Force quit the sneaky way.** Some programs, including the Dock, don't show up at all in the usual Force Quit dialog box. Your next attempt, therefore, should be to open the Process Viewer program (in Applications→Utilities), which shows *everything* that's running. Double-click a program to force quit it.

Tip: If all of this seems like a lot to remember, you can always force-restart the Mac. On desktop Macs, press the left-pointing triangle button on the front or side of the computer; on laptops, you press Control-⌘-power button.

Error Messages When Opening

If you get an error message when you try to *open* something (a program, a document, a folder), it may be that the *permissions* of either that item or something in your System folder have become muddled. It can happen to the best of us.

Open your Applications→Utilities folder, and launch Disk Utility. Click the First Aid tab, click your hard drive, click Verify, click Verify Disk Permissions, and then read an article while the Mac checks out your disk (see Figure 15-1).

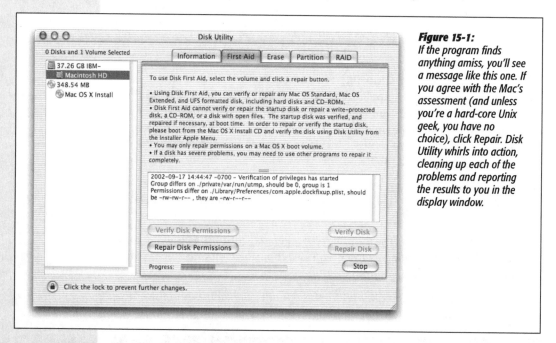

Figure 15-1:
If the program finds anything amiss, you'll see a message like this one. If you agree with the Mac's assessment (and unless you're a hard-core Unix geek, you have no choice), click Repair. Disk Utility whirls into action, cleaning up each of the problems and reporting the results to you in the display window.

The Wrong Program Opens

As noted in Chapter 4, the way documents are linked to the programs that can open them is very different in Mac OS X than it was before. Some documents have invisible, four-letter type and creator codes that tell them which programs they "belong to." Other documents lack these codes, and open up in whichever program recognizes its file name extension (.doc or .txt, for example).

Page 86 shows you how to choose which program opens a certain document (or kind of document). But that's not much help when you double-click a SimpleText document and have to sit there while SimpleText opens up—*in Classic,* mandating a 45-second wait.

The simple rule to remember here is that *creator codes override file name extensions.* In other words, a file called Contract.txt generally opens in Mac OS X's TextEdit—*if* it doesn't have a four-letter creator code behind the scenes. If that same file has SimpleText's creator code (ttxt), however, it opens in SimpleText (and Classic) no matter what its file name is.

In other cases, the quickest solution may be to *strip away* the type and creator codes. You can do that by dragging the troubled files' icons onto a program like Wipe Creator (available from the software page of *www.missingmanuals.com*). At that point, Mac OS X has only the document's file name extension to go on when choosing a program to open it.

Can't Empty the Trash

If emptying the Trash gives you "Could not be completed because this item is owned by Marge," you're trying to move or delete another Mac account holder's stuff. As you know, that's a big no-no in Mac OS X.

In that case, just make yourself the new owner of the file or folder, as described in the box on page 393.

Fixing Permissions Problems

Sooner or later, when you try to move, rename, or delete a certain file or folder, you may get an error message like this: "The folder 'Junk' could not be opened because you do not have sufficient access privileges." Or this: "The operation could not be completed because this item is owned by Chris" (or by *root,* which means by Mac OS X itself).

Both kinds of messages, with their awkward passive-voice construction, clank on the trained English-speaking ear. However, what they're trying to say is, you've run into a *permissions* problem.

As noted in Chapter 12, Mac OS X is designed to accommodate a number of different people who share the same Mac over time. Nobody is allowed to meddle with other people's files or folders. But even if you're the solo operator of your Mac, you still share it with Mac OS X itself (which the error messages may refer to as *root* or *system*).

In any case, if you're confident that whatever you're trying to do isn't some kind of nihilistic, self-destructive act like trashing the Applications folder, it's easy enough to get past these limitations. Just highlight the recalcitrant file or folder and then choose File→Get Info. In its window, you'll find an Ownership & Permissions panel that lets you reassign ownership of any icon to, for example, yourself (if you have an Administrator account, that is). Make sure your permission is "Read & Write." (Just don't perform this surgery on files in the System folder.)

Now you *own* that folder or file, and you can do whatever you like with it.

Application Won't Open

If a program won't open (if its icon bounces merrily in the Dock for a few seconds, for instance, but then nothing happens), begin by trashing its preference file, as described on page 390. If that doesn't solve it, reinstalling the program usually does.

Program Icons Turn to Folders

You may remember that in Mac OS X, almost every application, behind the scenes, is actually a folder. All you see (and double-click to open) is one icon called Mail, for example, but inside are dozens of folders, icons, and chunks of software code. The only way you'd ever know that a Mac OS X "application icon" is an optical illusion would be to Control-click the application and, from the pop-up menu, choose Show Package Contents.

Every now and then, though—most often after a power failure—Mac OS X puts on a much more showy display of this feature than perhaps you'd like: Suddenly *all* applications show up as folders, whose names bear the suffix *.app.* All very educational, of course, but now you have no way to actually *run* those programs, because the icon to double-click has disappeared.

Most of the time, the generic-folders problem stems from the corruption of three particular preference files in your Home→Library→Preferences folder: LSApplications, LSClaimedTypes, and LSSchemes. Throw them away, and then log out. When you log back in, your applications should all have been restored to their rightful conditions.

If that doesn't solve it, running the disk-checking program called Disk Utility (page 366) should clear it up.

Finally, it's conceivable that the permissions for your own Home folder have become hosed, meaning that Mac OS X believes that somebody else owns your Home folder.

Check its access privileges by highlighting your Home folder's icon and choosing File→Get Info. If *you* aren't identified as the owner (on the Ownership & Permissions panel), see "Fixing Permissions Problems" on page 393.

Startup Problems

Not every problem you encounter is related to running applications. Sometimes trouble strikes before you even get that far. For example:

Kernel panic

When you see the dialog box shown in Figure 15-2, you've got yourself a *kernel panic*—a Unix nervous breakdown.

(In such situations, *user panic* might be the more applicable term, but that's programmers for you.)

Kernel panics are extremely rare. If you see one at all, it's almost always the result of a *hardware* glitch: a memory board, accelerator card, graphics card, SCSI gear, or USB hub that Mac OS X doesn't like.

You need to restart your computer. Hold down the Power button for several seconds or press the Restart button.

Veuillez redémarrer votre ordinateur. Maintenez la touche de démarrage enfoncée pendant plusieurs secondes ou bien appuyez sur le bouton de réinitialisation.

Sie müssen Ihren Computer neu starten. Halten Sie dazu die Einschalttaste einige Sekunden gedrückt oder drücken Sie die Neustart-Taste.

コンピュータを再起動する必要があります。パワーボタンを数秒間押し続けるか、リセットボタンを押してください。

00:03:93:D6:70:AE   192.168.001.101

If restarting doesn't solve the problem, detach every shred of gear that didn't come from Apple. Restore these components to the Mac one at a time until you find out which one was causing Mac OS X's bad hair day. If you're able to pinpoint the culprit, seek its manufacturer (or its Web site) on a quest for updated drivers, or at least try to find out for sure whether the add-on is compatible with Mac OS X.

There's one other cause for kernel panics, by the way: moving, renaming, or changing the access permissions for Mac OS X's essential system files and folders—the Applications or System folder, for example. (See page 277 for more on permissions.) This cause isn't even worth mentioning, of course, because nobody would be that foolish.

Freezes during startup

If the Mac locks up during the startup process, you need to run Mac OS X's disk-repair program, as described below.

Forgotten password

If you or one of the other people who use your Mac have forgotten the corresponding account password, no worries: just read the box on page 276.

Fixing the Disk

As noted in the introduction of this book, the beauty of Mac OS X's design is that the operating system itself is frozen in its perfect, pristine state, impervious to conflicting system extensions, clueless Mac users, and other sources of disaster.

That's the theory, anyway. But what happens if something goes wrong with the complex software that operates the hard drive itself?

Fortunately, Mac OS X comes with its own disk-repair program. In the familiar Mac universe of icons and menus, it takes the form of a program in Applications→Utilities called Disk Utility.

Disk Utility can cure all kinds of strange ills, including these problems, among others:

- Your Mac freezes during startup, either before or after the Login screen.

- The startup process interrupts itself with the appearance of the text-only command line.

- You get the "applications showing up as folders" problem (see page 394).

Method 1: Disk Utility

The easiest way to check your disk is to use the Disk Utility program. Use this method if your Mac can, indeed, start up. (See Method 2 if you can't even get that far.)

Disk Utility can't check the disk it's *on*. That's why you have to restart the computer from the Mac OS X CD-ROM (or another startup disk), and run Disk Utility from there. The process goes like this:

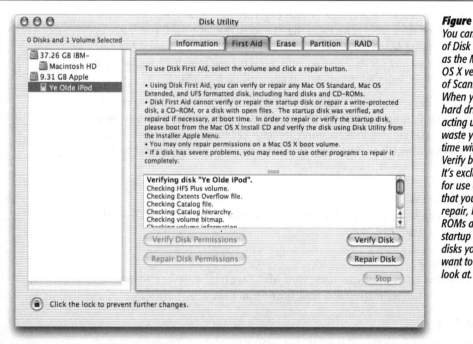

Figure 15-3:
You can think of Disk Utility as the Mac OS X version of ScanDisk. When your hard drive is acting up, don't waste your time with the Verify button. It's exclusively for use on disks that you can't repair, like CD-ROMs and the startup disk—disks you just want to have a look at.

1. **Start up the Mac from the Mac OS X CD or DVD.**

   The best way to do that is to insert the CD and then restart the Mac while holding down the C key.

   You wind up, after some time, at the Mac OS X Installer screen. Don't be fooled—installing Mac OS X is *not* what you want to do here. Don't click Continue!

2. **Choose Installer→Open Disk Utility.**

   That's the unexpected step. After a moment, the Disk Utility screen appears.

3. **Click the First Aid tab.**

   The program now looks like the illustration in Figure 15-3.

4. **Click the disk or disk partition you want to fix, and then click Repair.**

   The Mac whirls into action, checking a list of very technical disk-formatting parameters.

If you see the message, "The volume 'Macintosh HD' appears to be OK," that's meant to be *good* news. Believe it or not, that cautious statement is as definitive an affirmation as Disk Utility is capable of making about the health of your disk.

Note: Don't be alarmed. The message's last line says "Repair completed" whether or not any repairing was done at all.

Disk Utility may also tell you that the disk is damaged, but that it can't help you. In that case, you need a more heavy-duty disk-repair program like DiskWarrior *(www.alsoft.com)*.

Method 2: fsck at the console

Disk Utility isn't of much use when you can't find the Mac OS X CD, when your CD drive isn't working, or when you're in a hurry to get past the startup problems that are plaguing your machine. In these cases, you'll be glad that you can boot into the Mac's raw Unix underlayer to perform some diagnostic (and healing) commands.

Specifically, you'll be glad that you can run the Unix program *fsck,* for which Disk Utility is little more than a pretty faceplate.

Like any Unix program, *fsck* runs at the command line. You launch it from the all-text, black Unix screen by typing the command and pressing Enter.

Single-user mode (⌘-S at startup)

To get there in times of startup troubleshooting, press ⌘-S while the Mac is starting up. (If you're stuck at the frozen remnants of a previous startup attempt, you may first have to force-restart your Mac; see page 392.)

This technique takes you into *console mode,* shown in Figure 15-4. In console mode, Unix takes over your screen completely, white type against black, no windows or icons in sight. Abandon the mouse, all ye who enter; in console mode, you can't do anything but type commands.

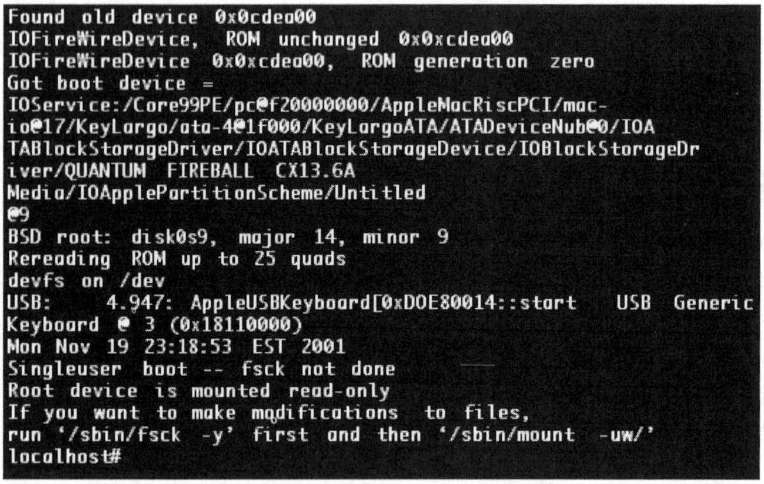

```
Found old device 0x0cdea00
IOFireWireDevice,   ROM unchanged 0x0xcdea00
IOFireWireDevice  0x0xcdea00,  ROM generation  zero
Got boot device =
IOService:/Core99PE/pc@f20000000/AppleMacRiscPCI/mac-
io@17/KeyLargo/ata-4@1f000/KeyLargoATA/ATADeviceNub@0/IOA
TABlockStorageDriver/IOATABlockStorageDevice/IOBlockStorageDr
iver/QUANTUM  FIREBALL  CX13.6A
Media/IOApplePartitionScheme/Untitled
@9
BSD root: disk0s9, major 14, minor 9
Rereading  ROM up to 25 quads
devfs on /dev
USB:    4.947: AppleUSBKeyboard[0xDOE80014::start    USB Generic
Keyboard @ 3 (0x18110000)
Mon Nov 19 23:18:53  EST 2001
Singleuser  boot -- fsck not done
Root device is mounted  read-only
If you want to make modifications  to files,
run '/sbin/fsck  -y' first and then '/sbin/mount  -uw/'
localhost#
```

Figure 15-4:
In console mode, your entire screen is a command line interface. Unix jockeys can go to town here. Everyone else can timidly type fsck -y *after the* localhost # *prompt—see this prompt on the very last line?—and hope for the best.*

When the technical-looking scrolling text finally stops at the *localhost #* prompt, you're ready to type commands. You're now in what's called *single-user mode,* meaning that the Unix multiple-accounts software has yet to load. You won't be asked to log in.

At the *localhost #* prompt, type *fsck -y* (note the space before the hyphen) and press Enter. (The *y* means "yes," as in "yes, I want you to fix any problems automatically.")

Now the file-system check program takes over, running through five sets of tests. When it's complete, you'll see one of two messages:

- **The volume Macintosh HD appears to be OK.** All is well. Type *reboot* and press Return to proceed to the usual Login screen and desktop.

- **File system was modified.** A good sign, but just a beginning. You need to run the program again. One *fsck* pass often repairs only one layer of problems, leaving another to be patched in the next pass. Type *fsck -y* a second time, a third time, and so on, until you finally arrive at a "disk appears to be OK" message.

Tip: Typing *reboot* at the prompt and pressing Return is how you get back to the familiar blue world of icons and windows.

Where to Get Troubleshooting Help

If the basic steps described in this chapter haven't helped, the universe is crawling with additional help sources.

Built-in Help

The Mac's built-in help system isn't what you'd call a veritable troubleshooting clinic. But at the very least, you'll read about how a feature is *supposed* to work, just in case you were mistaking that correct operation for eccentric behavior.

It's easy enough to use: At the desktop, choose Help→Mac Help. Type a search phrase into the bar and press Enter. You'll be shown the help pages that Apple considers most helpful to your search. (You use the list as you would a Web page.)

Help online

These Internet sites contain nothing but troubleshooting discussions, tools, and help:

- **MacFixIt** *(www.macfixit.com)*. A glorious resource for troubleshooting advice.
- **Mac newsgroups** (such as *comp.system.mac*). A newsgroup is an Internet bulletin board, which you can access using a program like Microsoft Entourage or Thoth *(www.thothsw.com)*. If you're polite and concise, you can post questions to the multitudes here and get more replies to them than you'll know what to do with.
- **Other Apple support resources** *(www.apple.com/support)*. Apple's help Web site also includes downloadable manuals, software updates, frequently asked questions, and many other resources.

The mother of all troubleshooting resources, however, is Apple's own Knowledge Base. This is the collection of 50,000 individual technical articles, organized in a searchable database, that the Apple technicians themselves consult when you call for help.

If you like, you can visit this library using your Web browser *(http://kbase. info.apple.com)* or right within Sherlock 3 (click the AppleCare icon). You can search it either by typing in keywords or by using pop-up menus of question categories.

Help by telephone

Finally, consider contacting whoever sold you the component that's making your life miserable: the printer company, scanner company, software company, or whatever.

If it's a Mac OS problem, you can call Apple at 800-275-2273 (that's 800-APL-CARE). For the first 90 days following your purchase of Mac OS X (which, as far as Apple knows, is the date of your first call), the technicians will answer your questions for free.

After that, unless you've paid for AppleCare for your Mac (a three-year extended warranty program), Apple will charge you to answer your questions—unless the problem turns out to be Apple's fault, in which case they won't charge you.

The "Where'd It Go?" Dictionary

All the words and pictures so far in this book are just great for leisure reading. But in a crisis of helplessness on your new Mac, this appendix may be more useful. It's an alphabetical listing of every common Windows function and where to find it in Mac OS X. After all, an operating system is an operating system. The actual functions are pretty much the same—they're just in different places.

About [This Program]

To find out the version number of the program you're using, don't look in the Help menu. Instead, look in the *Application* menu next to the menu—the one that bears the name of the program you're in. That's where you find the About command for Macintosh programs.

Accessibility Options Control Panel

The special features that let you operate the computer even with impaired vision, hearing, or motor control is called Universal Access in Mac OS X. It's in System Preferences (see Chapter 13).

Active Desktop

The Mac never displays Web pages directly on the desktop—and knowing Apple, that's probably a point of pride.

Add Hardware Control Panel

The Mac requires no program for installing the driver for a new external gadget. The drivers for most printers, mice, keyboards, cameras, camcorders, and other accessories are preinstalled. If you plug something into the Mac and find that it doesn't work immediately, just install the driver from the included CD (or the manufacturer's Web site).

Add or Remove Programs Control Panel

Here's another one you just don't need on the Macintosh. Installing a program onto the Mac is described on page 104. To remove a program, you generally just drag its icon to the Trash.

The exceptions are programs like Microsoft Office for the Mac, whose installers offer an Uninstall option for your convenience.

All Programs

There's no Programs menu built into Mac OS X, like the one on the Windows Start menu. The Dock is intended to serve as your list of *favorite* programs, and the Applications folder is your master list of *all* programs.

On the other hand, you can make a Programs menu of your own in five seconds. Just drag your Applications folder onto the right side of the Dock (page 67). Now its icon is a tidy pop-up menu of every program on your machine.

Alt Key

On the Mac, it's the Option key. You can substitute Option for Alt in any keystroke in most popular programs. The Options key has a number of secondary features on the Mac, too: It hides the windows of one program when you click into another, and so on.

Automatic Update

The System Preferences→Software Update panel does exactly the same thing.

Backspace key

It's in the same place on the Macintosh keyboard, but it's called the Delete key.

Battery Level

The status of the battery in your PowerBook or iBook laptop now appears in the menu bar, rather than in the system tray. (If you don't see it, open System Preferences→Energy Saver and turn it on.)

BIOS

You'll never have to update or even think about the ROM of your Macintosh (the approximate equivalent of the BIOS on the PC). It's permanent and unchanging. Your Macintosh does have some firmware that's quite similar to BIOS, and it occasionally has to be updated in order to work with a new version the Mac operating system or some dramatic new feature. You'll be notified on the screen (via the Software Update program) when the time comes—once every four years, perhaps.

Briefcase

Mac OS X doesn't have anything like the Briefcase, a Windows invention designed to help you keep your files in sync between a laptop and a desktop computer. On the other hand, if you sign up for a .Mac account (Chapter 5), you get a program called Backup that is similarly designed to keep folders synchronized between two machines. And you can use iSync (Chapter 14) to keep your calendar, addresses, and other items synced between multiple computers.

Calculator

The calculator program in Mac OS X is almost identical to the one in Windows XP, except that it can also perform conversions (temperature, distance, currency, and so on) and features an editable "paper tape." It sits in your Applications folder and is described in Chapter 14.

Camera and Scanner Wizard

When you connect a digital camera or scanner to your Mac, either iPhoto or Image Capture opens automatically and prepares to download the pictures automatically, just like the Camera and Scanner Wizard. Details on Image Capture in Chapter 14, and on iPhoto on page 343.

CDs

Chapter 8 offers the full scoop on working with discs on the Mac, but here's a quick summary:

If your Mac keyboard has an Eject or F12 key in the upper-right corner, you hold it down for a moment to open the CD drawer, or, if you have a slot-loading CD drive, to spit out the CD that's in it. There are various other ways to eject a disc, too, but the point is that you never do so by pushing the Eject button on the drive itself. (And unlike Windows, no drive icon ever appears on the Mac unless there's a disc *in* it.)

Character Map

This Windows program helps you find out what keys you need to press to trigger trademark symbols, copyright symbols, and other special characters. The equivalent on the Mac is Key Caps, which is in your Applications→Utilities folder—but the Character Palette (page 301) is even easier to use.

Clean Install

The Mac OS X installer can give you a fresh, virginal copy of the operating system, just as the Windows installer can. Instructions are in Appendix A.

Clipboard

The Macintosh clipboard works almost exactly like the one in Windows. In the Finder, you can choose Edit→Show Clipboard to see whenever you have most recently copied or cut.

Command Line

In Mac OS X, the command line is alive and well—but it speaks Unix, not DOS. You get to it by opening Terminal (page 376).

Control Panel

There is a Control Panel in Mac OS X—but it's called System Preferences and is represented on the Dock by a little light-switch icon. As in Windows XP, you can view these icons either by category or in a simple alphabetical list: just choose either Show All In Categories or Show All Alphabetically from the View menu. Details in Chapter 13.

Copy, Cut, Paste

When you're editing in a word processor or graphics program, the Mac OS X Cut, Copy, and Paste commands work exactly as they do in Windows.

At the desktop, however, there are a few differences. You can indeed copy icons and paste them into a new window using the Copy and Paste commands—you just can't *cut* them out of a window, as you can in Windows.

On the other hand, Mac OS X offers a handy secondary feature: If you paste into a word or text processor instead of into another desktop window, you get a tidy list of the names of the icons you copied.

Ctrl Key

On the Macintosh, you generally substitute the ⌘ key in keystrokes that would normally involve the Control key. In other words, the Save command is now ⌘-S instead of Ctrl-S, Open is ⌘-O instead of Ctrl-O, and so on.

Date and Time

You set your Mac's calendar and clock in the Date & Time Panel of System Preferences.

Delete Key (Forward Delete)

Desktop Mac keyboards have a forward-delete key exactly like the ones on PCs. On Mac laptops, you trigger the forward-delete function by pressing the regularly scheduled Delete key while pressing the Fn key in the lower-left corner of the keyboard.

Desktop

The Macintosh desktop is pretty much the same idea as the Windows desktop, with a few key differences:

• Disk icons show up on the Mac desktop as soon as they are inserted or connected. You don't have to open a window to see their icons.

• You change the desktop picture using the Desktop Panel of System Preferences.

• The Trash is an icon on the Dock, not loose on the desktop.

Directories

Most people call them *folders* on the Mac.

Disk Defragmenter

There's no such utility included with Mac OS X, although Norton Utilities for the Mac will do the job if you feel that it's essential to have your hard drive neatly defragmented. (A defragmenting program moves around the pieces of files on your hard drive in an effort to optimize their placement and speed of opening.)

Disks

Working with disks is very different on the Mac. Every disk inside, or attached to, a Macintosh is represented on the screen by an icon. Mac OS X does have something like the My Computer window (choose Go→Computer), but both the icons on the desktop and the icons in the Computer window reflect only the disks currently inserted in your Mac. You'll never see an icon for an empty drive, as you do on Windows, and there's no such thing as drive letters (because the Mac refers to *disks,* not to *drives*—and refers to them by name).

Display Control Panel

The functions of the Windows Display Control Panel lurk in the Mac OS X System Preferences program—just not all in one place. You set a desktop picture using the Desktop panel, choose a screen saver using the Screen Effects panel, and adjust your monitor settings using the Displays panel. (Mac OS X offers no ability to change the system-wide look of your computer, as you might using the Appearance tab in Windows.)

DLL Files

The Macintosh equivalent of DLL files—shared libraries of programming code—is invisible and off-limits. As a result, no Macintosh user ever experiences DLL conflicts or out-of-date DLL files.

DOS Prompt

There's a command line in Mac OS X, but it's Unix, not DOS. See page 376.

Drivers

Drivers, a living hell in the Windows world, are practically invisible and forgotten on the Mac. "My machine locked up because I had an outdated driver" is a virtually unheard-of utterance among Mac users.

Drivers for hundreds of mice, printers, disk drivers, and music players are built into Mac OS X, just as they are in current versions of Windows. Occasionally, you'll buy some oddball add-on equipment that requires you to run an installation CD, which deposits the necessary driver onto your Mac. Otherwise, though, you can pretend that drivers don't even exist on the Mac.

End Task Dialog Box

If some Macintosh program is hung or frozen, you escape it pretty much the same way you would in Windows: by forcing it to quit. To bring up the Force Quit dialog box, you press Option-⌘-Esc as described on page 79.

Exiting Programs

You can quit a program either by choosing Quit from the menu bearing its name (next to the menu), or by right-clicking its Dock icon (or Control-clicking, or click-and holding) and then choosing Quit from the pop-up menu.

Explorer

The Mac has its own "tree" view of the files and folders on your hard drive: list view. By expanding the "flippy triangles" of your folders, you build a hierarchy that shows you as much or as little detail as you like.

If you prefer the Explorer effect of clicking a folder in *one* pane to see its contents in the next, try column view instead. Both views are described in Chapter 2.

Favorites

In Mac OS X, there isn't one single Favorites menu that lists both favorite Web sites and favorite icons. The Favorites menu of Internet Explorer, the Web browser, lists only Web sites. The Favorites menu at the desktop lists only favorite files, folders, disks, and other icons.

Faxing

Not all Macs come with built-in faxing software—at this writing, only iBooks and iMacs do. (It's called FaxSTF, and if you have it it's in your Applications folder.) If you have another kind of Mac, consider installing the shareware program PageSender, the free Cocoa eFax, or any of the other faxing programs that come up when you search *www.versiontracker.com* for "fax."

File Sharing

See page 308 for an in-depth look at the Macintosh networking and file-sharing system.

Floppy Disks

Don't bother looking; you won't find floppy drives on Macs. They disappeared in about 1997. According to Apple, it's much more efficient to transfer files between machines using an Ethernet cable (page 308), a CD that you burned (page 194), or email (Chapter 10).

Of course, you can buy an external USB floppy drive for any Mac for under $45.

Folder Options

The Folder Options control panel in Windows is a crazy collection of unrelated settings that boil down to this:

- **General tab.** Exactly as in Windows, it's up to you whether or not double-clicking a folder opens up a second window—or just changes what's in the first one. On the Mac, you make these changes using the Finder→Preferences command. There you'll find the option called "Always open folders in a new window."

- **View tab.** Most of the options here don't exist on the Mac. For example, you can't opt to make all the invisible system files visible (at least not without add-on shareware). You can, however, choose whether or not you want to see the file name extensions in your desktop windows (like .doc and .html). Choose Finder→ Preferences, and turn "Always show file extensions" on or off.

- **File Types tab.** Just as in Windows, you can reassign certain document types so that double-clicking opens them up in the program of your choice. But on the Mac, you can reassign either a whole class of files at once, as on Windows, *or* one file at a time. To do it, you use the Get Info window as described on page 86.

- **Offline Files.** There's no equivalent feature on the Mac.

Fonts

The Mac and Windows both use TrueType, PostScript, and Open Type fonts. (In fact, your Mac can even use the exact font files you had on Windows.) A complete discussion is on page 188.

Help and Support

At the desktop, choose Help→Mac Help. In other programs, the Help command is generally at the right end of your menus, exactly as in Windows.

Hibernation

The Mac can't hibernate at all, as modern PCs do, cutting all power but remembering what programs and documents you had open for a faster restart later. Sleep mode is the closest it gets (see "Standby Mode" in this appendix).

Internet Explorer

The standard Web browser is in your Applications folder—or you can click its icon on your Dock. As noted on page 259, the Macintosh version of this browser offers a number of useful features not available in Windows.

Internet Options

On the Mac, you find the options for your Web browser by choosing Internet Explorer→Preferences. (There *is* an Internet panel in System Preferences, but the only browser setting you can change here is your preferred startup Web page.)

IRQs

Forget it. These, and their resulting conflicts, don't exist on the Mac.

Java

This interpreter of tiny programs written in the Java programming language is alive and well in Mac OS X. The Applet Launcher program in your Applications→Utilities folder, for example, is prepared to run any of these little programs that you happen to stumble across.

Keyboard Control Panel

You can make exactly the same kinds of settings—and more—on the Keyboard Panel of system Preferences.

Logging In

As it turns out, the multiple-accounts feature of Mac OS X is extremely similar to that of Windows 2000 and Windows XP. In either case, you can, if you wish, create a requirement to login with a name and password before using the computer. This arrangement keeps separate the documents, email, and settings of each person who uses the computer.

Mail Control Panel

Mac OS X comes with its own email program (see Chapter 10); all of its settings are contained within the program.

Maximize Button

On the Mac, clicking the Zoom button (the green button at the upper-left corner of a window) does something like the Maximize button in Windows: it makes your window larger. On the Mac, however, clicking the Zoom button never makes the window expand to fill the entire screen. Instead, the window grows—or *shrinks*—precisely enough to enclose its contents.

Menus

Here's one of the biggest differences between the Mac and Windows: On the Macintosh, there's only one menu bar, always at the very top of the screen. The menus change depending on the program and the window you're using, but the point is that the menu bar is no longer inside each window you open.

Tip: Just because you don't see the little underlines in the menus doesn't mean you can't operate all of the menus from the keyboard, as in Windows. See page 87 for details.

Minimize Button

You can minimize a Mac OS X window to the Dock, just the way you would minimize a Windows window to the taskbar. You do so by double-clicking its title bar, pressing ⌘-M, choosing Window→Minimize Window, or clicking the yellow Minimize button at the top left of a window. (Restore the window by clicking its icon on the Dock.)

Mouse Control Panel

The equivalent settings await you in the Mouse panel of system Preferences.

My Computer

The Mac's Computer window is very similar (choose Go→Computer), in that it shows the icons of all disks (hard drive, CD, and so on). On the other hand, it shows *only* the disks that are actually inserted or connected (see "Disks").

My Documents, My Pictures, My Music

The equivalent buckets for your everyday documents, music files, and pictures are the Documents, Pictures, and Music folders in your Home folder. (See page 20 for more on the Home folder.)

My Network Places

To see your "network neighborhood," choose Go→Connect to Server. All of the Macs and PCs on your network show up in the resulting list (see page 116).

Network Neighborhood

See the previous entry.

Notepad

There's no Mac OS X Notepad program. But give Stickies a try (page 354).

PC World

The sister publication is *Macworld (www.macworld.com)*, but you'll also get a lot out of magazines like *MacAddict* and *MacHome Journal*.

Personal Web Server

If you'd like to host your own Web site, you've come to the right place. Using the Sharing panel of System Preferences, you can turn your Mac into a Web server that's accessible from the Web browsers of people on your office network, the Internet at large, or both. That's because inside Mac OS X is *Apache*, one of the strongest and most popular Unix Web server programs—precisely the same one that drives 60 percent of the Internet's commercial Web sites (including Apple.com).

The bottom line: If you build it, they won't necessarily come. But at least you'll have the capacity to handle them if they do. Here's how you turn your Mac into a low-budget Web site:

1. **Put the HTML documents, graphics, and files you want to publish into your Home→Sites folder.**

   Your Web site's home page, by the way, must be named *index.html*. (Apple has already put an *index.html* document into your Sites folder, just to give you the idea; feel free to replace it.)

2. **Open System Preferences; click Sharing (Figure 16-1).**

   Open System Preferences by clicking its Dock icon or by choosing its name from the menu.

3. **Turn on the Personal Web Sharing checkbox.**

   You've just made the contents of your Web Pages folder available to anyone who connects to your Mac.

Tip: Take this opportunity to turn on Mac OS X's *firewall,* too (page 216). You wouldn't want Internet hoodlums to take advantage of your open Web connection.

IP Addresses and You

Every computer connected to the Internet, even temporarily, has its own exclusive *IP address* (IP stands for Internet Protocol). What's yours? Open the Sharing pane of System Preferences to find out (page 307). As you'll see, an IP address is always made up of four numbers separated by periods.

Some Macs with broadband Internet connections have a permanent, unchanging address called a *fixed* or *static* IP address. Clearly, life is simpler if you have a fixed IP address, because other computers will always know where to find you.

Other Macs get assigned a new address each time they connect (a *dynamic* IP address). That's virtually always the case, for example, when you connect using a dial-up modem. (If you can't figure out whether your Mac has a static or fixed address, ask your Internet service provider.)

You might suppose that Mac fans with dynamic addresses can't use any remote-connection technologies like the Web-sharing feature described on these pages. After all, your Mac's Web address *changes* every time you connect, making it impossible to provide a single, permanent address to your friends and co-workers.

The answer is a *dynamic DNS service* that gives your Mac a name, not a number. Whenever you're online, these free services automatically update the IP address associated with the name you've chosen (such as *macmania.dyndns.org*), so that your friends and colleagues can memorize a single address for your machine.

To sign up for one of these services, just go to their Web sites—*www.dyndns.org, www.dhs.org, www.dtdns.com, www.hn.org, www.no-ip.com,* and so on.

You'll also have to download and run a utility called an *update client,* which contacts your DNS service and keeps it up-to-date with your latest IP address, regularly and automatically. Check your DNS service's Web site for a list of compatible update clients.

Once you've got a fixed DNS name associated with your Mac, you'll be able to access it from elsewhere (provided it's online at the time) via File Sharing (page 308), the screen-sharing program called Timbuktu, the Web Sharing feature described on these pages, and so on.

(If you have a fixed address, you can also pay a few dollars a year to register your own *domain name,* a bona fide address like *www.yournamehere.com.* To register one [or to find out if the name you want is taken], visit a site like *www.networksolutions.com.*)

4. Note your IP address.

In general, your Mac's Web address is based on its IP address (or Network Address), the string of numbers separated by periods that appears near the top of the Sharing pane.

Tip: If you connect to the Internet via dial-up modem, you may not see an IP address here until you're online.

---

5. Email your new Web address to your friends and co-workers.

In this example, your address is *http://111.222.3.44/~chris/* (the number is your IP address, and the name should be your short user name). Don't forget the final slash. Tell your friends to bookmark it so they won't have to remember this address.

Tip: That IP address with all the numbers is the one that people on the *Internet* need. People on your local office network can use your Mac's Rendezvous name to connect instead—the name that appears on the Sharing pane of System Preferences. In this case, they'd type *http://office-mac.local/~chris* into their Web browsers, where *office-mac.local* is your Mac's Rendezvous name.

Figure 16-1:
Use the Web Sharing System Preferences pane to make designated folders on your hard drive available to anyone on the Internet. Note your Mac's IP address, indicated here. It's the basis for all of the fun Mac-sharing-over-the-Internet features described in this chapter.

Web sharing on/off   Your IP address

The easiest way to distribute files

Here's a handy secret: If there isn't a document whose name is *index.html* in your Sites folder (or Library→WebServer→Documents folder), then visitors see, in their browsers, a handy list of the files that *are* in that folder (see Figure 16-2).

Figure 16-2:
Here's a great way to make files available to other people on your network or collaborators across the Internet. Just put your files into the Sites or Library→ WebServer→Documents folder and make sure nothing is named index.html. *The Parent Directory link takes you to the folder that contains* this *one—if you've been given access to it, that is.*

This is a terrific convenience: It offers a quick, simple way for you to make a bunch of documents available for downloading. All your visitors have to do is click one of these file names. It downloads immediately, no matter what kind of computer your Web visitor is using.

More on Apache

As noted above, Apache is the most popular Web-serving software in the world. As you can well imagine, it's powerful, reliable—and very technical. It is, after all, a Unix program.

You can read more at any of these sources:

- **The Apache manual.** To open it up, type *http://localhost/manual/* into your browser's address bar. You won't get far reading this thing if you haven't spent some time at a technical college, but at least you'll know what you're up against.

- *Apache: The Definitive Guide.* A book from O'Reilly.

- **MacOSXHints.com.** Dozens of Mac OS X fans have posted specific Apache-tweaking tips and ticks at *www.macosxhints.com.*

Note, too, that $300 will buy you a graphic front end for the various Apache settings, in the form of Tenon's iTools program. It still requires an understanding of the technical aspects of Web hosting, but at least it spares you from having to type out Unix commands to make your changes.

Phone and Modem Options Control Panel

To find the modem settings for your Mac, open System Preferences. Click Network, choose Internal Modem from the Show pop-up menu, and click the Modem tab.

Power Options

To control when your Mac goes to sleep and (if it's a laptop) how much power it uses, use the Energy Saver panel of System Preferences (Chapter 13).

Printer Sharing

To share a USB inkjet printer with other Macs on the network, open the Sharing panel of System Preferences on the Mac with the printer. Turn on Printer Sharing.

On each of the other Macs, open the Print Center program (in the Applications→ Utilities folder). Click Add. When the printer list appears, choose Directory Services from the top pop-up menu, and make sure that Rendezvous is selected in the bottom one. Presto: The name of the USB printer, elsewhere on the network, appears in the list. You're ready to share.

Printers and Faxes

For a list of your printers, open the Print Center program in your Applications→ Utilities folder. You manage faxes using either FaxSTF or a shareware program (see "Faxing").

PrntScrn

You capture pictures of your Mac screen by pressing Shift-⌘-3 (for a full-screen grab) or Shift-⌘-4 (to grab a selected portion of the screen). Details on page 176.

Program Files Folder

The Applications folder (Go→Applications) is like the Program Files folder in Windows—except that you're not discouraged from opening it and double-clicking things. On the Macintosh, every program bears its true name. Microsoft Word is called Microsoft Word, not WINWORD.EXE.

Properties Dialog Box

You can call up something very similar for any *icon* (file, folder, program, disk, printer) by highlighting it and then choosing File→Get Info.

But objects in Macintosh *programs* generally don't contain Properties dialog boxes. (Microsoft Office is, as usual, an exception; these programs offer a File→Properties command.)

Recycle Bin

Mac OS X has a Trash icon at the end of the Dock. In general, it works exactly like the Windows Recycle Bin—and why not, since the Macintosh Trash was Microsoft's inspiration?—but there are a couple of differences. The Macintosh never auto-empties it, for example, no matter how full your hard drive gets. That job is up to you. (The simplest way is to Control-click it, or right-click it, and choose Empty Trash from the contextual menu.)

The Mac never bothers you with an "Are you sure?" message when you throw something into the Trash, either. In fact, it doesn't even ask for confirmation when you *empty* the Trash (at least, not when you empty it by Control-clicking). The Mac interrupts you for permission only when you choose File→Empty Trash—and you can even turn that confirmation off, if you like (in Finder→Preferences).

To put icons into the Trash, drag them there, or just highlight them and then press ⌘-Delete.

Regional and Language Options Control Panel

The close equivalent is the International panel of System Preferences.

Registry

There is no Registry on the Macintosh. Let the celebration begin!

Run Command

The equivalent command line is Terminal (page 376).

Safe Mode

There's no real equivalent to Safe Mode on the Mac. You can press the Shift key during startup to suppress the loading of certain software libraries, but that still doesn't produce a massively stripped-down machine like Safe Mode does.

ScanDisk

Just like Windows, the Mac automatically scans and, if necessary, repairs its hard drive every time your machine starts up. To run such a check on command, open Disk Utility (located in the Applications→Utilities folder), and then click the First Aid tab.

Scheduled Tasks

To schedule a task to take place unattended, use the *cron* Unix command in Terminal (page 376), or one of the scheduling programs listed at *www.versiontracker.com.*

Scrap Files

On the Mac, they're called *clipping files,* and they're even more widely compatible. You create them the same way: Drag some highlighted text, or a graphic, out of a program's window and onto the desktop. There it becomes an independent clipping file that you can drag back in—to the same window, or a different one.

Screen Saver

The Mac's screen savers are impressive. Open System Preferences and click the Screen Effects icon.

Search

In Mac OS X, you have two convenient ways to look for files. You can type into the Search bar at the top of every desktop window and then press Return (page 57), or you can choose File→Finder for a more complete search by almost any criterion, including words inside the files. Chapter 2 contains details.

Note that in Mac OS X, the Find program finds things *on your hard drive;* it doesn't search the Web, too, as the Windows Search command does. To find Web sites, you use Sherlock (page 245).

Shortcut Menus

They're called *contextual* menus in Mac parlance. You produce them by Control-clicking things like icons, list items, and so on. (If you have a two-button mouse, feel free to right-click instead of using the Control key.)

Shortcuts

On the Mac, they're known as *aliases,* and they're even more useful (and intelligent). See page 53.

Sounds and Audio Devices

Open System Preferences; click the Sound icon.

Speech Control Panel

The Mac's center for speech recognition and text-to-speech is the Speech panel of System Preferences. As Chapter 14 makes clear, the Mac can read aloud any text in any program, and it lets you operate all menus, buttons, and dialog boxes by voice alone.

Standby Mode

On the Mac, it's called Sleep, but it's the same idea. You make a Mac laptop sleep by closing the lid. You make a Mac desktop sleep by choosing →Sleep, or just walking away; the Mac will go to sleep on its own, according to the settings in the Energy Saver panel of System Preferences.

Start Menu

There's no Start menu in Mac OS X. Instead, you stash the icons of the programs, documents, and folders you use frequently onto the Dock at the bottom edge of the screen. (That is, it's *usually* at the bottom edge; you can also move it to either side of the screen using the →Dock submenu.)

Exactly as with the Start menu, you can rearrange these icons (drag them horizontally) and remove the ones you don't use often (drag them away from the Dock and then release). To add new icons of your own, just drag them into place (applications go to the left of the Dock's divider line, documents and folders to the right).

StartUp Folder

To make programs launch automatically at startup, include them in the list of Login Items in the System Preferences→Login panel.

System Control Panel

The Mac has no central equivalent of the System window on a Windows PC. But its functions have analogs here:

- **General tab.** To find out your Mac OS X version number and the amount of memory on your Mac, choose →About This Mac.

- **Computer Name tab.** Open System Preferences, click Sharing, and edit your computer's network names here.

- **Hardware tab.** The closest thing the Mac has to the Device Manager is Apple System Profiler (page 359).

- **Advanced tab.** In Mac OS X, you can't easily adjust your virtual memory, processor scheduling, or user profile information.

- **System Restore tab.** This feature isn't available in Mac OS X. On the other hand, there's less need for it: Because the System folder is essentially fixed under glass, you don't run into the kind of "uh-oh, my last driver installation just hosed my machine" problems that require "rewinding" your system in Windows.

- **Automatic Updates tab.** Open System Preferences and click Software Updates.

- **Remote tab.** These features are unavailable in Mac OS X. (Apple does, however, sell something called Apple Remote Desktop, a program that lets you control other Macs remotely—anywhere on an office network, an AirPort wireless network, or even across the Internet. It's available from Apple's Web site.)

System Tray

The perfect Mac OS X equivalent of the System Tray (also called the notification area) is the row of *menulets* at the upper-right corner of your screen; see page 15.

Taskbar

Mac OS X doesn't have a taskbar, but it does have something very close: the Dock (Chapter 3). Open programs are indicated by a small black triangle beneath their icons on the Dock. If you hold down your cursor on one of these icons (or Control-click it, or right-click it), you'll get a pop-up list of the open windows in that program, exactly as in Windows XP.

Control-clicking a folder or disk icon on the Dock is even more useful. It produces a pop-up menu of everything inside that disk or folder—a terrific form of X-ray vision that has no equivalent in Windows.

On the other hand, some conventions never die. Much as on Windows, you cycle through the various open programs on your Dock by holding down the ⌘ key and pressing Tab repeatedly.

Taskbar and Start Menu Control Panel

To configure your Dock (the equivalent of the taskbar and Start menu), choose ⌘→Dock→Dock Preferences, or click the Dock icon in System Preferences.

"Three-Fingered Salute"

Instead of pressing Ctrl-Alt-Delete to jettison a stuck program on the Mac, you press Option-⌘-Esc. A Force Quit dialog box appears. Click the program you want to toss, click Force Quit, confirm your choice, and then relaunch the program to get on with your day.

ToolTips

Small, yellow identifying balloons pop up on the Mac almost as often as they do in Windows. Just point to a toolbar icon or truncated file name without clicking. (There's no way to turn these labels off.)

TweakUI

The closest equivalent for this free, downloadable, but unsupported Microsoft utility for tweaking the look of your PC is TinkerTool 2 for Mac OS X. You can find it at, and download it from, *www.versiontracker.com.*

User Accounts Control Panel

Like Windows 2000 and Windows XP, Mac OS X was designed from Square One to be a multiuser operating system, keeping the files, mail, and settings of each person separate. You set up and manage these accounts in System Preferences→Accounts (Chapter 12).

Window Edges

You can enlarge or shrink a Mac OS X only by dragging its lower-right corner—not its edges.

WINDOWS (or WINNT) Folder

Mac OS X's operating system is largely invisible. Its files sit in various corners of your hard drive, off-limits to tampering, but one location bears some resemblance to the Windows folder: the folder called System, which sits in your main hard drive window. As in recent Windows versions, you're forbidden to add, remove, or change anything inside. Also as in Windows, most of it is invisible anyway.

Windows Logo Key

The Mac has no equivalent for the Windows logo key on most PC keyboards.

Tip: If you hook up a USB Windows keyboard to your Mac, the Windows key behaves like the Mac's ⌘ key (see page 17).

Windows Media Player

The Mac comes with individual programs for playing multimedia files:

- **QuickTime Player** (Chapter 14) to play back movies and sounds.

- **iTunes** (Chapter 8) to play CDs, Internet radio, MP3 files, and other audio files. (As a bonus, unlike Windows XP, iTunes can even *create* MP3 files.)

- **Apple DVD Player** (Chapter 8) to play DVDs. If your Mac does, in fact, have a DVD player built in, this program is in the Applications folder.

(On the other hand, there's also a Mac version of Windows Media Player; see page 178.)

Windows Messenger

Mac OS X doesn't come with built-in videoconferencing and voice conferencing software, as Windows XP does.

For regular typed chat, however, you can use either iChat, described in Chapter 11, or the Mac OS X versions of MSN Messenger, AOL Instant Messenger, or Yahoo Messenger.

WordPad

The TextEdit program (in the Applications folder) is a bare-bones word processor like WordPad. It can't, alas, open Word files, as WordPad can (although it does open RTF files).

Zip Files

Zip files exist on the Mac, too, although StuffIt files are much more common. See page 105 for a discussion of software compression standards on the Mac.

The Master OS X Keystroke List

Month after month, magazines like *PC World* publish secret tips and tricks that Microsoft buried inside Windows: keys that you press at special times to produce special functions and shortcuts. Mac OS X offers a long list of similar keystrokes, including many that you can press during startup. Clip and post to your monitor—unless, of course, you got this book from the library.

Startup Keystrokes

Keys to Hold Down	Effect
C	Start up from a CD
D	Start up from the first partition
N	Start up from network server
T	Enters FireWire Target Disk mode (page xx)
X	Starts up in Mac OS X (if 9 is on the same disk)
Shift	Prevents startup items from opening
Option	Shows icons of all startup disks, so you can choose one for starting up
⌘-Option-P-R	Zaps the parameter RAM (PRAM), a troubleshooting tactic. (Hold down until second chime.)
⌘-V	Show Unix console messages during startup
⌘-S	Start up in single-user (Unix) mode
mouse down	Ejects a stuck CD or DVD

In the Finder

⌘-Option-W	Closes all Finder windows
right arrow, left arrow	Expands or collapses a selected folder in list view
Option-right arrow	Expands a folder in a list view *and* all folders inside it
Option-left arrow	Collapses folder *and* all folders inside it
⌘-up arrow	Opens parent folder
⌘-Option-Shift-up arrow	Selects the Desktop
⌘-down arrow	Opens the selected icon
Option-click the flippy triangle	Expands or collapses all folders within that window
Tab	Selects next icon alphabetically
Shift-Tab	Selects previous icon alphabetically
⌘-Delete	Moves highlighted icons to the Trash
⌘-Shift-Delete	Empties the Trash
Space bar	Opens the disk or folder under mouse immediately (during a spring-loaded folder drag)

Power Keys

On keyboards with a power key

⌘-Control-power	Forces a restart
Control-⌘-Option-power	Shuts down
⌘-Option-power	Put recent models to sleep

On machines without a power key

Control-Eject	Bring up dialog box for shutdown, sleep or restart
⌘-Control-Eject	Forces a restart
Control-⌘-Option-Eject	Shuts down
⌘-Option-Eject	Puts the Mac to sleep

Managing Programs

⌘-Tab	Press and release: Switches back and forth between current and previous open program
⌘-Tab	Hold down ⌘: Press Tab repeatedly to cycle through open programs on the Dock. (Add Shift to cycle *backward* through open programs on the Dock)

⌘-~	Switches to next open window in this program
Option-⌘-Esc	Opens the Force Quit dialog box (to close a stuck program)
Shift-⌘-3	Captures the screen image as a PDF file on your desktop
Shift-⌘-4	Produces a crosshair; drag to capture a selected portion of the screen as a PDF graphics file. (Press Space to get the "camera" cursor that snips out just a menu, icon, or window.)
⌘-Space	Switches keyboard layout (if more than one is installed)
Option-"Empty Trash"	Empties the trash without being asked "Are you sure?" (also nukes locked files)
Option-click a Dock icon or open window	Switches to new program and hides previous one
⌘-Option drag	Scrolls a Finder window in any direction
⌘-drag	Rearrange or remove menulets or toolbar icons
⌘-click window title	Opens a pop-up menu showing the *folder path*
Option-click the Zoom button	Enlarges the window to full screen
Option-click the Minimize button	Minimizes all Finder windows
Option-click Close button	Closes all Finder windows
Shift-click the Minimize or Close button	Minimizes or closes window in slow motion
⌘-Option-D	Hides/shows the Dock
⌘-click a Dock icon	Reveals its actual Finder icon
⌘-Option-click a Dock icon	Switches to this program and hides all others
Control-click (or click and hold on) a Dock icon	Opens a contextual menu
⌘-drag an icon onto a Dock icon	Prevents Dock icons from moving, so that you can drop your icon onto one of them
⌘-Option-drag an icon onto the Dock	Forces a Dock program icon to open the icon you're dropping

Index

Colophon

Due to an annoying and permanent wrist ailment, the author wrote this book by voice, using Dragon Naturally Speaking on a Windows PC. The Microsoft Word files were then transferred (courtesy of Mac OS X's ability to see PCs on the same network) to a Power Mac G4 and a PowerBook G4, where they were edited and transmitted to the book's editors and technical reviewers.

The screenshots were captured with Ambrosia Software's Snapz Pro X *(www. ambrosiasw.com)* on the Mac, and SnagIt *(www.techsmith.com)* in Windows. Adobe Photoshop and Macromedia Freehand *(www.adobe.com)* were called in as required for touching them up.

The book was designed and laid out in Adobe PageMaker 6.5 on a PowerBook G3 and Power Mac G4. The fonts used include Formata (as the sans-serif family) and Minion (as the serif body face). To provide the and ⌘ symbols, a custom font was created using Macromedia Fontographer.

The book was generated as an Adobe Acrobat PDF file for proofreading and indexing, and finally transmitted to the printing plant in the form of PostScript files.

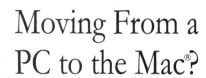